ID0850364

By referring to the tradition of scholarship directed at the so-called "latitudinarians," this collection of essays attempts a revision of intellectual–historical approaches to mid- to late-seventeenth-century English culture. "Latitudinarianism" (a phenomenon which is still loosely defined) is often seen as the product of changing attitudes to knowledge, faith, and politics during the Interregnum, especially as they were expressed by the Cambridge Platonists. It is also thought of as an orthodoxy of sorts emerging during the Restoration, and confirmed by the institutional triumph of the broad Anglican church after 1688. It is thus a useful device to re-open numerous questions, concerning the relations between the Cambridge Platonists and their intellectual successors, and concerning the nature of Restoration thought as such, both before and after the Glorious Revolution. Dividing into two parts, this collection accordingly focuses first on the Cambridge Platonists, especially Cudworth and More, and then moves on to the later seventeenth century, culminating in essays on the philosopher John Locke.

Taken as a whole, these new contributions argue for the need to apply interdisciplinary methods to the study of English culture between 1640 and 1700. And they also reveal that one such method is to attend to questions of discourse and language as a medium of cultural exchange. The variety of approaches serves to illuminate the cultural fluidity of the period, in which inherited models and vocabularies were forced to undergo revisions, coinciding with the formation of many cultural institutions still governing English society.

Philosophy, science, and religion in England
1640–1700

Philosophy, science, and religion in England 1640–1700

Edited by

Richard Kroll, Richard Ashcraft, Perez Zagorin

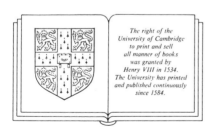

The right of the
University of Cambridge
to print and sell
all manner of books
was granted by
Henry VIII in 1534.
The University has printed
and published continuously
since 1584.

Cambridge University Press

Cambridge
New York   Port Chester
Melbourne   Sydney

Published by the Press Syndicate of the University of Cambridge
The Pitt Building, Trumpington Street, Cambridge CB2 1RP
40 West 20th Street, New York, NY 10011–4211, USA
10 Stamford Road, Oakleigh, Melbourne 3166, Australia

First published 1992

Printed in Great Britain at the University Press, Cambridge

*A cataloguing in publication record for this book is
available from the British Library*

Library of Congress cataloguing in publication data

Philosophy, science, and religion in England, 1640–1700 / edited by
Richard Kroll, Richard Ashcraft, and Perez Zagorin.   p.   cm.
Includes index.
ISBN 0-521-41095-9 (hardback)
1. Latitudinarianism (Church of England – Congresses. 2. Cambridge
Platonists – Congresses. 3. Philosophy, British – Congresses. 4. Science –
England – History – 17th century – Congresses. 5. England – Intellectual life –
17th century – Congresses. 6. England – Religion – 17th century – Congresses.
7. Great Britain – History – Stuarts, 1603–1714 – Congresses.
I. Kroll, Richard W. F. II. Ashcraft, Richard. III. Zagorin, Perez.
BX5126.p48   1991
001'.1'094209032 – dc2091-2387 CIP

ISBN 0 521 410959 hardback

UP

Contents

Notes on contributors

RICHARD ASHCRAFT is Professor of Political Science at the University of California, Los Angeles. He is the author of *Revolutionary Politics and Locke's Two Treatises of Government* (1986), *Locke's Two Treatises of Government* (1987), and numerous articles on political theory. He has recently completed editing *John Locke: Critical Assessments* in four volumes (Routledge, 1990).

ALLISON P. COUDERT teaches in the Honors College at Arizona State University. Her research and publications have focused on early modern science, witchcraft, and women. She is currently at work on an intellectual and cultural biography of Francis Mercury van Helmont (1614–98).

ALAN GABBEY is Reader Emeritus and former departmental Head in History and Philosophy of Science, Queen's University, Belfast. He is a *membre effectif* of the Académie Internationale d'Histoire des Sciences. His interests lie mainly in renaissance and seventeenth-century philosophy and science, especially natural philosophy and the philosophy of mind. Currently he is completing an edition of the More–Descartes correspondence and an inventory of the manuscripts and papers of Roberval, and is working on a study of the mechanical philosophy.

MICHAEL HUNTER is Reader in History at Birkbeck College, University of London. His books include *Science and Society in Restoration England* (1981) and *Establishing the New Science: The Experience of the Early Royal Society* (1989). His current research is focused on Robert Boyle. His paper, "Alchemy, magic, and moralism in the thought of Robert Boyle," recently appeared in the *British Journal for the History of Science*; and (with Edward B. Davis and Antonio Clericuzio) he is preparing a new edition of Boyle's complete works.

SARAH HUTTON is Senior Lecturer in the Division of Cultural and Historical Studies of the School of Education and Humanities at the Hatfield Polytechnic. Her research centers on seventeenth-century English thought, in particular the Cambridge Platonists. She is the editor of *Henry More (1614–1687): Tercentenary Studies* (1990), and *New Perspectives on Renaissance Thought: Studies in the History of Science, Education and Philosophy in Memory of Charles Schmitt* (with J. Henry, 1990). Forthcoming publications include a revised edition of *Conway Letters: the Correspondence of Anne Viscountess Conway, Henry More, and their Friends 1642–1684* (original editor, M. H. Nicolson, 1991), and *Plato and the English Imagination* (with A. Baldwin, 1993).

RICHARD KROLL is the Associate Professor of English at the University of California, Irvine. He is author of *The Material Word: Literate Culture in the Restoration and Early Eighteenth Century* (1991). He has published on Restoration drama, as well as other aspects of Restoration culture, with especial focus on Hobbes and Locke. He has most recently written on Davenant, Hobbes, and Dryden, and is at work on two anthologies of critical essays on intellectual and literary history, and a study of eighteenth-century notions of dissent provisionally entitled *Writing, Institutions, and Dissent from Rochester to Austen.*

JOSEPH M. LEVINE is Professor of History at Syracuse University. He is the author of a number of books and articles on English intellectual history in the early modern period, including *Dr. Woodward's Shield: History, Science, and Satire in Augustan England* (1977), and *Humanism and History: Origins of Modern English Historiography* (1987). He has just completed a new work entitled *The Battle of the Books: History and Literature in the Augustan Age* (1991).

JOHN MARSHALL is a Visiting Professor of History at the University of Oregon (1990–91). He was formerly a Research Fellow of Peterhouse, Cambridge and a member of the Faculty of History of Cambridge University. He is currently adapting his doctoral thesis, "John Locke in context: religion, ethics and politics" (John Hopkins University 1990), into a series of books and articles.

MARGARET J. OSLER is Associate Professor of History at the University of Calgary. Her research and publications have focused on seventeenth-century philosophies of nature and their relationship to theology. She is presently completing a book provisionally entitled

Theology and the Mechanical Philosophy: Gassendi and Descartes on Divine Will and the Philosophy of Nature.

G. A. J. ROGERS is Reader in Philosophy at the University of Keele. He has published many articles and books on seventeenth-century philosophy and intellectual history, and is the editor (with the late Peter Nidditch) of John Locke's *Drafts for the Essay concerning Human Understanding and other Philosophical Writings* (1990) for the Clarendon edition of *The Works of John Locke*. He is editor of the *British Journal for the History of Philosophy*.

PEREZ ZAGORIN is Joseph C. Wilson Professor of History at the University of Rochester. His fields of study include both early modern English and European political, intellectual, and cultural history. Among his publications are *The Court and the Country* (1969), *Rebels and Rulers* (1982), and a number of articles on Thomas Hobbes. His most recent work is *Ways of Lying: Dissimulation, Persecution, and Conformity in Early Modern Europe* (1990).

Preface

The essays collected in this volume were originally presented at a four-day conference held at the William Andrews Clark Memorial Library, Los Angeles. The Clark Library is one of the finest collections extant of rare books and manuscripts from the period 1640 to 1750, providing an ideal setting. It was also appropriately the place where the conference originated. A forum for reappraising the English latitudinarians was the brainchild of Richard H. Popkin, whose *History of Scepticism from Erasmus to Spinoza* could be said to inform much of what follows. During the 1982–83 academic year, Richard Popkin served as the Clark Professor; and in that context he proposed the idea to two Clark Library Fellows, James E. Force and Richard Kroll, who subsequently organized and ran the conference under the rubric, "Latitudinarianism, science, and society."

We now entitle this collection, representing a sample of some of the papers read at the conference, *Philosophy, Science, and Religion in England, 1640–1700*. The change of title occurs for two reasons. It responds to those academic constraints which might lead a reader to suppose that a volume discussing latitudinarianism is narrowly engaged in theological disputes, whereas the topic necessarily engages much broader cultural and intellectual issues, affecting our general interpretation of the Interregnum and Restoration. The second reason is intrinsic to the nature of the debate about latitudinarianism both as it occurs within seventeenth-century historiography and as it developed through four days of a California spring. Richard Kroll's introduction suggests that it became increasingly evident to all the participants that the debate surrounding latitudinarianism eventually translates into the question of how best to describe cultural change and cultural practice between 1640 and 1700. The inelegance of the label and the arcana of theological specifics variously disguise how the topic of latitudinarianism serves to organize a comprehensive series of historical and methodological concerns.

The papers that follow, then, often refer to latitudinarianism as a sociological, intellectual, or cultural category. We have selected these papers with an eye to the period (1640–1700), the culture (England), and the larger issue at hand (shifts in ideas and cultural practices from the mid to the later seventeenth century). The result fortuitously mirrors the conventional division of the period into the Interregnum and Restoration, even though many of the papers included seek to challenge or reorganize the rationale for that division. The book is accordingly divided into two sections: one deals predominantly with the Cambridge Platonists; the other with aspects of Restoration thought, culminating in two papers on Locke, whose death in 1704 acts conveniently as a *terminus ad quem*.

The introduction seeks more fully to establish the context within which all the papers are operating; it summarizes and coordinates the arguments of the essays to follow; and, finally, Richard Kroll presents his perspective on a major issue with which all the essays are at least implicitly engaged, proposing that an attention to language as a medium of cultural exchange supplies a revealing instrument for examining the period in question. This section of his introduction represents, of course, his own, not necessarily his coeditors' or the contributors' opinions.

The original participants in the conference were as follows: Richard Ashcraft ("Latitudinarianism and toleration: historical myth versus political reality"); Jackson I. Cope ("The semiotics of narrative and the survival of stylistics: the progress of Bunyan and the latitudinarians"); Allison Coudert ("The limits of latitudinarianism: Henry More's reaction to the Kabbala and Quakerism"); Mordechai Feingold ("Apologetics without science? The Boyle lectures revisited"); James E. Force ("Sir Isaac Newton, 'man of wide swallow': Newton and the latitudinarians"); Lila Freedman ("Latitudinarianism in the colonies"); Jack Fruchtman, Jr. ("Late latitudinarianism: the case of David Hartley"); Alan Gabbey ("The mechanical analogy in latitudinarian thought"); Michael Hunter ("Latitudinarianism and the early Royal Society"); David Kubrin ("'Burning times': Isaac Newton and the war against the earth"); Joseph M. Levine ("Latitudinarians, neoplatonists, and the ancient wisdom"); John Marshall ("John Locke and latitudinarianism"); James Moore ("Liberal Huguenots, latitudinarians, and the Pyrrhonian controversy"); Richard Olson ("Richard Hooker and the roots of the latitudinarian movement"); Margaret Osler ("Voluntarism and latitudinarianism in the thought of Robert Boyle"); Richard Popkin ("Glanvill: sceptical neoplatonist?"); John Rogers ("Locke and the latitude-men: ignorance as a ground of toleration"); Barbara Shapiro ("The historiography of latitudinarian studies"); William Spellman ("Locke and the latitudinarian perspective on original sin"); Jan van den Berg ("Between platonism and enlightenment: Simon Patrick"); Theodore Waldman ("Further studies in reasonable doubt"); and Perez Zagorin ("Cudworth and Hobbes on Is and Ought").

Respondents and moderators included (apart from names cited above): Leland Carlson, Robert Frank, Jr., James Jacob, Margaret Jacob, Richard Kroll, Maximillian Novak, M. A. Stewart, Norman Thrower, John Wallace, and Robert Westman.

Thanks go to the University of California, Los Angeles for hosting the conference and generously providing funds. The National Endowment for the Humanities and the Ahmanson Foundation equally generously supported the event. We also received invaluable help from the UCLA Seventeenth- and Eighteenth-Century Studies Center, and the librarians and staff of the William Andrews Clark Memorial Library, especially Carol Briggs and Susan Green. And thanks, finally, to Erin Everson and Diana Secker for their assistance in proofing the manuscript.

1 Introduction

Richard Kroll

> One of the most dangerous ideas for a philosopher is, oddly enough, that we think with our heads or in our heads.
>
> The idea of thinking as a process in the head, in a completely enclosed space, gives him something occult.

Ludwig Wittgenstein, Zettel, nos. 605–6

The problem

In 1662, one S.P. (commonly held to be Simon Patrick) issued from Cambridge a twenty-four page epistolary tract addressed to an Oxonian friend ("G.B."). *A Brief Account of the New Sect of Latitude-men, Together with Some Reflections upon the New Philosophy* has by now achieved the status of a classic in English intellectual and cultural history, and has spawned many volumes many times its size. The tract has drawn, and continues to draw such inordinate attention partly because it claims to report on cultural phenomena at a historical juncture between the Interregnum and the Restoration for which historians of most kinds still possess no satisfactory model. *A Brief Account* has also drawn attention because of its peculiarly negative status as evidence, which has often made it a site of many different forms of methodological and ideological projection, and accordingly a litmus-test of the current state of scholarship. Rather than describing a concrete group of individuals in entirely positive language, it describes in the broadest, even the vaguest terms, a series of generic attitudes within a group S.P. wishes to defend. In response to G.B.'s reports of rumors that a potentially dangerous and subversive group has emerged at Cambridge (Sig. A2^r), S.P. discovers a number of Cambridge divines who seek to cultivate a distinctive mode of ecclesiastical, social, and epistemological moderation (a "vertuous mediocrity" [7]), who seek to preserve the instituted structure and ceremonies of the Church of England, and who seek, within the confines of orthodoxy, to adapt the newest philosophical (or "scientific") movements to the conditions of English life. But, as with Thomas Sprat's

History of the Royal Society (1667), which Michael Hunter discusses below, the reliability of *A Brief Account* is heavily qualified by the tract's polemical motives, which make it an extremely complicated item of evidence upon which to have founded an entire historiography. In fact, especially as S.P. closes with his vision of the new philosophy displacing Aristotelian systematizing, it becomes difficult if not impossible to gauge the extent to which S.P. is speaking on his own behalf or reporting attitudes among his still-unnamed group of Cambridge churchmen.

I begin this introduction with *A Brief Account* because, reflecting their origins as conference papers, many of the essays that follow refer explicitly to "latitudinarianism," a tag S.P. seems to have bequeathed to church history and the history of science, if he did not invent it. But like S.P.'s tract, the term has remained excruciatingly vague. Nevertheless, like so many other devices, it has a venerable heuristic status in historical studies dealing with mid- to late-seventeenth-century England, a field which has achieved nothing like the scholarly attention devoted to the early Stuarts. Broadly speaking, "latitudinarianism" connotes a distinctively English phenomenon – intellectual, social, political, or all three – which began to organize itself during the Civil War and Interregnum, and came into its own after the Restoration, becoming a virtual orthodoxy after 1688.[1] Some scholars see the roots of the movement in Richard Hooker's *Of the Lawes of Ecclesiasticall Politie* (1593–97); even more trace them to the Great Tew circle and its finest utterance, William Chillingworth's *The Religion of Protestants a Safe Way to Salvation* (1638). Still others – notably James and Margaret Jacob – argue that latitudinarianism in its Anglican incarnation became the defining ecclesiastical mode of the Whig settlement after 1688. But the looseness of the term seems not to have compromised its appeal for scholarly discourse, and its more local power to have drawn scholars from a variety of disciplines to the Clark Library, Los Angeles, in the spring of 1987. What was interesting at that event, however, was the extent to which four days of often intense discussion yielded surprisingly little substantive or methodological agreement about the putative object of our pursuit.

For this reason alone, the title of our volume purposefully omits reference to "latitudinarianism." But the essays that follow demand the more general grouping suggested by the present title. Not only do they, negatively, reveal the elusiveness of terms like "latitudinarian" as a means to examine specific, local, historical issues; but they positively constitute an engagement with an historiographical conundrum that casual allusions to "latitudinarianism" have tended to camouflage. That is, they are engaged with one of the single most culturally fluid and most underexplored regions of English history, namely the period immediately leading up to and including what we now call the Restoration. This is an era of extraordinary cultural fertility, in which inherited models and vocabularies are still patently visible, yet are under revision at a time when, by coincidence or otherwise, many of the cultural institutions that have subsequently governed English life are being formed. An obvious example is Samuel Pepys' almost single-handed transformation of English naval administration.[2] In the absence of a canonical historiographical model to which to respond (Christopher Hill or Lawrence Stone for the early seventeenth century; J. H. Plumb for the eighteenth) we are left in an arguably more interesting and healthy intellectual situation. Scholars must formulate for themselves by what methods, devices, or vocabularies they can examine and describe the changes in cultural attitudes, in social, in political, in scientific, and in literary behavior that undeniably occurred between the onset of the English Civil War and the Restoration. This encompassing question has usually been divided and apportioned among different academic disciplines, which have accordingly limited its scope. Church historians ask what happens to religious ideas, to theology and ecclesiology between the death of Cromwell and the great fire or the 1688 revolution; there is a well-established tradition of inquiry concerned with the rise and establishment of English science; there have been attempts, some quite venerable, to link "religious" with "scientific" ideas and motives (though the largely modern categories of "religion" and "science" have received less scrutiny); and political scientists have tried to develop a calculus of relations among church, court, science, the growth of party-politics, and dissent, to name only the most obvious candidates. To put the question in a slightly different way, one that S.P.'s *A Brief Account* is often implicitly called upon to answer, how can we discriminate not only what the later seventeenth century inherited from what appears to us a clearly visible and well-explored series of events in political history distinguishing the middle of the century, but also how, by what mechanisms of adaptation and appropriation, did it do so? This is, structurally, the central concern examined in different ways by each essay reproduced below, in the same way that it is a similar concern of a similar volume of essays, *Occult and Scientific Mentalities in the Renaissance*, which engages more exclusively with the historiography of science.[3] As Brian Vickers shows there in great detail, when we disturb the comfortable boundaries between the "occult" and "scientific" which have helped to organize our allegories of scientific advance during the sixteenth and seventeenth centuries, we see at once how such dualisms demonstrably did not operate socially or rhetorically as dichotomies in those "transitional" periods in question, whatever their appeal to us.[4] And as Perez Zagorin effectively puts the question in his essay here, how can we describe in responsible terms the move from some pre-modern argument about the nature of political rights and obligations in Cudworth, to something that, in Hobbes, Zagorin – following a venerable interpretive tradition – chooses to call "modernity"? A *locus classicus* of this descriptive conundrum within the history of science is, of course, Joseph Priestley's "discovery" of oxygen, which – as Thomas Kuhn points out – was not in some real sense a "revolution," because it occurred within an experimental context determined by a vocabulary that could not manifest that discovery to the eighteenth century as the revolution we now take it to be.[5]

Moreover, Brian Vickers implies in his introduction to *Occult and Scientific Mentalities*, such a collection also provides an occasion on which to examine the differences between intrinsic and extrinsic modes of explaining change, and, more importantly, develop a logic or method by which we can set them into some mutual and productive relation, since, Pocock has argued, they are neither identical nor necessarily in conflict.[6] Thus Richard Ashcraft takes strategic exception to an "intrinsic" tendency to take the rhetorical claims of Restoration texts at face value, a tendency which too readily ignores the social, one might even say ideological function which those texts, in practical and concrete ways, were made to serve.

The historiography of latitudinarianism, and the religion-and-science debate

It is instructive, then, to abandon an exclusive interest in "latitudinarianism," and make it an occasion for discussing the more general and tantalizing problem of how we can describe cultural and intellectual change between roughly 1640 or 1650 and the high Restoration. I will therefore first describe the historiography of "latitudinarianism" because it articulates the narrative many of the essays printed here assume, and because the fortunes of that historiography, I want to argue, reveal better than most the interpretive challenge facing historians of the period in question. What we find, predictably, is that the historiography falls into distinct phases, reflecting different academic fashions. What is perhaps less expected is that the late-Victorian historians, who recognizably established this field of inquiry within church history, reveal a subtlety of approach lost to a later generation who have subsequently, in a number of fields, defined the conduct of the enterprise. Like the essays in *Occult and Scientific Mentalities*, however, I would also suggest that, with significant variations in their assumptions, scholars are once again recuperating something of the complexity of analysis the field once possessed.

In the preface to his elegant and passionate work, *Rational Theology and Christian Philosophy in England* (1872), John Tulloch proposes to "describe a movement hitherto imperfectly understood" (vii).[7] Into the drama which pitched royalists against parliamentarians, "Anglicans" against "puritans," all wearing sharply distinguishable regalia, Tulloch insinuates a third cast of actors. The movement he reveals is embodied, in his narrative, almost exclusively in the Great Tew Circle before the onset of the Civil War, and in the Cambridge Platonists, whose period of most cohesive activity (Tulloch implies) came to an end before the Restoration. It is easy to dismiss Tulloch's achievement if we see only his idealist, progressivist, and establishmentarian bias. For, in his first volume, he discovers in the Great Tew circle (especially Falkland, Hales, and Chillingworth) an "ideal element" of Christian moderation (I: x), a strain of thought developed in reaction to increased Catholic and Calvinist propagandizing in the early years of the seventeenth century. And he discovers in Holland a parallel movement, this time embodied in the Remonstrants' refusal at the Synod of Dort (1618) to bow to strict Calvinist predestinarianism which sought (in the Arminian view) fatally to abrogate certain elements of human will in favor of systematic and doctrinal purity. By hinting that toleration achieved a "virtual triumph" after the revolution of 1688 (I: viii), and implying that he is speaking in some historical period "after the triumph of toleration" (II: 458), Tulloch sets a precedent for one view of what the "latitudinarians" (as he rarely calls them) achieved for posterity. Tulloch's choice of "rational" and "liberal" as epithets to apply to the figures and ideas he discusses further amplifies his idealist and progressivist strain, which he attaches to a weak Hegelian view of history as moving erratically between a dogmatic and critical spirit. For Tulloch (as for Matthew Arnold) criticism is the informing spirit of what is best for modern social institutions.

Tulloch's book weighs heavily on interpretations of mid to late seventeenth-century church history. Like Mark Pattison's great biography of Isaac Casaubon, which appeared only three years after *Rational Theology*,[8] it is a seductive experience, not only because it forges a polemic against epistemic and political dogmatism in favor of a certain kind of moderation, but also because it remains quite clear-sighted about the fact that claims to moderation occur within institutional, social, and political contexts.[9] If there is any purity in moderation, it is to be found only in the individual cultivation of character: Falkland, Hales, Chillingworth, and Smith seem to have achieved such a stance, but three of these men died young, and before their commitments could be tested over time under political pressure. Tulloch holds that, for all their attachment to a rhetoric of toleration, his rational theologians would never countenance the full expression of dissent from instituted social forms. This we can read to reflect Tulloch's fears for church integrity threatened by Gladstonian reform. More realistically and descriptively, however, I take Tulloch to register the impossibility of constructing liberal or libertarian ideals *outside* institutional motives, a position that at a theoretical level the social sciences are once again asserting.

Tulloch's analysis reveals its sophistication by maintaining a tactical balance between, on the one hand, the view that moderation, rationality, liberty, are properties that we can at any time choose to promote or destroy; and, on the other, the view that the historian can only hypothesize these properties as conditions either of individual character, or of the confluence and conflict of local historical forces. Moderation or rationality is not, then, as some historians of science seem to have assumed, a reified category in itself: it is the condition of lived experience. But neither are the interested motives of persons or parties solely sufficient to describe why we still recognize those categories as (possibly) recurring and (usually) desirable. So Tulloch begins his narrative with a double aetiology, one describing the possibility of criticism or the critical spirit within post-Reformation theology, and the other, where his narrative truly begins, charting the local convergence of opposed pressures in early Stuart England. The conflicting forces of puritan and Catholic polemic created a reaction among an unusual group of individuals gathered around the perennially eloquent figure of Lucius Cary, Second Viscount Falkland at his house at Great Tew outside Oxford. "Moderation," whose vocabulary draws upon a number of different intellectual inheritances, only becomes a reality in this case by a kind of glorious accident, a chance convergence of like-minded individuals. So, apart from Falkland himself, who operated in reaction to religious pressures *within* his family, Tulloch talks most about Hales and Chillingworth. Hales had personally attended those violent debates at the Synod of Dort involving the Calvinists and the Arminians or Remonstrants headed by Simon Episcopius, and, in the course of reporting back to England as an observer, seems to have become persuaded of the force of the Arminian critique of Calvinist dogma. Chillingworth, too, experienced a conversion, briefly becoming a Catholic, and then reconverting to Anglicanism, later to write his famous defense of moderate protestantism against the Jesuit Father Knott with the aid of Falkland's library at Great Tew. In closing the first volume of his narrative, Tulloch discusses Jeremy Taylor and Edward Stillingfleet only insofar as their individual publications reflect or reiterate a position clearly derived from the Tew Circle. Tulloch effectively avoids having to account for "latitudinarianism" after the Restoration: Jeremy Taylor's [*Theologia eklectikē*] *A Discourse of the Liberty of Prophesying* (1647) and Edward Stillingfleet's *Irenicum. A Weapon-Salve for the Churches Wounds* (1661) are publications that (like the heroes of the Tew Circle) stand at some distance from established party politics, not only because Taylor and Stillingfleet were Anglicans, but because both publications appeared before the re-establishment of the church, which returned the Anglicans to power. Tulloch knows that Stillingfleet was later embarrassed by his most liberal tract, and evidently holds that the appropriation of its intellectual tropes by post-Restoration institutions damaged their original critical power and purpose. (He writes, "Unhappily, their voice was unheard, or at least uninfluential" [I: 462].)

Tulloch's second volume follows the same pattern of argument. The scene of activity shifts from Oxford to Cambridge, and Tulloch concentrates his energy on the Cambridge Platonists. His major point is that their capacity to elaborate a rhetoric earlier developed by the Great Tew Circle, depended substantially on their marginal, merely "academic" position (II: 276). And further, where the earlier rhetoric of moderation responded to conflictual pressures (resulting in Civil War), the Cambridge Platonists, who came into their own during the Interregnum, were forced to respond to a choice between sectarian radicalism and Hobbesian materialism (II: 38). If, in a qualified way, Tulloch admits Culverwel, Worthington, Rust, Patrick, Fowler, Glanvill, and Norris into his discussion of the Cambridge Platonists, he is careful to emphasize a decline from "the new speculative spirit" that accompanied their rise (II: 15). Indeed, he refuses to remark except dismissively on "the new political type of latitudinarianism which came into vogue at the Revolution" (II: 410) – it remains ambiguous whether Tulloch means to refer to 1660 or 1688, but within his argumentative economy, either will do. If moderation became a property of party-political alliances, Tulloch finally will not judge how this might transpire, remaining skeptical about the later *quality* of the appeal to moderation. So, unlike a later and more fearless generation, Tulloch reserves judgment on the accuracy of S.P.'s *A Brief Account* as a reliable report on the fortunes of "moderation" and "science" between 1658 and 1662, that crucial moment in the formation of what we now call the Restoration period.

With all its strengths and weaknesses, I would argue that Tulloch's work sets the pattern for another monumental history, W. K. Jordan's *The Development of Religious Toleration in England*, published in four volumes between 1932 and 1940.[10] Like Tulloch's soft Hegelianism, the idea of development advertised by Jordan's title raises the specter of a kind of Whig history, in which toleration came by an organic process to manifest and vindicate itself. Of course, this parodic view of Whig progressivism holds as little for Jordan as for Tulloch. For like our experience of Tulloch, what strikes us about Jordan's analysis is precisely the balance between, on the one hand, treating toleration as some social or political ideal of behavior or expression that we can legitimately derive from the past; and, on the other, demonstrating that toleration, inasmuch as it is ever attained, is the condition of various social, political, legal, or theological disputes. Now accounting in microscopic detail for all elements of the polity, including Roman Catholics, Jordan nevertheless follows a similar organizational pattern to Tulloch: he first establishes the existence of and the local pressures upon a given group, then explains in more systematic, analytic terms the theoretical claims that the group or representative polemicists made. The subtitle of Jordan's last volume, published during World War II, is symptomatic: there he describes the "attainment of the theory and accommodations in thought and institutions." Toleration, in sum, is constituted by and as a claim to be recognized within a highly charged political situation, as indeed the period 1600–60 can only be said to have been. "Toleration" emerged or developed, it is evident, because for each group involved (the Great Tew Circle, the Catholics, the radical sects), toleration could become known only as a demand to be recognized within a contestatory political cosmos. That Jordan distinguishes "theory" from practical "accommodations in thought and institutions" is to resist, however, reducing the *idea* of toleration merely to a set of local positions established by conflicting motives, in, say, 1641. If toleration can become palpable only by accommodation to political practice, that fact does not prevent our treating it as nevertheless capable of retaining its own discursive and critical integrity, relative to the motives of those wishing to appropriate it. This complicated symbiosis (even dialectic) between theory and practice informs Jordan's striking allegory about the rise of European fascism that comprises that preface to the third volume of his study, published in 1938: if toleration were not an idea, he implies, a rhetorical possibility within and yet beyond the local machinations of institutions, then we would at this critical historical juncture have no verbal means of appeal against the new political tyrannies. To say that all humans and all institutions behave irrationally is not to say that rationality is neither desirable nor, on occasion, possible.

The second major phase in the study of cultural and intellectual changes from the mid to later seventeenth-century England set in just as Jordan's massive work was making its appearance. This is a well-documented historiographical moment lucidly discussed by T. K. Rabb, H. F. Kearney, and Douglas S. Kelmsley.[11] The 1930s saw a series of articles by Dorothy Stimson which proposed, in the most famous, "that Puritanism was an important factor, hitherto little regarded, in making conditions in England favorable to the new philosophy headed by Bacon."[12] This thesis immediately received exhaustive exposition in 1936, when R. F. Jones published his massively influential *Ancients and Moderns: A Study in the Rise of the Scientific Movement in Seventeenth-Century England*,[13] and Robert K. Merton published his article, "Puritanism, pietism, and science," which sketched in miniature the thesis fully developed in his monograph for *Osiris*, "Science, technology and society in seventeenth-century England" (1938).[14] Inasmuch as they describe relations among politics, science, religion, and literature, and inasmuch as they propose a clear relationship between puritanism and science, these two studies have determined the main directions of Interregnum and Restoration studies, if only by reaction. For example, because he brings to his view of literary history an impressive range of scholarship in the history of science, Jones's interpretation of Restoration culture has, so far with little dissent,[15] remained canonical within literary studies. Though the shapes of their respective arguments have produced different scholarly stemma, Jones and Merton jointly engage in important methodological shifts away from Tulloch and Jordan. The effect is partly tonal: by introducing "science" into social and religious movements, their arguments assume as if by osmosis a new scientistic method and confidence in themselves. And their scientistic presumptions tend to foster nakedly progressivist allegories of the change between 1640 and the Restoration. Admittedly, Jones and Merton offer unitary and extraordinarily cohesive interpretative mechanisms; but they also discard the complicated interplay between intrinsic and extrinsic modes of explanation informing Tulloch and Jordan. The conclusion to *Ancients and Moderns* epitomizes Jones's positivist vision of progress, which he propounds by establishing, like the book's title, a series of functional antinomies graphically controlling his evidence (science vs. imagination; rhetoric vs. plain style, and so on). Like the ideology of American progressivism of which his book is a symptom, Jones holds firmly to the ideal of "progress" (the modern), although ineluctably it demands the sacrifice of "humanistic and cultural" values (the ancient). It is a sacrifice that Jones can ultimately make without regret: with Bacon as its patron saint, and accompanied by the hard-headed political, religious, and "utilitarian" ideals of the Commonwealth, "the obsequious submission to the authority of antiquity" yielded to the new "science [which] could find a place in the sun," a critical moment, evidently, in "the history of the liberation of the mind" (268).[16]

Though differently expressed, Merton's optimism is of a similar kind. Like Jones, upon whom he draws, Merton's thesis vindicates the superiority of the "puritan" world-view as the chief catalyst in the development of modern science. Where Jones's method is largely intrinsic – Baconian and puritan *ideas* establish the necessary conditions for scientific ideas – Merton's is more extrinsic. Influenced by Weber, Merton forges links between puritanism and science by arguing, at a typical juncture, that "the acceptance of every great change of belief depends less upon the intrinsic force of its doctrines or the personal capabilities of its proponents than upon the previous social changes which are seen – *a posteriori*, it is true – to have brought the new doctrines into congruence with the dominant values of the period" (464). Merton supports his sociological explanation for the rise of science on statistics derived from the *Dictionary of National Biography* (a secondary vehicle of evidence whose biases he ignores), which themselves lend the argument the positivistic authority of "social science." In sociological terms, Merton develops Jones's thesis about a tectonic shift to a new "practical empiricism" whose virtues the overly stabilized application of "utility" and "technology" serve to validate.

Both because of the analytical reductions I describe, and because those reductions informed Christopher Hill's enthusiastic support of the "puritanism" and "science" thesis in the early 1960s,[17] a number of critics, notably Rabb and Kearney, emerged. Their main points I have already anticipated: in order to argue a coherent, stable, and constructive alliance between "puritanism" and "science," the operative terms must be so reified, simplified, or broadened as either to render them useless as descriptions of recognizable historical phenomena, or to create illusory causal explanations from at best loosely analogical relations, or both. Scholars were, so to speak, left holding two bags, one denoting the recognizable phenomena of the rise and establishment of science, and the other, the multiple, cultural, political, and theological conditions of the Interregnum and early Restoration. Though Charles Webster refashioned the puritanism-and-science thesis in his epic *The Great Instauration* as late as 1975,[18] Kearney had already a dozen years before suggested a possible direction for revising it that was to receive its fullest expression in an article by Barbara Shapiro (1968) and in her book on John Wilkins (1969).[19] Deeply uncomfortable about Hill's treatment of science and puritanism as virtually synonymous, Kearney pointed out that men like William Harvey, Robert Boyle, John Williams, and Seth Ward, key figures in the establishment of Restoration science, hardly merited the epithet "puritan" in any exact sense, and that rather they are "best described as latitudinarian or moderate."[20] This hint developed its own logic in Shapiro's seminal article, "Latitudinarianism and science in seventeenth-century England." Rehearsing the now well-established criticism of the puritanism-and-science thesis, Shapiro argued for the existence of "a broad middle category of divines, scholars, and politicians who wanted mild reforms in the church and sought moderate means of accomplishing them," and, further, that "nearly all of the seventeenth-century English scientists and scientific movements are to be found within this moderate category" (19). And writing that the organizing category, "moderation *qua* moderation" thus managed to focus the relationship between mid-century figures and the establishment of science, Shapiro offered Wilkins as her chief example (21). The final chapter of Shapiro's book on Wilkins, which appeared a year later (1969), amplified the theme: true science and true moderation managed to forge, after the Interregnum, a functionally a-political climate of inquiry which avoided the pitfalls of party-politics because it consciously limited its claims to knowledge in such a way as to preclude any dogmatic political platform.[21]

The a-political tendencies in Shapiro's early work – deliberately or otherwise – created a response that reasserted the interested nature of the relationship between religion and science in the mid to later seventeenth century. I have just mentioned Charles Webster's *The Great Instauration*, which appeared in 1975, articulating at length a version of the puritanism-and-science thesis. But the work of James and Margaret Jacob effectively established a new phase in the argument: taking Shapiro's hint that the establishment of science was the product of "latitudinarian" commitments developed during the Interregnum, the Jacobs, in a series of articles and two books, argued that the cosmologies propounded by, respectively, Boyle (in the early Royal Society) and Newton (for the early eighteenth century) responded to particular, concrete sets of political circumstances, becoming by the same token the vehicles of establishment "ideology."[22] Thus for example we find the Jacobs arguing not for the "puritan" or "latitudinarian" but "the Anglican origins of modern science," whereby the "new Anglicanism [in formation by the end of the Interregnum] with its supportive science and natural philosophy was crucially defined by the dialectics of revolution" such that "puritanism was transformed into liberal Anglicanism during and because of the Revolution."[23] What is attractive about the Jacobs' thesis is that it accounts for the institutional dimension of "science" as practiced within concrete social and political circumstances. It is clearly one stimulus in Shapin and Schaffer's impressive and influential book about Boyle's vigorous exclusion of all things Hobbesian from the early Royal Society, centrally because Hobbes's plenist cosmology was interpreted as the physical expression of Hobbes's political absolutism.[24] However, the Jacobs' gestures towards "dialectics" and "ideology" have remained – as Michael Hunter points out below – frustratingly vague. To what extent can we take a given text, utterance, or idea to be the expression of "ideology" in the conscious sense often implied by the Jacobs' method of presentation? And to what extent, by contrast, does it contribute to "ideology" in the sense of a political unconscious? These are questions that have continued to plague interpretations of S.P.'s *A Brief Account* or Sprat's *History of the Royal Society* as signifying or representing some larger social, political, "ideological" movement.

The present volume

My historiographical survey establishes the point, I trust, that we are in a position once again not unlike that recognized by Tulloch and Jordan, in which the simple analytical dualisms provided by Jones and Merton have, in the subsequent half century, been eroded. During the 1970s and early 1980s, the Jacobs' work once again complicated the science-and-religion question, just as historians of science were finding that the simple demarcation between "religion" and "science," between "science" and "magic" or the occult no longer holds.

The essays that follow are all confronted by this renewed sense of complexity in cultural and political analysis, and seek, in their different ways, to confront it in turn. They are arranged in two groups, the first concentrating heavily on the Cambridge Platonists, and their relations with the past (fictional or otherwise), their contemporaries, or later and different thinkers like Hobbes and Stillingfleet; and, following Richard Ashcraft's more general essay on the latitudinarians, the last four essays deal with high Restoration figures like Boyle and Sprat, on the one hand, and Locke, with whom we conclude, on the other.

The opening group of essays – by Allison Coudert, Sarah Hutton, Joseph Levine, Alan Gabbey, and Perez Zagorin – all ask how we can legitimately treat the Cambridge Platonists as either beholden to the past, centrally the high renaissance topoi of occult knowledge, alchemy, the ancient wisdom (tropes which also sustained a currency at mid-century); or as anticipating the future, a new mode of organizing reason, knowledge, and science represented, here, by Stillingfleet and Hobbes. Coudert, Hutton, and Levine all deal with the relations between Cambridge Platonism and the topoi of the Kabbala (Coudert), the *prisca theologia* (Hutton), and the ancient wisdom (Levine). The figure of More, we discover in all three essays, as well as Gabbey's discussion of the mechanical analogy, sits most uncomfortably between a high renaissance occultism (which Coudert charts in scrupulous detail and relates to Quaker and even radical sectarian thought), and some more recognizably "modern" possibility that Zagorin discovers in Hobbes's conventionalist arguments for political obligation. As Coudert, Hutton, Levine, and Gabbey are explicitly aware in their studies, it is not that More is internally divided, but that he poses a threat to scientistic ways of reading the period between 1640 and 1660. After we have negotiated Coudert's map of More's peculiar allegiances, which he then gradually revises,

Hutton presents us with Stillingfleet re-reading More, as it were, revising those features of More's use of the *prisca theologia* which conflict with his immediate requirements (intellectual? political? social?), ones which his two different versions of *Origines Sacrae* serve to highlight. Stillingfleet retreats decisively from More's assumption that we have access to some ancient mode of knowledge, not least, as Hutton points out, because Stillingfleet employs a more decided skepticism about the possibility of recuperating the past. In Hutton's allegory of the change, the epistemological issue is clearly significant.

Joseph Levine seeks to revise the view – most vigorously articulated in Jones's *Ancients and Moderns* – that the "scientific" spirit commanded the abandonment of the ancients. Levine's case in point is the Cambridge Platonists, who constitute, according to his claim, nothing if not a revival of interest in the ancients. But the argument, like Hutton's, also becomes a means of mapping attitudinal shifts within this difficult period, represented by the difference between Tuckney and Whichcote: the *way* the ancients are admitted into orthodox Christian concerns (or whether they were admitted at all) distinguishes one attitude from the other. More exemplifies the Cambridge Platonists' anxiety to mediate between the free and self-evidencing power of reason (which they associated with Hobbes's rationalist heterodoxy), and a view that Christian revelation, which cannot value ancient knowledge in any form, monopolizes reason. The ancient wisdom makes a certain postulate of reason available to us, outside and yet in harmony with Christian revelation: reason discovers itself as a permanent value, discernible however by weighing and authorizing the ancient wisdom in the light of Christian knowledge. Cudworth closes Levine's essay, since his *True Intellectual System of the Universe* (1678) represents a late expression of this particular project to accommodate the ancient wisdom to the necessities of orthodoxy.

Alan Gabbey's essay on Cudworth and More deploys a double strategy. It reconstructs what their seventeenth-century contemporaries meant to describe when they referred – often polemically – to the "latitudinarians." And in discovering an internal tension within the latitudinarians' distinction between the essentials of religion and its "negotiable externals," Gabbey lights upon a theoretical instability that More was trying to resolve within his cosmology. The second half of Gabbey's essay is thus given over to an analysis of More's use of the mechanical analogy, which reveals (like his interest in the neurospast), More's determination to preserve *both* an access to the spiritual principles of things *and* a respect for the outward constitution of our physical and social knowledge, while avoiding the reductions of pure spiritual determinism (whereby God directly manipulates every atom of the world and human experience) or pure mechanism.

Perez Zagorin develops the view of much scholarship – and articulated in Levine's and Gabbey's essays – that a defining feature of Cambridge Platonism was its reaction to Hobbes. This provides an occasion to examine the distinctions between Cudworth's and Hobbes's attitudes to the human sense of a moral imperative. In questioning Cudworth's assumption that Hobbes's conventionalism necessarily implies complete relativism, Zagorin reconstructs Hobbes's argument from its premises, showing that, despite his contractual view of obligation, he still accords authority to a trans-cultural and trans-historical capacity for reason, which establishes the law of nature as partly independent of the dictates of the sovereign. What is reasonable is not always what the sovereign dictates it to be. Hobbes thus constructs an internal tension in his argument which saves it from complete relativism, though its economy is utterly distinct from Cudworth's view that moral properties inhere in the cosmos.

The second section of this collection discusses the Restoration proper, and individual figures like Boyle, Sprat, and Locke. Richard Ashcraft's article incorporates distinct methodological aims by eroding the boundaries among political history, intellectual history, and the history of science. Rehearsing the methodology of his study, *Revolutionary Politics and Locke's "Two Treatises of Government,"*[25] Ashcraft writes that latitudinarianism in no way *functionally* contributed to modern political practice in ways that other historians have often assumed. The passage of the Toleration Act after 1688 registered less a triumph of toleration than a violently anti-Catholic reaction uniting otherwise warring religious sects. In any case, up to that point, "latitudinarian" appeals to moderation and reason merely rationalized highly oppressive mechanisms of political hegemony. By contrast, the dissenters employed a radically different view of reason – almost a rationalistic one – where the individual can apprehend divine purposes for himself, and so embarrasses any claim by the magistrate to intervene between the common man and the sources of truth and power. The latitudinarian assault on enthusiasm is an attempt to limit, if not deflate, that argument. Thus Ashcraft takes issue with Tulloch's "rational theology" as applied to the seemingly "moderate" church tradition he describes, and appropriates it for the nonconformists. As Barbara Shapiro's work suggests, religion, politics, and claims to "rationality" (and "science") constitute a single ideological and cultural formation; so that it becomes vital to examine not what parties in a contested field claim for themselves, but to see how their claims are used as effective instruments of policy.

Taking her cue from an important article by J. E. McGuire, Margaret Osler argues the influence of Gassendi on Boyle by virtue of their shared voluntarism, the view that God can, by an arbitrary exercise of will, potentially intervene in the physical workings of the universe. The God shared by Gassendi and Boyle is no *deus absconditus*; nor is he, however, the powerfully immanent God of the inspirationalists, infusing every particle of matter. In a fashion resembling More's equilibria as Gabbey describes them, God's reasonable dealings with humankind require him to allow considerable regularity in what we observe, so that we can negotiate with the world that represents divine activity; and God's omnipotence allows him to suspend those laws at will. Thus like Coudert's essay on More's complicated dealings with various continental figures, Osler's too helps to correct the impression that the relations of science and religion in mid-century England is interpretable by reference exclusively to English thinkers.

Michael Hunter, however, does return to the English scene. By referring with great exactitude to manuscript material, some since purloined, but reproduced here as an appendix to his essay, Hunter argues that given its provenance, Sprat's *History of the Royal Society* cannot be taken to express Royal Society "ideology," if by that we mean an official advertisement for the attitudes of the body as a whole. This challenges a standard assumption about the usefulness or representative quality of the work, by showing (i) that only portions of the *History* were officially authorized by other members of the Royal Society (like Evelyn); and (ii) that the Royal Society as a body cannot be said to represent, in its constitution and attitudes, a single "ideology" in the sense implied by the Jacobs' use of the term.

We close with two essays on Locke. John Rogers takes a strictly "internalist" approach, showing how part of this argument for toleration is indebted to an earlier nexus of views holding that since human knowledge is by its nature limited, no individual or single group within the polity can reasonably or consistently impose its interpretations of truth – political or otherwise – on others. Like several contributors to this volume, Rogers finds More to represent an important fulcrum in the shift from an earlier transcendentalism (represented here by Vaughan) to the view that knowledge can operate only by appearances, which is to say nominally. Like Shapiro, Levine, Gabbey, or like Gerard Reedy's *The Bible and Reason*, which discusses Restoration hermeneutics,[26] Rogers stresses that the "reason" employed by More is not rationalist, since it operates within clearly defined skeptical parameters. Thus Locke's modified notion of reason, which also owes something on his own admission to Chillingworth, stands in marked contrast, for example, to that of Leibniz.

Where Rogers primarily emphasizes Locke's indebtedness to the past,

John Marshall depicts the extent to which Locke's theological and ecclesiological views were influenced by the "latitudinarians," and by the same token, those significant points where he diverges from them. Like the "latitudinarians," Locke adopted the familiar distinction between essentials and non-essentials in religion, and emphasized the moral over the preceptual features of belief. Marshall points out, however, that Locke focused on theological matters only after his exile to Holland in 1683, and in the process began more radically to differentiate himself especially (partly on the manuscript evidence Marshall presents) on the issue of the trinity and soteriology after 1684–85. From *The Reasonableness of Christianity* onwards, Locke did not maintain a trinitarian position, and rejected orthodox accounts of original sin and Christ's satisfaction. By this time, we are indeed a long way from Henry More's presuppositions. If in the middle of this volume, Levine and Gabbey depict the complexities of a philosophical and attitudinal change from the Cambridge Platonists to later figures, Marshall demonstrates a further shift in Locke, from a distinct set of theological views articulated during the Restoration, to Locke's own peculiar and late positions which questioned orthodox attitudes to the trinity and salvation. Whether, as in many canonical histories, Locke thus establishes the terms for a later age, is not the aim of the present volume to decide.

"Moderation," language, and society

Ever since Jones's and Merton's classic studies on mid-seventeenth-century science, most scholars have recognized that important Restoration figures – Sprat, Wilkins, Boyle, Locke – are engaged as fully with the question of language as anything else. The seventeenth-century interest in language schemes is only a small symptom of a much wider phenomenon. But, in a peculiar way, Jones's formulations have prevented a thorough exposition of the way contemporary attitudes to language might provide an access to the cultural shift occurring between 1640 and 1660. The reasons are two-fold. First, Jones suggested not only that the rise of science affected linguistics (which is undeniable), but also that it accompanied not so much a corresponding distrust as an active *dislike* of words, resulting in the cultivation of a plain style, by which Jones designates an anti-rhetorical ideal of transparent referentiality. Since "science" requires a "utilitarian" grasp of things, language must be forced more radically to *refer* to objects in the world. The slightly lurid terms in which Jones and Merton cast the equation connotes the degree to which the scientistic ideals of knowledge and language they projected onto their evidence (Sprat's *History* being a classic case) derived less from a Restoration than a modern, industrial ("utilitarian") bias.[27] For them, language is the handmaiden, not the condition of knowledge.

The other obstacle to treating language as a vehicle and index of "scientific" attitudes in the mid to later seventeenth century arose from the organization of modern lines of inquiry. However misconceived the details of their interpretations, Jones and Merton still tended to accord language considerable prominence in their discussions; and though Shapiro has admitted a similar interest, it is only in her most recent work that she questions the view that the rise of science required an anti-poetical, anti-metaphorical purge of aesthetics. For the most part, however, more conventional historians of science have adopted Jones's description as a convenient appendix to what they see as more substantial and rewarding lines of inquiry. There is some fear that a concern with language (mere literature) will distract our attention from cultural, social, political, or scientific actualities. Seventeenth-century linguistics or philosophies of language have been chiefly the concern of specialists in those subjects.[28] One clear exception is Brian Vickers' attempts directly to revise Jones's baleful influence on literary studies, and to reintroduce the linguistic question into the historiography of science, for example in his excellent contribution to *Occult and Scientific Mentalities in the Renaissance*. But Vickers, like Jones himself, occupies an uneasy place somewhere between the "literary" field, within which he (like Jones) operates on a daily basis, and the history of science, a field usually policed by the claims and methodology of social science. What Quentin Skinner has described as the "return of grand theory to the social sciences" in various guises like Foucaultian, post-structuralist, or post-Marxist theory has however succeeded in drawing certain groups and individuals in the social sciences back to the question of language. One hesitates to judge the range and depth of the consequences, but one recent example of this shift in the history of science is Shapin and Schaffer's *Leviathan and the Air Pump*, where the authors examine the concrete social and ideological conditions and consequences of deploying one metaphor (the existence of the void as a physical hypothesis) at the expense of another (Hobbes's plenist view of matter). Because this is a contest of metaphors (since both cosmologies were for all intents and purposes hypothetical), the issue of language is central to the argument. Attending to the way certain metaphors are used as vehicles of desire and prohibition seems in this case to offer an extremely sensitive instrument for gauging the kinds of changes this volume describes and examines.

I want therefore to close my introduction by highlighting the issue of language, not because many or most of the essays that follow overlook or ignore it, but because, for the most part, their attentions are directed elsewhere. As I have already implied, the focus on language holds a very real methodological promise for our understanding of the Restoration, not merely in "linguistics." And it is demonstrably of vital concern to figures in the period because it involves the issue of who gets to control and disseminate knowledge, and under what conditions. Since the vehicle of knowledge is language, the political and religious stakes in the linguistic question are understandably high. Like Alan Gabbey's essay below, Shapin and Schaffer's example should already indicate how, at the methodological level, the persuasive, rhetorical force of certain metaphors, conscripted by certain individuals (here Boyle) or institutions (the Royal Society) can achieve a high degree of descriptive precision. Intellectual history, in this turn, becomes, as Bouwsma puts it, the history of meaning.[29] But however useful we might find the approach, we still need to ask whether and to what extent this attitude to language itself informs the texts we describe. That is, is there some distinction between our contemporary view that cultural metaphors are socially constitutive, and early Restoration attitudes to language? Didn't the authors Jones discusses in fact cherish something like the transparent referential ideal he imputes to them, which would prevent them seeing what was at stake?

Several of the essays below recognize that language was of vital importance to the figures they describe. In their different ways, Ashcraft, Gabbey, and Levine indicate that the actors involved knew that different views about the nature of language would reflect and reinforce different attitudes towards the powers of the mind, towards religious, scientific, and social apprehension.[30] Rogers, for example, recalls More's discomfort at Vaughan's transcendentalism, which would legislate a direct and unmediated grasp of the natures of bodies, thus disposing those forms of representation by which we can only *infer* the properties of things, amounting to a denial of language as a medium intervening between human desires and aspirations, and those perfect forms of apprehension they seek. So it is evident that the Restoration did recognize that language was important as a cultural and political issue; and it defended language not as some transparent vehicle between mind and world (a view which dates from the nineteenth, not the eighteenth century), but as some opaque, inescapably rhetorical medium. If the essays that follow are correct, More is especially pertinent, since he wishes to enforce the condition by which humans must inevitably negotiate with external forms (of the world, of social institutions) in a contingent mode; and yet he wishes to preserve his faith in the accessibility of reason and the divine.

The fact and necessity of institutions to human experience is a central part of the argument about representation (and so about language), for, as several essays below stress, the latitudinarians (whether we mean the

Cambridge Platonists or later Anglican divines) are committed to Anglicanism, if not as an inevitable and necessary condition of spiritual expression, certainly as an inherited and public, though imperfect, arena of religious and social participation. In a peculiar, even unexpected way, Hobbes fits in at this point, because the political thesis of *Leviathan* can be said to presuppose the inevitable fact of human institutions, for which the first was always, for Hobbes, language.

Like Jones, then, I would argue that language is always of central and special concern for studies of the period 1640 to 1660, and not only within literary history or the history of linguistics. But unlike Jones, we should see the development of the issue, at that moment in time, in terms which pit a rhetorical view of language – an inevitably formal and contingent artefact – against a view that, despite our linguistic condition, argues that we can gain access to the true properties of bodies, or alternatively the mind of God. The emergence of probability, charted variously by Van Leeuwen, Hacking, Shapiro, and Patey, proves to characterize the emergence not of a view that language can and should be the transparent, referential vehicle of knowledge, but of language signifying our limited and highly circumscribed condition.[31] The widespread attack on metaphor does not seek to erase language or poetry as such, but expresses a discomfort at those epistemologies – associated with gnostic and socially divisive truth claims like those made by religious "enthusiasts" – which aimed by a radical kind of referentialism to inspect and (it was feared) potentially to police the nature of matter and the inward conscience.

What looks like an exclusively linguistic concern thus signifies a highly defined nexus of political motives. And because the social sciences have characteristically tended to ignore or dismiss linguistic issues as "merely" a question of rhetoric, they have not been, until relatively recently, sufficiently alive to the cultural symbiosis between debates about language and politics in our period. The defense of a rhetorical view of language, in the sense in which I have defined it, becomes the instrument of those interests best served, for whatever reasons, by preserving inherited or reconstituted institutions. The rhetoric of "moderation" by which certain Anglican divines characterized themselves, is descriptively exact when applied to their epistemological presuppositions. They are anti-essentialists in epistemology, physics, and language, and limit, indeed *moderate*, the powers of reason fully to apprehend and chart reality. But just as it would be a mistake to dismiss their claims for *epistemological* moderation as an empty lie, it would be equally a mistake to confuse this epistemic with political moderation. The moderate argument about knowledge is the exact corollary to a defense of institutions: since knowledge is only ever nominal, that is, operates by recourse to appearances, to what can be externally, publicly represented, then it becomes all the more inevitable that claims to a private language, a non-negotiable trans-linguistic reality be embarrassed by accusing them of flirting with an epistemological impossibility. And this amounts to the charge that special claims to private or gnostic knowledge constitute an act of social irresponsibility: the private is, on this view, a-social, hence anti-social. Consequently, the well-recognized attack on enthusiasm, which serves concrete, institutional motives, is part of that same argument about language, since what is centrally the most disturbing feature of enthusiasm is its resistance to representation, the refusal to perform all individual acts under the social gaze. What is historically in Hobbes, and analytically in Wittgenstein (who supplies my epigraph) a linguistic *condition*, becomes, by this logic a prescription for social behavior.

This is precisely the point of contention between John Owen and Richard Baxter on the one hand, and even "moderate" Anglicans on the other. The tension between certain presbyterian and Anglican positions is suggested by the Savoy Conference, which failed (according to Burnet) on the question of external forms of worship. When the Anglicans insisted on compulsory kneeling at communion, the presbyterians wanted such issues to remain voluntary. Examined closely, this is a debate about the relationship of representation (by implication, language) to politics: the Anglicans, who emphatically do not agree with the Catholics that certain forms of worship are efficacious in salvation or sanctification (which would be idolatry or superstition), demand certain compulsory "gestures" as denoting the necessary, formal, and public conditions of engaging in the polity. What most fundamentally disturbs them about the presbyterian position is the potential for *ad hoc* innovations to religious ceremonies to interrupt and thus subvert the formal continuities by which all people worship, and – most important – *can be seen* to worship God. This constitutes in effect a defense of verifiability, in its nice sense. Tulloch quite correctly reports that the "moderate" latitudinarians could not truly countenance dissent, and the rationale is frequently this. They support public institutions, not because they are endowed with special spiritual powers, but because they represent the proper arena for public acts of symbolism, including especially divine worship. One imagines that this rationale operates as a powerful logic within the "latitudinarians'" attraction to Erastianism.

That the participants within this cultural moment understood the relationships I have described is demonstrated by the two authors most commonly cited along with S.P. as witnesses to the existence and character of early "latitudinarianism," namely Gilbert Burnet and Edward Fowler. Gilbert Burnet's *History of His Own Time* establishes many of the most recognizable features associated with the latitudinarians: their moderation, their Arminianism, their commitment to Anglican institutions, their anti-Catholicism, their loathing of enthusiasm, and, as Burnet's brief account proceeds, their style, to which, Burnet writes, he himself is indebted.[32] What is clear is that the "method" he sees defined by this set of attitudes finds its corollary in a certain prose style exemplified in Burnet's own *History*. It is easy to interpret Burnet's quite typical language as an expression of some referential and transparent linguistic ideal, especially coming as it does with an allusion to Tillotson's and Lloyd's participation in Wilkins' language schemes.[33] Thus Lloyd, we read, "looked further into a natural purity and simplicity of style, than any man I ever knew," helping in the process to correct "the common errors of language" (I: 347).

But Burnet evidently recognizes that this ideal of a "pure" and "natural" style is itself a highly rhetorical conception, not only because it is expressed as the artificial outcome of a distinct attitude to knowledge and the polity, nor because it is a prose habit that Burnet has consciously cultivated, but because – as applied to preaching – it establishes a rhetorical mean between "very flat and low" delivery and "a false pitch of a wrong sublime" (I: 348). The "plain style" does not foster the idea that individual nouns or words can or should refer unproblematically to the world, but embodies a complicated effect that shuns different rhetorical extremes. It mediates, significantly, between a merely uninteresting prose style (approximating, incidentally, the scientistic prose Jones understood by "plain style"), and a sublime style, namely one so overly clotted with figural intensity that it overwhelms the hearer. Both instances sacrifice the capacity for individual judgment and assent: the prose either simply escapes the reader's focus or "attention," or so overstimulates him or her that he or she cannot pause to consider the terms of the proposition being presented. That is, the poetics of the plain style, like Church custom itself, perpetuates the necessity of forensic, public scrutiny, whether applied to literate experience or participation within the polity.

This argument is more carefully and explicitly developed in Edward Fowler's *A Defence of the Resolution of this Case, viz. Whether the Church of England's Symbolizing so far as it doth with the Church of Rome, makes it Unlawfull to hold Communion with the Church of England* (1684), which seeks to defend Anglicanism against nonconformist charges of Romanism. Written by the author of a tract often cited in the literature on latitudinarianism (*Principles and Practices* [1670]), this pamphlet accompanies a series of such defenses in *A Collection of Cases and Other Discourses Lately Written to Recover Dissenters to the Communion of the Church of England* (1685). Fowler's co-authors include at least three others often characterized as "latitudinarians," namely Stillingfleet, Tenison, and Patrick. Fowler passionately denies the charge that Anglican uses of liturgical forms amount to idolatry: they are, he emphasizes, only inherited *customs*, so that the Anglican church "*imposeth her Rites not* (as the Church of *Rome* does *her's*) *as necessary, and as parts of Religion, but as merely indifferent and changeable things*" (5). Since these customs constitute merely contingent formal rules for social and religious engagement, it is virtually impossible to reconcile rigid nonconformism with a "humble and modest and peaceable" character (7), the principle being that "those who will by no means be prevailed with, to conform to the Laws of the Society of which they are Members, shall be cast out of it" (6). Laws have no *absolute* ground of epistemic or political authority, but rather offer instruments by which to regulate individual participation in society in an orderly and decent fashion. Obstinate nonconformism thus amounts to an anti-social, individual pathology rather than a defensible ethic, since it implicitly rests on a claim to private and certain knowledge about social and political truths; and these, given certain skeptical premises, can only be illusory. (The contrary side of the argument is the subject of Richard Ashcraft's essay: he shows that the nonconformist critique of Anglican hegemony did indeed constitute a qualified resistance to a limited epistemology.)

Viewed from a linguistic vantage, Fowler is preserving a criterion of explicitness: knowledge can and must only occur as a public, scrutable condition. Fowler thus responds to nonconformist charges that, in reading the communion service facing the altar, the Anglican minister cannot be heard by the people, which constructs his position as a site of arbitrary and privileged clerical authority. But this potential acoustic difficulty Fowler carefully distinguishes from deliberate acts of Catholic obfuscation represented by reading the service in Latin ("*an unknown tongue*" [9]). English is a freely available, public medium of exchange; Latin preserves knowledge only for a clerical elite.

Fowler's rehearsal of the distinction between things indifferent and things necessary leads to a further elaboration of his linguistic argument. He claims that the nonconformists cannot consistently use the notion of things indifferent to argue that because the Church of England aspires to regulate things indifferent, it is committing an act which *naturally* contradicts divine purposes. By alluding to St. Paul's argument about food offered to idols (1 Cor. 10:14–11:1), Fowler establishes the view that all cultural symbols, in which he includes language, are human artefacts. Just as Paul writes that "All things are lawful for me, but all things are not expedient" (1 Cor. 10:23[a]), what validates or invalidates a given sign is not some essential, inward constitution, but the way it is used or organized within the political, social, or moral forum. Fundamentally, we cannot recover some "natural" ground of knowledge, which would require a notion either of referential transparency or incantatory power invested in the word, as if a sign carried within it an *intrinsic* power or significance. That is, for Fowler, the question of idolatry has nothing to do with the (supposedly) mysterious power of images, but their function within public, organized systems of cultural meaning. Signs become idols solely by virtue of their association with pagan practices, but that still cannot bestow on them the intrinsic power to corrupt. The test is, as Fowler puts it, a matter of "action" (social context) or "end" (social purpose).

Turning to Leviticus 18, Fowler asks why certain "Mixtures of Seeds *and of* Linnen and Wollen" associated with the "*Magical Exploits*" of the Egyptians were forbidden the Hebrews. Again, we discover that it is not the particular organization of materials into symbols *per se* that endow them with power to corrupt the chosen people, but "the doings of those people, whom they [the Israelites] were exceedingly prone to *imitate*, even their greatest Immoralities" (18–19).

Fowler's brief excursus into comparative cultural criticism returns him directly to the narrower linguistic question, if by "linguistic" we mean a consideration of words as opposed to other systems of signs or symbols. Why, in Hosea 2:16–17, does God demand to be called "*Ishi*" and "*no more Baali*"?[34] The question is pointed because "Baali" like "Adonai" "*doth...signifie...my Lord*" and no more: "*Adonai is of the same signification, by which name it was never unlawful to call God*" (19).[35] The distinction, it transpires, is not intrinsic to the words themselves, but their cultural and circumstantial *position* in a double sense. In the first place, the utterance "*Thou shalt call me* Ishi, *and shalt call me no more* Baali" (20) depends, for a correct interpretation, on its performative context not as a command, but as a promise, one made on the basis that God will no more punish but will love his people. And since "Baali" is the name given to a God whose actions inspire fear, such a name can no longer apply to a God who will, after initiating this promise, act in love towards his people: "there shall no more be an occasion given you from my severe usage of you, to call me by a name that signifies, a *hard Lord*, or he would be to them like such a Lord as *Baal* was, but he would shew them the kindness of a tenderly loving Husband, for the time to come" (20).

Like other cultural and religious symbols (Anglican ceremonies, Egyptian signs), language acquires significance only by "occasion," its circumstances determining whether an utterance has the force of a promise or a command, and establishing the context by which even individual nouns possess a given semantic. This linguistic view is anti-essentialist: in themselves, symbols are arbitrary, entirely neutral counters like casual strokes of a pen on paper. What endows them with moral and ideological force is their organization into a grammar by and within social practices. Against the nonconformists whom he depicts as attached to the notion that signs have intrinsic (perhaps even rational) weight quite apart from the conditions under which they are used, Fowler supposes a view strikingly like that of Hobbes (on the one hand) and modern attitudes to language (on the other) which see it as an artificial medium, a reflection and reinforcement of social and cultural practices. By implication, and in contrast, to dream that we can escape our linguistic condition so understood is to construct for ourselves an untenable fiction of epistemological security. Inasmuch as this "latitudinarian" position is an analysis of knowledge, it is indeed moderate because it defines limits for human understanding. Inasmuch, however, as it becomes a prescription flowing from the recognition that we are universally implicated in social relations, it could become, as Richard Ashcraft argues it did, the rationale by which to legislate a universal submission to the visible religious practices of the Anglican church. If religion, science, and society mutually cooperate in Fowler's text, they do so because they share in his analysis of how all three must use language.

Notes

1 I wish to express thanks to Dr. Roy Porter and Professor T. K. Rabb for their generous comments on the original draft of this introduction. In his historiographical commentary on the scholarship, T. K. Rabb expresses his discomfort at the exclusive focus on the English character of the phenomenon, suggesting that latitudinarian ideas must be understood in relation to earlier continental movements. That project, however, is outside the scope of this collection. For a detailed commentary on the institutional fortunes of the latitudinarians in the Restoration and eighteenth century, see John Gascoigne, *Cambridge in the Age of the Enlightenment: Science, Religion and Politics from the Restoration to the French Revolution* (Cambridge, 1989). Gascoigne presents the most detailed reading of the latitudinarians' relations with Cambridge to date, arguing that they succeeded as a group during the Restoration by moving to London, achieving national prominence only after 1688. Gascoigne also argues that the latitudinarians provided one rationale for late eighteenth-century political radicalism. (See "Anglican latitudinarianism and political radicalism in the late eighteenth century," *History* 71 (1986): 22–38.) In a series of articles, Michael Heyd sketches some possible genealogies which connect large-scale continental movements to the English latitudinarians. See "The emergence of modern science as an autonomous world of knowledge in the protestant tradition of the seventeenth century," *Cultural Traditions and Worlds of Knowledge: Explorations in the Sociology of Knowledge* 7 (1988): 165–79; "The new experimental philosophy: a manifestation of 'Enthusiasm' or an antidote to it?," *Minerva* 25 (1987): 423–40; "Protestantism, enthusiasm, and secularization in the early modern period: some preliminary reflections," in *Religion, Ideology and Nationalism in Europe and America* (Jerusalem, 1986), pp. 15–27.

2 See Richard Ollard, *Pepys* (Oxford, 1984), for an excellent account.

3 Brian Vickers, ed. *Occult and Scientific Mentalities in the Renaissance* (Cambridge, 1984).

4 A notable example of such historiographical revision is, of course, Keith Thomas, *Religion and the Decline of Magic* (New York, 1971). See also, Charles Webster, *From Paracelsus to Newton* (Cambridge, 1982).

5 See for example, Thomas S. Kuhn, *The Structure of Scientific Revolutions*, 2nd ed. (Chicago, 1970), pp. 156–57.

6 J. G. A. Pocock, "The history of political thought: a methodological enquiry,"

in *Philosophy, Politics, and Society* (second series), ed. Peter Laslett and W. G. Runciman (New York, 1962), pp. 183–202.

7 I use the second edition of Tulloch (2 vols. Edinburgh and London, 1874). Citations appear in the text.

8 Mark Pattison, *Isaac Casaubon, 1559–1614* (London, 1875).

9 This is a point made in effect by Tulloch's own strident anti-Catholicism. For him, conversion to the Church of Rome constitutes a "perversion."

10 W. K. Jordan, *The Development of Religious Toleration in England*, 4 vols. (Cambridge, Mass., 1932–40).

11 See, for example, H. F. Kearney, "Puritanism, capitalism and the scientific revolution," *Past and Present* 28 (1964): 81–101; "Puritanism and science: problems of definition," *Past and Present* 29 (1965): 104–10; Douglas S. Kelmsley, "Religious influences in the rise of modern science: a review and criticism, particularly of the 'protestant-puritan ethic' theory," *Annals of Science* 24 (1968): 199–226; T. K. Rabb, "Puritanism and the rise of experimental science in England," *Journal of World History* 7 (1962): 46–67; "Religion and the rise of modern science," *Past and Present* 31 (1965): 111–26.

12 Dorothy Stimson, "Puritanism and the new philosophy in England," *Bulletin of the Institute of the History of Medicine* 3 (1935): 321.

13 R. F. Jones, *Ancients and Moderns: A Study in the Rise of the Scientific Movement in Seventeenth-Century England* (St. Louis, 1936). In the light of my argument about Jones's scientistic leanings, it strikes me as apt that the second edition of *Ancients and Moderns* was published in 1961, at the dawn of the Kennedy era, a high moment of American progressivism.

14 Robert K. Merton, "Puritanism, pietism, and science," *The Sociological Review* 28 (1936): 1–30; and "Science, technology and society in seventeenth-century England," *Osiris* 4 (1938): 360–632.

15 Informed exceptions, in the last ten years or so, include Joseph M. Levine and Brian Vickers. See Joseph M. Levine, "Ancients and moderns reconsidered," *Eighteenth-Century Studies* 14 (1981): 72–89; *The Battle of the Books: History and Literature in Augustan England* (Ithaca, 1991); and Brian Vickers' contributions to *Occult and Scientific Mentalities*, cited above; also "The Royal Society and English prose style: a reassessment," in *Rhetoric and the Pursuit of Truth: Language Change in the Seventeenth and Eighteenth Century* (Los Angeles, UCLA, 1985), pp. 3–63.

16 One might also make similar criticisms about G. R. Cragg's church history of the period. Speaking in theological terms, Cragg moves quite decisively between regretting the loss of the magic of some former (pre-scientific) world, and comforting himself with the thought that we got science in its place. See especially Gerald R. Cragg, *The Church and the Age of Reason, 1648–1789* (Harmondsworth, 1970), esp. pp. 68–74; and *From Puritanism to the Age of Reason: A Study in Changes in Religious Thought within the Church of England, 1660–1700* (Cambridge, 1950).

17 See for example, Christopher Hill, "Science, religion and society in the sixteenth and seventeenth centuries," *Past and Present* 31 (1965): 97–103. This is one item in a debate that had been conducted intensely in the pages of *Past and Present*, especially in volumes 27–29.

18 Charles Webster, *The Great Instauration: Science, Medicine and Reform, 1626–1660* (London, 1975).

19 Barbara Shapiro, "Latitudinarianism and science in seventeenth-century England," *Past and Present* 40 (1968): 16–41; *John Wilkins: An Intellectual Biography, 1614–1672* (Berkeley, 1969).

20 Kearney, "Puritanism, capitalism, and the scientific revolution," p. 95.

21 For example, Shapiro writes: "Here we find an explicitly stated and highly developed body of thought, which from the standpoint of science formulated a moderate, nondogmatic religion compatible with scientific knowledge, and from the standpoint of religion elaborated an approach to the epistemology and methodology of science compatible with religious belief" (*John Wilkins*, p. 224).

22 Shapiro was directly criticized by Lotte Mulligan, in "Anglicanism, latitudinarianism and science in seventeenth-century England," *Annals of Science* 30 (1973): 213–19; and "Civil war politics, religion and the Royal Society," in Charles Webster, ed. *The Intellectual Revolution of the Seventeenth Century* (London, 1974), pp. 317–46. This collection includes several pieces relevant to the debate. In chronological order, the Jacobs' output is as follows (the list is selective): James R. Jacob and Margaret C. Jacob, "Scientists and society: the saints preserved," *Journal of European Studies* 1 (1971): 87–92; JRJ, "Restoration, reformation and the origins of the Royal Society," *History of Science* 8 (1975): 155–76; MCJ, *The Newtonians and the English Revolution, 1689–1720* (Ithaca, 1976); JRJ, *Robert Boyle and the English Revolution: A Study in Social and Intellectual Change* (New York, 1977); JRJ and MCJ, "The Anglican origins of modern science: the metaphysical foundations of the Whig constitution," *Isis* 71 (1980): pp. 251–67.

23 J. R. and M. C. Jacob, "The Anglican origins," p. 258.

24 Steven Shapin and Simon Schaffer, *Leviathan and the Air Pump: Hobbes, Boyle, and the Experimental Life* (Princeton, 1985). I do not mean to agree with Shapin and Schaffer's interpretation of Hobbes in this manichean model: many readers of Hobbes would disagree with their contention that Hobbes's plenism, his determinism, and his absolutism cooperate as metaphorical templates of each other, and some would doubtless argue that some of these postulates do not actually exist in Hobbes, at least in any simple form. Indeed, it is Hobbes who (along with, for example, Boyle and Hooke) articulates most clearly the rhetorical model for culture I depict below. Shapin and Schaffer are nevertheless important for my argument in exemplifying an entire historiographical approach to the difficult period I am discussing.

25 Richard Ashcraft, *Revolutionary Politics and Locke's "Two Treatises of Government"* (Princeton, 1986).

26 Gerard Reedy, S. J., *The Bible and Reason: Anglicans and Scripture in Late Seventeenth-Century England* (Philadelphia, 1985).

27 An attitude propagated by Robert Adolph, *The Rise of Modern Prose Style* (Cambridge, Mass., 1968), as well as Jones's essays on language and style in *The Seventeenth Century: Studies in the History of English Thought and Literature from Bacon to Pope* (Stanford, 1951).

28 See for example, Hans Aarsleff, *From Locke to Saussure: Essays in the Study of Language and Intellectual History* (Minneapolis, 1982); Murray Cohen, *Sensible Words: Linguistic Practice in England, 1640–1785* (Baltimore, 1977); James Knowlson, *Universal Language Schemes in England and France, 1600–1800* (Toronto, 1975); Vivian Salmon, *The Study of Language in*

Seventeenth-Century England (Amsterdam, 1979); and M. M. Slaughter, *Universal Languages and Scientific Taxonomy in the Seventeenth Century* (Cambridge, 1982). Of these, only Aarsleff, and more particularly Slaughter, attempt to relate linguistic change to the history of science as a discipline.

29 Bouwsma, "From the history of ideas to the history of meaning," *Journal of Interdisciplinary History* 12 (1981): 279–91.

30 I should add that although she writes about language less directly in this collection than elsewhere, Allison Coudert has dealt with this problem, for example in "Some theories of a natural language from the Renaissance to the seventeenth century," *Studia Leibnitiana* 7 (1978): 56–114.

31 See Ian Hacking, *The Emergence of Probability: A Philosophical Study of Early Ideas about Probability, Induction, and Statistical Inference* (Cambridge, 1975); Henry Van Leeuwen, *The Problem of Certainty in Seventeenth-Century England, 1630–1690* (The Hague, 1963); Douglas Lane Patey, *Probability and Literary Form: Philosophical Theory and Literary Practice in the Augustan Age* (Cambridge, 1984); Barbara Shapiro, *Probability and Certainty in the Seventeenth Century* (Princeton, 1983).

32 Bishop Burnet, *History of His Own Time*, 6 vols. (Oxford, 1833). References to this edition will appear in the text.

33 I do not mean to imply that Wilkins' language schemes sought such an ideal in actuality, only that they are often assumed to do so.

34 I reproduce the biblical text as cited by Fowler in his tract.

35 T. K. Rabb points out that Fowler's translations of Hebrew nouns are incorrect. This may be unfortunate, but it does not alter the consequences of his argument either for his or my purposes.

Part I

The Cambridge Platonists: philosophy at mid century

2   Henry More, the Kabbalah, and the Quakers

Allison P. Coudert

A discussion of Henry More's understanding of the Kabbalah and Quakerism must begin with some indication of how More came to be involved with either; and that leads to More's meeting with the enigmatic Dutchman, Francis Mercury van Helmont, in October 1670. Through his subsequent friendship with van Helmont, More's previous, though cursory, interest in both the Quakers and the Kabbalah became deeper and more personal. But before discussing the substance of this friendship, its improbable nature is worth a moment's consideration.

How could Henry More, that implacable enemy of enthusiasm and sectarianism, have developed such close personal and intellectual ties with a man whose life and thought seem so profoundly inimical to everything that More stood for? Van Helmont, whose quixotic, paradoxical spirit was attested by everyone, was an archetypal enthusiast. Born a Catholic, he had, in the years before his meeting with More, frequented many of the sects tacitly tolerated in Amsterdam, although persecuted elsewhere – the Mennonites, Collegiants, Seekers, Labadists, and Quakers. Van Helmont's quest for spiritual enlightenment ignored more than denominational boundaries, it transcended the limits of Christianity itself and took as its province all theology: ancient and modern, orthodox and heretical, Christian and non-Christian. Within this mix, the single most important and consistent influence on van Helmont's thought was the Lurianic Kabbalah. His commitment to the Kabbalah was responsible for his arrest and imprisonment by the Roman Inquisition in 1661 on the charge of "judaizing."[1] But neither his imprisonment nor the intervening years had dampened van Helmont's enthusiasm for the Kabbalah. When he arrived to dine with More in his chambers at Christ's College, the Kabbalistic doctrine of reincarnation was the main topic of conversation.[2]

Van Helmont's religious enthusiasm was plain for all to see, including More, but no less evident was his reputation as an enthusiast in science. He was the son of Jan Baptista van Helmont and an exponent in his own right of that "Familiasticall-Levelling-Magicall temper"[3] so loudly decried by all those who denounced, as More did, the radicalism of the

31

Civil War period. Van Helmont was a practicing alchemist. His very name, Mercury (Francis was only added later), was redolent with alchemical associations and a lasting reminder that he had been born shortly after his father claimed to have transmuted eight ounces of base metal into pure gold.[4] The younger van Helmont grew up in a household in which Hermeticism was figuratively and literally his daily bread. From earliest infancy he was fed drops of a beverage distilled by his father from cedars of Lebanon.[5] One can only add that he lived until the age of eighty-four.

While More welcomed his eccentric guest to his chambers, one wonders if he remembered his earlier contention that all "chymists" suffered from "flatulent melancholia," a diagnosis of partial insanity he had subsequently dropped in favor of straight diabolism.[6] As a neoplatonist Henry More shared the repugnance felt by his Greek mentors for things manual and empirical. Some years before his meeting with van Helmont he had rather tactlessly told that indefatigable empiricist William Petty exactly how inane he judged the work of experimental scientists to be.[7] Yet under the influence of van Helmont, More would soon become an experimentalist himself.[8]

These obvious temperamental and intellectual incompatibilities should have precluded the friendship between More and van Helmont. Even more to the point, however, is the fact that More's eventual rejection of van Helmont's philosophy appears in retrospect to have been something of a replay of his earlier reaction to Thomas Vaughan, whom More had called, among other things, a "chymicall monkey."[9] The More–Vaughan controversy revolved around the same issues that More was to bring up later in connection with van Helmont, the Quakers, and the Kabbalah. In the books More wrote against Vaughan in the 1650s he charged Vaughan with being an enthusiast, a pantheist, and a materialist. These charges were of profound significance because in More's estimation they inevitably led to atheism, and for More atheism was synonymous with anarchy.[10] As we shall see, these were precisely the charges More later levelled against Quakers and Kabbalists.

For all their ostensible differences, there were, nevertheless, definite reasons why More should have been attracted to van Helmont and through van Helmont to the Kabbalah and Quakerism, just as there had been reasons why More had been attracted to Vaughan's philosophy. The violence of More's reaction in both cases is, I would suggest, a measure of this attraction. In the end, however, More rejected as excessive doctrines he had once been tempted to embrace.[11]

In *Radical Religious Movements in Early Modern Europe* (1980), Michael Mullet has drawn up a list of traits characteristic of the "lay religious impulse" of the period. His list is suggestive because so many of the traits apply equally well to the religious outlook of Henry More, Francis Mercury van Helmont, and even George Fox, the founder of the Quakers. What divides these men is not so much the substance of their thought, but the degree of emphasis they placed on individual points. Mullett's list includes:

1 an emphasis on immediate contact with God, either through Scripture or the spirit within
2 a stress on experience rather than established truth
3 a refusal to accept the orthodox teaching of the Trinity
4 speculation about the existence of heaven and hell
5 a tendency towards limiting or rejecting the doctrine of predestination and a consequent leaning toward the Pelagian view that man can contribute to his own salvation
6 the rejection of the distinction between priest and layman as well as the notion of an established church
7 hostility to tithes.

Mullet suggests other consistent themes as well, such as the persistence of millenarianism, the fight for liberty of conscience, an emphasis on practical morality, and an attack on privilege. Out of this comprehensive list only a few points are not consonant with the thought of Henry More. He did not dispute the doctrine of the Trinity; nor as a staunch defender of the Anglican Church, did he advocate its disestablishment or object to tithes. More importantly, by no stretch of the imagination can Henry More be accused of political radicalism. He was not infected with a "levelling" temper, but accepted class privilege as natural and just. More's political and social conservatism was undermined to a large extent, however, by the implicit radicalism of his critique of the hypocrisy and aridity of the established Church and by his advocacy of a religion that came from the heart.[12] More speaks as frequently as any Quaker of the "inner light."[13] Morality, not theology, was the center of More's religious universe. With his emphasis on the practical fruits of religious beliefs, he had more in common with the Quakers than he himself realized. He was both surprised and offended when he heard that George Keith attributed his conversion to Quakerism to reading More's *Grand Mystery of Godliness*.[14] But there was much in More's book, as well as in his other writings, that would have been entirely acceptable to a Quaker. More's emphasis on the primacy of love among the divine attributes, for example, was a theme he and Quaker apologists shared. Like the Quakers and so many other sectarians, More rejected the doctrine of predestination. His description of his disaffiliation from Calvinism while on the playing fields of Eton points to the consistent optimism and humanity characteristic of his subsequent religious outlook.[15] The emphasis that More placed in all his writings on the goodness and compassion of God led him to de-emphasize the idea of eternal torment and to accept the possibility of reincarnation as a way of providing sinners with another chance. That the pre-existence of souls was the subject of More's first conversation with van Helmont suggests their common interests and orientation.

I have discussed More's reaction to the Kabbalah and Quakerism elsewhere;[16] but I would like to continue the discussion here by describing in more depth the reasons why More was attracted to the Kabbalah and to a lesser extent to Quakerism in the first place. The most obvious reason for More's initial interest in both was his relatively tolerant attitude,[17] an attitude illustrated by his eclectic methodology. More described himself as "a fisher for Philosophers, desirous to draw them to or retain them in the Christian faith."[18] He was willing to consider diverse philosophical and religious ideas with a view to selecting those which best suited his ecumenical purpose. This attitude typified his approach to the Kabbalah. "I do not doubt," he wrote to his friend Lady Conway, "but there is pretious gold in this Cabbalisticall rubbish, which the discerning eye will easily discover."[19] Commenting on a reference made to him as a "latitudinarian," More indicates both the conciliatory and propagandist purpose behind his tolerance:

As for me, I have never allowed myself to be swallowed up by any sect. I am content with the name of the primitive Christian, just as you profess yourself an Evangelical. Nor am I a Latitudinarian in any other sense than that I have the broadest sympathy towards all men altogether with a sentiment well-disposed not only towards our own Reformed, but also towards Pontificals, Jews, Turks, and even Pagans. Nevertheless I reprove and attack the errors of them all.[20]

More's tolerant stance, which Alan Gabbey aptly describes as "a rule of suspension of judgement,"[21] only applied to those doctrines which were, in More's estimation, relatively unimportant, doctrines such as the pre-existence of the soul or the infinity of the world. On matters that he considered essential, More was both adamant and passionate, as one can see from the six treatises he eventually wrote rejecting most aspects of the Kabbalah as dangerously atheistical.[22]

There is a less obvious, but no less important, reason for More's interest in the Kabbalah and Quakerism as well. Certain aspects of More's neoplatonic orientation make his initial attraction to both entirely comprehensible. Elements of the ancient gnostic belief in the perfectibility of man and in universal salvation survive in both the Kabbalah and in

Quakerism. These same gnostic elements appear in the neoplatonic philosophy that so attracted More as a Cambridge undergraduate. More's neoplatonism made him receptive to these ideas, but his commitment to Christian theology proved stronger in the end. As much as More tried to combine the two, the task was essentially impossible. He eventually rejected those aspects of neoplatonic thought which greatly attracted him but which he came to recognize as incompatible with Christian theology.

More and Cartesian dualism

More's initial reaction to the Kabbalah was favorable largely because his knowledge of genuine Kabbalistic thought was negligible and based on second-hand and heavily neoplatonized sources. As Brian Copenhaver has pointed out, More's concept of space incorporated the Kabbalistic idea that place (*maqom*) is an attribute of God, an idea he discovered in Agrippa's *Occult Philosophy* (hardly a genuine Kabbalistic text) and found useful in his refutation of Descartes.[23] Following his initial enthusiasm for Descartes, More became preoccupied with what he identified as the atheistical implications of Cartesian dualism, and he employed what little he knew about the Kabbalah to combat this dualism.[24] If only matter and not spirit was extended, as Descartes maintained, then in More's view spirit was non-existent. For in order to exist an entity had to be located in a physical place. More labelled those who rejected the notion that spirit was extended "nullibists," or "nowhere-ists," and argued that such a view inevitably fostered atheism.[25] By adopting the Kabbalistic view that space was a divine attribute, More believed he had discovered an apt example of an entity that was extended though immaterial. In this instance the Kabbalah provided More with evidence to support his contention that spiritual substances were extended.

More's rejection of Cartesian dualism was part of his rejection of exclusively mechanical explanations in science. If all the events in the natural world could be explained in terms of matter in motion, divine Providence was meaningless and the way would be open, first, for materialism but, ultimately, for atheism. A major objective in all More's writings from the 1650s to the end of his life was to prove that spiritual forces were responsible for material change.[26]

Brian Vickers has made the cogent observation that the whole tenor of renaissance neoplatonism and occultism is "a progressive reification of the immaterial."[27] The elaborate series of emanations in the various neoplatonic and hermetic creation myths basically served to explain how the One became the many, or how spirit was gradually transformed into matter. Ficino's neoplatonic magic, for example, was based on the assumption that the world spirit was material enough to be consumed, inhaled, or absorbed in various foods, drinks, perfumes, or sounds, each one of which possessed power to ennoble the spirit of a practicing Magus. As Ficino defined the *spiritus mundi* it was something of a hybrid between matter and spirit; consequently, it was a perfect bond between the two: "[Spirit is] a very subtle body; as it were not a body and almost a soul. Or again, as it were, not a soul and almost a body."[28]

More admitted that there had been a time in his life when he became temporarily infatuated with "Marsilius Ficino, Plotinus...and Mercurius Trismegistus."[29] More's early poetry was clearly influenced by Ficino's *Theologia Platonica*.[30] One suspects, however, that More's infatuation was cut short by his realization that in the final analysis neoplatonism and Christian theology were not compatible. Neoplatonic monism simply does not fit with the essentially dualistic view of matter and spirit inherent in orthodox Christianity. However unhappy More was with Cartesian dualism, he was unable to overcome it. As Lady Conway pointed out, he simply replaced it with something similar. In her one book, published after both her and More's death, Lady Conway offers a perceptive analysis of the inconsistencies involved in More's concept of spirit. (More was always the first to speak of the acuity of Lady Conway's intellect.[31]) If spirit possessed both motion and sense, as More believed, then body would be superfluous:

But if they alledge, that Body and Spirit do agree in some Attributes, as Extension, Mobility, and Figurability; so that Spirit hath Extension, and can reach from one place to another, and also can move itself from place to place and form itself into whatsoever figure it pleaseth, in which cases it agrees with a body, and a Body with it.[32]

Furthermore, soul and body must be one and the same or else the soul would be able to remove itself whenever the body was hurt and therefore avoid feeling pain:

Moreover, Why is the Spirit or Soul so passible in corporal Pains? for if when it is united with the Body, it hath nothing of corporeity, or a bodily Nature, Why is it grieved or wounded when the body is wounded, which is quite of a different Nature? For seeing the Soul can so easily penetrate the Body, How can any Corporeal Thing hurt it? If it be said, the Body only feels the pain, but not the Soul; this is contrary to their own Principles, because they affirm, that the Body hath neither Life nor Sense: But if it be granted, that the Soul is of One Nature and Substance with the Body, although it is many degrees more excellent in regard of Life and Spirituality, as also in swiftness of Motion, and Penetrability, and divers other Perfections; then all the aforesaid difficulties will vanish, and it will be easily conceived how the Body and Soul are united together, and how the Soul moves the Body, and suffers by it and with it.[33]

Lady Conway had enlisted More's help in studying Descartes. As an apt and enthusiastic pupil, she may have discovered something that More overlooked; for in his *Meditations on First Philosophy* Descartes points out that the one area where mind–body dualism does not seem to hold is pain:

Nature also teaches me by these sensations of pain, hunger, thirst, etc. that I am not only lodged in my body as pilot in a vessel, but that I am very closely united to it, and so to speak so intermingled with it that I seem to compose with it one whole. For if that were not the case, when my body is hurt, I, who am merely a thinking thing, should not feel pain, for I should perceive this wound by the understanding only, just as the sailor perceives by sight when something is damaged in his vessel.[34]

Lady Conway's own experience of pain – she suffered from incapacitating headaches from the age of eighteen until her death – might well have made this passage stand out in her mind. Though admittedly more orthodox (and perhaps for that very reason), More was a less rigorous philosopher and less in fact of a neoplatonist than his pupil. Lady Conway took her own criticisms of More's philosophy to heart and followed van Helmont's lead in adopting a consistent, but hardly Christian, philosophy of spiritual monism.

Both van Helmont and Lady Conway maintained that matter and spirit were simply opposite poles on either end of a continuum. They accepted the neoplatonic view of matter as privation, as a negative entity without real existence. In a small treatise entitled *A Cabbalitical Dialogue* written as an explicit answer to More's criticism of the Kabbalah, van Helmont outlines his and Lady Conway's position:

these are our Positions, 1) That the Creator first brings into being a spiritual Nature. 2) And that either arbitrarily (when he pleases) or continually, as he continually understands, generates, etc. 3) That some of these spirits, for some certain cause or reason, are slipt down from the state of knowing, or Penetration. 4) That these Monades or single Beings being now become spiritless or dull, did cling or come together after various manners. 5) That this coalition or clinging together, so long as it remains such, is called matter. 6) That, out of this matter, all things material do consist, which yet shall in time return again to a more loosened and free state. No contradiction is involved in all these. Hence the Creator may also be said to be the efficient cause of all things materiated or made material, although not immediately.[35]

The idea that matter was essentially spirit provided the basis for van Helmont's and Lady Conway's millennial vision of a future time when every particle of matter would be restored to its pristine spiritual condition. In this scheme of universal salvation there was no place for the orthodox Christian doctrine of Hell. In Lady Conway's opinion no sin committed by a finite creature against an infinite God could be punished indefinitely. God's love, as well as his justice, required that punishment be "medicinal" and last only long enough to "cure" sinful creatures and redirect them towards the good.[36]

Lady Conway accepted this idea in a very personal way. By seeing pain as the inevitable prelude to redemption, she found justification and consolation for her own suffering. There was no greater symbol of the value of pain and suffering than the figure of Christ crucified and resurrected. Alchemists incorporated this idea into their art, making it an axiom that the physical suffering and death of the compounds they employed were the essential steps in their purification and transmutation. With his alchemical background and unorthodox Christian beliefs van Helmont came to view pain as a necessary but transitory state in the drama of universal salvation. In convincing Lady Conway of this truth he gave her help as a philosopher where he could not give it as a physician.

The sources for van Helmont's and Lady Conway's monistic philosophy lie in neoplatonism, alchemy, and the Kabbalah. They were acquainted with the latter through the work of renaissance Kabbalists such as Pico, Reuchlin, and Postel; but their most important and immediate source of Kabbalistic doctrine came through the translations published by van Helmont's good friend Christian Knorr von Rosenroth (1636–1689) in his monumental *Kabbala Denudata*.[37] Von Rosenroth addressed the preface to this work "to the lover of Hebrew, Chemistry, and Philosophy" ("ad Lectorem Philebraeum, Philochymicam, & Philosophum"), an unlikely combination of interests by our lights but one that made perfect sense in the seventeenth century. Von Rosenroth's ideal reader would quite naturally combine an interest in the Kabbalah, alchemy, and platonic or neoplatonic philosophy because such a person would be attracted to the view that matter was essentially spirit and that consequently humans were perfectible, salvation universally attainable, and the millennium inevitable. The mix of alchemical[38] and Kabbalistic ideas in the *Kabbala Denudata*, as well as in van Helmont's and Lady Conway's philosophy, encouraged an exhilarating faith in the ability of man to save himself and the world. The Hermetic Magus at the center of Florentine neoplatonism reappears in the seventeenth century in the guise of a Christian Kabbalist.

Alchemy and the doctrine of perfectionism

Much of the esoteric or spiritual side of alchemy came from gnostic and neoplatonic ideas that had been expunged from orthodox Christianity.[39] This is particularly clear in the case of the early Greek gnostic practitioners of alchemy, Bolos of Mendes, Zosimos, Cleopatra, and those who wrote in the name of the legendary founder of alchemy in the West, Hermes

Trismegistus. Legend credits Trismegistus with some thirty-six thousand original works, but by far the most famous is the enigmatically brief *Emerald Table*, which consists of a series of brief, oracular precepts. The following precept establishes the fundamental alchemical doctrine that every created thing emanates from a single divine substance that assumes innumerable forms in the course of endless transformations:

And as all things were produced by the one word of one Being, so all things were produced from this one thing by adaptation.[40]

Alchemists appropriated the ancient symbol of the ouroboros, or tail-eating serpent, to illustrate their conviction that all matter is essentially one. The Greek phrase all-in-one, or the one-in-all, is frequently written inside or around the ouroboros. The phrase became an alchemical motto, constantly repeated: "for there is only one substance, in which all is hidden," writes Lambspring in his seventeenth-century book of alchemical emblems.[41] Basil Valentine, another seventeenth-century alchemist, writes more enigmatically: "More I may not say about All-in-All, since all is comprehended in all."[42] Elias Ashmole, who described his own election as an alchemical adept, took as his heraldic motto, "ex uno omnia."[43] Francis Mercury van Helmont designated himself as "philosophus per Unum in quo Omnia."[44]

The alchemical goal of transmutation was based on the Aristotelian axiom that everything in nature strives for perfection. In the same way that an acorn strives to become an oak and a child a man, the six base metals strive to become perfect gold. The function of the alchemist was to help nature along by speeding up this natural development though various processes of purification. The chemical operations which gave alchemists the greatest certainty that they were on the right track were distillation and sublimation, or what alchemists themselves were more likely to call "rarefaction," "exaltation," and "condensation." When alchemists saw vapors rise in their vessels, condense, and revaporize, they thought they were witnessing a miraculous transformation in which the souls of matter separated from its body and reunited with it in a more refined and pure state.[45] A dualistic conception of matter and spirit tends to disappear in alchemical descriptions of these processes.

The "reification of the immaterial," which Vickers takes as characteristic of renaissance occultism, is thus a basic aspect of alchemical thought and one that influenced the alchemical and physical theories of Paracelsus and his most famous follower, Jan Baptista van Helmont. Paracelsus describes the creation of the world as a series of chemical coagulations in which astral matter becomes increasingly material. Paracelsian medicine was based on the assumption that immaterial thoughts and passions were reified into corrosive physical substances that coagulated in the body as malignant tartar. Walter Pagel, Paracelsus's and the elder van Helmont's most knowledgeable expositor, remarks on the tendency towards monism in the thought of both men.[46]

Alchemists shared the gnostic, but for Christians heretical, vision of man as potentially divine. In gnostic thought man is a spark of divinity who has fallen into the world of matter. He has temporarily forgotten his divine nature but can be made to remember it through the experience of *gnosis*, in which he suddenly "knows" what his real condition is (hence the term gnostic, or "one who knows"). The gnostic regenerative experience is described in one of the Hermetic dialogues first translated in Latin by Ficino. *Nous*, the universal mind, explains to Hermes Trismegistus the power that man possesses to become God:

See what power, what swiftness you possess. It is so that you must conceive of God; all that is, he contains within himself like thoughts, the world, himself, the All. Therefore unless you make yourself equal to God, you cannot understand God: for the like is not intelligible save to the like. Make yourself grow to a greatness beyond measure, by a bound free yourself from the body; raise yourself above all time, become Eternity; then you will understand God. Believe that nothing is impossible for you, think yourself immortal and capable of understanding all, all arts, all sciences, the nature of every living being. Mount higher than the highest height; descend lower than the lowest depth. Draw into yourself all sensations of everything created, fire and water, dry and moist, imagining that you are everywhere, on earth, in the sea, in the sky, that you are not yet born, in the maternal womb, adolescent, old, dead, beyond death. If you embrace in your thought all things at once, times, places, substances, qualities, quantities, you may understand God.[47]

The Greek alchemist Zosimos experienced *gnosis* as a result of his alchemical visions. "I found that I understood it well," he wrote describing the marvelous moment in which he grasped the mysterious unity behind the endless flux of material existence.[48] The Elizabethan Magus John Dee gained a similar insight into the unity of creation through his *Monas*, a talisman whose very name expressed the basic alchemical doctrine of the "all-in-one." Dee praised God for allowing men to have, via the *Monas*, "Such great wisdom, power over other creatures and large dominion."[49] This optimism quite obviously clashed with the Christian doctrine of original sin and emphasis on man's fallen nature. It represented Pelagianism taken to extremes.

In some forms of gnostic thought man not only has the power to become divine himself but because he is the microcosm and contains the whole of creation within himself, he also has the power to redeem matter as well. Many alchemists viewed themselves as gnostic saviors whose job was to redeem base matter. Agrippa believed as much:

Geber teaches in his book the *Sum of Alchemy*[50] that no one can reach perfection in that art without having recognized its principles within himself, indeed, the more each man understands himself, the greater the power of attraction he attains, the greater and more wonderful the work he does, and he rises to such perfection that he becomes a Son of God, and is transmuted into the image of God, and is united with him in a way which is granted neither to angels, nor the world, nor any creature save only man himself; in short, he can become a Son of God, and united with God. And moreover, when man is united with God, everything in that man is also united with the divine – firstly his mind then his spirit and his animal faculties, his vegetative faculty and the elements, right down to matter; indeed, he draws with him even the body, whose shape remains, transferring it to a better destiny and a celestial nature, so that it may be glorified in immortality; and this gift, as we have just mentioned, is peculiar to man, for whom the glory of being made in God's image is truly his own, and not shared with any other creature.[51]

This inflated view of man's role in the universe was encouraged by the parallel alchemists drew between the philosopher's stone and Christ and by their conviction that both were in man. "Christ, that most noble cornerstone, is in us," wrote Robert Fludd, who was, among other things, a staunch proponent of spiritual alchemy.[52] For alchemists like Fludd transmutation was a process that transformed the alchemist from an ordinary mortal immersed in the physical world into a superior being fully conscious of the mystery of life and death.

Von Rosenroth and van Helmont came to their reading of the Kabbalah with minds steeped in renaissance neoplatonism, hermeticism, and alchemy. They were syncretists in the best renaissance tradition of Pico, Postel, and Reuchlin. What they found in the Kabbalah confirmed what they already knew. The alchemical concept of transmutation as a regenerative experience for both matter and the alchemist has striking similarities with the concept of restoration, or *tikkun*, elaborated by the sixteenth-century Kabbalist Isaac Luria; and the Hermetic vision of the alchemist as a gnostic savior who could redeem base matter has astonishing parallels with the incredible powers attributed to man in the Lurianic Kabbalah.

The sixteenth-century Lurianic Kabbalah, which provided the focus for von Rosenroth's, van Helmont's, and Lady Conway's Kabbalistic studies, differed from earlier Kabbalistic thought in concentrating on the end rather than the creation of the world. Gershom Scholem has explained Luria's preoccupation with the redemption and the millennium on historical grounds as a reaction to the Jews' traumatic expulsion from Spain. He attributes the appeal of the Lurianic Kabbalah to Luria's creative interpretation of exile as a preliminary state in a process of universal redemption.[53]

In one Lurianic creation myth, evil entered the world with "the breaking of the vessels" (*Shevirath Ha-Kelim*) that had been created by God to contain rays of divine light. In Luria's mythopoetic explanation once the vessels were broken, the shattered pieces fell down becoming the dregs, husks, or shells of the material world, while the purest part of the divine light, which the vessels were meant to hold, fled back to the heavens. Some spark of light, however, fell with the vessels and became immersed in matter. These were souls in exile. Freeing these souls, or sparks of light, and reuniting them with the divine light constituted the work of redemption, or restoration, a word which van Helmont and Lady Conway use frequently.[54] Because the process of redemption involves progressive purification, it is long and arduous and in that sense very like the process of alchemical transmutation. Souls are required to suffer repeated transmigrations or reincarnations (*gilgul*) before they can escape from the material world and return to heaven as pure spirit.

Luria's concept of *tikkun*, or restoration, is similar, though far more elaborate in its detail, to the Christian concept of *apocatastasis*, or universal salvation. This doctrine is usually associated with Origen, who was anathematized for it at the Council of Constantinople in 553 A.D., but it had a firm biblical grounding in Acts 3:21 ("the times of the restitution which God hath spoken by the mouth of all his holy prophets") as well as the assent of other Church Fathers.[55] Before the seventeenth century there were genuine moral scruples which dictated against the revival of the belief in universal salvation: such a belief brought into question the accepted Christian concepts of retributive justice, the eternity of hell, and the redemption of the just alone. As D. P. Walker points out, all three concepts are related; if one is questioned, so are the others. There were also less exalted political and social scruples militating against the doctrine. People were literally terrified that by denying the eternity of hell and preaching universal salvation, they would plunge the world into moral anarchy. Only in anonymous, posthumous, or chiliastic writings does one come across the belief in universal salvation and a modification, or elimination, of the traditional view of Hell.[56] During the seventeenth century, however, the idea of universal salvation became widespread and the acceptance of the belief coincided with a vast improvement in Origen's reputation, which had begun in the sixteenth century.[57]

The idea of universal salvation was particularly congenial to Dutch Arminians and Cambridge Platonists. Henry More was extremely partial to Origen, whom he described as "that miracle of the Christian world."[58] In 1661 *A Letter of Resolution Concerning Origen and the Chief of his Opinions* appeared in which the anonymous author revived Origen's belief in reincarnation and presented a penetrating criticism of the concept of hell and perpetual damnation. George Rust is thought to have been the author of this book, which makes it particularly interesting because Rust was on the fringe of the Cambridge Platonists and a friend of More. More never realized that the book was by Rust (if, indeed, it was), but he praised it for its "wit and learning"[59] and annotated and republished it along with Joseph Glanvill's *Lux Orientalis*, a work that also argued in favor of reincarnation. Although More did not reject the idea that hell might be a place of eternal punishment, he clearly leaned toward the idea that it was not. For Christian Kabbalists like van Helmont and Lady Conway, however, the similarity between the Christian concept of *apocatastasis* and the idea of *tikkun*, or restoration, in the Lurianic Kabbalah gave the latter added legitimacy.

Luria's vision of a restored and perfected universe is closely related to his animistic philosophy. The nature and relationship between spirit and matter is as ambiguous in the Lurianic Kabbalah as it is in alchemy. Luria believed that everything is alive and full of souls. Luria's disciple Hayim Vital set forth Luria's belief in a treatise included in the *Kabbala Denudata*: "There is nothing in the world, not even among silent things, such as dust and stones, that does not possess a certain life, spiritual nature, a particular planet, and its perfect form in the heavens."[60] Lurianic Kabbalists envisioned creation as a concatenation of innumerable souls in different states of spiritual awareness and development, an idea borrowed by van Helmont and Lady Conway. A later Kabbalist describes Luria's theory that souls rise up the ladder of creation until they are finally freed from the cycle of birth and rebirth:

And God gradually raises these [souls] from step to step. In the *gilgul* [reincarnation] he first brings them to life as stones, and from these as plants, from there as animals, and from there as pagans and slaves, and from there as Jews.[61]

The pious Kabbalist in Luria's system possesses powers remarkably similar to those of the Hermetic Magus and alchemical adept. In his recent work on the Kabbalah, Moshe Idel emphasizes the important role of theurgy in Kabbalistic thought. Idel believes that while major trends in Kabbalistic theurgy originated in classical Rabbinic sources, the more extreme forms go back to pre-Rabbinic sources that went underground and reappeared in the Kabbalah.[62] In both the Talmud and Midrash the belief exists that by fulfilling the commandments, pious Jews are able to induce the divine presence, or *Shekhinah*, to dwell among the Jewish people. Idel suggests that the Temple service may originally have been such a theurgical activity.[63]

These ideas were greatly magnified in the Kabbalah, where man is held responsible for maintaining the connection between God and the world.

Gikatilla, whose treatise *The Gates of Light* appears in the *Kabbala Denudata*, outlines the essential role played by holy men (*Zaddikim*) in maintaining a balance of divine forces in the world:

If men defile and remove themselves from the Torah and the commandments and do wickedness, injustice and violence, then the attribute of the righteous stands to look and watch and survey their deeds. And when he sees that they reject the Torah and the commandments and do injustice and violence, then the attribute of righteous is removed and gathers itself [above] and ascends higher and higher. Then all the channels and influxes are interrupted.[64]

Idel labels this Kabbalistic view of man's function in the universe, "universe maintenance activity!"[65]

One of the principle ways available to Kabbalists for drawing down the divine powers was by pronouncing combinations of Hebrew letters. Abulafia, who perfected this technique, describes the process as well as the effects it has on Kabbalists:

Be prepared for thy God, oh Israelite! Make thyself ready to direct thy heart to God alone. Cleanse thy Body and choose a lonely house where none shall hear thy voice. Sit there in thy closet and do not reveal thy secret to any man. If thou canst, do it by day in the house, but it is best if thou completest it during the night. In the hour when thou preparest thyself to speak with the Creator and thou wishest Him to reveal His might to thee, then be careful to abstract all thy thought from the vanities of this world. Cover thy self with thy prayer shawl and put *Tefillin* on thy head and hands that thou mayest be filled with awe of the Shekhinah which is near thee. Cleanse thy clothes, and, if possible, let all thy garments be white, for all this is helpful in leading the heart towards the fear of God and the love of God. If it be night kindle many lights, until all be bright. Then take ink, pen and a table to thy hand and remember that thou art about to serve God in joy and gladness of heart. Now begin to combine a few or many letters, to permutate and combine them until thy heart be warm. Then be mindful of their movements and of what thou canst bring forth by moving them. And when thou feelest that thy heart is already warm and when thou seest that by combinations of letters thou canst grasp new things which by human tradition or by thyself thou wouldst not be able to know and when thou art thus prepared to receive the influx of divine power which flows into thee, then turn all thy true thought to imagine the Name and His exalted angels in thy heart as if they were human beings sitting or standing about thee.[66]

The idea that the Kabbalist must prepare his limbs for the indwelling of the divine spirit, or *Shekhinah*, is common in Kabbalistic thought.[67] Christian Kabbalists could easily interpret this idea along the line of the "inner Christ," or "Christ within," as the Quaker George Keith did.[68]

The Kabbalists who followed Abulafia's directions for combining the letters of the Hebrew alphabet were doing on a small scale what God had done on a much larger scale. According to the unidentified author of the *Sefer Jesira* – a favorite book among Kabbalists – the letters for the Hebrew alphabet were the building blocks from which God had constructed the universe. Napthali ben Jacob Bacharach, the author of *The Valley of Kings*, brings out the magical implications in the *Sefer Jesira*. He gives a recipe for making a three-year-old heifer, probably a covert reference to the making of the *golem*. He is understandably reticent about the exact nature of the process, but he describes how each part of the heifer's body can be produced through various combinations of letters and vowels with the divine *Tetragrammaton*, the four letter name of God.[69] In their capacity as creators, Kabbalists were very like alchemists who envisioned their labors as mirroring those of God, the master alchemist.[70] Both the Arabic alchemist Jabir ibn Hayyan and Paracelsus attempted to create the *homoculus*, the alchemical equivalent of the *golem*.

The myth of the gnostic savior takes on a novel form in Luria's interpretation of Jewish dietary laws. According to Luria, while eating and drinking an individual performs a sacred duty that affects the fate of numerous souls:

he who is a wise disciple and eats his food with proper attention is able to elevate and restore many revolving souls. Whoever is not attentive will not restore anything, but he will sustain damages.[71]

Luria's conviction that the souls in food could be elevated by the gustative attentions of wise and pious men convinced him that idiots should be forbidden meat since they could not hope to elevate it. Luria's ideas are reflected in van Helmont's and Lady Conway's contention that each individual consists of myriads of souls, or individual monads (a term they both used),[72] each one of which ascends or descends the scale of creation.

All these examples illustrate the astonishing powers attributed to man in Kabbalistic thought. As Idel comments:

The focus of Kabbalistic theurgy is God, not man; the latter is given unimaginable powers to be used in order to repair the divine glory or the divine image; only his initiative can improve Divinity...the Jew is responsible for everything, including God, since his activity is crucial for the welfare of the cosmos.[73]

Idel contrasts this Kabbalistic view that God is dependent on man with the Christian concept of man's utter dependence on God. He believes that Christian Kabbalists ignored the theurgical aspects of the Kabbalah and concentrated on the theosophical:

One of the crucial differences between the original Kabbalistic texts and their perception by the Christian Kabbalists was the neutralization of the theurgical aspect, so central for the Jewish Kabbalah, with the concomitant acceptance of Kabbalistic theosophy as the ultimate message of Jewish mysticism.[74]

But clearly some Christian interpreters of the Kabbalah recognized the similarity between Kabbalistic and Hermetic theurgy. Von Rosenroth and van Helmont were among these Christian cognoscenti.

More's contemporaries, together with modern scholars, frequently point to the affinity between radical sectarianism, Hermeticism, and Paracelsian–Helmontian science. To this list we may also add the Lurianic Kabbalah. However different in particulars all these various philosophies shared a common belief in perfectionism – in man's inherently divine nature and in his ability to restore the earth to its prelapsarian state. They also shared the belief that it was each individual's mission and responsibility to contribute to the process of redemption. Hermetic Magi and mystical alchemists were engaged in a process of personal and cosmic purification. Kabbalists were convinced that the destiny of the world depended on their least word, thought, or action. A similar emphasis on the potential impact of an individual's behavior provided the rationale for the continual, intense, and in some instances pathological, self and social scrutiny characteristic of much protestant thought. The idea of a sacred community enshrined in covenant theology made it essential for everyone to be his brother's keeper lest one erring individual spoil everyone's chance at heaven.

The Quakers and the doctrine of perfectionism

The common millenarian orientation and implicit perfectionism in much radical religious and philosophical thought in the seventeenth century helps to explain why van Helmont was attracted to the Quakers and why George Keith became such an enthusiastic Kabbalist. Quakers tended to internalize the Christian drama of Christ's death and resurrection and to think of heaven and hell as internal states. In this respect they thought in ways remarkably similar to mystical alchemists whose goal was an internal transmutation. G. F. Nuttall was the first to point out the similarities between the Quakers' belief in man's capacity to transcend sin and the Hermetic view of man as the divine microcosm.[75] The Quaker emphasis on the "inner light," or on "Christ within," led some Quakers to believe they were God or possessed miraculous powers. The shaking, or quaking, that earned Quakers their name, was a sign of divine possession. James Nayler identified so completely with this spirit of "Christ within" that he rode into Bristol on the back of a donkey, while Quaker women threw palm fronds in his path. Other Quakers claimed to possess the same miraculous healing powers as the Apostles and Christ. George Fox kept a book listing the cures he had effected – some one hundred and fifty, among which were cases of toothache, gout, blindness, scrofula, small-pox, the stone, paralysis, headaches, ulcers, and even a broken neck. Several Quaker women claimed to have experienced painless childbirth, a clear indication that in their minds they had returned to the prelapsarian time before God had cursed Eve. A few Quaker men attempted to resurrect the dead, apparently on the assumption that they, too, had returned to the prelapsarian world in which death was unknown. Ralph Josselin reports in his diary that a group of Quakers travelled to Colchester to see the resurrection of their fellow Quaker James Parnell.[76] Fox describes a Worcester Quaker who exhumed the body of a Quaker apprentice and "commanded him in the name of the living God to arise and walk."[77]

Henry More was convinced that the Quakers had descended from the Familists.[78] Like many of his contemporaries he bracketed the Familists and Quakers together in a blanket condemnation of enthusiasm and sectarianism. Even if More's purpose in identifying the Quakers with Familists was tendentious, he probably was correct. The emphasis that Henry Nicholas, the founder of the Familists, placed on love, the "inner light," and the ability of man to conquer sin and become divine had a great deal in common with later Quaker thought. The connection between the Quakers and Familists is doubly interesting because it suggests the Familists as a possible source for the traces of Hermeticism discovered by Nuttall and others in Quakerism. The Familist John Everard (1575–1650?), for example, has been seen by Christopher Hill, among others, as an exponent of ideas later associated with the Quakers.[79] Everard was also a neoplatonist, an alchemist, and a Hermeticist. He made the first English translation of the *Corpus Hermeticum* and of the *Asclepius*, which was published after his death in 1657. His sermons are heavily influenced by neoplatonic and Hermetic ideas. In his first sermon, Christ is identified as Nous, or Mind. Everard also translated the *Emerald Table* of Hermes Trismegistus and the alchemical works of Basil Valentine.[80]

In his combination of interests, John Everard is remarkably like Francis Mercury van Helmont and George Keith. As Henry More said, he was not at all surprised that Keith, the Quaker, should have found the Kabbalah "as sweet and pleasing ... as new milk to any kitten."[81] More meant by this that one enthusiasm invariably leads to another. But we are in a position to see more clearly just why Keith could believe that the Kabbalah and Quakerism were compatible. As Quaker theology developed, however, and as the Quakers became increasingly conservative in their struggle for respectability, the notion of man's perfectibility was eliminated and with the disappearance of that idea went the link to Kabbalistic, Hermetic, and alchemical thought.

Henry More and the doctrine of perfectionism

At this point one might well ask what this long and somewhat circuitous discussion of the perfectionist doctrines in alchemy, the Kabbalah, and Quakerism has to do with Henry More? The answer I would suggest is a great deal. A hallmark of the Cambridge Platonists was their rejection of the Augustinian and Calvinist emphasis on man's depraved and fallen nature and the reassertion of the renaissance theme of the dignity of man. The optimistic and inherently Pelagian outlook of the Cambridge Platonists was reflected in their preference for the writings of the Greek philosophers and Greek Church Fathers over those of Augustine and later Churchmen. As Patrides has said, "The deification of man is one of the most thoroughly Greek ideas espoused by the Cambridge Platonists."[82] Plato believed that men had the capacity "to become like God."[83] Plotinus believed it possible for man to merge with the one and "to be God."[84] Origen, St. Gregory of Nyssa, and St. Athanasius accepted this thoroughly Greek idea.[85] Although refuted by Augustine and again by Calvin, the idea of man's kinship with God and his consequent perfectibility kept reappearing in Christian writings, but always on the borders of heresy, if not well beyond. As a result of his reading of platonic and neoplatonic philosophers, particularly Plotinus, More invested the orthodox Christian belief that man was made in God's image with the platonic idea that man could become divine. As an orthodox Anglican More could not accept the inherent divinity of man as openly and completely as alchemists and Kabbalists because it so obviously clashed with the Christian doctrine of original sin. But there is enough evidence in More's writings to suggest that his orthodoxy was not always in control. Take, for example, the following expostulation:

How *lovely*, how *Magnificent* a *State* is the *Soul* of *Man* in when the *Life of God* inactuating her, shoots her along with himself through Heaven and Earth; makes her *Unite* with, and after a Sort feel herself animate, the whole World... This is to become *Deiform*, to be thus suspended (not by Imagination, but by Union of Life... joining Centers with God) and by a sensible Touch to be held up from the clotty dark Personality of this Compacted Body. Here is *Love*, here is *Freedom*, here is *Justice* and *Equity* in the *Super-essential Causes* of them. He that is here looks upon All things as One; and on himself, if he can then mind himself, as a part of the Whole.[86]

This passage appears in a treatise in which More attacks Thomas Vaughan as an enthusiast, a charge that Vaughan had previously levelled against More. More adopts a strange defense against Vaughan's accusation. First he simply denies that he is an enthusiast: "Nor am I at all, Philalethes, Enthusiastical." But he then goes on to write one of the more enthusiastic passages on record, in which he seems quite consciously to wish to surpass *Nous* in his soliloquy to Hermes Trismegistus quoted above (p. 40):

For God doth not ride me as a Horse, and guide me I know not whither myself; but converseth with me as a *Friend*: and speaks to me in such a *Dialect* as I understand fully, and can make others understand, that have not made Shipwrack of the Faculties that God hath given them, by *Superstition* or *Sensuality*... For God hath permitted to me all these things; and I have it under the Broad Seal of Heaven. Who dare charge me? God doth acquit me. For He hath made me full lord of the Four Elements; and hath constituted me Emperour of the World. I am in the *Fire of Choler*, and am not burn'd; in the *Water* of *Phlegm*, and am not drown'd; in the *Airy Sanguine*, and yet am not blown away with every blast of transient Pleasure, or vain doctrines of Men; I descend also into the sad *Earthly Melancholy*, and yet am not buried from the sight of my God. I am, *Philalethes*, (though I dare say thou takest me for no bird of Paradise) *Incola Coeli in Terra*, an *Inhabitant of Paradise* and *Heaven* upon Earth – I sport with the Beast of the Earth; the Lion licks my Hand like a Spaniel; and the Serpent sleeps upon my Lap and stings me not. I play with the Fowls of Heaven; and the Birds of the air sit Singing on my Fist. All these things are true in a Sober Sense. And the *Dispensation* I live in, is more *Happiness* above all Measure, than if thou couldst call down the moon so near thee by thy *Magick* Charms that thou mayst kiss her, as she is said to have kiss'd *Endymion*; or couldst stop the course of the Sun; or which is all one, with one Stamp of thy foot stay the Motion of the Earth.[87]

This rhapsodic passage brings to mind the Hermetic vision of man as the microcosm with the power to comprehend the macrocosm because it lies within himself. It also suggests that More had absorbed the platonic view that man has the capacity to become divine. In this connection it is interesting to note that one of the people who read the draft of Ward's life of More complained that not enough was said about More's mystical experiences and their contribution to his attainment of spiritual perfection: "Why must we have no account or Journal of the Holy discipline of *Divine Wisdom* upon this Early Devoto; whereby he *became Perfect*, as the Author of Wisdom expresseth it, ch. 4.13 *in a short time*?"[88] That More did believe perfection was attainable, at least in his more enthusiastic moments, is suggested by other passages in his writings dealing with purification.

Purification is a consistent theme in More's work. As Staudenbaur has pointed out, when More discusses purification he mixes together the essentially incompatible treatments of the subject in Christian and neoplatonic thought. As More says, helpfully citing his sources while describing his spiritual crisis as a Cambridge undergraduate:

It fell out truly very *Happily* for me, that I suffer'd so great a *Disappointment* in my *Studies*. For it made me seriously at last begin to think with my self; whether the *Knowledge* of things was really that *Supreme Felicity* of Man; or something *Greater* and *More Divine* was; Or supposing it to be so, whether it was to be acquired by such an *Eagerness* and *Intentness* in the *reading* of Authors, and *Contemplating* of things; or by the *Purging* of the *Mind* from all sorts of vices whatsoever; Especially having begun to read now the *Platonick* Writers, *Marsilius Ficinus*, *Plotinus* himself, *Mercurius Trismegistus*; and the *Mystical Divines*, among whom there was frequent mention made of the *Purification* of the *Soul*, and of the Purgative Course that is previous to the *Illuminative*; as if the Person that expected to have his Mind *illuminated* of God, was to endeavour after the *Highest Purity*.[89]

For Christians purification is a moral and ethical matter, while for neoplatonists, Hermeticists, and alchemists, purification is an essentially physical act. The physical nature of More's notion of purification is evident in the following passage. Here More describes regeneration in terms of the purification of the blood and spirits by means of the world spirit inhaled during prayer. Not all prayers, however, can effect such purification, but only

such [prayers] as *deep Sighs* from the very bottom of the Soul do also accompany with the most *vehement Aspirations* after God and virtue. For by these Labours and passions we ventilate and purge the blood and Spirits, and draw in larger Draughts of the pure air or *ether* on them; by which we strengthen and increase the *Luciform Body*, (that which *Hierocles* calls also the *Spiritual* and *attenuate* Vehicle) and imbibe with them at length *God himself*, in a sort into our *Souls*.[90]

More outlined a "philosophical hypothesis touching the mystery of regeneration," an essentially physical process described by Ward as follows:

he ever had a great Care, to keep in good Order what the *Platonists* call the *Luciform Vehicle* of the Soul; in which the Boniform *Faculty*, as they term it, resides. And here it will not be amiss to acquaint the Reader with some Peculiar *Maxims* of His upon this subject. He laid a great stress upon what he calls the *Divine Body*, as well as the *Divine Life* itself; and upon the *former* because of the *latter*: For he supposeth that it always *dwells* in it, and is no where fixable out of it; and that by how much any Person partakes more of *Righteousness* and *Virtue*, he hath also greater Measure of this *Divine Body*, or *Coelestial Matter*, within himself. Of this he particularly discourseth in the Beginning of his Fourth *Dialogue* ... and tells us, of what great Moment it is; and that *by our sincere* Devotions, *and* Breathings towards God, and *in* Virtue of Our real Regeneration, *we imbibe both the* divine Life, *and the* Divine Body *at once*. And in a MS I have seen, he observes on this Head, *that there* is a *holy* Art of Life, *or certain Sacred Method of attaining unto great and Experimental* Praegustations, of the Highest Happiness, that *our Nature is capable of*; and *that the* Degrees of Happiness *and* Perfection *in the* Soul *arise, or ascend, according to the* Degree *of* Purity and Perfection *in that* Body or Matter *she is united with*: So that we are to endeavour *a Regress from the baser Affections of* the Earthly Body; *to make our* Blood *and* Spirits *of a more refined consistency; and to replenish our* Inward Man *with so much larger Draughts of* Aethereal or Coelestial *Matter*.[91]

More's conscious effort at an early age to suppress his obvious interest in natural philosophy reflects his commitment to platonic epistemology and to the concomitant conception of purification as a process of eradicating the grosser aspects of the body:

> that insatiable Desire and Thirst of mind after *Knowledge* of things was wholly almost extinguish'd in me; as being solicitous now, about nothing so much as a more full *Union* with this *Divine* and *Coelestial Principle*, the inward flowing Well-spring of *Life eternal*: With the most fervent Prayers breathing often unto God, that he would be pleas'd thoroughly to set me free from the dark Chains and this so sordid captivity of my *own Will*.
>
> But here openly to declare the Thing as it was; when this inordinate Desire after the *Knowledge* of things was thus lay'd in me, and I aspir'd after nothing but this sole *Purity* and *Simplicity* of *Mind*, there shone in upon me daily a greater Assurance than ever I could have expected, even of those things which before I had the greater Desire *to know*; Insomuch that within a few years, I was got into a most *Joyous* and *Lucid* State of *Mind*; and such plainly as is *ineffable*; though according to my custom I have endeavoured to express it.[92]

More's enhanced spiritual state, produced by the regenerative processes he himself describes, was accompanied in turn by unusual physical manifestations: his urine had the "Flavour of Violets"; his breast and body "sent forth flowery and Aromatick Odours."[93] Such claims, which suggest the close association between body and spirit in More's thinking, together with his own enthusiastic statements, led people to accuse him of enthusiasm, a charge that Ward felt compelled to explain and refute.[94]

I am not suggesting that More was a Hermeticist or that he accepted perfectionist ideas, simply that there are aspects of his thought that lean in the direction of perfectionism and that consequently may have made him more aware and critical of the doctrine when he met it head on. More's most passionate diatribes are directed at those who, in his estimation, misunderstood the doctrines that he cherished. He attacked Thomas Vaughan for distorting true platonism with "preposterous and fortuitous imagination."[95] He attacked the Lurianic Kabbalah because it, too, went beyond the boundaries of the kind of neoplatonized Christianity that he deemed acceptable. More constantly tried to fit Kabbalistic philosophy to the procrustean bed of his brand of Christian neoplatonism. In the letters and treatises that More sent to von Rosenroth, who was then in the process of editing the *Kabbala Denudata*, More draws repeated parallels between Kabbalistic and neoplatonic doctrines, only to have them rejected by von Rosenroth.[96]

Through van Helmont and von Rosenroth More was exposed for the first time to genuine Kabbalistic thought. His earlier and enthusiastic book on the Kabbalah, the *Conjectura Cabbalistica* (1653), had been written in virtual ignorance of authentic Kabbalistic texts. The two Jewish authorities More cites most frequently (and presumably the only ones he actually read) are Philo and Maimonides, neither of whom can by any stretch of the imagination be described as Kabbalists.[97] When More wrote his *Conjectura Cabbalistica* he had not read the *Zohar*, the book that was at the heart of Kabbalistic thought and a fundamental text for all Kabbalists, including van Helmont and von Rosenroth. In a letter to Lady Conway, More candidly admits that his Kabbalah was the product of his own imagination:

Though the Conceptions in the Cabbala be most what my own, yet I do what I can in my Defense to gette Godfathers all long to these births of my own braine, and so to lessen the odium of these inventions by alleging the Authority of Ancient Philosophers and Fathers, and therefore the Defense is longer than other wise it had needed to have been.[98]

The "godfathers" More found are none other than his favorite Greek philosophers, Pythagoras, Plato, and the neoplatonists. Like most Christian interpreters of the Kabbalah, More used the term to designate a philosophy which he considered particularly enlightening.[99] For More this was his ingenious analysis of the first three chapters of Genesis as an up-to-date scientific text based on the principles of Descartes. More's Kabbalistic work had, therefore, the apologetic purpose of integrating platonism and Judaism within a Christian and scientific framework. More subscribed to the view of renaissance neoplatonists and Christian Kabbalists that Moses had been the mentor of Pythagoras and Plato. Platonic philosophy therefore had an impeccable pedigree; whatever deviations appeared in it resulted from the fact that Plato and Pythagoras had "mingled their own fooleries" with the pure source of Mosaic philosophy.[100]

More's early Kabbalistic work represents a phase of his thought in which he still had high hopes for the mechanical philosophy of Descartes and felt that Christianity could absorb pagan and Jewish influences. As he became older his views narrowed. He recognized greater difficulty in harmonizing science and religion and he began to suspect that too much philosophizing could undermine essential Christian beliefs. Through his association with van Helmont and correspondence with von Rosenroth, he came into contact with genuine Kabbalistic thought and his early enthusiasm faded. His mind revolted against such elaborate doctrine. How, he asked, in a treatise that von Rosenroth published in the *Kabbala Denudata*, can the Kabbalah pretend to explain difficult passages in Scripture when it is itself so abstruse? Allegories and enigmas are not explained by further allegories and further enigmas.[101] After carefully reading the treatises included in the *Kabbala Denudata*, More concluded that the Kabbalah had almost nothing to offer Christianity. He levelled three basic criticisms against the Kabbalah: (1) its doctrines were unnecessarily complex and made faith difficult when it should be simple; (2) its philosophy was flagrantly materialistic and pantheistic; and (3) the Kabbalah was tantamount to atheism.

More expressed these criticisms in six short treatises which are included in the *Kabbala Denudata*.[102] The most lively of these treatises is the sixth one entitled, *The Fundamentals of Philosophy, or the Cabbala of the Eagle, the Boy and the Bee*. This short critique of the Kabbalah begins dryly enough with a list of sixteen axioms that More attributes to Kabbalists. All of these elaborated the idea that matter and spirit are interchangeable, an idea accepted, as we have seen, by Luria, van Helmont, and Lady Conway. The depth of More's distaste for the Kabbalah only appears towards the end of the treatise, when More describes the nightmare that provided him with the bizarre title of his work. More dreamt that he was in a strange room looking out of a window facing east. He observed an eagle flying toward him and when he opened the window, the bird flew in. The room turned into a garden and More found himself sitting under a tree. The bird perched tamely on his hand like a hawk and allowed More to stroke him. More observed that the bird seemed to consist solely of dry bones without any muscle, and he was surprised by the strange shape of the bird's beak, flatter than a duck's and bent at an acute angle. To More's amazement the bird began to speak. He then turned suddenly into a small boy with dirty blue and white hair and a dirty tunic in matching colors. Hoping to discover whether the boy was a good or bad spirit, More asked him if he believed in one God. The boy's negative reply, given with a condescending smile, proved too much for More, who descended from the philosophical heights, and, to use his own words, "ordered Satan to be gone and assailed the boy with repeated kicks."[103] The boy immediately transformed himself into a bee, but More continued to kick as the bee buzzed around his shins. More did not think that a "trivial matter" could have reduced him to such a frenzied state. When he began to analyze his dream, he realized that the only thing that might have upset him so thoroughly was the Kabbalah, precisely because it preached both materialism and pantheism.[104]

By the time More finished his last Kabbalistic critique in 1675 he had read Spinoza and was profoundly disturbed by the pantheistic implications of both Spinoza's philosophy and the Kabbalah. In fact More criticizes both philosophies in almost identical terms. His criticisms led him to the conclusion that there was a clear and unbridgeable difference between matter and God, or matter and spirit, though not of the kind proposed by Descartes. He could not accept van Helmont's and Lady Conway's contention that everything was essentially spirit and that matter was simply spirit in a debased or "congealed" state. He emphasizes the absurdities to which this doctrine leads. If God had not created the world out of matter that was totally distinct from his essence, then the world would somehow have emanated from God and be God. God would then be divisible, which in More's philosophy was utterly impossible since divisibility was *the* property that distinguished matter from spirit. More was shocked and appalled by the pantheistic doctrines he discovered in the Kabbalah: "no one can fail to see how monstrously discordant the idea is that God can become stones, dung, a little louse, a toad, a devil, etc."[105] If everything was essentially spirit, as van Helmont and Lady Conway argued, everything would feel and it would be impossible to carry out the simplest tasks: "Since all matter is a mass of sleeping souls, it ought to be considered how much pain axes, saws, and files cause these creatures. That a part of God can sink down into this sleep and pain, how ridiculous and horrible."[106] More had levelled the same criticism in similar words against Spinoza.[107]

More picked out other examples of "gross," "crass," and essentially pantheistic thought in the Kabbalah. He took exception, for example, to the Kabbalistic description of the unfolding of the ten sefiroth, or divine emanations:

The three ways in which the emanations of the Sefiroth of the Cabbalists are said to be made, namely, together, one above the other, joined in a heap, or in three distinct columns, or, finally, disposed as circles within circles seems to me altogether gross and crass, as if the divine powers were not spirit but body.[108]

The mythologizing talents of Lurianic Kabbalists held no charm for Henry More.

More's attack on materialism was nothing new. Some of his most vigorous, as well as his earliest, poetry and prose had been directed against materialist philosophies.[109] More's increasingly outspoken criticisms of Cartesian philosophy was based on his growing awareness of its materialist implications.[110] His great interest at the end of his life in substantiating the existence of witches, ghosts, and poltergeists was simply part of his larger campaign to discredit materialism.[111]

With all his criticism More did not totally reject the Kabbalah. As his disturbing nightmare shows, he believed that there were traces of divine wisdom represented by the "bones" of the eagle, who was after all a royal – though in this instance, a decrepit – bird. He also thought that the Kabbalah might prove of some use in converting the Jews. But, as we might expect from his methodology, More was far more interested in fitting Kabbalistic ideas into a neoplatonic–Christian framework than in understanding them in any detail on their own terms.

In the end, More reverted to his own brand of Kabbalah and to the

Pythagorean hermeneutic he had employed in the *Conjectura Cabbalistica*. He simply rejected all those Kabbalistic doctrines he disliked on the grounds that they were not a genuine part of the ancient Kabbalah received by Moses and passed down to Pythagoras. More attributed the corruptions and distortions in the Lurianic Kabbalah to the taint of Aristotelianism and to the fact that later Jewish Kabbalists were "ignorant of prophetic style."[112] He believed that the Jews had lost the old, genuine Mosaic Kabbalah in the repeated and various disasters befalling them throughout their history. Because Pythagoras had lived four to five centuries before these disasters had distorted the Mosaic Kabbalah, More was convinced that he and his followers provided a better source for the rediscovery of original Kabbalistic doctrine than later Jewish writers. While van Helmont and von Rosenroth were suspicious of the Greeks and subscribed to the *Graecia mendax* tradition especially prevalent among sixteenth-century protestants, More was not and did not.[113] He began as a neoplatonist and he ended up a neoplatonist, although by the end of his life, he had clearly and consciously subordinated his philosophical interests to theology.

The tendency in neoplatonic thought to reify the immaterial and to materialize the spiritual was therefore finally and forcefully rejected by More. He became an outspoken dualist and only accepted those elements of neoplatonic philosophy that were compatible with the Christian concept of creation *ex nihilo* and with the Christian belief in the transcendence of God. In his mind there was a fundamental and essentially moral difference between matter and spirit. Matter was inherently "vile," "low," "mean," and "crass," all words used by More, while spirit was the opposite. This was the basis for More's ambivalent attitude towards empiricism. The empirical investigation of nature was not only a low-level activity because it dealt with material things, it was also deceptive and misleading. Empiricism resulted in the kind of false philosophy that More excoriated in his criticisms of the Kabbalah. More argued that the Kabbalists had ended up with a totally erroneous view of God, matter, and the creation because they had confused two incompatible methodologies, the rational and the empirical. In More's criticism of what he takes to be this confused Kabbalistic epistemology, one can observe his platonic bias:

To speak briefly of the methods involved in these two kinds of philosophizing. The first arises from a certain perception and intellectual acuteness; the second from a dull imagination and bodily sensation.... To the first source are referred all the innate ideas in the human intellect, or the accurate notions of things, which no external sense is able to perceive, such as [the idea] of a triangle, of a circle, or a tetrahedron, or of a most perfect being, and the like. Included in this group are purely intellectual axioms, or immediate truths of logic, ethics, mathematics. ... the human mind perceives truth by means of its sagacity alone, without the benefit of the corporeal imagination or of the external senses, which are not able to perceive eternity, nor necessity, nor infinity, nor finally, the notion of God....

As for the other source [of philosophizing], one may attribute the following concepts to it: that a substance is perceived in length and breadth, that all corporeal matter is extended (with its contrary, that spirit is nowhere); that nothing can be made without preexisting material, or, what amounts to the same thing, that nothing can be created; that the movement of one body is caused by another; that everything that occurs in the world results from mechanical causes alone; that bodies are held together by the union of hooked atoms; and an infinite number of similar ideas, found especially among the followers of Democritus, Epicurus, and Lucretius, among others. When I read these ideas as a young man, I thought immediately afterwards that I had heard some old satyr or ape philosophizing, in as much as all things were deduced from the external senses and the crass imagination.[114]

More's commitment to the superiority of platonic epistemology is clear: reasoning from sense impressions is worthy of brute beasts, not men; the true apprehension of reality can only come from the innate ideas lodged in the mind.

The gulf that existed between matter and the mind, or matter and spirit, in More's philosophy paralleled the gulf between man and God. Although More had a far higher opinion of human nature than Calvin, he ultimately rejected the kind of perfectionism characteristic of alchemy, the Lurianic Kabbalah, and radical sectarianism.

Conclusion

It is significant that More's most enthusiastic period was in the 1640s and 1650s, a time when enthusiasm was widespread and the doctrine of perfectionism an inherent aspect of the prevalent millenarianism accompanying the political confusion and unrest. "Why may we not have an Heaven here and Heaven hereafter too?" asked Gerrard Winstanley. Although a Leveller when he asked this question (and hence an extremist by definition), Winstanley echoed the views of many of his more moderate contemporaries, millenarians in their own right, who concluded that the millennium was a prize to be won by their own efforts.[115] As the ultimate expression of cosmic democracy, Winstanley's pantheism was even more revolutionary: "The whole creation of Fire, Water, Earth and Aire and all the varieties of bodies made up thereof, is the cloathing of god."[116] What is so interesting in the context of this paper is the similarity of Winstanley's pantheism to that of van Helmont and Lady Conway. Even more pertinent is the similarity between the radicalism of extremists like the Ranters and the Levellers and that of the Quakers. The Quakers' opposition to landlords, their refusal to pay tithes and to take oaths, and their contempt for social conventions (exemplified in the famous "hat controversy"[117]) enhanced their radical reputation and, with it, the distrust they inspired. The result was a concerted drive against them, which began in 1656 when Cromwell and Monck purged the Quakers in the New Model Army.[118]

Geoffrey Nuttall has asked why the puritans, who shared so many common ideas and attitudes with the Quakers, turned so strongly against them in the late 1650s. He answers his own question with both a political and a psychological explanation. During a period when religious conformity was synonymous with political loyalty and political loyalty rested on the taking of oaths, Quakers were bound to be perceived as disloyal. The religious question was therefore part of larger political issues and as the political situation changed, so did puritan attitudes. By the late 1650s and on into the 1670s, as stability and the restoration of order became the primary goals in both political and religious life, the second Civil War generation turned against the enthusiasm of the Civil War period. Puritans rejected their own enthusiastic past, which had so much in common with the Quakers, in much the same way that Quakers were later to reject theirs.

Winthrop Hudson has suggested another reason for the growing fissures between religious groups with initially similar outlooks and beliefs. He argues that two essentially incompatible impulses lay behind the emphasis on mystical religion in the puritan commonwealth. As these incompatible impulses revealed themselves with increasing clarity, division and dissention inevitably followed. The first impulse was rooted in an emphasis on practical piety and on direct communion with God. The inward, spiritual nature of religious experience was stressed above the letter. A second and entirely different source of mysticism lay in the attempt to recreate, or rediscover, the original, primitive Christian community. This attempt led individuals on spiritual odysseys that often took them from one group to another in search of the true Church. Such a pilgrimage could lead to disillusionment with all institutional forms of worship and to complete surrender to the spirit within. According to Hudson, these two impulses attracted different people. The first was more congenial to those like Henry More who accepted established religious institutions (and the clerics who staffed them) but hoped to revitalize them from within. The second tradition was potentially far more radical, anti-clerical, and even antinomian. The Quakers, van Helmont, and Lady Conway fit into this group. Hudson correlates the two traditions with the existing class structure: "The first [tradition] was largely a middle-class movement, expressing middle-class ideas; the second was what we would now term proletarian in outlook and ideology and involved a strong element of social protest."[119] The problem with this economic and class analysis is that it does not fit the Quakers. According to Reay, while there were a substantial number of poor Quakers, hearth-tax returns reveal that the majority belonged to the relatively comfortable middle section of the community.[120] In seventeenth-century England religion was an extremely powerful force and not solely a function of economics. Van Helmont's and Lady Conway's conversion to Quakerism is a case in point. Even if the majority of Quakers were middle class, it was still a momentous step, as the Quakers themselves recognized, for a Baron and a Lady to renounce their class privileges and join a group intent on recreating the equality of the first Christian communities. (Hence the Quakers' use of "thee" and "thou," which was expressly intended to obliterate class distinctions.)

Both Nuttall's and Hudson's analyses help to explain Henry More's growing conservatism. As a result of the sectarianism and extremism of the Civil War period, More came to appreciate the dangers of enthusiasm. More's emphasis in later years on morality and the adherence to traditional values reveals his distrust of the esoteric, arcane knowledge to which he was so clearly drawn by temperament. The last of More's writings reveal a kind of anti-intellectualism at odds with his earlier work. More's conservatism may also have been stimulated, at least in part, by the extreme skepticism and fideistic arguments of Catholic apologists who took great pleasure in emphasizing exactly where the rejection of tradition had gotten protestants. More appears to have concluded that if no absolute moral standards could be established by reason, the best course would be to conform to existing laws and conventions.[121]

In the end More could not accept the Kabbalah nor could he accept Quakerism; but the time and energy he expended trying to understand both is a measure of his humane and tolerant outlook. More's tolerance was certainly limited by modern standards, restricted as it was to an individual's private conscience.[122] Even then it did not extend to atheists,[123] Jews, professed enthusiasts,[124] and even Presbyterians,[125] all of whom could not be trusted because by More's tendentious definition they were not guided by reason.[126] But, in an age when intolerance was clearly still the rule, More was more tolerant than many of his contemporaries. As he says, "That there is a Right of every Nation and Person to examine their Religion, to hear the Religion of Strangers, and to change their own, if they be convinc'd. That those Nations that acknowledge this Right and act accordingly, have naturally a Right to send out Agents into other Nations."[127] More's tolerance was a function of his faith in reason. Reason would, he believed, eventually lead reasonable men to accept the kind of reasonable religion he supported.[128] Such a belief appears naive, tautologous, and self-serving now, but More's emphasis on the reason-ableness of *his* Christianity did have the effect of downplaying the role of revelation, a tendency that eventually led to the non-dogmatic Christianity of late seventeenth-century deists such as Toland, Collins, and Tindal. Tolerance was only possible once the concept of unique, unquestionable truth of revelation had been abandoned. More took a tentative step in that direction.

More's eventual rejection of the Kabbalah and Quakerism was one aspect of his emphasis on reason, even, or especially, in religion. He faulted both Quakers and Kabbalists for their lack of reason, for their excessive enthusiasm, and for their resulting sectarian spirit. Instead of encouraging charity and concord, he accused both groups of pretending to have some special insight into divine wisdom, an insight that made them superior and unique. More found this abhorrent. As he says in the annotations he made to Glanvill's *Lux Orientalis*:

But because a fancy has taken a man in the head, that he knows greater Arcana than others, or has a more orthodox belief in things not necessary to salvation than others have, for him to affect to make others Proselytes to his Opinion, and to wear his badge of wisdom, as of an extraordinary Master in matters of Theory, is a mere vanity of spirit, a ridiculous piece of pride and levity, and unbeseeming either a sober...man or a good Christian. But upon such pretenses to gather a Sect, or set up a church or Independent Congregation, is intolerable Faction and Schism, nor can ever bear a great and strict examination according to the measures of the truest Morals and Politicks.[129]

In a sense one could say that More's tolerance led him to reject the Kabbalah and Quakerism on the grounds that both were too specialized and esoteric in their theology, too uncompromising in their claim to special truth, and ultimately too intolerant of alternative views. An even more basic reason for his rejection of both, however, lay in his political and social conservatism and Calvinist training. In the final analysis More was unable to accept the optimistic, radical Pelagianism inherent in the occult philosophies to which he was otherwise so obviously drawn.

Notes

1 Allison Coudert, "A Quaker-Kabbalist controversy: George Fox's reaction to Francis Mercury van Helmont," *Journal of the Warburg and Courtauld Institutes* 39 (1976): 171–89; F. M. van Helmont, *Memoirs*, Sloane MS 530, British Library, London.

2 Marjorie H. Nicolson, *The Conway Letters* (New Haven, 1930), p. 323.

3 Thomas Hall, *Vindiciae Litterarum* (London, 1655), p. 199.

4 J. B. van Helmont, *Oriatrike, or Physick Refin'd* (London, 1662), pp. 751–52.

5 "The nourishing of an infant for long life," *ibid.*, pp. 797–99.

6 Thomas H. Jobe, "The Glanvill-Webster debate: the devil in restoration science," *Isis* 72 (1981): 343–56.

7 Charles Webster, "Henry More and Descartes: some new sources," *British Journal for the History of Science* 4 (1969): 365.

8 Allison Coudert, "Henry More and witchcraft," *Of Mysticism and Mechanism: Tercentenary Studies of Henry More, 1614–1687*, ed. Sarah Hutton (Dordrecht, 1990).

9 *Observations Upon Anthroposophia Theomagica* (London, 1650).

10 On the question of atheism and the anxiety and fear it generated, see Michael Hunter, *Science and Society in Restoration England* (Cambridge, 1981), ch. 7.

11 In her article, "Henry More, Thomas Vaughan and the late renaissance magical tradition," *Ambix* 27 (March 1980): 36–57, Arlene Guinsberg argues that More actually came to accept in later life many of Vaughan's ideas. Serge Hutin takes a more extreme position in *Henry More: Essai sur les doctrines theosophiques chez les Platoniciens de Cambridge* (Hildesheim, 1966), where he argues that More was an outright theosophist in the tradition of Vaughan and van Helmont. Hutin is able to do this because he mistakenly attributes van Helmont's opinions to More. See C. A. Staudenbauer's review of Hutin in *The Journal of the History of Ideas* 35 (1974): 157–69.

12 "O *Philopolos*, he that is a Candidate for the Kingdom of God, let him above all things cultivate the Heart; for through this only is the Inlet into the Kingdom of Light" (*The Divine Dialogues*, London, 1668, Vol. 2, p. 37).

13 "The Quakers Principle is the most safe and reasonable here, to keep close to the Light within a Man" (Richard Ward quoting a letter written by More in his biography, *The Life of the Learned and Pious Dr. Henry More*, London, 1710, p. 247).

14 Nicolson, *Conway Letters*, p. 341.

15 Ward, quoting letters by More, pp. 5–7.

16 Allison Coudert, "A Cambridge platonist's Kabbalist nightmare," *The Journal of the History of Ideas* 35 (1975): 633–52.

17 The idea that the Cambridge Platonists were tolerant is challenged by Richard Ashcraft in his stimulating article in this volume.

18 *The Apology of Dr. Henry More...Wherein is Contained as well a More General Account of the Manner and Scope of his Writings* (London, 1664), p. 494.

19 Nicolson, *Conway Letters*, p. 351.

20 More to Christian Knorr von Rosenroth, Herzog August Bibliotek, Wolfenbüttel, Cod. Guelf. 30.4, 57v.

21 Alan Gabbey, "Philosophia Cartesiana Triumphata: Henry More (1646–1671)," *Problems of Cartesianism*, ed. T. M. Lennon, et al. (Montreal, 1982), pp. 183–4.

22 See below, p. 52.

23 Brian P. Copenhaver, "Jewish theologies of space in the scientific revolution: Henry More, Joseph Raphson, Isaac Newton and their predecessors," *Annals of Science* 37 (1980): 523.

24 Alan Gabbey has shown that More's attitude towards Descartes was critical from the start and that consequently one cannot say that More rejected Cartesian philosophy after an initial infatuation (n. 21).

25 *The Divine Dialogues* (London, 1668), 1: Ar.

26 This objective explains More's intense interest in witchcraft. See my article, "Henry More and witchcraft."

27 Brian Vickers, "Analogy and identity," *Occult & Scientific Mentalities in the Renaissance*, ed. Brian Vickers (Cambridge, 1984), p. 117.

28 Ibid., p. 117.

29 Ward, p. 12.

30 Geoffrey Bullough, ed., *Philosophical Poems of Henry More* (Manchester, 1931); C. A. Staudenbaur, "Galileo, Ficino, and Henry More's *Psychathanasia*," *The Journal of the History of Ideas* 46 (1968): 565–78; Alexander Jacob, "Henry More's *Psychodia Platonica* and its relationship to Marsilio Ficino's *Theologia Platonica*," *The Journal of the History of Ideas* 46 (1985): 503–22.

31 More maintained that he had "Scarce ever met with any Person, Man or Woman, of better Natural parts than Lady Conway." Ward, p. 193.

32 *The Principles of Ancient and Modern Philosophy, concerning God, Christ, and the Creatures, viz. of Spirit and Matter in General: whereby may be resolved all those Problems or Difficulties, which neither by the School nor common Modern Philosophy, nor by the Cartesian, Hobbesian or Spinosian could be discussed* (London, 1692; originally published in Latin in Amsterdam in 1690), ed. with an introduction by Peter Loptson (International Archives of the History of Ideas, no. 101. The Hague, 1982), p. 202.

33 Ibid., p. 132.

34 *Meditation VI, The Philosophical Works of Rene Descartes*, ed. E. S. Haldane and G. R. T. Ross (New York, 1967), Vol. 1, p. 192.

35 *A Cabbalistical Dialogue in Answer to a Learned Doctor in Philosophy and Theology that the World was made of Nothing* (London, 1682), p. 4. Lady Conway took an identical position in chapters 6 and 7 of her book.

36 *The Principles of Ancient and Modern Philosophy*, ch. 6.

37 *Kabbala Denudata seu Doctrina Hebraeorum transcendentalis et metaphysica atque theologia ... Apparatus Cujus Pars prima continet Locos Communes Cabbalisticos ... Pars secunda vero constate e Tractatibus variis ...* (Sulzbach, 1677). *Kabbalae Denudatae Tomus Secundus, Id est Liber Sohar Restitutus ...* (Frankfurt, 1684).

38 Von Rosenroth was a practicing and a mystical alchemist. He and van Helmont wrote an alchemical mask that was performed at Sulzbach for Prince Christian August. Von Rosenroth included a Hebrew alchemical treatise in the first volume of the *Kabbala Denudata* entitled *Compendium Libri Cabbalistico-Chymici, Aeschmezareph dicti, de Lapide Philosophica, etc.* Cf. Gershom Scholem's article on von Rosenroth in *Encyclopedia Judaica* (Jerusalem, 1971); Raphael Patai, "Esh M'tzaref – a Kabbalistic–alchemical treatise," *Occident and Orient. A Tribute to the Memory of A. Scheiber* (Leiden, 1988), pp. 299–313.

39 Alchemy was known as *the* "Hermetic" art; but Hermeticism was basically a derivative of gnostic and neoplatonic thought, with bits of popular magic and astrology thrown in. A-J Festugière, *Corpus Hermeticum*, text établi par A. D. Nock et traduit par A-J Festugière, 2 vols. (Paris, 1945).

40 Quoted in John Read, *From Alchemy to Chemistry* (New York, 1966; originally published 1937), p. 54.

41 *The Book of Lambspring*, In *The Hermetic Museum*, ed. A. E. Waite. 2 vols. (London, 1973; originally published 1893), Vol. 1, p. 274.

42 Ibid., p. 323.

43 Quoted in C. H. Josten, *Elias Ashmole (1617–1692). His Autobiographical Notes, his Correspondence and other Contemporary Sources relating to his Life and Work*, 2 vols. (Oxford, 1966), Vol. 1, p. 88.

44 Foreword to his edition of his father's *Ortus medicinae*, ed. F. M. van Helmont (Amsterdam, 1648).

45 Another precept in the *Emerald Table* presents a cryptic description of reflux distillation: "Ascend with the greatest sagacity from the earth to heaven, and then again, descend to earth and unite together the powers of things superior and things inferior. Thus you will obtain the glory of the whole world, and obscurity will fly away from you." Quoted in Read, *From Alchemy to Chemistry*, p. 54. Cf. Dietlinde Goltz, "Zur Geschichte der Sublimation," *CIBA* Rundshau (1970–73): 38–48.

46 Walter Pagel, *Paracelsus: An Introduction to Philosophical Medicine in the Era of the Renaissance* (Basel, 1958), p. 208; *Jan Baptista van Helmont: Reformer of Science and Medicine* (New York, 1982).

47 *Corpus Hermeticum*, Vol. 1: pp. 147ff. Translated and paraphrased in Frances Yates, *Giordano Bruno and the Hermetic Tradition* (London, 1964), p. 32. This was the text that inspired Pico della Mirandola to write his radically Pelagian *Oration on the Dignity of Man*.

48 F. S. Taylor, "The visions of Zosimos," *Ambix* 1 (1937): 90.

49 C. H. Josten, "A translation of John Dee's *Monas Hieroglyphica* (Antwerp, 1564), with an introduction and annotations," *Ambix* 12 (1964): 84–221.

50 Actually he does not. As Martin Plessner has pointed out, Agrippa must have found this idea in a treatise belonging to the Arabic corpus of Jabir. Cf.

"Geber and Habir ibn Hayyan: an authentic sixteenth-century quotation from Jabir," *Ambix* 16 (1968): pp. 113–18.

51 Ibid., 115. Cf. H. C. Agrippa, *Three Books of Occult Philosophy*, tr. J. F. (London, 1651), p. 460.

52 C. H. Josten, "Truth's golden harrow. An unpublished alchemical treatise of Robert Fludd in the Bodleian Library," *Ambix* 3 (1949): 91–150. Cf. C. G. Jung, "The Lapis-Christ parallel," *Psychology and Alchemy*, tr. R. F. C. Hull (Princeton, 1968), pp. 345–431.

53 Gershom Scholem, *Major Trends in Jewish Mysticism* (New York, 1974; first published 1955). Moshe Idel has questioned this interpretation in his book, *Kabbalah: New Perspectives* (New Haven, 1988), pp. 258ff. From my reading of Jonathan Israel's *European Jewry in the Age of Mercantilism* (Oxford, 1985), it still seems reasonable to follow the main outline of Scholem's interpretation. Israel documents the traumatic effect repeated expulsions had on Jews of the sixteenth and seventeenth centuries. Although Idel may be right that the Lurianic Kabbalah did not have the broad appeal that Scholem describes and was not therefore solely and directly responsible for the Sabbatian movement, it does still stand as a creative interpretation of exile and the existence of evil, an interpretation that had great appeal for certain Jews as well as for the small band of Christian Lurianic Kabbalists I am describing.

54 Cf. Lady Conway's *The Principles of Ancient and Modern Philosophy*, pp. 188, 193.

55 Cf. C. A. Patrides, "The salvation of Satan," *Journal of the History of Ideas* 28 (1967): 467–78.

56 D. P. Walker, *The Decline of Hell* (Chicago, 1964).

57 Erasmus, for example, considered Origen vastly superior to Augustine. Cf. Edgar Wind, "The revival of Origen," in *Studies in Art and Literature for Bella da Costa Greene*, ed. D. E. Miner (Princeton, 1954), pp. 412–24.

58 *A Collection of Several Philosophical Writings* (London, 1662), pp. xxi–xxiii.

59 H. More, *Annotations upon the Two Foregoing Treatises, Lux Orientalis ... and The discourse of Truth* (London, 1682).

60 "De Revolutionibus Animarum," *Kabbala Denudata*, Vol. 2, pt. 2, p. 415.

61 Josef Salomo Delmedigo, quoted in Gershom Scholem, "Seelenwanderung und Sympahthie der Seelen in der judischen Mystik," *Sonderdruck aus Eranos Jahrbuch* 24 (1956): 103.

62 Moshe Idel, *Kabbalah: New Perspectives*, chs. 7 and 8.

63 Ibid., p. 167.

64 Ibid., p. 183. The idea of removal of the attribute of the righteous is remarkably similar to the myth of Astrea in Ovid's *Metamorphoses*, Bk. 1.

65 Ibid., p. 170.

66 Quoted in Gershom Scholem, *Major Trends in Jewish Mysticism*, pp. 136–37.

67 Idel, *Kabbalah*, p. 169.

68 Nicolson, *Conway Letters*, pp. 408, 415, 417, 420, 431.

69 "Introduction pro melior Intellectu Libri Sohar ... Vallem Regiam," *Kabbala Denudata*, Vol. I, pt. 1, pp. 220–21. Gershom Scholem, "Golem," *Encyclopedia Judaica*; "The Idea of the Golem," in *On the Kabbalah and its Symbolism*, tr. Ralph Manheim (New York, 1965), ch. 5; "Die Vorstellung

vom Golem in ihren tellursichen und magischen Beziehungen," *Eranos Jahrbuch* 22 (1954): 235–89. In the Talmud there is a legend of two Rabbis who made a calf for themselves every Sabbath by using the *Sefer Jesira* and who then ate it! (*Sanhedrin* 65b). According to L. Goldschmidt there is a story in the Jerusalem Talmud of a Rabbi who boasted that with the help of the *Sefer Jesira* he could make stags and roe stags out of cucumbers and pumpkins (*Sepher Jesirah: Das Buch der Schopfung*, Frankfurt a. M., 1894, p. 4).

70 Allison Coudert, *Alchemy: The Philosopher's Stone* (London and Boulder, Co. 1980), pp. 80, 208.

71 *Kabbala Denudata*, Vol. II, pt. 2, p. 419. On the subject of eating, swallowing, and devouring as a metaphor for the *Unio mystica*, see Idel, *Kabbalah*, pp. 70ff; Louis Jacobs, "Eating as an act of worship in Hasidic thought," *Studies in Jewish Religious and Intellectual History presented to Alexander Altmann* (Tuscaloosa, Ala., 1979), pp. 157–66.

72 For example, see above p. 37 and Lady Conway's *Principles*, p. 163.

73 Idel, *Kabbalah*, p. 179.

74 Ibid., p. 262.

75 G. F. Nuttall, "Unity with the creation: George Fox and the Hermetic philosophy," *Friend's Quarterly* 1 (1947): 134–43.

76 *The Diary of Ralph Josselin, 1616–1683*, ed. A. Macfarlane (London, 1976), p. 367.

77 *George Fox's "Book of Miracles,"* ed. H. J. Cadbury (New York, 1973), pp. 14–15; K. L. Carroll, "Quaker attitudes towards signs and wonders," *Journal of the Friends Historical Society* 54 (1977): 74ff.; B. Reay, "Quakerism and society," *Radical Religion and the English Revolution*, ed. J. F. McGregor and B. Reay (London, 1984), pp. 141–64.

78 *Conway Letters*, pp. 304–7, 342, 328, 379, 382, 408, 415, 417, 421.

79 Christopher Hill, *The World Turned Upside Down: Radical Ideas during the English Revolution* (New York, 1972), p. 149.

80 Nuttall thinks Fox read Everard's translation of the *Divine Pymander*. On Everard cf. Robert M. Schuler, "Spiritual alchemies of seventeenth-century England," *The Journal of the History of Ideas* 41 (1980): 293–318.

81 *Conway Letters*, p. 415.

82 C. A. Patrides, *The Cambridge Platonists* (Cambridge, 1970), p. 19.

83 *Theatetus*, p. 176b.

84 *Enneads*, Vol. I, pt. ii, p. 6.

85 "The Son of God was made man so that we might be made Gods" (Athanasius, *De Incertitudo*, Vol. LIV). Origen believed that Christ had assumed manhood so that "by fellowship with divinity human nature might become divine" (*Contra Celsus*, Vol. III, p. 28).

86 Ward, pp. 89–90.

87 Ibid.

88 Ibid., preface.

89 Ibid., p. 12.

90 Ibid., p. 103.

91 Ibid., pp. 39–40.

92 Ibid., p. 15.

93 Scolia to *Enthusiasmus Triumphatus*, section 58; Ward, p. 147.

94 "And if in the high Warmeth, and Letting out of his Pen at this time, some Expressions fall from him that may seem to be over-adventurous and unwarrantable; or if he shall appear in some things to be even *Enthusiastical*, though against Fantasy and *Enthusiasm* it self; He hath offer'd so good an *Account* thereof, and so sober an *Apology*, in that Letter of *Mastix* before cited; that it will abundantly Satisfy the judicious and Ingenuous; and leave the thing (however he seem'd afterwards to neglect it himself) a Beauty and not a Blemish in his *Writings* and *Character*" (Ibid., p. 51).

95 *Observations upon anthroposophia Theomagica*, preface.

96 For example, More argued repeatedly that the ten Kabbalistic *sefiroth* were essentially the three neoplatonic hypostases (*Opera Omnia*, Vol. II, p. 432).

97 Although in his *Conjectura Cabbalistica* More does refer to "The Rabbines" (pp. 143, 147) and to "R. Abraham Ben Ezra" (p. 129), as well as to the Schools of Hillel and Samai" (p. 150), his knowledge of these sources was second-hand. As More says at one point, "Vatablus observes out of the Hebrew Doctors" (p. 113). Philo was of particular interest to More because of his allegorical interpretation of Scripture, his reconciliation of platonism and Judaism, and his emphasis on ideas as causal factors. More's attraction to Maimonides lay in their similar emphasis on reason as an integral aspect of all religious experience, including revelation and prophecy.

98 *Conway Letters*, p. 83.

99 Marjorie H. Nicolson, "Milton and the Cabbala," *Philosophical Quarterly* 6 (1927): 1–18.

100 *Conjectura Cabbalistica*, p. 83.

101 *Kabbala Denudata*, Vol. I, pt. 2, p. 179.

102 These six treatises were published both in the *Kabbala Denudata* and later in More's Latin edition of his collected works.

   1 *Aditus tentatus rationem reddendi Nominum & Ordinis decem Sephirotharum in duabus Tabulis Cabbalisticis, ex Scriptura, Platonismo, Rationeque libera* (*KD*, Vol. I, pt. 2, pp. 14–27).

   2 *Quaestiones et Considerationes paucae brevesque in Tractatum primum libri Druschim.* (*KD*, Vol. I, pt. 2, pp. 62–72).

   3 *Ulterior Disquisitio* (*KD*, Vol. I, pt. 2, pp. 173–224).

   4 *Visionis Ezechieliticae sive Mercavae Expositio* (*KD*, Vol. I, pt. 2, pp. 225–73).

   5 *Catechismus Cabbalisticus sive Mercavaeus* (*KD*, Vol. I, pt. 2, pp. 274–92).

   6 *Fundamenta Philosophae sive Cabbalae Aeto-Paedo-Melissaeae* (*KD*, Vol. I, pt. 2, pp. 293–312).

103 *Fundamenta Philosophiae, sive Cabbale Aeto-Paedo Melissaeae*, pp. 298–300.

104 For a fuller discussion of this nightmare, see "A Cambridge Platonist's Kabbalist nightmare."

105 *Fundamenta Philosophiae*, p. 298.

106 Ibid., p. 297.

107 "Whence if there is no substance which is God, or a Being entirely and absolutely perfect, but only a matter, as *Spinoza* would have it, then this *Spinozan* god is like a Goose among Geese, an Ass among Asses, a Toad among Toads, a Louse among Lice, a Tortoise among Tortoises, a Man

among Men, a Fool among Fools, a Maniac among Maniacs, a *Spinoza* in *Spinoza*" (*Demonstrationis duarum Propositium, Opera Omnia* London, 1679, p. 627).

108 *Quaestiones et Considerationes*, p. 64.
109 The entire purpose of his *Psychodia* was to combat materialism.
110 In his preface to *An Explication of the Grand Mystery of Godliness* (1660), More says that he wrote his *Antidote against Atheism* (1653) because he realized that mechanistic materialism fostered atheism.
111 Coudert, "Henry More and witchcraft."
112 *Opera Omnia*, Vol. II, pp. 452–72; *Kabbala Denudata*, Vol. I, pt. 2, pp. 177–224.
113 D. P. Walker, *The Ancient Theology: Studies in Christian Platonism from the Fifteenth to the Eighteenth Century* (London, 1972), pp. 96ff.
114 *Fundamenta Philosophia*, pp. 302–4.
115 For an overall view of the way in which millenarianism contributed to the idea of scientific progress, see Charles Webster, *The Great Instauration* (London, 1975).
116 Gerrard Winstanley, *Works*, ed. G. H. Sabine (London, 1953), p. 451.
117 Quakers refused to doff their hats in the presence of their social superiors, taking the notion that all men were equal in the eyes of God to one logical conclusion.
118 B. Reay, "Quakerism and society," *Radical Religion in the English Revolution*, ed. J. F. McGregor and B. Reay (Oxford, 1984), p. 155.
119 Winthrop S. Hudson, "Mystical religion in the puritan commonwealth," *Journal of Religion* 28 (1948): 51–6.
120 B. Reay, "The social origins of early Quakers," *Journal of Interdisciplinary History* 11 (1980).
121 Richard H. Popkin, *The History of Skepticism from Erasmus to Spinoza* (Berkeley, 1979). In a recent article Popkin describes More as an "incurable skeptic," which would make his increasing conservatism even more understandable. I believe that More's skepticism was not incurable, merely expedient. For both views see Richard H. Popkin, "The spiritualistic cosmologies of Henry More and Anne Conway," and Allison Coudert, "Henry More and witchcraft," in *Of Mysticism and Mechanism: Tercentenary Studies of Henry More, 1614–1687*, ed. Sarah Hutton (Dordrecht, 1989), pp. 97–114; 115–36.
122 In this respect More's tolerance was similar to that permitted in Thomas More's *Utopia*.
123 Because atheists did not believe in heaven or hell, they could not be trusted to act morally. Like the majority of his contemporaries, More believed that most men had to be compelled to be good and that a belief in hell was a deterrent to sin (*The Grand Mystery of Godliness* in *Theological Works*, London, 1708, p. 361). On this whole question, see D. P. Walker, *The Decline of Hell*.
124 *The Grand Mystery of Godliness*, p. 368.
125 *The Apology of Dr. Henry More*, pp. 513–14.
126 *The Grand Mystery of Godliness*, p. 369.
127 As Rosalie Colie points out, More took this economic argument from Henry

Robinson, who argued that free trade requires toleration and that those nations denying freedom of worship should not send out agents to the countries discriminated against (Robinson, *A Short Answer to A. S.*, London, 1645). Rosalie L. Colie, *Light and Enlightenment: A Study of the Cambridge Platonists and the Dutch Arminians* (Cambridge, 1957).

128 More believed that Christian magistrates should build schools and foster "humane learning" with the aim of promoting a more rational understanding of scripture (*The Grand Mystery of Godliness*, p. 369). Cudworth advocated the same thing in *A Sermon Preached Before the Honorable House of Commons*, London, 1647).

129 *Annotations upon the two foregoing Treatises, Lux Orientalis ... and The Discourse of Truth*, pp. 147–48.

Edward Stillingfleet, Henry More, and the
    decline of *Moses Atticus*: a note on
    seventeenth-century Anglican apologetics

Sarah Hutton

The theological legacy of the Cambridge Platonists to the liberal
Anglicanism of the second half of the seventeenth century was
acknowledged by their later contemporaries. Gilbert Burnet recognized
them as the fathers of the broad church movement nicknamed
latitudinarianism.[1] John Ray draws on Henry More and Ralph Cudworth
in his masterpiece of natural theology, *The Wisdom of God in the Works
of Creation* (1691).[2] Like their liberal-minded successors, the Cambridge
Platonists sought to defend the faith by rational argument. While they
were fairly eclectic in their philosophical sources, and receptive to
contemporary philosophical and scientific developments,[3] the Cambridge
Platonists show a marked preference for neoplatonism as the philosophical
under-pinning of religion. A specifically platonic element in their legacy
can be observed among their latitudinarian followers, especially Simon
Patrick.[4] Indeed, the importance of platonism as the *ancilla theologiae
christianae* is insisted upon by Simon Patrick in his *A Brief Account of the
New Sect of Latitude men*, where he claims that "True *Philosophy* can
never hurt sound *Divinity*," and makes an appeal for Christianity to be
allowed to "choose her Servants where she best likes; let her old loving
Nurse the *Platonick Philosophie* be admitted again into her family."[5] The
other defender of the latitude men, Edward Fowler, insists in his *The
Principles and Practices of Certain Moderate Divines of the Church of
England* that most of the "Basic Tenets of Christian Religion" are found
in pagan writings, "especially in the writings of the Platonists."[6] Fowler
also quotes Henry More in this work.[7] Nonetheless this admiration for
neoplatonism is modified in later Anglican apologetics and absent from
some, notably the Boyle lectures. One major difference between the
Cambridge Platonists and Anglican apologists of the late seventeenth
century is that the latter were less inclined to accept a synthesis of
neoplatonism and Christianity as a basis for a philosophical defense of
religion. Among the successors to the Cambridge Platonists, Edward
Stillingfleet offers an interesting case study because his defense of religion
anticipates this change. He was closely connected to Cambridge

Platonists, yet his differences from them are clear to see. In particular, it is possible to detect in Stillingfleet a distancing from Henry More. The aim of this paper is to examine the way in which Edward Stillingfleet's perception of the link between neoplatonism and Christianity differed from that of the Cambridge Platonists, particularly Henry More. By examining this one strand of Anglican thought I hope to clarify one aspect of the relationship between the Cambridge Platonists and their successors, a relationship which has, in the words of Barbara Shapiro, "puzzled scholars."[8] But first a few words on Henry More's syncretic apology for religion.

Like the other Cambridge Platonists, especially Cudworth, Henry More belongs to the platonic tradition in Christian theology deriving from the Fathers, according to which ancient pagan philosophy, especially platonism and neoplatonism, can be integrated with Christianity. The apparent attractiveness of neoplatonism for the Cambridge Platonists and latitudinarians like Patrick and Fowler was that it appeared to echo the truth of revelation. More himself, in his *Mystery of Godliness*, regards the "Platonick Philosophie" as "more than human in the chief strokes thereof."[9] More, Fowler and probably also Patrick defined platonism with some latitude to include all that we now understand by neoplatonism. The virtuous pagans in More's listing include Pythagoras, Socrates, Plato, Plotinus and Plutarch. He accounts for the particular closeness of platonism to the true religion by claiming that the platonists derived true doctrine from the Hebrews, "by conversing with the Jews, or by conversing with them that had conversed with them."[10] To demonstrate echoes of scriptural truth in the writings of pagan philosophers was not just to identify useful common ground between philosophy and theology. It was also a way of arguing the essential rationality of Christianity (including some of its more mysterious tenets, such as belief in the Trinity or in the Resurrection). More's commendation of the ancient philosophers is consistent with the principles of the rational defense of Christianity which he sets out in his *Apology*.[11] As with other liberal theologians of the Renaissance, the particular synthesis of pagan philosophy and Christianity which the Cambridge Platonists adopted was that known now as the *prisca theologia*, the ancient theology.[12] This explained the apparent occurrence of orthodox Christian doctrine in heathen philosophy as a pagan tradition of religious truth deriving from Moses and transmitted through a succession of virtuous pagans. Among these, Plato was supposed a key figure, whence the title *Moses atticus* from Numenius' description of him as Moses talking Attic Greek.[13] There were variations in the supposed line of transmission from the ancient Hebrews,[14] but one of the most detailed accounts is to be found in More's *Defence of the*

Philosophick Cabbala published with his *Conjectura cabbalistica* in 1653 and considerably elaborated in his *An Appendix to the Philosophick Cabbala* printed in his *A Collection of Several Philosophical Writings* in 1662.[15] Here More incorporates an ancient philosophy of nature along with the ancient theology as a *scientia perennis* deriving from and discernible in the text of Genesis. More and Cudworth were not the last to subscribe to this kind of syncretic account of the relationship of pagan philosophy and true religion. But they did so in the face of the historical criticism of the seventeenth century which had exploded the supposed antiquity of prominent *prisci*, most notably Hermes Trismegistus.[16] Furthermore, a rational defense of religion based on ancient wisdom rather than contemporary science and philosophy was bound to seem rather dated in the mid seventeenth century.

Edward Stillingfleet (1635–99) began his studies at St. John's College, Cambridge in 1653. While at Cambridge he met Henry More, Simon Patrick and others who were to become leading latitudinarians.[17] Although at first he was, apparently, inclined to Presbyterianism, he took steps to get himself ordained, and, after the Restoration embarked on an ecclesiastical career. His first book, *Irenicum, a Weapon salve for the Churches Wounds* (1659), was well received. As the title suggests, it was eirenic in spirit, clear evidence of Stillingfleet's latitudinarian outlook. Stillingfleet's *Origines sacrae* was published in 1662,[18] the same year as Patrick's *Brief Account* and More's *A Collection of Several Philosophical Writings*, which contains the fullest version of the *Conjectura cabbalistica*. It was published at a fairly critical moment in More's career as a theologian, at a time when he had been obliged to defend his more tolerant theology against attacks from Joseph Beaumont, master of Peterhouse, Cambridge. More's *Apology*, published with his *A Modest enquiry into the Mystery of Iniquity* in 1664, replies to Beaumont's unpublished attack on his *An Explanation of the Grand Mystery of Godliness* (1660).[19] It was this controversy which probably occasioned Patrick's and Fowler's defences of latitudinarianism. Accident of publication date alone suggests that Stillingfleet's *Origines sacrae* might shed light on the link between More and the latitudinarians. And indeed, *Origines sacrae* marks a discrete but nonetheless emphatic shift of position from that of the Cambridge Platonists, especially Henry More. For, among other things, it contains a critique, albeit a modest one, of Henry More on the subject of the transmission of divine wisdom from the ancient Hebrews to classical paganism. Later in life, Stillingfleet started work on a second version of *Origines sacrae* which he never completed.[20] Although the revised version is only a fragment of the projected whole, it does suggest a redrawing of Stillingfleet's apologetic strategy such that, taken together, the two versions demarcate a development of Stillingfleet's apologetic to take more account of seventeenth-century thought than of ancient wisdom. It is on Stillingfleet's distancing of himself from More over this issue that I shall now concentrate.

Origines sacrae is a work of immense erudition. In its day it was reckoned one of the best defenses of religious belief in general and of Christianity in particular.[21] In six hefty books, Stillingfleet sets out to prove the primacy of scripture by demonstrating its authenticity when compared with other types of evidence, chiefly historical, and dating chiefly from antiquity, that is from records of events purportedly contemporaneous with biblical history. Stillingfleet places himself in the platonic tradition of Christian apologetics when, in the *Preface* to *Origines sacrae*, he mentions Mornay and Grotius as his forbears.[22] Like More, he states the need for a fuller and more rational defense of religion to suit the philosophical temper of his time. His main objective is to demonstrate the primacy of scripture. The main thrust of his argument is aimed at discrediting all non-biblical testimony, whether philosophical or historical. His argument is a version of the seventeenth-century hebraizing interpretation of all pagan writings as derivations from or corruptions of the original biblical account.[23] He does not reject pagan testimony out of hand, but uses it as negative confirmation of the original truth of the Bible.

Wherein we shall observe the same method, which Thales took in taking the height of the pyramids, by measuring the length of their shadow; so shall we the height and antiquity of truth from the extent of the fabulous corruptions of it.[24]

What Stillingfleet offers by way of ancient pagan testimony is not different as to substance from the content of the *prisca theologia*, but different as to the relationship which pagan testimony bears to its supposed original. He dispenses with any idea of a secret or hidden transmission of the truth as also with the notion of a Mosaic succession – that Moses was the key transmitter of revealed truth to the pagan philosophers. Instead of being the best preservers of these snippets of revelation, the Greeks were the worst corrupters of it. Nevertheless, Stillingfleet acknowledges that the fact that some pagans entertained "sublimer notions concerning God and the soul of man" was evidence of a "wonderful discovery of Divine Providence" to prepare the gentiles for the gospel.[25] He commends the early Christians for pointing out parallels between pagan philosophy and Christian doctrine which show "that Christianity did not rase out, but only build upon those common foundations, which were entertained by all who had any name for reason."[26] However, his doubts about the value of this are strong, since, without the help of revelation, the ancient heathens were misled into idolatry and superstition by their groping reason. The result was that, horrified by the unnatural, absurd and execrable practices of their idolatrous peers, intelligent heathens spurned all religion (and, so to speak, threw out the baby of true doctrine with the bath-water of false religion). Or else, for the sake of the truth, they accepted the false doctrines in which it was embedded (and so kept both baby and bath-water).[27] It is not surprising, therefore, to find Stillingfleet complaining about the over-valuing of platonic philosophy.[28]

Prominent in Stillingfleet's aim to discredit gentile testimony are arguments to show, as he does on the subject of the origin of the world, "The lamentable perplexities the ancient philosophers were about it, what meanders they were lost in for want of a clue to guide them through."[29] He does not deny the value of platonism. Indeed, using the example of Ammonius, whom he takes to be Christian, he sees the conjunction of platonism and Christianity as potentially beneficial.

It is an easy matter to conceive what an excellent improvement might be made of the ancient Platonic philosophy by the advantage of the Scriptures, by one who was so well versed in both of them as Ammonius is supposed to have been; and how agreeable and becoming would that philosophy seem which had only its rise from Plato, but its height and improvement from those rich and truly Divine truths which were inlaid with them?[30]

Nevertheless Stillingfleet charges the platonists with failing to acknowledge their debt to scripture, with stealing and corrupting divine truths,

and it is more than probable...that whatever is truly generous and noble in the sublimest discourses of the Platonists, had not only its primitive rise, but its accession and improvement from the Scriptures, wherein it is still contained in its native lustre and beauty, without those paintings and impure mixtures which the sublimest truths are corrupted with in the Platonic writing.[31]

One of Stillingfleet's most serious charges against Plato is that he wrote in an obscure way in order to disguise his thefts from scripture and make them more palatable to his Greek audience. "His great fault" was

that he wrapt up and disguised his notions in such a fabulous and ambiguous manner, that partly it might be less known from whence he had them, and that they might find better entertainment among the Greeks, then they were ever like to do in their plain and native dress.[32]

On all these points, perhaps especially the last, Stillingfleet takes issue with the *interpretatio christiana* of neoplatonism as embodied in the *prisca theologia*. The idea that Plato deliberately veiled his doctrines in mythical form was fundamental to the *prisca theologia*. Among other things, it made it easier to foist Christian doctrine on to Plato. Another important factor is the supposed line of transmission of divinely revealed truth by

Moses to the Egyptians and thence to the Greeks. Believers in the *prisca theologia* made much of Plato's alleged sojourn in Egypt where he was thought to have had contact with the Egyptian sages who had learned so much from Moses. Stillingfleet is conscious of the difficulties involved in demonstrating contact between ancient philosophers and the ancient Hebrews. He does not deny that there may have been some contact, that Pythagoras, for instance, may have been acquainted with the Jews. But he rejects the supposition that Pythagoras conversed with Hebrew prophets on Mount Carmel.[33] He also rejects another attempt to explain links between Moses and the neoplatonists by identifying Moschus, the Sidonian mentioned by Iamblichus, as Moses.[34] And he takes pains to discredit Hermes Trismegistus, another key figure in the renaissance construction of the ancient theology, and one whose authority had been definitively called into question by Isaac Casaubon in 1614.[35]

Stillingfleet's rejection of important aspects of the *prisca theologia* seems to me to entail specific criticism of Henry More. He makes no reference to More by name when discussing the neoplatonists, although he does refer to him by name in other connections.[36] But the details he gives of the Mosaic succession point to More's *Conjectura cabbalistica*, especially his *Defence of the Philosophick Cabbala* and the Appendix to it published in his *Collection of Several Philosophical Writings* in 1662. In addition to those points I have already mentioned (but not including the case of Hermes Trismegistus) Stillingfleet specifically rejects any idea that "the Pythagoric numbers should be adequate to the days of creation." He also denies that belief in the pre-existence of souls can be attributed to Moses.[37] These points feature prominently in More's attempt to read the first three books of Genesis as natural philosophy in code, as an allegory of the natural philosophy revealed by God in the account of the creation. In the course of his discussion in the *Appendix to the Defence of the Philosophic Cabbala*, More posits a line of transmission for this revealed wisdom through Moses, Pythagoras, Sidonius and Democritus, even including Descartes as a latter-day exponent. He goes to some lengths to explain Pythagorean numbers as having evolved from the number six of the days of creation, and he adduces support for his belief in the pre-existence of souls.[38] Furthermore, Stillingfleet derides this account of ancient wisdom as a "secret cabala of the creation."[39] To impute some sort of occult meaning to the Mosaic text contradicts their manifest plainness. On the subject of pre-existence Stillingfleet comments:

But it cannot but seem very strange, that an hypothesis capable of being reconciled to the plain literal sense of the Scriptures (delivered by a person who useth great artifice and cunning to disguise his opinions, and such a person withal, who...is supposed to have been very conversant with the writings of Moses) should be taken in its literal sense, as it really imports preexistence of each particular soul in the grossest manner; and this should be made a part of the philosophic *cabala* of the writings of such a person, who useth not the least artifice to disguise his sense, nor gives us any where the intimation that he left behind him such plaited pictures in his history of the beginning of the world, that if you look straight forward, you may see a literal *cabala*; on the one side a philosophical, and on the other a moral.[40]

This reference to a tripartite cabala must be an allusion to More. Stillingfleet proposes to turn the supposed cabala on its head. Instead of hunting for scraps of philosophy hidden in the text of Genesis, he says, it would be more logical to see platonism as a collection of occulted biblical truths. It is Plato who should be read allegorically, not Moses. Stillingfleet relocates More's cabala in platonism instead of Genesis.

And it seems far more rational to me to interpret those persons' opinions to a cabalistical or an allegorical sense, who are known to have written designedly in a way obscure and ambiguous, than to force those men's expressions to *cabalas*, who profess to write a plain history, and that with the greatest simplicity and perspicuity ... But now if we remove the *cabala* from Moses to Plato, we may find no incongruity or repugnancy at all, either as to Plato's way of writing, or the consonancy of the opinion so interpreted to the plain genuine sense of Moses.[41]

In place of a clearly traceable *prisca theologia*, Stillingfleet proposes a general and universal tradition by which revealed but reasonable truth was derived either from the ancient Hebrews or from earliest times and disseminated in a multiplicity of ways:

for I do not see any reason to aver, with so much confidence as some do, that those philosophers who spake with any thing consonantly to Moses, must presently converse with the Jews, transcribe their opinions out of the Scriptures, or have them conveyed to them in some secret cabala of the creation, as it is affirmed of Pythagoras and Plato, and may with no less reason of Thales. But this I suppose may be made evident to any considerative person, that those philosophers of Greece, who conversed most abroad in the world, did speak far more agreeably to the true account of things, than such as who only endeavoured by their own wits to improve or correct those principles which were delivered by other philosophers; which I impute not so much to their converse with the Mosaic writings, as to that universal tradition of the first ages of the world, which was preserved far better among the Phoenecians, Egyptians, Chaldeans and others, than among the Greeks.[42]

Stillingfleet observes that parallels to the Mosaic account of creation may be found in the thought of the ancient heathens, but suggests that these are more likely to be cases of concurrence with than derivation from Genesis. Such is the case, according to him, with the founders of the two Greek schools of natural philosophy, the Ionic and the Italic.[43] He does not, however, dispense completely with the suppositions that underlie the construction of the ancient wisdom. He acknowledges that the platonic tradition contains many parallels with biblical truth, and he does suppose some kind of transmission, albeit by a different name. Indeed he allows for a cross-fertilization between Christianity and later platonism. Stillingfleet accounts for the "higher strain" with which philosophers like Plotinus, Porphyry, Iamblichus and Hierocles wrote about "many weighty and important truths" by claiming that they were influenced by "that great restorer of philosophy, Ammonius of Alexandria ... who living and dying a Christian ... did communicate to his scholars the sublimer mysteries of Divine revelation, together with the speculations of the ancient philosophers."[44]

The dismantling of the *prisca theologia* is taken still further in the second version of *Origines sacrae*, of which only two chapters were written. But the aim of this version is much the same as the first, namely a "vindication of the truth and authority of the holy Scriptures."[45] The contents list, together with the first two extant chapters indicate a re-organization of his material as a result of a shift in his apologetic strategy. Instead of starting with a comparative account of pagan and biblical historical testimony, Stillingfleet begins with "A General Discourse in Vindication of the Principles of Natural and Revealed Religion, with an answer to the Objections of Atheists and Deists." Where the first version reserves arguments about natural religion till the third book, this one commences with a reasoned defense of religion, progressing from natural to revealed religion and taking account of what he calls "the modern atheistical hypotheses," that is to say, Hobbes, Descartes and Spinoza. Prior to tackling these moderns who undermine Providence and "attribute too much to the mechanical powers of matter and motion,"[46] Stillingfleet deals with the ancients. His argument is not confined to ancient materialists, but extends to others, including Hermes Trismegistus, Orpheus, Socrates, Aristotle and Pythagoras, among them some of the key figures from the *prisca theologia*. The argument is not directed against the ancient theology as such, but rather against atheists who claim that religion is the invention of politicians. In the course of the arguments he discredits Orpheus and Hermes by conceding that they were inventors of religious cults. However, having established this, he proceeds to use it as evidence for the naturalness of religion. For Hermes did not invent religion. Rather, he introduced a cult which involved the perversion of pre-existing religion.[47] Orphic corruptions failed to overthrow religion thanks to "some very great reason in nature to have kept the notion of a Deity in men's minds."[48] It was *universal* tradition that preserved religion from Orphic and Hermetic corruption. There was no *occult* tradition in which Orpheus and Hermes played a key part as preservers of

Mosaic orthodoxy. Thus, while refuting the charge of the atheists, Stillingfleet undermines the fabric of the *prisca theologia*.

Stillingfleet's critique of the ancient theology can be seen as a kind of ground-clearing exercise. For one thing the ancient theology as a philosophical defense of religion was an anachronism in the later seventeenth century when ancient philosophy no longer commanded undisputed esteem but had to contend with the rival attractions of new and vigorous philosophies. The *prisca sapientia* could not assimilate contemporary philosophy (though More did try to fit Descartes into it). Besides, as an apology for religion the ancient theology was never unproblematic even among its adherents.[49] In all probability, the use made of it by the perceived enemies of religion, the deists in particular, did nothing to recommend it to believers.[50] In conceding the doubtful authenticity of some of its key figures and in acknowledging that even the best of the *prisci* were purveyors of suspect doctrine, Stillingfleet recognizes the dubiousness of its benefit to Christian apologetics. It is, of course, only fair to note that his critique amounts to more than a caution against the extravagant speculations of Henry More. His views on Hermes Trismegistus and Orpheus, which undoubtedly take account of the criticisms of Casaubon and Vossius, could well have been written with Cudworth in mind.

Stillingfleet's doubts about the value of ancient wisdom as *ancilla theologiae* are also consistent with his view of the limited capacity of human reason.[51] However, his position is not radically different from More's. Not only does he make use of More's arguments on occasion, but, like More, he still subscribes to a thorough-going hebraizing interpretation of all ancient wisdom as deriving from the Jews. His critique of the *prisca theologia* is really just a reshuffling of the same pack. Nor was he alone in proposing a variant on the old model. As D. P. Walker has shown, the late-seventeenth-century Jesuit missionaries to China extended the ancient theology to include the Chinese.[52] They did not, however, derive the Chinese ancient theology from Moses. Others who did not subscribe to the idea of a *philosophia perennis* as such believed in the Oriental origins of learning. Thomas Sprat, for instance, mentions "the ancient Testimony of History, that all Learning and Civility were derived from the Eastern parts of the World."[53] And Sir William Temple speculated as to a pedigree of learning derived from the Chinese via the Indians, Ethiopians and Arabs.[54] Stillingfleet still belongs within the same Anglican platonizing tradition as More, the roots of which are traceable to Laudians like Thomas Jackson as much as to William Chillingworth.[55] The major difference from More is that Stillingfleet seeks to generalize the *consensus gentium* argument (of which the *prisca theologia* is a specialized form) by appealing to a universal, instead of a particular tradition. Further, in the second version of *Origines sacrae*, he emphasizes and updates the argument from design, citing Harvey, Ray, Boyle, Swammerdam, Loewenhoek and Redi to illustrate the workings of Providence so as to counter the old atheist claim that the world came into existence by chance.[56] Clearly new strategies were required for facing the challenge of the new philosophies. Stillingfleet's response to this challenge is evident in his later insistence that proof of the existence of God was insufficient unless accompanied by demonstration of His providence. Thus the second version of *Origines sacrae* takes Descartes to task for rejecting final causes and Hobbes for founding religion on fear. And by introducing a defense of ancient natural philosophy alongside his critique of the ancient theologians, Hermes and Orpheus, Stillingfleet also sharpens up his contention that knowledge of natural philosophy is a guarantee against superstition. His prime example is Anaxagoras who, he claims, believed in God, "not for want of understanding natural causes" but as a direct result of his "skill in philosophy." Moreover, Anaxagoras' "skill in philosophy" leads him to recognize a providential Deity. For, by giving a natural explanation of meteors, Anaxagoras "took away an ignorant superstition" and demonstrated the "effects of Divine Providence, which ordered the affairs of mankind for the best, as well as the meteors in the air."[57]

Stillingfleet's critique of More and of the well-worn renaissance model for reconciling philosophy and theology was neither radical nor new. Others, including Joseph Beaumont, had derided More for his cabalistic flight of fancy.[58] And, as already observed, the platonizing syncretism of the *prisca theologia* had always had its critics.[59] But Stillingfleet's arguments do, I think, anticipate the way Anglican apologetics would go, at least on the subject of the use of ancient philosophy. It is striking that the Boyle lecturers, renowned for their advocacy of Newtonian science,[60] have little use for ancient philosophy and none for the *prisca theologia*. Among the few who do refer to the ancients, John Harris justifies the citing of ancient opinions concerning God as a *consensus gentium* argument for the rationality of belief in God and immaterial substance.[61] Samuel Bradford insists that the ancient heathens had only imperfect notions of the deity because, "where Revelation was or is wanting, Men have generally fallen into very gross and vile mistakes."[62] When parallels are noted between Scripture and ancient philosophy, they are most often explained by the idea of common tradition going back to earliest times.[63] Even so, pagan renderings of scriptural truth are demonstratively corrupt, or poor seconds to the biblical counterpart.[64] This is the opinion of John Woodward who acknowledges the excellence of some ancient pagans.[65] It is only in Woodward that there is any allusion to the *prisca theologia*, and that is dismissive, when he says of Hermes Trismegistus, "The Pillar of Faith needs not the prop of fiction."[66] In two cases lecturers distinguish the later from the earlier pagan philosophers, claiming that the former had the advantage of direct contact with Jews or Christians, whereas the latter were dependent on general tradition for their approximations of scriptural truth.[67] Of these two, only John Williams acknowledges Stillingfleet as a source.[68] But it is probable that the others drew from similar latitudinarian sources.

By contrast with those theologians who popularized his science as the handmaid of Anglican apologetics, Isaac Newton believed in the existence of a genuine *prisca sapientia*, in the sense of a body of truth known to wise men in remote antiquity.[69] He also believed in universal plagiarism from Hebrew sources by the gentiles.[70] But within the scheme of history as he appears to have constructed it, Plato and his followers figure not as careful disseminators of revealed truth, but as its worst corrupters.[71] Paradoxically, therefore, while proponents of Newtonianism like the Boyle lecturers quietly ignored the *prisca theologia*, Newton himself sought to disinter the ancient theology and to re-instate Moses/Moschus. Even so, Newton's view of the *prisci*, especially of Plato, was perhaps closer to Stillingfleet than to Henry More.

Notes

1 Gilbert Burnet, *History of My Own Time*, ed. O. Airy (Oxford, 1897), Vol. I, pp. 334–35. This was first published 1723–34. On the theological legacy of the Cambridge Platonists, see H. R. McAdoo, *The Spirit of Anglicanism: A Survey of Anglican Method in the Seventeenth Century* (London, 1965); G. R. Cragg, *From Puritanism to the Age of Reason* (Cambridge, 1950). Cf. also J. Tulloch, *Rational Theology and Christian Philosophy in England in the Seventeenth Century* (Edinburgh, 1872), Vol. II, p. 6.

2 In particular, Ray draws from More's *Antidote against Atheisme* to reinforce the argument from design. See Robert Crocker, "Henry More: a biographical essay," in S. Hutton (ed.), *Henry More (1614–1687): Tercentenary Studies* (Dordrecht, 1989), p. 11. On Ray generally, see C. E. Raven, *John Ray, Naturalist*, 2nd ed. (Cambridge, 1986).

3 On the reception of seventeenth-century philosophy by the Cambridge Platonists, see *inter alia*, Rosalie Colie, *Light and Enlightenment: A Study of the Cambridge Platonists and Dutch Arminians* (Cambridge, 1957); J. E. Saveson, "Descartes' influence on John Smith," *Journal of the History of Ideas* 20 (1959): 258–63; "Differing reactions to Descartes among the Cambridge Platonists," *Journal of the History of Ideas* 21 (1960): 560–67; S. L. Mintz, *The Hunting of Leviathan: Seventeenth-century Reactions to the Materialism of Thomas Hobbes* (Cambridge, 1962); D. B. Sailor, "Cudworth and Descartes," *Journal of the History of Ideas* 23 (1960): 133–40; A. Pacchi, *Cartesio in Inghilterra: Da More a Boyle*, (Bari, 1973); Alan Gabbey, "Philosophia Cartesiana Triumphata: Henry More 1646–71," in *Problems in Cartesianism* ed. T. M. Lennon, J. M. Nicholas, J. W. Davis (Kingston and Montreal, 1982).

4 See J. van den Berg, "Between platonism and enlightenment: Simon Patrick (1625–1707) and his place in the latitudinarian movement," *Nederlands Archief voor Kerkgeschiedenis*, 68 (1988): 164–79.

5 S[imon] P[atrick], *A Brief Account of the New Sect of Latitude men* (London, 1662). I accept the identification of S. P. as Simon Patrick. On this see T. W. Birrell's introduction to the reprint of *A Brief Account*, Augustan Reprint Society Publication 100 (Los Angeles, 1963).

6 Edward Fowler, *The Principles and Practices of Certain Moderate Divines of the Church of England (Greatly Misunderstood) Truly Represented and Defended...in a Free Discourse between Two Intimate Friends* (London, 1670), pp. 79–82. Some copies of this book substitute the phrase "*Abusively Called*

Latitudinarian" for the words "*Greatly Misunderstood*" in the title. Fowler's *Design of Christianity* (London, 1671) is a sequel to this defense.

7 E.g. ibid., p. 132.

8 Barbara Shapiro, *Probability and Certainty in Seventeenth Century England: a Study of the Relations Between Natural Science, Religion, History, Law, and Literature* (Princeton, 1983), p. 106. Cf. also Shapiro, *John Wilkins, 1614–1672. An Intellectual Biography* (Berkeley and Los Angeles, 1969), p. 153.

9 More, *An Explanation of the Grand Mystery of Godliness* (London, 1660), Preface, p. vi.

10 Ibid., p. 68.

11 More, *The Apology of Dr. Henry More*, in *A Modest Enquiry into the Mystery of Iniquity* (London, 1664), pp. 483ff.

12 See especially, D. P. Walker, *The Ancient Theology, Studies in Christian Platonism from the Fifteenth to the Eighteenth Century* (London, 1972), and C. B. Schmitt, "Prisca theologia e philosophia perennis, due temi del Rinascimento e la loro fortuna," in his *Studies in Renaissance Philosophy and Science* (London, 1981).

13 Numenius apud Clemens Alexandrinus, *Stromata*, Vol. I, p. xxii. Cf. John Wallis, *Three Sermons Concerning the Sacred Trinity* (London, 1691), p. 100: "*Plato* hath borrowed so much of his Philosophy, History, and Theology, from *the Jewish* learning, as that he hath obtained the title of Μωσῆς Ἀττικίζων *Moses disguised in Greek dress*."

14 See Walker, *Ancient Theology*, ch. 6 for some seventeenth-century French variants.

15 *Conjectura Cabbalistica or, A conjectural Essay of Interpreting the Minde of Moses According to a Threefold Cabbala: viz. Literal, Philosophical, Mystical or Divinely Inspired* (London, 1653). More expands his original account of the "Philosophick Cabbala of Moses" by adding twelve chapters in his *An Appendix to the Defence of the Philosophic Cabbala*, in his *A Collection of Several Philosophical Writings* (London, 1662).

16 On the dating of the writings of Hermes Trismegistus, see F. A. Yates, *Giordano Bruno and the Hermetic Tradition* (London, 1964), ch. 21, and A. Grafton, "Protestant versus prophet: Isaac Casaubon on Hermes Trismegistus," *Journal of the Warburg and Courtauld Institutes* 46 (1986): 78–93.

17 For Stillingfleet's biography see *The Life and Character of That Eminent and Learned Prelate Dr. Edward Stillingfleet, Lord Bishop of Worcester* (London, 1710), probably by Timothy Godwin, and also printed in *The Works of... Dr. Edward Stillingfleet* (London, 1707–10), Vol. 1, pp. 1–46; *Dictionary of National Biography* s.v. "Stillingfleet, Edward"; R. T. Carroll, *The Common Sense Philosophy of Religion of Bishop Edward Stillingfleet* (The Hague, 1975). See also R. H. Popkin, "The philosophy of Bishop Stillingfleet," *Journal of the History of Philosophy* 9 (1971): 303–19.

18 Edward Stillingfleet, *Origines sacrae: or a Rational Account of the Grounds of the Christian Faith, as told to the Truth and Divine Authority of the Scriptures, and the Matters therein Contained* (London, 1662).

19 On More's controversy with Beaumont, see Marjorie Nicolson, "Christ's College and the latitude men, *Modern Philology* 27 (1929): 35–53, and H. C. Foxcroft, *A Supplement to Burnet's History of My Own Time* (Oxford,

1902), pp. 463–64. Marjorie Nicolson describes More's *Apology* as "the highest point in the Cambridge Latitudinarian Movement." Beaumont was not satisfied with More's reply and published his dissatisfaction as *Observations upon the Apologie of Dr. Henry More* (Cambridge, 1665).

20 *Origines sacrae: or a Rational Account of the Grounds of Natural and Revealed Religion: wherein the Foundations of Religion and the Authority of the Scriptures, are Asserted and Clear'd with an Answer to the Modern Objections of Atheists and Deists*. This fragment was apparently written in 1697 and was first printed in Stillingfleet's collected *Works* (1707–10), Vol. II. Stillingfleet laid aside this second version of *Origines Sacrae* when he commenced his controversy with John Locke. Stillingfleet is best known nowadays on account of his involvement in this controversy. But, since in the judgment of history and philosophy, he was the loser, it has earned him dubious fame. See, however the studies by R. H. Popkin and R. T. Carroll (esp. pp. 86–100), (see above n. 17) and J. W. Yolton, *John Locke and the Way of Ideas* (Oxford, 1956), pp. 124–28 and 132–40.

21 See *Life* in Stillingfleet's *Works* (see above n. 17), Vol. 1, p. 5. Also Burnet, *History*, (see above n. 1), Vol. I, p. 326.

22 *Origines Sacrae*, Vol. I, p. xii (Preface). All references to the two versions of this work are to the nineteenth-century edition, *Origines Sacrae or, a Rational Account of the Grounds of Natural and Revealed Religion* (Oxford, 1836) (editor unknown). I shall refer to the first version as 1 *OS* and to the second as 2 *OS*, giving volume and page numbers from this edition, but also supplying book, chapter and section numbers in parentheses so as to facilitate cross-referencing to other editions.

23 For an account of this kind of hebraizing harmonization of biblical and gentile sources, see F. E. Manuel, *Isaac Newton, Historian* (Cambridge, 1963) chs. 6 and 7. John Wallis, Regius Professor of Geometry at Oxford, also espoused the view "that much of the Heathen Learning (their Philosophy and Mythology) was borrowed from the Jews," *Three Sermons* (see n. 13 above), p. 99. Theophilus Gale is a seventeenth-century example of an English hebraizer. His *Court of the Gentiles* (London, 1669–78) draws on Stillingfleet in Gale's attempt to derive all ancient learning from the Jews. Another well-known seventeenth-century exponent of similar views is Samuel Bochart, whose *Geographiae Sacrae, seu Phaleg et Canaan* (1646) was used by Stillingfleet.

24 1 *OS*, Vol. I, p. 17 (I, i, 14).

25 Ibid., Vol. I, p. 10 (I, i, 8).

26 Ibid., Vol. I, p. 11 (ibid.).

27 Ibid., Vol. I, p. 12 (I, i, 9) and 1: 15 (I, i, 13).

28 Ibid., Vol. II, p. 102 (III, iii, 12).

29 Ibid., Vol. II, p. 106 (III, iii, 14).

30 Ibid., Vol. II, pp. 101–2 (III, iii, 13).

31 Ibid., Vol. II, p. 102 (ibid.).

32 Ibid., Vol. II, p. 103 (ibid.).

33 Ibid., Vol. II, p. 7 (III, ii, 2).

34 Ibid. On Moses/Moschus see J. E. McGuire and P. M. Rattansi, "Newton and the 'Pipes of Pan'," *Notes and Records of the Royal Society of London* 21 (1966): 108–43.

35 See n. 16 above. Stillingfleet does not make specific mention of Casaubon when discounting the antiquity of Hermes Trismegistus. When repudiating Hermes as a source of Egyptian wisdom, he pours particular scorn on his reputation as the founding father of chemistry, citing Hermann Conring's *De hermetica Aegyptiorum vetere et Paracelsicorum nova medicina liber unus* (Helmstadt, 1648). See 1 *OS*, Vol. I, pp. 146–47. He also criticizes Francesco Patrizi for his admiration of Hermes.

36 Especially as an authority on Cartesianism, e.g. 1 *OS*, Vol. II, p. 60, where he cites *An Antidote against Atheisme, The Immortality of the Soul*, and the letters to Descartes of "that judicious philosopher Dr. H. More." Cf. also ibid., Vol. I, p. 491 and Vol. II, pp. 55–56.

37 1 *OS* Vol. II, p. 7 (III, ii, 2).

38 More, *Appendix to ... the Philosophick Cabbala*, chs. 1–7, in *A Collection* (op. cit. n. 12) Vol. II. Cf. also "The preface general", pp. xvi–xviii and pp. xx–xxvi, ibid., Vol. I.

39 1 *OS*, Vol. II, p. 5 (III, ii, 1).

40 Ibid., Vol. 2, p. 108 (III, iii, 15). The 1662 edition uses More's spelling, "*Philosophick Cabbala.*"

41 Ibid.

42 Ibid., Vol. II, p. 5 (III, ii, 2).

43 Ibid., Vol. II, pp. 8–11 (III, ii, 3).

44 Ibid., Vol. II, p. 101 (III, iii, 13).

45 2 *OS*, Vol. II, p. 247 (I, i).

46 Ibid., Vol. II, p. 405 (I, ii).

47 Ibid., Vol. II, pp. 251ff. (I, i).

48 Ibid., Vol. II, p. 269 (I, i).

49 The dangers of Platonizing Christianity were felt by both Platonizing theologians and their critics. See Walker, *Ancient Theology*, pp. 2–3, 111–13 etc. A particularly vexed issue was the Trinity. See S. Hutton, "The neoplatonic roots of Arianism: Ralph Cudworth and Theophilus Gale," in *Socinianism and its Role in the Culture of the Sixteenth to the Eighteenth Centuries*, ed. L. Szczucki (Warsaw/Łodz, 1983), pp. 139–45.

50 e.g. Edward, Lord Herbert of Cherbury and John Toland. See Walker, *Ancient Theology*, ch. 5, and G. Cherchi, *Satira ed Enigma: due saggi sul Pantheisticon di John Toland* (Lucca, 1985).

51 When explaining "why philosophy and idolatry did increase so much together," Stillingfleet argues, "though right reason, fully improved, would have overthrown all those cursed and idolatrous practices among the heathens; yet reason, only discerning some general notions, without their particular application and improvement, did only dispose the most ordinary sort of people to a more ready entertainment of gross idolatry." 1 *OS*, Vol. I, p. 10 (I, i, 8).

52 Walker, *Ancient Theology*, ch. 6.

53 Sprat, *History of the Royal Society* (London, 1667), p. 5.

54 Temple, *An Essay upon the Ancient and Modern Learning* (1690) in *The Works of Sir William Temple* (London, 1740) Vol. I, pp. 151–69.

55 Thomas Jackson (1579–1640) combined a rational approach to theology with a penchant for neoplatonism. The full extent of his influence has yet to be

ascertained, but he did influence the Cambridge Platonists and the latitudinarians, especially Simon Patrick. See S. Hutton, "Thomas Jackson, Oxford platonist, and William Twisse, Aristotelian," *Journal of the History of Ideas* 34 (1978): 635–52.

56 Stillingfleet's line-up of contemporary scientific authorities bears striking similarity to that of Richard Bentley in the first series of Boyle lectures, *A Confutation of Atheism from the Structure of Human Bodies* (London, 1652) and *A Confutation of Atheism from the Origin and Frame of the World* (London, 1693). The difference is that Stillingfleet's argument and use of detail are much fuller. I deal with this aspect of Stillingfleet's apologetics in my forthcoming article, "Science, philosophy and atheism: Edward Stillingfleet's defense of religion."

57 2 *OS*, Vol. II, p. 331 (1, i). Stillingfleet also credits Anaxagoras with recognizing "gravitation as the main foundation of union and composition," and with rejecting vortices, as if he were some kind of ancient-Greek, anti-Cartesian Newtonian (2 *OS*, Vol. II, p. 328).

58 Beaumont, *Observations*, p. 6.

59 Cf. n. 49 above. For a seventeenth-century attack on Platonizing theology, see William Twisse, *A Discovery of Dr. Jackson's Vanity* (Amsterdam, 1631), which is discussed in my article cited in n. 55 above. The kinds of danger inherent in platonism perceived by a theologian like Twisse, who was concerned about heresy, are of a different order from those perceived by Thomas Sprat, whose objection to the Fathers' use of arguments of heathen philosophers is that they introduced disputatiousness, as opposed to false doctrine, into religion. Sprat, *History*, pp. 11–12.

60 On the Boyle lectures see J. J. Dahm, "Science and apologetics in the early Boyle lectures," *Church History* 39 (1970): 172–86; M. C. Jacob, *The Newtonians and the English Revolution, 1689–1720* (Brighton, 1976), which is constructively criticized by G. Holmes, "Science, reason and religion in the age of Newton," *British Journal for the History of Science* 11 (1978): 164–71.

61 J. Harris, *Eight Sermons*, The Boyle lectures for 1698, published in *A Defence of Natural and Revealed Religion: Being a Collection of Sermons Preached at the Lectures Founded by the Honourable Robert Boyle, Esq; (from the Year 1691–1732)*, ed. Sampson Letsome and John Nicholl (London, 1739), 1: 392–93. (Referred to hereafter as *Boyle Lectures*.)

62 S. Bradford, *The Credibility of the Christian Revelation from its Intrinsick Evidence*, In *Boyle Lectures*, Vol. I, p. 465. Cf. W. Berriman, *The Gradual Revelation of the Gospel: from the Time of Man's Apostasy* in *Boyle Lectures* [for 1730], Vol. III, p. 598.

63 W. Berriman, ibid.; J. Williams, *Twelve Sermons Preached at the Honourable Robert Boyle's Lectures*, ibid., Vol. I, pp. 169–71; T. Burnet, *The Demonstration of the True Religion*, [for 1725], ibid., Vol. III, p. 567.

64 T. Burnet, ibid.

65 J. Woodward, *Eight Sermons Preached at the Lecture Founded by the Honourable Robert Boyle, Esq.*, *Boyle Lectures*, Vol. II, pp. 506–7.

66 Ibid., p. 509. Other fictitious props mentioned by Woodward are Hystapes, Lentulus, Pilate and the St. Paul–Seneca correspondence.

67 J. Williams, *Boyle Lectures*, Vol. I, p. 194.

68 Ibid.
69 On this see especially McGuire and Rattansi, "Newton and the 'Pipes of Pan.'"
70 See F. I. Manuel, *Isaac Newton, Historian*, ch. 6.
71 On Newton's opinion of Plato as a corrupter of religious truth, see F. E. Manuel, *The Religion of Isaac Newton* (Oxford, 1974), Vol. II, pp. 68–76. In his unpublished "Theologia gentilis origines philosophicae," Newton explains polytheism as the result of the idolatrous divinization of Noah and his progeny. See R. S. Westfall, *Never at Rest: A Biography of Isaac Newton* (Cambridge, 1983; first published 1980), pp. 350–56.

4 Latitudinarians, neoplatonists, and the ancient wisdom

Joseph M. Levine

I

It took a long time in the England of rebellion and civil war for the still small voice of Anglican moderation to be heard. Even after the Restoration the violence of religious and political debate continued to obscure the call to reason and the growing desire for peace among protestants. Eventually, however, the cry was heard across the land and it was discovered that there had been there, all along, a doughty little band of scholars quietly but earnestly pleading the cause. "I can come into no Company of late," wrote an Oxford friend to Simon Patrick in 1662, "but I find the chief Discourse to be about a certain new Sect of Men call'd Latitude-Men." According to Patrick, who immediately returned one of the first and best descriptions of the movement, it had arisen at Cambridge in "opposition to that hide-bound, strait-laced Spirit that did then prevail." The latitudinarians, he reported, desired to settle religion in a "virtuous mediocrity" between the puritans and the papists on the one hand and the skepticism and materialism of the atheists on the other. He emphasized their attempt to conciliate the claims of reason and revelation and their plea for toleration and the virtuous life above any ceremonial scruples. And he noticed their preference for the church fathers before any modern divines and for the platonists beyond any other philosophers.[1]

It is the appeal of the "platonic" philosophy, or rather one particular strand in that ancient tradition of thought, that I should like to consider here. There were, of course, platonists long before there were latitudinarians and there were soon to be latitudinarians who were no longer platonists, but for a short time the two became nearly synonymous. It appears that at Cambridge during the Interregnum the platonic teaching was found especially helpful in serving the cause of protestant accommodation by furnishing a fresh armory of philosophical arguments for the occasion, as well as a reservoir of ancient learning to bolster it. Gilbert Burnet remembered the first of these Cambridge teachers and perhaps the most influential, Benjamin Whichcote, setting his young students to reading the ancient philosophers, "chiefly Plato, Tully and Plotinus,"[2] and although Whichcote did not himself put much weight on scholarship, he seems to have succeeded in encouraging among his followers an appetite for the whole works of ancient Alexandria and modern Florence. Increasingly, the young men at Cambridge drew draughts upon that rich tradition and more and more upon that peculiar conviction in it that there had once been an ancient wisdom or perennial philosophy. They thus attempted, at one and the same time, to combine arguments from reason and authority, from the ancients and the moderns, to defend their theological position against their enemies on all sides.

It is true that platonism had turned up in England more than a century before in the days of Erasmus and Thomas More, and it had led a lively existence among the poets and a marginal life in the universities at least from the days of Queen Elizabeth. Its protean character, so evident in that astonishing syncretism of the Florentines who first mediated between Plato, the ancient Alexandrians and modern Europe, made it attractive to many, and the idea of an ancient wisdom (an idea ancient in itself) found appeal across a wide range of opinion: from the Catholic, Baronius, and the Huguenot, Philippe de Mornay, to the Arminian, Richard Montagu, and that skeptical magus, Sir Walter Ralegh.[3] As a result, in the early seventeenth century there was hardly anyone who did not know that there had once been a body of truth in the world that had been transmitted through the ages, from Moses or earlier through the Egyptians, Brahmans, Magi, and sibylls to the Greeks and beyond; and that the course of true knowledge had passed from East to West, from pure light to darkness and renewal. At Emmanuel College, Whichcote certainly accepted the notion and turned his attention back upon the sources. At Christ's College, the moderate puritan, Joseph Mede, devoted his great learning to the idea. And in 1641, an obscure fellow of Trinity College, named John Sherman, published a small book which he entitled suggestively, *A Greek in the Temple*.

Sherman turned to the ancient wisdom in order to defend the pagan writers against their critics – an issue once again after fifteen hundred years of wrangling. Apparently, some of the more radical puritans were once more detecting danger in the classics and Sherman was fortified by the old arguments he discovered in St. Augustine and the familiar examples of Moses spoiling the Egyptians and St. Paul answering the pagans in kind.[4] His chief concern was to vindicate the autonomy of reason, "nature's light," without diminishing either the authority or uniqueness of the Scriptures, and thus show that the pagans had something to offer – though not quite enough – to Christian truth and learning. At the same time, he saw that the only way to answer either pagans or atheists was on their own ground by appealing to the reason in all men. It was this perilous middle ground, half way between the modern puritans and the modern unbelievers, that was to appeal so much to the platonists of the Interregnum and to their followers at the Restoration.

Sherman believed that one proof that human reason could achieve some understanding of God was the many striking parallels that existed between pagan and Christian teaching. The Hebrews, he conceded, had learned nothing from the Greeks; their knowledge was all divinely inspired and uncontaminated. But had the Greeks learned anything from the Hebrews? The many correspondences in thought between the pagans and the Jews – between Moses and Solon, Plutarch and the Psalms, Matthew and Hesiod, etc. – could only be explained, he imagined, in one of two ways. Either they had each been arrived at independently by reason or else the Greeks had borrowed directly from the Jews. Sherman thought that there might be something to both of these possibilities. The pagans could well have employed both reason and scripture, the one which they shared equally with the Jews, the other which they might well have borrowed. Reason could have told them much about God and the world, for example about God the creator and the immortality of the soul, though less about God the redeemer. There was, to use Sherman's own words, "a cognoscibility of God by humane understanding without any supernatural doctrine,"[5] just as some of the fathers and schoolmen had declared. But he agreed that revelation could have told them something more both about what was reasonable and what was beyond reason. Sherman does not, however, pretend to the scholarship that would be required to assess that debt precisely, preferring to quote from Zanchius, that "Pythagoras and Trismegist and Plato had read some part of Scripture, and peradventure had learned some notions from the Jews," particularly that Hermes had taught the Trinity more clearly than the Old Testament.[6] Since it was generally agreed that that mystery was impossible to attain by reason alone, it seemed tolerably clear to Sherman that that notion at least must have been borrowed from revelation.

In short, it looked to Sherman, despite some hesitation, as though much of the ancient wisdom had been available to the pagans both through reason and the reading of the Old Testament. That this was still insufficient, however, he was ready to concede and that was why he thought that the revelation of the New Testament was also required. His argument thus allowed for, but also delimited, the reasonableness of Christianity; it opened the door to pagan learning and allowed the Greeks into the Temple without losing sight of the priority of scriptural proof. To Sherman, it seemed a shame, for example, to give up the pagan poets whose admittedly fabulous histories nevertheless supplied some useful "allusions into real things before the flood, as if in a manner they would redeeme the losse of the history of the world." Like many of his contemporaries, he believed that the stories of the pagan gods concealed the history of the ancient heroes. Thus Christians and pagans each had something to offer the other; for if there were some heathens like Hermes who seemed almost Christian, there were plenty of Christians who seemed even more like heathen, and if "we might use some of their science, they needed some of our Scripture."[7]

In general then Sherman's little work anticipates the main position of the neoplatonists, though without their erudition. He knew the importance of reading the original texts but he was unable somehow to make the effort himself.[8] He knew that Dionysius the Areopagite had been eliminated as an apostolic saint by Valla and Erasmus who had exposed the anachronisms in the text. But he was not willing to allow the same kind of arguments against Hermes and the sibylls. He knew that their works had been challenged too as pious frauds (presumably by Isaac Casaubon whose famous exposé had appeared in 1614), but he argues nevertheless from the mention of the sibylls in Cicero and from the authority of the humanist, Reuchlin, and the Byzantine, Suidas, that they were genuine. He remained uncertain only whether their knowledge derived merely from reason, "or whether they sprang from some other light, either of Divine revelation or Diabolicall."[9]

What the young men in Sherman's audience thought about this I cannot say, nor whether Whichcote read or perhaps inspired the little work that slipped into the world on the eve of the revolution. Certainly there were others around who shared some of its sentiments; for example, Robert Greville, Lord Brooke, who had been to Cambridge with Whichcote and written a neoplatonic book on *The Nature of Truth* in 1640; and his two young friends, John Sadler and Peter Sterry, "the first," we are told, "that were observ'd to make a public Profession of Platonism in the university." The parallelism between the Scriptures and Greek learning was almost a commonplace at this time.[10] Perhaps it does not matter; the position Sherman had staked out for himself had long been familiar in Western Europe and was available to the neoplatonists from many sources. But the timing is instructive; Cambridge at least was awake to the possibilities of ancient wisdom. And if Sherman had only limited weapons to employ in the ensuing battle, there would soon be others on the scene ready to use the whole armory of contemporary learning to support their cause – modern philology as well as ancient philosophy.

II

If Sherman in 1642 was already trying to steer a middle course between puritans and "atheists," between those who insisted on the exclusive truths of scripture and those who preferred an unrestricted reason, by

1651 the matter had become very much more urgent. By then the radical puritans had seized power and executed the king; they had tried to reform religion through the Westminster Assembly and education by a purge of the universities. The rule of the saints seemed close at hand. In 1651, Anthony Tuckney, an old-fashioned Emmanuel puritan, finally lost patience with his old student, Benjamin Whichcote, and denounced the neoplatonist in public. In the same year, Thomas Hobbes published his *Leviathan*.

Whichcote had been a tutor at Emmanuel since 1634. Though he published little, he delivered through the years a set of Sunday sermons that became famous. Despite his liberal views, he somehow escaped persecution and was eventually elected vice-chancellor. On that occasion, he delivered a deeply felt sermon that proved the last straw for his old tutor, now become master of Emmanuel. Tuckney was a Calvinist, but he was more tolerant than many. "In the assemblie," he explained to Whichcote in 1651, "I gave my vote with others that the Confession of Faith, putt out by Authoritie, should not bee required to bee sworne or subscribed-too; we having bin burnt in the hand in that kind before."[11] Later, at St. John's College, he resisted pressure to weed out students for their religious convictions. "He was determined to choose none but scholars, adding very wisely, they may deceive me in their godliness, they cannot in their scholarship."[12]

The exchange of views in 1651 was therefore bitter but civilized. Tuckney remembered Whichcote as a boy, willing, pious, and obedient, but already somewhat cloudy and obscure in expression. Unfortunately, the young man had put aside his useful studies to undertake philosophy and metaphysics. He had mistakenly read the Anglican divines: Field and Hammond, Hooker and Chillingworth, and Thomas Jackson – the last another early platonist with a confident belief in the early wisdom. Worse yet, on becoming a fellow of Emmanuel, he had cast himself "into the conspiracie of very learned and ingenious men, whom I fear, at least some of them, studied other authors, more than the scriptures, and Plato and his Schollars, above others."[13] Here, apparently, was the chief source of Whichcote's heresies.

Tuckney did not mince words. Since Whichcote had become Vice-Chancellor, Tuckney had heard him time and again repeat the words, "divinest reason" and "mathematical demonstration." It was, he complained, a pernicious doctrine, bound to corrupt the young, that preferred reason, "the candle of the Lord," as Whichcote called it, to the "certainties of divine testimonie, and faith in it." Similarly, Tuckney was alarmed to find Whichcote supporting freedom of the will against predestination and the "liberty of prophecying" against discipline. It was no more than a newly minted "moral divinitie," a platonic faith, with only a little tincture of Christ added. It did not help that the new doctrine proved exceedingly popular with the students.[14]

Whichcote tried to rebut his old master point by point, though accepting the main charge. He claimed that his views "concerning natural light and the use of reason" had first been pronounced many years before. Since then, he had consistently urged "that the truth declared by God, concerning our relief by Christ, was amiable, gratefull, acceptable to minde and understanding." Reason was indeed "the Candle of the Lord," and could never contradict faith. As for liberty of prophesying, "Truth is Truth, whosoever hath spoken itt, or however it hath bin abused."[15] In short, Tuckney was right that Whichcote believed in the importance of reason, the efficacy of freedom of the will, toleration of Christian speculation, and the usefulness of pagan philosophy. He had been wrong only in arguing that this must contradict revelation and confound true religion.

Tuckney was no obscurantist and did not mean to extinguish philosophy altogether. He was, we are told, "a man of great reading, and much knowledge, a ready and elegant Latinist."[16] Before an ignorant audience he was ready to defend the cause of learning; but before a university audience he thought it better to decry the ignorance and errors of the philosophers, as he believed the Bible had done, rather than exaggerate their virtues. Whichcote, on the other hand, was no pagan and did not mean to extinguish revelation either, which he explained elsewhere, is "superadded" to reason to reinforce and improve upon it. "The greatest Things of Reveal'd Truth, tho' they be not of Reason's Invention, yet they are of the prepar'd mind readily entertain'd and receiv'd."[17] He made no effort to defend his erudition – which would probably not have impressed Tuckney anyway – and he avoids mentioning Plato altogether. He is content for the moment to argue simply from reason and revelation and to overlook the perennial philosophy and the argument from pagan authority.

Yet there was no avoiding the implication. Reason, after all, belonged to all men at all times, to pagans as well as Christians, Arminians as well as puritans, perhaps even to Mohamet. Something of the truth then, and the good life, must have been available, quite apart from revelation, to all men from the beginning of time.[18] In this context, the idea of an ancient wisdom was unavoidable however much it was bound to frighten Tuckney and his friends by prejudicing the self-sufficiency of the Bible, and there are a number of passages in Whichcote's sermons that refer directly to it.[19] In one, Whichcote notices again the many parallels between sacred and secular history, the latter apparently borrowed from the former, "as Nisus's hair in imitation of Samson's, Deucalion's Flood in imitation of

Noah's, Hercules in imitation of Joshua, etc."[20] It appeared that many of the pagans, "not corrupted by Education or Interest or the Strain of Time, do relate many things that are consistent with those that are in the Bible." According to Augustine and others there was ample evidence of the platonists in the New Testament. As a result, there were "many things in prophane stories in several Ages that give Testimony and Light to Parts of Reveal'd Truth." Elsewhere, he recalls the argument by universal consent for Christian morality, true again for all men at all times.[21] Whatever differences might sometimes appear in these matters, they were never about essential things, "but all...in points of very curious and nice Speculation, or in Arbitrary Modes of Worship." Whichcote's "latitude" was thus meant to be wide indeed. Natural religion, he concludes, was written on man's soul at the very moment of his creation.[22] The *prisca theologia* had been there from the beginning of time.

III

It is evident, then, that the first target of the Cambridge Platonists was those puritan colleagues who seemed to threaten anew the pagan classics and the life of reason. But the platonists were soon aware of the danger from the other flank. They saw that the "new philosophy" posed at least equal peril to the precarious balance that they desired. Thus they read Francis Bacon with dismay when he proposed a radical separation between religion and natural science; and they drew back from Descartes when they discovered in his materialistic physics what seemed to be a threat to the life of the spirit.[23] But when Thomas Hobbes printed the *Leviathan* in 1651 their worst fears were confirmed.[24] Reason unrestrained, like faith unalloyed, seemed to have gone amok. According to Burnet, Hobbes's main principles (though disguised a bit to deceive unwary readers) were: "that all men acted under an absolute necessity...that souls were material; thought being only a subtil and imperceptible motion...that interest and fear were the chief principles of society; and all morality in the following that which was our own private will or advantage." *Leviathan* was popular, Burnet believed, because of its very novelty and boldness. It was the Cambridge Platonists, he remembered, who had first set out systematically to refute the "atheistical" philosopher.[25]

The problem, then, was how to delimit reason even while defending it, to answer the "mere naturalists" as well as the extreme puritans.[26] And here, no doubt, lay the peculiar appeal of the ancient wisdom. The truths of Christianity had now to be defended against men who were not even Christians and could not depend on revelation alone. Pagans required a pagan testimony which the platonists found ready to hand in the venerable notion of an ancient tradition of truth handed down through the generations. "I have made it appear at large," Whichcote wrote triumphantly, "that the great notices of natural knowledge and the main articles of the Christian faith have had a very great acknowledgement in the world in the several ages of it: and this is an argument to prevail with the atheist and infidel."[27] The platonists were convinced that the Mosaic teaching was essentially rational, and comprehended, besides most Christian doctrine and ethics, much history and natural philosophy. But it contained also matters which, while not unreasonable, could never have been discovered by reason, such crucial things as the history of the world from creation through fall and flood to the resurrection of Christ and the mystery of the Trinity.[28] All that was required therefore was to show that the ancient pagans had known these things too – though not necessarily as well as their sources – to prove that they must have received them from the revealed tradition. It was up to the ingenuity of neoplatonic scholarship to ferret out the evidence to make the case.

It would require a large volume to show just how the Cambridge company took up this task in that apparently endless series of works that they began to produce from the 1650s. They were determined to defend the realm of reason and spirit against all comers: philosophically, by developing platonic notions about space, matter and ideas; empirically, by assembling every instance of ghostly and spiritual behavior, including witchcraft; and historically, by retrieving the whole testimony of the ancient wisdom from the Hermetic corpus to the Hebrew Cabala. They were delighted to discover in the course of their researches that even their philosophical opponents, the materialists, atheists, and socinians, had all been anticipated and answered in antiquity, and that not even Hobbes could pretend to anything new. And all the time they tried to guard their flanks against the enemies on both sides, attempting valiantly to steer a middle course between a too exclusive faith and an unrestrained reason, a too exuberant "enthusiasm" and a desiccated spirit. Perhaps it will suffice for this brief pre-history of the latitudinarians to retrace the early career of that most famous of these platonic "latitude-men," Henry More, so that we may see how his ideas developed out of this same contemporary situation and the hints of his predecessors.

In a brief autobiography written long afterward More himself tried to describe the genesis of his ideas. He explained there how he was brought up "under Parents and a Master that were great Calvinists (but withall very pious and good ones)"; how he was sent afterward to Eton College, not for the sake of religion but to improve his Latin and Greek, "but neither there nor anywhere else, could I ever swallow down that hard

Doctrine of Fate"; how his parents and older brother insisted on predestination and did not spare the rod but only ended up in confirming what he maintained was his "innate idea" of freedom.[29] From Eton, More went on to Christ's College just a little after John Milton attended, with the scene already set for the great rivalries of the Interregnum.[30] He found there, according to a contemporary, three influential men contending for the loyalties of the students: William Power, William Chappell and Joseph Mede. "Power's pupils that were thought but too loose, like their Tutor, were called Powritans; Chappell's thought too precise, call'd Puritans; and Mede's that kept the medium between both, Medians."[31] Archbishop Laud tried hard to encourage the first; Milton reinforced his own convictions under the second; but More was drawn to Mede and imbibed from him not only religious moderation but a respect for scholarship and a consuming interest in the Old Testament. According to Mede's biographer, John Worthington, More's good friend and fellow platonist, Mede "applied himself to the more usefull study of History and Antiquities, particularly to a curious enquiry into those Mysterious Sciences which make the ancient Chaldeans, Egyptians and other Nations so famous, tracing them so far as he could, having any Light to guide him, in their Oriental Schemes and Figurative expression, as likewise in their Hieroglyphics."[32] For More and Worthington it was a great privilege to study under this man, so modest and humane, devoted to his studies and his university.

No doubt it was perfect training for a defender of the ancients, though Mede himself was probably more concerned about the future than the past and wrote as his magnum opus, a key to the biblical prophecies that was still standard in the days of Isaac Newton and that long afterward inspired both More and Worthington to something of the same kind. More traced his own vocation back to his days at Eton and boasted having an "immoderate thirst after Knowledge" from the beginning, especially in natural philosophy and metaphysics. At Cambridge, he read all the appropriate works, both ancient and modern, and ended up a skeptic, rather like his great French contemporary, René Descartes. In despair, he seems to have had a conversion induced by a study of the neoplatonists, possibly under Whichcote's inspiration. He discovered that contemplation had to be accompanied by a moral purification, "especially having begun to read over the Platonick Writers, Marsilius Ficinus, Plotinus himself, Mercurius Trismegistus and the Mystical Divines." He remembered purchasing a copy of the *Enneads* as a junior master for sixteen shillings, "and I think I was the first that had either the luck or the courage to buy him." Typically, he does not mention Plato directly.[33]

Autobiography is a notoriously defective genre, particularly when it is written for apologetical purposes, and More may well have simplified his story to make his polemical (platonic) point, i.e. that his fundamental ideas were innate and needed only to be reawakened. Perhaps it should be noted that at Eton More was under the mastership of the "ever memorable" John Hales, one of the most influential of the pre-latitudinarians, and we have heard other platonic voices at Cambridge besides Whichcote who might well have influenced his thinking.[34] Apparently, under their inspiration, More abandoned skepticism, re-covered his naturally "joyous and lucid" state of mind, and never again lost his serenity.

The first fruits of More's conversion were some poems which he published in 1642 and then more elaborately and with notes in 1647.[35] The verse was modeled on the *Fairie Queen*; the sentiments were thoroughly neoplatonic; but the fusion was not altogether successful. More soon gave up poetry for a torrent of prose, sometimes infused still with poetic fancy and occasional flights of inspiration but more often shapeless and a little obscure. The trouble was that he wrote too fast and never blotted a line. "His first draft, he would say, must stand."[36] It is not easy to describe the great body of work that he left behind him at his death in 1687, especially since More not infrequently changed his mind on basic matters. On a few things, however, he stood fast, not least his conviction in the basic truth of the ancient wisdom.

It was about 1647 that More met Anne Finch, the future Lady Conway, and began a life-long friendship and correspondence. Lady Conway's first letters were prompted by the notes to More's poems and show a surprising philosophical curiosity. She became More's devoted pupil, though eventually she went her own way. When she wrote to her father-in-law after meeting More, she was quite prepared to defend the ancient wisdom herself, and sent him an elaborate account of its transmission through the ages, no doubt inspired by the sentiments of her tutor who had written in his *Psychozoia*, that Plato's school,

> ...well agrees with learned Pythagore,
> Egyptian Trismegist, and th'antique roll
> Of Chaldee wisdome, all which time hath tore
> But Plato and deep Plotin do restore.[37]

More had meant to write, he explained in the notes to his poem, "as a Reporter of the Wisedome of the Ancients rather than a Warranter of the same," but in fact he had acted as an advocate. It was no contemptible argument, he insisted, "that the Platonists, the best and divinest of Philosophers, and the Christians, the best of all that do professe religion, do both concur that there is a Trinity." God had not left the heathen without witness to himself. "To speake the Truth, Stoicisme, Platonisme, and Pythagorisme are gallant lights...so near Christianism if a man will look on them favorably, that one would think they were baptized."[38] Consequently, all the best things in modern times seemed to him mere revivals of the ancient wisdom: Copernicus had restored the hypothesis of Pythagoras about the motion of the earth, and the modern platonists, Ficino, for example, or himself, were simply reenacting the ancient struggle against atheism (or Epicureanism). Throughout the poems More employs that ingenious synchretistic talent that he had learned from the Florentines and which finds agreement everywhere: in the sibylline oracles with Moses, Hermes Trismegistus with Marcus Aurelius, even Galileo and Descartes with Plato. If there is something troubling about this all too easy reconciliation, it is largely a result of More's underlying presupposition: truth is unchanging and rational – available to all men at all times – a conviction that accounts for his method, so hopelessly unhistorical to our present taste. "I think all men are to interpret Plato and all men at their best, and rather make what of undoubted truth they aime at, then quarrel and entangle themselves in disputes about the manner of expressing which no man can reach into."[39] Lady Conway could not have agreed more.[40]

More was thus learned but no scholar; he mined antiquity for its present use, indifferent to the nice distinctions of philological learning. No wonder that Hermes Trismegistus and the sibylls could survive for him without equivocation and despite criticism.[41] His life work was a determined effort to defend the rationality of Christian truth, particularly the existence and providence of God and the immortality of the soul, and for this he was prepared to employ all means and take on all comers, ancient and modern. According to his biographer, John Ward, he developed his theories out of four principal sources which he wove together into a synthesis. The result was a large and oddly impressive achievement which for a time overwhelmed the London bookmarket – but the synthesis proved to be inherently unstable.

In the first place, according to Ward, More drew upon the "free Exercise of his own Reason and Faculties."[42] No doubt More thought this primary, although he qualified his rationalism by insisting on the need for internal moral purification and the guidance of a sound Christian spirit. He was alarmed by the ease with which reason unrestrained could slide into skepticism or atheism and had won his own peace of mind by reading the mystics, particularly the *Theologia Germanica*.[43] The good life always took precedence for him over correct ideas, ethics over metaphysics, though in fact More devoted most of his attention to the latter. Reason without guidance could too easily become unreasonable. On the other hand, More felt the danger of exaggerating interior illumination and turned vigorously first against the latest devotees of natural magic,

Thomas Vaughan in particular, and then the Quakers, especially after Lady Conway began to favor them.[44] The problem here as elsewhere was to maintain the *via media*, to build a cosmology that was objective and rational and that would reinforce the truth of God's existence and providence without losing the way or retreating into mysticism. More hoped that his own system of the world, his physics and metaphysics, with its splendid notions about matter and space, infinity, the pre-existence of the soul, etc., would do the trick, and he remained unruffled in old age by criticism and competing theories, issuing and reissuing his works in Latin as well as English, and accepting the plaudits of a considerable following.

In the second place, according to Ward, More drew "partly from the sense of such ancient Sages as have ever been in greatest Honour and Esteem for their Wisdom and Virtue." Here, of course, is our theme, and we have seen something of More's indebtedness to this neoplatonic argument even in his early poems. He never gave up this self-conscious affiliation of ideas, the sense, as he put it in his collected works (1662), that his own rational philosophy was a "restitution of that ancient and venerable wisdom" of Moses and his Egyptian and Greek successors. More, however, did not believe that correct ideas about God and the world were *dependent* on the succession of the ancient wisdom; rather he thought that they were merely *confirmed* by it. The good reasonable man was capable of finding his way to wisdom at all times and places and hence could restore the ancient ideas without employing any scholarship – accidentally as it were – by discovering them for himself. Needless to say, it was immensely encouraging to find one's reasoning anticipated by the sages of the past, to find "very noble Patronage for the cause among the ancients,"[45] but the implication was that the moderns (More included) could actually rival the ancients in their wisdom because of the same fundamental and unchanging truths and through an equal capacity to reason.

This is borne out by More's third source which according to Ward was "partly from the Discoveries of the New Philosophy." More's commitment to reason meant that although he upheld the ancients, he could not overlook the possibilities of contemporary speculation. In particular, he was much taken by the Frenchman, René Descartes, whose views began to circulate widely in England in the 1640s.[46] Descartes was, of course, *the* modern *par excellence* and in the *Discourse on Method* (translated into English in 1649), he argued unequivocally for a fresh start to all knowledge and boldly called into question the entire received tradition, historical and philosophical. It was just this point that angered his critics and one of them (also soon translated into English) poured scorn on the philosopher's "injurious and dishonorable disesteem for reverend antiquity."[47] Nevertheless, for the moment, Descartes even more than Francis Bacon, seemed to promise everything for the advancement of learning.

Now it looks as though More was attracted to Descartes *despite* his avowed modernity. "I must confess," he wrote in 1662, "that the very newness alone is occasion enough, even to those that are truly ingenious, to make a stand, that which is strange having something of the face of what is hostile."[48] It was not the modernity – which turned out upon inspection to be largely illusory – but the rationality of the Cartesian system that attracted him initially. Descartes had shown what More confidently expected to find in the 1640s, that the world reflected a God of reason, that nature was fully intelligible because it was mathematical and mechanical. He thought he had found the Frenchman set upon the same purpose as himself, though from the opposite direction. Whereas More, reasoning like the platonists, had begun to explore the world of ideas, Descartes had chosen to pursue the world of material nature. "That which enravishes me most is that we both setting out from the same lists, though taking several wayes, the one travelling in the lower road of Democritisme, amidst the thick dust of Atoms and flying particles of Matter; the other tracing it over the high and aeiry Hills of Platonisme, in that more thin and subtil Region of Immateriality, meet together notwithstanding at last." (Descartes, needless to say, had adamantly refused to accept any classical pedigree.)[49] The conjuncture, according to More, was in an understanding of Scripture, the last of the four sources that Ward assigned to the making of More's thought. Platonism and Cartesianism together, he argued, offered "the most approvable Philosophical Interpretation of the first chapters of Genesis as ever was yet offered to the World since the loss of the Judaical Cabala."

More's final source of inspiration, then, was "from either the open Expression, or else more secret Interpretations of Holy Scripture."[50] He had not forgotten revelation, though in emphasizing reason and nature he had nearly lost the need for it. He had wanted to insist that Scripture itself was only fully intelligible to reason, that it required the combined ingenuity of platonism and Cartesianism to unlock the secrets encapsulated first of all in the Mosaic text, and interpreted afterward by the Cabala. All that was needed to tidy up this unlikely synthesis was to show first that Descartes was merely reiterating what had already been divined in antiquity by reason – for the idea of a new truth seemed always self-contradictory to More – and next that Genesis rightly understood was precisely agreeable to the findings of reason.

The outlines of this projected synthesis were already visible in the philosophical poems; More spent the next decade working them out. The first exchange of letters with Lady Conway was about Descartes, as More tried to coax his reluctant student into sympathy with his mentor. However, the Cartesian emphasis on mechanism in nature already threatened More's sense of the spiritual and a correspondence between the two just before Descartes died in 1649 suggests that there were indeed real differences between them. (Was the human body, as Descartes insisted, simply a machine? Were animals mere automata? Were there no spiritual forces at large in nature? etc.)[51] Nevertheless, More's initial reaction was enthusiastic, as we have seen, and More remained an advocate at least until 1662.[52] So when More was confronted with a criticism of Descartes by William Petty, who preferred Francis Bacon, he firmly defended his choice. The experimental method had some use but More would not suffer the general principles of nature to be "hermetically imprison'd in some narrow neck'd glasse."[53] Was there an experiment that could confute Descartes? As for Baconian utility, More was satisfied that the true end of philosophy was contemplation. It was temperance and humility, not power and material well-being that mattered in the end. Here anyway was one form of modernity that More would not countenance, though on occasion he did try an experiment.[54]

In 1652 More turned his new philosophical weapons directly against the enemy in a work dedicated to Lady Conway, *An Antidote against Atheisme*. "Atheisme and Enthusiasme, though they seeme so extreamly opposite one to another, yet in many things do very nicely agree."[55] He claimed (echoing Whichcote) that the existence of God was as clearly demonstrable as a geometrical theorem. Later, he looked back upon "those times wherein excess of Liberty, and the dangerous abuse thereof to Atheism and Prophaneness... forced me to encounter those strutting Giants and Defiers of Heaven at their own weapon, as they boastingly pretend, I mean Free Reason and Philosophy." He used the ontological argument supplied by Descartes, but set aside the rest, substituting his own views about the way in which nature revealed the hand of providence. Lady Conway was very pleased; the most obstinate atheist, she told him, must be compelled to submit to his arguments.[56] Among other things, More devoted a whole long passage to assembling the evidence for spirit in the world (witches, ghosts, miraculous cures, etc.). "It is not to be imputed to any vain credulity of mine," he hoped, "or that I take a pleasure in telling strange stories, but that I thought fit to fortify and strengthen the Faith of others." He came to feel in time that this was the most persuasive evidence for the truth of religion. As in affairs of state, some argued, "no bishop, no king," so More was certain in matters of religion, "no Spirit, no God."[57] The rift with mechanists like Thomas Hobbes or the Greek atomists was thus insuperable, although the rupture with Descartes, for whom the worlds of spirit and matter were equally real but incompatible, was still postponed.

In the following year (1653), More responded to a request by Lady Conway to interpret the allegory of Adam and Eve with an even more elaborate treatise. Once determined, he could not stop till it was done. Her letter had "injected such a peremptory purpose in me of interpreting the three first Chapters of Genesis with a continuall paraphrase by verse according to a triple sense, Litteral, Philosophicall, and Morall." He called it *Conjectura Cabbalistica*.[58] More was fearful that the story of Creation taken by itself might actually foster atheism by helping the unregenerate to think that the whole business of religion was no more than a fable. What was required therefore was an allegorical interpretation. More found the way in an old device of the platonists. (John Colet had already employed it in England in the days of Erasmus and Thomas More.) Moses had to be seen as a political leader facing a rude and ignorant populace. Prudence dictated that he address his audience in a language that was immediately intelligible, or else lose his chance to convert them. So the crafty politician dictated the literal story of the creation as we find it in Genesis, at the same time concealing beneath its surface a rich philosophical and moral meaning for the few who might become sophisticated enough to want a rational understanding of the universe.

As a result, More had only to employ his own reason to discover in the text of Scripture the physics and metaphysics that lay concealed there. A mere naturalist might be surprised to discover that Moses was thus, "Master of the most sublime and generous Speculations that are in all Naturall Philosophy,"[59] but More was confident that it was so. All knowledge, he explained, whether natural or divine, had been given first to Adam, "then revived or confirmed again to Moses," then transmitted to the ancient pagans and Jews, where it could still be seen in the writings of Plato and Pythagoras and the rabbis, "who in things where prejudice need not blinde them, I should think as fit as any to confirm the Cabbalistic sense." He concedes that some "fooleries" and corruptions must have entered into the tradition and would have to be weeded out in any new revival.[60] It was therefore natural that More should find now that the Cartesian philosophy only looked good insofar as it had "interwoven into it that noble system of the World according to the tradition of Pythagoras and his Followers, or if you will of the most ancient Cabbala of Moses." All the rest was "enormously and ridiculously false." Meanwhile More was delighted with his own work; when he reissued it, some years later (with additions), he wrote proudly to Lady Conway that he had "confirm'd the reasonableness of my Philosophick Cabbala even to my own amazement!"[61] It was about that time, incidentally, that he and his friends began to be branded with the nickname latitudinarians.[62]

The original *Conjectura* had only taken a few months to write. It is characteristic of More that it was only when the work was done that he thought to give it its ancient patrimony. "Though the conceptions in the Cabbala be most my own," he explained to Lady Conway, "yett I do what I can in my Defense to gette Godfathers all along to these truths of my owne braine, and so lessen the odium of these inventions by alledgeing the Authority of Auncient Philosophers and Fathers."[63] When later, he wrote his *Ethics*, he did much the same thing. His intention, he said there, was "to pour fourth the Sense and Emanations of his own Mind upon this Subject"; but when he discovered once again that the ancients had anticipated him, he decided to quote them copiously. This was all to the good, since, "he had not so much affected Singularity in this Undertaking, as a restitution of Morals to their pristin state."[64] For More, neither the appeal to antiquity or to novelty was sufficient of itself and it was possible to see merit in both the ancients and the moderns without worrying about progress or decline. In all things, reason alone was sovereign, not least in its basic indifference to the mere "critical and grammatical skill" that was so prized by scholars but which More confined simply to the literal (and least significant) aspect of the text. The *Conjectura Cabbalistica* may be the fullest and best exposition of the ancient wisdom in Henry More's voluminous works but as a historical defense of traditional knowledge it still left something to be desired.

Indeed More himself was sensible of the need to do more and from time to time he contributed to the task. But on the whole he was satisfied to leave the great work of erudition to his learned Cambridge friend, Ralph Cudworth. (The *Conjectura* had in fact been dedicated to Cudworth who was encouraged to "make up out of your rich Treasury of Learning, what our penury could not reach to, or our Inadvertancy may have omitted.") The work that resulted eventually, Cudworth's *True Intellectual System of the Universe* (1678), was thus the natural culmination of a collaborative effort to ground the latitudinarian middle way on reason *and* the *prisca theologia*. In this remarkable work, Cudworth was able to gather together the whole immense store of classical and Christian learning that had accumulated since the Renaissance in order to show how the knowledge of essential things had been transmitted through the ages against all the old enemies of reason and true religion. Reason and tradition were now *demonstrated* to be one and it must be a bold skeptic or a very great scholar who would have the nerve or the knowledge to criticize it.[65]

If, unfortunately, this whole large enterprise, this heroic attempt to marry reason and tradition, philosophy and scholarship, into a consistent whole, now seems a little pointless and its massive scholarship tedious at best and usually wrong, it remains that that great labor once seemed absolutely essential to the latitudinarian cause and the best strategy that could be used to justify it. Indeed, of all the arguments that the moderates then employed,[66] it was probably the hardest to answer in its own time, and it took a long while before critical learning became competent enough to dismiss it altogether.[67] But by then the latitudinarians had won the political battle and disappeared from view, the victims in part of their own success and the progress of modern scholarship. The *prisca theologia* was gradually banished to the margins of the European consciousness and the neoplatonic strand in English thought slowly submerged and forgotten. The reconciliation of reason and tradition is always hard to make and inherently unstable and the Enlightenment was not the first age – or the last – to split them asunder and have to face the consequences.

Notes

1 *A Brief Account of the New Sect of Latitude Men* (1662), ed. T. A. Burell (Los Angeles, 1963). Cf. Edmund Fowler, *The Principles and Practice of certain Moderate Divines of the Church of England* (London, 1670). For the platonists in general, see John Tulloch, *Rational Theology and Christian Philosophy in England in the Seventeenth Century*, 2 vols. (Edinburgh, 1874), Vol. II, pp. 31ff.; J. H. Muirhead, *The Platonic Tradition in Anglo-Saxon Philosophy* (London, 1931); Ernst Cassirer, *The Platonic Renaissance in England*, trans. James P. Pettigrove (Edinburgh, 1953); *The Cambridge Platonists*, ed. C. A. Patrides (London, 1969).

2 Gilbert Burnet, *History of My Own Time*, ed. Osmund Airy, 2 vols. (Oxford, 1897), Vol. I, p. 331.

3 The idea of an ancient wisdom is already employed by the church fathers, Lactantius, Eusebius, Augustine, etc., before it was revived in the Italian Renaissance by Ficino, Pico, et al. See D. P. Walker, *The Ancient Theology* (Ithaca, 1972). For the influence of platonism on Elizabethan philosophy, see Charles Schmitt, *John Case and Aristotelianism in Renaissance England* (Kingston and Montreal, 1983), pp. 47–51, 163–67. Other references to the ancient wisdom may be found in Charles Schmitt, "Perennial philosophy: from Agostino Steucco to Leibniz," *Journal of the History of Ideas* 27 (1966): 505–32; Jeanne Harrie, "Duplessis-Mornay, Foix-Candale and the Hermetic religion of the world," *Renaissance Quarterly* 31 (1978): 499–524; Danton B. Sailor, "Moses and atomism," *Journal of the History of Ideas* 25 (1964): 3–16; Karl H. Dannenfeldt, "The pseudo-Zoroastrian oracles in the Renaissance," *Studies in the Renaissance* 4 (1957): 7–30; Erik Iverson, *The Myth of Egypt and its Hieroglyphics* (Copenhagen, 1961); Frances A. Yates, *Giordano Bruno and the Hermetic Tradition* (London, 1964).

4 John Sherman, *A Greek in the Temple, Some Commonplaces delivered in Trinity College Chapell in Cambridge* (Cambridge, 1641), Vol. III, pp. 20–21. Compare John Milton, *Areopagitica* (London, 1644) in *Works*, Vol. IV (New York, 1931), pp. 306–10. About Sherman there is not much to say, except that he went to school in London at the Charterhouse and then to Queen's College, where he later became fellow and President. He wrote this little work, he says, many years before he delivered it. He seems to have died about 1663 to judge from the letter of Thomas Pierce to Sherman's "executor," prefixed to Sherman's *Infallibility of the Holy Scripture* (London, 1664).

5 Sherman, pp. 36–37.

6 Ibid., pp. 30, 73. Jerome Zanchius (1516–90) was an Italian protestant

theologian who migrated to Strassburg, Heidelberg, and elsewhere, and wrote a great number of theological works, including a famous commentary on Genesis and a treatise on the Trinity. His collected works appeared at Geneva in 1613 and was popular in England; see Arnold Williams, *The Common Expositor: An Account of the Commentaries on Genesis 1527–1633* (Chapel Hill, 1948), pp. 31, 34–36. For some early news about Hermes, see J. S. Gill, "How Hermes Trismegistus was introduced to renaissance England: the influence of Caxton and Ficino's *Argumentum* on Baldwin and Palfreyman," *Journal of the Warburg and Courtauld Institutes* 47 (1984): 222–25.

7 Sherman, pp. 25, 32.

8 "Let me reade the originall; translations may vary...interpretations may be as perplexed as the text," ibid., p. 48.

9 Ibid., pp. 14–15, 28–30. For the exposure of the fraudulent Hermetic writings, see Isaac Casaubon, *De rebus sacris et ecclesiasticis exercitationes XVI* (London, 1614), pp. 70–87; and the discussion in Frances A. Yates, *Giordano Bruno and the Hermetic Tradition* (1964, reprinted, New York, 1969), pp. 398–402, and especially, Anthony Grafton, "Protestant versus prophet: Isaac Casaubon on Hermes Trismegistus," *Journal of the Warburg and Courtauld Institutes* 46 (1983): 78–93.

10 Brooke's work has been reprinted with a useful introduction by Vivian de Sola Pinto (Farnborough, 1969); it is full of references to Plato and the platonists, especially Ficino, and includes at least one to the ancient wisdom and another to Hermes Trismegistus, pp. 30, 143. In 1641, he wrote in favor of toleration in *A Discovery Concerning the Nature of that Episcopacy which is Exercised in England*. Sadler and Story may have collaborated on the *Nature of Truth*, Sadler writing the preface which is signed J. S. It was Thomas Baker who credited them with their neoplatonic priority; see Vivian de Sola Pinto, *Peter Sterry: Platonist and Puritan* (Cambridge, 1934), p. 10. Other neoplatonists who entered Emmanuel College in these years included, besides Whichcote (1626), Sterry (1629), and Sadler (B.A. 1633), Smith (1626), Worthington (1632), Cudworth (1632), and Culverwel (1633). Although there were differences in the degree of their commitment to reason, they would probably all have agreed with Sterry, that "we speak the Language of the general stream of Divines, Philosophers, Poets, Heathen and Sacred, through all the Ages," Pinto, *Sterry*, p. 98. For the correspondence between Hebrew and Greek learning, see James Duport (Regius Professor of Greek at Cambridge from 1639), *Homeri Gnomologia duplici Parallelismo illustrata* (Cambridge, 1660).

11 Tuckney to Whichcote, October 8, 1651, *Eight Letters* in *Moral and Religious Aphorisms of Dr. Whichcote*, ed. Samuel Salter (London, 1753), p. 76.

12 Tuckney's "puritan" views may be derived from his sermons printed posthumously by his son and dated; see Anthony Tuckney, *Forty Sermons* (London, 1676).

13 Tuckney to Whichcote, September 15, 1651, *Eight Letters* pp. 17–40. For Jackson, see Sarah Hutton, "Thomas Jackson, Oxford platonist, and William Twisse, Aristotelian," *Journal of the History of Ideas* 39 (1978): 635–52. Jackson (1579–1640) wrote a series of *Commentaries upon the Apostle's Creed* (1613–57) full of references to the *prisca theologia* and extolling *recta ratio*.

14 *Eight Letters*, Vol. II, pp. 38–39. "Most men of parts here," wrote Thomas

Smith to Samuel Hartlib in November of 1648, "Have their thoughts so taken up with Platonisme, or other high and aery speculations of Divinity or Philosophy they will scarce vouchsafe to cast a glance on ... anything which is not in their way or aim," Charles Webster, *The Great Instauration* (London, 1975), p. 148. Tuckney seems to have read Whichcote's address (which has not survived) as an attack on his own commencement address, delivered the year before. It probably did not help that the radical independent, and new Arminian, John Goodwin, should choose to dedicate his *Redemption Redeemed* to Whichcote and his friends in the same year. Pelagianism urgently needed rebuttal. See Ellen More, "John Goodwin and the origins of the new Arminianism," *Journal of British Studies* 22 (1982): 67–69.

15 *Eight Letters*, pp. 99, 112. See also Whichcote, *Moral and Religious Aphorisms*, ed. Samuel Salter (1753, reprinted London, 1930), nos. 916, 644, 877–78, 943. The Whichcote–Tuckney exchange is discussed fully with other useful information in James D. Roberts, *From Puritanism to Platonism in Seventeenth Century England* (The Hague, 1968). See also Tulloch, Vol. II, pp. 45–98; J. B. Mullinger, *The University of Cambridge* (Cambridge, 1911), Vol. III, pp. 588–96; H. C. Porter, *Reformation and Reaction in Tudor Cambridge* (Cambridge, 1958), pp. 422–28; Robert A. Greene, "Whichcote, Wilkins, 'ingenuity' and the reasonableness of Christianity," *Journal of the History of Ideas* 42 (1981): 227–52.

16 Salter's life of Tuckney in ibid., p. xii. For anti-intellectualism among the puritans, see Anthony Wood, *Life and Times*, ed. Andrew Clark, Oxford Historical Society (1891), "Of the endeavors used to pull down Academies," p. 64. The title of one popular work is suggestive, Samuel How, *The Sufficiency of the Spirit's Teaching, without human Learning* (1640). In general, see Leo F. Solt, "Anti-intellectualism in the puritan revolution," *Church History* 24 (1956): 306–16; Richard L. Greaves, *The Puritan Revolution and Educational Thought* (New Brunswick, 1969), pp. 122–25.

17 See *Aphorisms*, no. 542. "The great materials of natural light are first in reason, and then reinforced in scripture. The articles of faith are first in scripture, and being there revealed, are after justified in reason; there is no true reason against them, but there is full satisfaction in them," Whichcote, The *Works*, 4 vols. (Aberdeen, 1751), Vol. I, p. 380. Several of Whichcote's sermons were published first by the third Earl of Shaftesbury (London, 1698), then more fully by John Jeffery and Samuel Clarke, 4 vols. (London, 1701–4) and afterward reprinted in the edition cited here. Whichcote's "spiritual is most rational" (*Eight Letters*, p. 108) may be compared with Richard Sibbes, "it is the greatest reason to yeeld reason to Faith," see Patrides, pp. 9–10.

18 Whichcote, *Works*, Vol. II, p. 319; Vol. IV, pp. 290, 437.

19 Ibid., Vol. II, pp. 160, 173; Vol. III, pp. 319–20.

20 Ibid., Vol. III, p. 25.

21 Ibid., Vol. II, p. 233.

22 Ibid., Vol. II, p. 319; *The Cambridge Platonists*, ed. E. Campagnac (Oxford, 1901), p. 24.

23 See John Smith, "The excellency and nobleness of true religion," *Select Discourses*, ed. John Worthington (London, 1660), pp. 377–451, in Patrides, p. 187; Marjorie Nicolson, "The early stage of Cartesianism in England," *Studies in Philology* 26 (1929): 356–74.

24 See Samuel I. Mintz, *The Hunting of Leviathan* (Cambridge, 1962), pp. 80–109.

25 Burnet, Vol. I, p. 333. Burnet visited Cambridge in 1663, met the platonists, and was impressed by Whichcote and More in particular; see T. E. S. Clarke and F. C. Foxcroft, *A Life of Gilbert Burnet* (Cambridge, 1907), pp. 38–39.

26 Whichcote, *Works*, Vol. II, p. 312. Cf. Henry Oldenberg to John Beale, 4 September 1660, *The Correspondence of Henry Oldenberg*, ed. and trans. A. Rupert Hall and Marie Boas Hall, Vol. I (Madison, 1965), pp. 384–87.

27 Whichcote, *Works*, Vol. III, p. 42.

28 Whichcote, *Works*, Vol. II, p. 2. Tuckney denies (1646) that the Greeks knew any of the basic Christian truths, "The wisest men of the East (whatever they were called before) began to be truly wise when they came to seek after Christ," *Forty Sermons*, p. 23. Elsewhere he inveighs against, "all over-bold and curious prying into the Ark of God's secrets, measuring his Concils by our Thoughts and the wisdom of them by our reason which instead of sticking to know Christ hath stretched many mens wits into wild and tedious disputes." The whole sermon seems a rebuke to Whichcote, ibid., p. 32. See also the sermon, January 17, 1657/58, ibid., pp. 248ff.

29 The autobiography was prefixed to the *Opera Omnia* (1675) and is translated by Richard Ward in *The Life of Henry More* (London, 1710), pp. 5–16. See also Serge Hutin, *Henry More: Essai sur les doctrines Theosophiques chez les Platoniciens de Cambridge* (Hildesheim, 1966); Aharon Lichtenstein, *Henry More: The Rational Theology of a Cambridge Platonist* (Cambridge, Mass., 1962); John Henry, "A Cambridge platonist's materialism: Henry More and the concept of the soul," *Journal of the Warburg and Courtauld Institutes* 49 (1986): 172–95. There is a useful bibliography of More's works in More's *Philosophical Writings*, ed. Flora I. Mackinnon (New York, 1925), pp. 234–45.

30 See C. C. Brown, "Henry More's deep retirement: new materials on the early years of the Cambridge platonist," *Review of English Studies* n.s. 20 (1969): 445–54; Marjorie Nicolson, "Christ's College and the latitude men," *Modern Philology* 27 (1929): 35–53.

31 Thomas Leigh in John Peile, *Christ's College* (London, 1900), p. 138.

32 John Worthington, "Life of Mede," in *Works*, 2 vols. (London, 1664), Vol. I, p. x.

33 Ward, p. 12.

34 We should not overlook Robert Gell, another of More's tutors, who succeeded Chappel as Hebrew Lecturer in 1634 and Mede as Greek Lecturer in 1638. He too became a friend of Lady Conway and showed a decided predilection for the ancient wisdom, though too alchemical and astrological for the mature More. In 1649, he delivered a sermon before the Society of Astrologers describing the "foure Schooles of Wisemen famous throughout the World": the Gymnosophists of Ethiopia, the Brachmans of India, and the Babylonian and Persian magi.

35 *Psycholodia Platonica: or a Platonicall Song of the Soul*, in *Philosophical Poems* (Cambridge, 1647); ed. Geoffrey Bullough (Manchester, 1931) (but without the notes added later by More).

36 Ward, p. 153.

37 *Philosophical Poems* (Bullough), p. 12. Anne Conway to her father-in-law, in *Conway Letters*, ed. Marjorie Nicolson (New Haven, 1930), pp. 36–38. The poem was written early in 1640; for the poet's indebtedness to the platonic

tradition, see C. A. Staudenbauer, "Galileo, Ficino and Henry More's *Psychathanasia*," *Journal of the History of Ideas* 29 (1968): 565–78; Alexander Jacob, "Henry More's *Psychodia Platonica* and its relationship to Marsilio Ficino's *Theologia Platonica*," ibid., 46 (1985): 503–22.

38 *Philosophical Poems* (1647), "To the reader," and "Notes upon *Psychozoia*," p. 371.

39 Ibid., p. 352.

40 See Lady Conway's own platonic essay, *Principles of the Most Ancient and Modern Philosophy*, trans. J. C. (London, 1692). It was printed first in Latin in Amsterdam (1690) and won the admiration of Leibniz.

41 See for example, *The Immortality of the Soul* (1659), Vol. II, ch. 12, in *A Collection of Several Philosophical Writings* (London, 1662), pp. 113–14.

42 Ward, p. 26.

43 Ibid., p. 12.

44 Thomas Vaughan's *Works* have been edited by Arthur Waite who includes an appendix on the More–Vaughan debate (1919, reprinted New Hyde Park, 1968), pp. 468–73. One of More's several contributions, *Enthusiasmus Triumphatus* (1656), has been reprinted with an introduction by M. V. De Porte (Los Angeles, 1966). See Frederic B. Burnham, "The More–Vaughan controversy: the revolt against philosophical enthusiasm," *Journal of the History of Ideas* 35 (1974): 33–49; Noel L. Brann, "The conflict between reason and magic in seventeenth century England: a case study of the Vaughan–More debate," *Huntingdon Library Quarterly* 43 (1980): 103–26. For More's attitude to the Quakers, see Marjorie Nicolson, "George Keith and the Cambridge Platonists," *Philosophical Review* 39: 36–55; *Conway Letters*, pp. 378ff.

45 Henry More, *Democritus Platonismus* (1646), ed. P. G. Stonewood, (Los Angeles, 1968): sig. A2.

46 See Nicolson, "Early stages"; Sterling Lamprecht, "The role of Descartes in seventeenth century England," Columbia University, *Studies in the History of Ideas* III (New York, 1935): 181–243.

47 *Reflections upon Monsieur Des Cartes's Discourse*, trans. John Davies (London, 1653). Cf. Descartes, *Rules for the Direction of the Mind* (1628, posthumously published, 1701), rule III, "In the subjects we propose to investigate, our inquiries should be directed, not to what others have thought ... but to what we can clearly and perspicuously behold and with certainty deduce; for knowledge is not won in any other way," *The Philosophical Works*, trans. Elizabeth S. Haldane and G. R. T. Ross (Cambridge, 1911), Vol. I, pp. 5–8.

48 *A Collection*, general preface, p. xi.

49 Ibid., p. 12. Descartes, *Principles of Philosophy* (Latin, 1644; French, 1647), Vol. IV, p. ccii.

50 Ward, p. 26.

51 Leonora D. Cohen, "Descartes and Henry More on the beast-machine, a translation of their correspondence pertaining to animal automation," *Annals of Science* 1 (1936): 48–61. See also Leonora Cohen Rosenfield, *From Beast-Machine to Man-Machine* (1940, reprinted New York, 1968). To the Conway letters printed by Marjorie Nicolson should be added now three more; see Alan Gabbey, "Anne Conway et Henry More: letters sur Descartes (1650–51)," *Archives de Philosophie* 40 (1977): 379–404.

52 Charles Webster, "Henry More and Descartes: some new sources," *British Journal for the History of Medicine* 4 (1969): 365. In 1662, More still admires Descartes; see *A Collection*, gen. pref., p. xi; by 1668, he has strong doubts; see the publisher (More) to the reader, *Divine Dialogues*; by 1671 he is ready to lump him with Hobbes, see the *Enchiridion Metaphysicum* (London, 1671), ad lect., sect. 10. By then he was worried "how prejudicial Descartes's mechanical pretensions are to the belief of a God"; see More to Boyle, *The Works of Robert Boyle*, Vol. VI (London, 1772), pp. 513–15. Alan Gabbey argues after a thorough review of the evidence that More did not so much change his mind about Descartes (whom he always criticized) but his strategy, as the danger from "atheism" seemed to grow; "*Philosophia Cartesiana Triumphata*: Henry More (1646–71)," *Problems of Cartesianism*, ed. Thomas M. Lennon, et al. (Kingston and Montreal, 1982), pp. 171–250.

53 The full exchange (1648–49) is given by Webster, "More and Descartes," 367–72.

54 See Robert A. Green, "Henry More and Robert Boyle on the spirit of nature," *Journal of the History of Ideas* 23 (1962): 451–74.

55 *An Antidote against Atheisme* (London, 1653), pref., sig. A. For the date of publication, see Gabbey, "*Philosophia*," p. 198n.

56 *Conway Letters*, pp. 70–71; *An Apology of Dr. Henry More* (1664), pp. 488–89; Gabbey, "*Philosophia*," p. 230.

57 *Antidote*, in *A Collection*, p. 142.

58 *Conjectura Cabbalistica or a Conjectural Story of Interpreting the Mind of Moses according to the Three-Fold Cabbala* (London, 1653). A second edition (with additions) appeared in *A Collection* (1662) and a third in the *Opera Omnia* (London, 1679). More did not yet know the Jewish cabbalistic writings; when he discovered them later, he was forced to disavow them. See Allison Coudert, "A Cambridge Platonist's Kabbalist nightmare," *Journal of the History of Ideas* 36 (1975): 633–52.

59 Ibid., preface, sig. B2; see too the general preface to *A Collection*, pp. xvi–xix. For the genesis of this idea and More's use of it, see Sailor, "Moses and Atomism," n. 3 above.

60 *Defence of the Three-Fold Cabbala*, pref., 83.

61 *Conway Letters*, p. 200; *Divine Dialogues*, Vol. I, "Publisher to the reader"; Gabbey, "*Philosophia*," p. 242.

62 See Nicolson, "Christ's College and the latitude-men," 49.

63 More to Lady Conway, August 9, 1653, *Conway Letters*, p. 83.

64 "Epistle to the reader," *An Account of Virtue* (London, 1690). This is a translation, probably by Robert Southwell, of More's *Enchiridion Ethicum* (1660).

65 *The True Intellectual System of the Universe: Wherein all the Reason and Philosophy of Atheism is Confuted; and its Impossibility Demonstrated* (London, 1678).

66 Cudworth's work should be compared with Theophilus Gale, *Court of the Gentiles* (1669–77) and with the works of Edward Stillingfleet.

67 The platonists received their first serious criticism from Samuel Parker, *A Free and Impartial Censure of the Platonick Philosophers* (Oxford, 1666). In 1733, Johann Lorenz von Mosheim turned Cudworth into Latin with critical and explanatory notes and this version was turned back into English by John

Harrison in three volumes (London, 1845). For the persistence of some of these ideas, see for example, Edmund Dickinson, *Physicus vetus et vera* (London, 1702). What happened afterward remains pretty much *terra incognita*. For a resurrection of some of these notions, however, see Cyrus H. Gordon, *The Common Background of Greek and Hebrew Civilization* (New York, 1965).

5 Cudworth, More and the mechanical analogy

Alan Gabbey

And like an Engin mov'd with wheel and waight,
His principles being ceast, he ended straight.

John Milton, "On the University Carrier" (*alter*)

An intriguing feature of Simon Patrick's *A Brief Account of the new Sect of Latitude-Men* (1662) is its conspicuous inclusion of *some reflections upon the New Philosophy*, as the full title puts it, meaning the new natural philosophy, the new science, that characterized the first half of the seventeenth century. A priori, there is no obvious reason why we should have expected Patrick to make a connection between characteristically latitudinarian positions and recent advances in natural philosophy. The latter seem to belong exclusively to the scientific domain, the former to areas of controversy within Anglicanism. Yet *A Brief Account* linked the latitude-men directly with an important feature of the "new philosophy" by crediting them with having "introduced" into England new doctrines of mechanical explanation of natural phenomena as correctives of the explanatory tautologies of peripatetic physics.[1] Patrick illustrated the contrast between the mechanical and the peripatetic philosophies with a lengthy parable of a farmer's faulty clock, the fruitless attempts of "a certain Peripatetick artificer" to mend it, and the intervention of "an ingenuous Gentleman" who, understanding perfectly the mechanical workings of clocks, was able to show the farmer why he needed a new one, and what he should do in future with any other clock that might go out of kilter.

It is not wholly clear from Patrick's pamphlet, which contained the first appearance in print of the terms "latitude-men"[2] and "latitudinarian," who exactly the latitude-men were. On the one hand, he writes that "*the greatest part* of the men that seem to be pointed at under that name [latitude-men], are such, whose fortune it was to be born so late, as to have their education in the University [of Cambridge], since the beginning of the unhappy troubles of this Kingdom."[3] Taking "the unhappy troubles" to refer broadly to the Civil Wars (1642–46, 1648–51) or possibly to the exploits of the Long Parliament (3 November, 1640–16 March, 1660), these lines imply that the Cambridge Platonists, usually taken to have been *the* latitudinarians, must have been very much in a minority as latitude-men. None of them commenced B.A. later than 1640, and only one (John Smith, M.A. 1644) commenced M.A. later than 1639.

On the other hand, Patrick's claim that the latitude-men "introduced a new Philosophy" surely refers only to the Cambridge Platonists, whose espousal of the new (mainly Cartesian) mechanical philosophy was the first in England, and predated any comparable philosophical predilections of younger candidate latitude-men such as Patrick himself, Tillotson, Stillingfleet, Fowler or Glanvill, whose university education (whether in Cambridge or Oxford) took place after the beginning of the kingdom's unhappy troubles.

I assume that Patrick is in fact describing what Burnham calls "first-" and "second-generation" latitude-men, the former being mostly or entirely Cambridge Platonists, the latter being "those who were formed under them,"[4] that is, younger men such as Patrick, Tenison, Tillotson, or Fowler.[5] Latitudinarianism is not the central theme of this essay, and I will be dealing with just two Cambridge Platonists, Ralph Cudworth and Henry More. Yet part of the value of Patrick's *Brief Account* is that it highlights and confirms latitudinarianism as a proper context within which to investigate the relations between theology and natural philosophy in seventeenth-century England. Accordingly, the latitudinarian framework will enable us to appreciate the significance of a mechanical analogy or simile used to striking rhetorical effect in their respective writings by both Cudworth and More.

In his defense of the latitude-men, Patrick saw polemical value in reminding his readers that "the Theater of nature" had become "much enlarged since *Aristotles* time,"[6] so he included mention of discoveries in mechanics, optics, microscopy, and chemistry, and he highlighted in particular the discoveries of Galileo, Scheiner, and Tycho in astronomy, of Gilbert in magnetical science, Boyle in pneumatics, Harvey in physiology and embryology, and of Descartes and Gassendi in mechanical philosophy. In short, the advances in the natural sciences had been the triumph of Freedom and Reason: why should the religious life not witness the same triumph?

In some quarters, not surprisingly, alarm had been caused by the perceived attunement of the latitude-men's intellectual complexion to the innovative spirit that informed these advances. In turn, this alarm partly motivated the contemporary censure that occasioned Patrick's public rejoinder. The fear was that *"new Philosophy* will bring in *new Divinity*; and freedom in the one will make men desire a liberty in the other."[7] The latitudinarian response was that natural philosophy and theology are distinct yet mutually compatible ways of enlisting free-ranging reason[8] in the search for God and His Works. Accordingly, they can and must be brought into harmony with each other.[9] Patrick himself believed that "true Philosophy can never hurt sound Divinity,"[10] a sentiment that found a ready echo in Henry More: "I can *ex animo* avow to all the world, that there is no real clashing at all betwixt any genuine Point of Christianity and what true Philosophy and right Reason does determine or allow, but that, as Aristotle somewhere speaks... there is a perpetual peace and agreement betwixt Truth & Truth, be they of what nature or kind so ever..."[11] And the most promising candidate for the title of "the true philosophy" was the mechanical philosophy, the most successful way of doing science that had come within the latitude-men's experience. In their eyes it was uncovering more truths about nature than could ever have been recovered from the effete subtleties of peripatetic physics. Clearly, the latitudinarian interest in the mechanical philosophy was more than just a polemical stratagem relying on simple emulation of the progressive tendencies in contemporary science.

Yet the mechanical philosophy was not an unmitigated blessing for latitudinarian – or at least platonizing – sensibilities. "Sound divinity" demanded that remedies be found for the serious weaknesses that were evident in the mechanical philosophy: the claim to provide purely mechanical explanation of all natural phenomena, for example, or the exclusion of spirit from the physical world, which it was feared would smooth the path to materialism and godlessness.[12] It was precisely because of these weaknesses, and the consequent necessity of introducing into the corporeal world some kind of plastic nature as an instrument of Providence, that Cudworth and More saw in the mechanical philosophy (if rightly understood) the best remedy for the disease of atheism. More's remedy was his "Spirit of Nature," which produces "such *Phaenomena* in the World, by directing the parts of the Matter and their Motion, as cannot be resolved into mere Mechanical powers."[13] Cudworth's remedy was his "Plastick Nature," which "as an Inferior and Subordinate Instrument, doth Drudgingly Execute that Part of his Providence, which consists in the Regular and Orderly Motion of Matter...[though] this *Plastic Nature* cannot act *Electively* nor with *Discretion*"[14]

To see how the mechanical philosophy could be employed to illustrate and fortify latitudinarian values, I begin with the unsurprising fact that although the Cambridge Platonists were the earliest group to be labelled as latitude-men by their adversaries, none of them welcomed the reproachful cognomen or used it in their opponents' sense to refer to themselves. The latitudinarian clan contained no self-confessed members. Those tracts that defended them admitted the name only *pro tempore* for the purpose of exculpating the group so maligned; they cannot be read as manifestos of a sect or faction,[15] nor can their authors be assumed to be admitting to the name or to the reputed doctrinal delinquencies associated with it.

An instructive instance of a refusal to wear the latitudinarian label occurs in an unpublished letter (*c.* 1671) from More to Christian Knorr von Rosenroth, which forms part of a series of exchanges on the Kabbala and other matters. Living in Sulzbach, Knorr von Rosenroth had been receiving from England, through the good offices of Francis Mercury van Helmont, books by Joseph Mede, Glanvill, Francis Potter, John Lightfoot, and More (the poetical as well as the theological and philosophical works). Also included in his reading list were some works of the latitude-men, including at least *A Brief Account* and George Rust's *Letter of Resolution Concerning Origen* (1661). Knorr von Rosenroth duly wrote to More to express his pleasure at receiving More's works together with "a few other things published by your latitudinarians [*à Latitudinariis vestris editis*]."

As a foreigner, von Rosenroth was probably innocent of the mild incivility in assuming on More's behalf, and to his face so to speak, sodality with the latitudinarians so-called. More's response was polite yet pointed. After some comments on three transmitters of antique philosophy – Fludd, Spenser, and Chaucer as translator of Boethius – More continued:

I understand Mr. van Helmont will be sending you all these authors, as well as a book showing the quality of certain men who against their will have been called latitudinarians by certain persons.[16] As for me, I have never allowed myself to be absorbed into any sect. I rest content in the name of primitive Christian, just as you confess yourself an Evangelical. And I am not a Latitudinarian in any sense other than that I harbour the greatest latitude of goodwill towards all men whatever, and do so with a kindly disposition of mind, not only towards our own Reformed, but also towards Pontificials, Jews, Turks and even pagans. Nonetheless I attack and censure the errors of them all, and not without a certain briskness of mind and discourse, so that stirred from their slumbers they might at last open their eyes and acknowledge the truth...[17]

Few latitude-men would have dissented from the spirit of this declaration of goodwill to all men, whether or not made also with an eye to doctrinal redress, and few would have been strangers to the spirit of toleration we feel moves between the lines of More's letter. Yet goodwill by no means exhausts the latitude-men's characteristic qualities, and indeed the latitudinarian temper is not the same thing as toleration, whether in its post- or pre-Restoration manifestations.[18] Exhibiting a seeming laxity in their attitudes to liturgy, rites and ceremonies, or Church government, the targets for the abusive nickname "latitude-man" shared ineradicable convictions more sharply focused than the pan-religious benevolence blandly avowed by More in this letter to von Rosenroth. There were changeless truths of greater spiritual moment which they would have held it an impiety to describe as "latitudinarian" and an impossibility to disregard in pleas for toleration, and which took precedence over sectarian shibboleths, "the externals of religion," or points of doctrine at odds with the counsels of well-tuned reason.

In his sermon on "The Use of Reason in Matters of Religion," Whichcote had advised his listeners that "in the great Matters of Righteousness, there is no Variation; but in *Positives* and *Institutes* there is a Latitude of Sense, Interpretation, Time, and Observance. Institutes were never intended to be in Compensation or Recompence for Failure in *Morals*: but for *their* better Security."[19] More might say of rites and ceremonies that "none of these things were so good as to make men good, nor so bad as to make men bad, but might be either good or bad according to the hands into which they fell."[20] There were however some things absolutely unqualifiedly good that could not but make men good, if only they would heed none but God's voice.

An exceptionally vigorous expression of More's views appears in his letter to Samuel Hartlib of December 30 (*o.s.*), 1649, written at a time of personal anguish for More. The letter is of particular importance in that it constitutes documentary proof that More subscribed to the Engagement, presumably some time between October 12 and December 10, 1650.[21] Hartlib had sent him two publications for perusal and comment, the first of them being one of the large number of printed contributions to the Engagement controversy, then at its height. Unfortunately, Hartlib's covering letter is lost, and More does not mention the title, though there is every possibility that Hartlib had sent him a copy of John Dury's *Considerations Concerning the Present Engagement* (1649), or his *A Case of Conscience Resolved* (1649):[22]

That in the blew cover in my conceit is such as may become a man of much sobriety and judgement, to have writt. It came to my handes just immediately after I had taken the engagement, and is written so much according to my minde and sense that if I were to give an account to any for this act of mine, I should referre them to this treatize, as to my own, it explicitly speaking out what I had more closely couched in my own minde concerning this matter; but I am more peculiarly pleased with what is contained in yᵉ 10ᵗʰ and 11ᵗʰ pages of the sayd treatize.

The other publication seems not to have been about the Engagement controversy, at least not directly, but had to do with reconciliation between contending religious factions. As we read More proclaiming his primal latitudinarian message, we can sense in the tirade the chagrin of a natural royalist who, despite the comfort of the pages between the blue cover and even possibly the comforts of being without "a conscience most ridiculously boggling,"[23] had just engaged to be true and faithful to the Commonwealth of England, as it was then established, without a King or House of Lords:

As for the other, viz ye loose sheet concerning a Truly and so forth, it is a very honest and Christian designe he drives at, if the partyes thus exasperated were any way at all reconcilable. That which is deplorable in this notion is this. That those men that make the greatest cry about relligion, and count themselves the onely conspicuous godly in the Kingdome, and think themselves even acted by God himself, and that they are zealous sincerely for the honour of his name, that all this zeal and heat which they spread and expresse, are about such thinges as are not at all essentiall to Godlinesse, nay are indeed nothing else but childish humours, and melancholick impressions upon their disturbed spiritts, or the stubborn effect of prevelant education or covetousnesse or pride or almost any thing rather then what they themselves, not examining themselves to the bottom, conceite it to be. But from this inept and unskillfull prosecution of matters of religion,[24] much scandal is given to the world, even to ye hazard of all religion, or els bringing back the dark dispensations of Popery. But would this were writt up every where in capitall letters, that THOSE THAT UNFEIGNEDLY LOVE GOD AND HIS CHRIST, THAT IT IS IMPOSSIBLE BUT THAT THOROUGH THAT LOVE THEY BEAR TO THESE, THAT THEY SHOULD SO TENDERLY AND AFFECTIONATELY LOVE ALL THOSE THAT ARE CONFORMABLE TO THE UNDOUBTED ESSENTIALLS OF CHRISTIANITY IN LIFE AND DOCTRINE, THAT THEY WOULD LEAVE OTHER THINGES AS FREE TO THINKE SPEAKE OR DOE, WITHOUT ANY CENSURE OR BITTERNESSE, MUCH LESSE DESIRE OF DESTRUCTION AND BLOODSHED. And those that are otherwise minded, I think I may speak it without rash-nesse, they are so far from being the eminent Godly of the land, that they are in truth but peevish, ignorant and untamed Hypocrites, as troublesome to men as detestible before God.[25]

Unswerving conformability to the undoubted essentials of Christianity lay at the heart of the latitude-men's spirituality. Whatever the full complement of those essentials, they included the quest for true godliness through keeping Christ's commandments and obeying the law of the spirit within us, that spirit which is "the candle of the Lord," perhaps the most cherished image of the Cambridge Platonists' faith.[26] All else, including the products of reason within the natural domain, is secondary to this inalienable duty, and what God has not commanded is not necessary for the authentic life of the spirit. As Whichcote expressed it in his sermon on "The Manifestation of Christ and the Deification of Man," "... there is no Superstition in using Things not commanded by God, *even in the Worship of God*; if they be Comely, and such as Reason doth allow of. But, there is Superstition in assuming to our selves *Authority to use them, as necessary Peices of Religion*, and as *sanctified* by Divine Institution; when they are not of God's Appointment."[27]

For the most extended homily on this theme, I turn to Ralph Cudworth's House of Commons sermon of March 31, 1647, delivered in St. Margaret's, Westminster, for which Cudworth took his text from 1 John, chapter 2:3–4: "And hereby we do know that we know him, if we keep his commandments. He that saith, I know him, and keepeth not his commandments, is a liar, and the truth is not in him." This was one of the series of regular Fast Sermons engineered (with the fasts themselves) by the Long Parliament, and which were preached, two at a time, on the last Wednesday of each month from February 23 (*o.s.*), 1642 to February 28 (*o.s.*), 1649.

There is some dispute as to the intended purpose of the Fast Sermons. Trevor-Roper argues that the fasts "were always regarded as party propaganda," the sermons being used by the leaders of the Long Parliament "both to declare long-term aims and to inaugurate temporary shifts of policy," at least as long as Parliament was united under effective leadership.[28] Yule takes a different view, arguing that although fast preachers often promulgated particular party lines and were at times specifically chosen for that purpose, in general they "endeavoured to see that reformation of religion was the first priority, and if any theme could be said to run through the Fast Sermons this would be it."[29] Trevor-Roper's case may hold good for the sermons he adduces as evidence, but seemingly not for all fast sermons, not only in the light of Yule's persuasive counter-arguments, but also because Cudworth's sermon (which neither Trevor-Roper nor Yule mentions) does not urge any specific political doctrine. The sermon ends with an "inward Reformation of the heart" being the *prerequisite* for achieving the sought-after "true Reformation" of "outward Government," thus providing support for Yule's case and for his observation that there is "hardly a sermon that does not end with an exhortation to help in the reformation of the church, and the reason given is that the state may prosper as well."[30]

On the other hand, Cudworth's sermon can hardly be said to have been preached at a time of Parliamentary unity, so perhaps Trevor-Roper's qualification of his own thesis (see above) applies at least to it: "Pym and his friends, even Vane, St. John, and Holles, might 'tune the pulpits' in order to keep Parliament and people together along a prepared line; but how could this be done when Parliament was at the mercy of its own warring parties, and of military force?... In such circumstances clergymen hardly knew what to say. There were too many tuners and no agreement about the musical notes."[31] Cudworth knew what notes to play, and upon what ground. What was more fundamental to the Christian life, in the midst of religious or political strife, than the keeping of Christ's commandments?[32]

Yet if knowing Christ rests on keeping His commandments, then it is to be suspected, Cudworth proclaims, that there are many whose souls are in darkness. There is such a plethora of tomes and discourses, of controversies and questions, all concerning Christ and the union of His divine and human natures,

> that our bookish Christians, that have all their religion in writings and papers, think they are now compleatly furnished with all kind of knowledge concerning Christ; and when they see all their leaves lying about them, they think they have a goodly stock of knowledge and truth, and cannot possibly misse of the way to heaven; as if Religion were nothing but a little *Book-craft*, a mere *paper-skill*. But if S. Johns rule here be good, we must not judge of our knowing of Christ, by our skill in Books and Papers, but by our keeping of his Commandments.[33]

The opposition between the essentials of religion and its negotiable externals, which for Cudworth include the activities of theological scribblers and system-mongers, is the grand theme on which he exercises his homiletic skill to build a multitude of variations throughout the sermon, employing naturally on the way simile and analogy as telling rhetorical devices.

One of these analogies is especially significant in that it illuminates the main theme of the sermon through an appeal to the notion of an internal "principle of life." "Inke and Paper can never make us Christians," Cudworth declaims, "can never beget a new nature, a living principle in us; can never form Christ, or any true notions of spirituall things in our hearts. The Gospel, that new Law which Christ delivered to the world, it is not merely a *Letter* without us, but a *quickning Spirit* within us." Mere words, dead words and maxims, dry argumentation, he continues, cannot encompass the mysteries of the divine life within. A painter may convey the shape and color of a rose, but never its fragrancy. He may paint a flame, but not convey its heat; he cannot draw a sound.[34] But further: "All the skill of cunning Artizans and Mechanicks, cannot put a principle of Life into a statue of their own making."[35]

This mention of mechanics and their statues comes across as something more than simply another figure of speech. Recalling Cudworth's writings on natural philosophy, particularly the "atomical philosophy," we read further into the sermon in hopeful pursuit of a more informative elaboration of the intriguing coupling of the mechanical and the spiritual. We are not disappointed. Much later in the sermon, Cudworth returns to the idea, now in the form of a simile, preceding it by a related simile borrowed from music:

the Law written upon *Tables of stone* without us...though it work us into some outward Conformity to Gods Commandments, and so hath a good effect upon the World; yet we are all this while, but like dead Instruments of Musick, that sound sweetly and harmoniously, when they are onely struck, and played upon from without, by the Musicians Hand, who hath the Theory and *Law* of Musick, *living* within himself. But...the *living* Law of the Gospel, the *Law of the Spirit of Life* within us, is, as if the *Soul of Musick*, should incorporate it self with the Instrument, and live in the Strings, and make them of their own accord, without any touch, or impulse from without, daunce up and down, and warble out their Harmonies. They that are acted only by an outward Law, are but like Neurospasts; or those little Puppets that skip nimbly up and down, and seem to be full of quick and sprightly motion, whereas they are all the while moved artificially by certain Wiers and Strings from without, and not by any Principle of Motion, from themselves within: or else, like Clocks and Watches, that go pretty regularly for a while, but are moved by Weights and Plummets, or some other Artificiall Springs, that must be ever now and then wound up, or else they cease. But they that are acted by the *new Law of the Gospel*, by the *Law of the Spirit*, they have an inward principle of life in them, that from the Centre of it self, puts forth it self freely and constantly into all obedience to the will of Christ...[36]

The explanatory role of the *neurospaston* from its classical origins through to modern times, and the related question of the characteristics that distinguish (in relevant senses) a puppet from the person or animal it represents, would make for an instructive chapter in the history of the mechanical philosophy. In *Noctes Atticae* Aulus Gellius relates the anti-astrological views of Favorinus (*ob.* mid-second century A.D.), who argued that men would not be rational beings, "but a species of ludicrous and ridiculous puppets [*neurospasta*], if it be true that they do nothing of their own volition or their own will, but are led and driven by the stars."[37] Clearly, Gellius was one classical source of the *neurospaston* idea for seventeenth-century writers. It does not matter greatly, however, whether Cudworth came across it in Gellius, in Plato's fable of the puppets,[38] in some other pre-seventeenth-century writer,[39] or in Henry More; or, conceivably, whether More took it from Cudworth. The significant point is that Cudworth and More (and Favorinus) invoked the puppet image for strikingly similar purposes.

More's purpose in book 1, canto 2 of *Psychathanasia, or The Immortality of the Soul*, the second poem of *A Platonick Song of the Soul*,[40] is to establish the respective natures of the souls of men, beasts, and plants, and to find "wherein all souls agree." All souls share the property of being self-moving, or "autokinetical," whether they be spermatical (vegetative beings, also plastic powers in animals), bestial (or sensitive), or rational (stanza 25). Nature displays many examples of soul as self-moving substance: plants and flowers, for example, their seminal centers awakened by solar warmth, shoot up and blossom through their internal vital force (stanzas 27–31).

[32]
But it's more plain in animalitie.
When fiery coursers strike the grassie ground
With swift tempestuous feet, that farre and nigh
They fill mens ears with a broad thundring sound
(From hollow hoof so strongly it doth rebound)
What's that that twitcheth up their legs so fast,
And fiercely jerks them forth, that many wound
They give to their own mother in their hast?
With eager steps they quickly mete the forrest wast.

[33]
That outward form is but a neurospast;[41]
The soul it is that on her subtile ray,
That she shoots out, the limbs of moving beast
Doth stretch straight forth, so straightly as she may.
Bones joynts and sinews shap'd of stubborn clay
Cannot so eas'ly lie in one straight line
With her projected might, much lesse obey
Direct retractions of these beames fine:
Of force, so straight retreat they ever must decline.[42]

If the souls of animals are "self-moving forms," "...That souls of men / Should be more stupid, and farre lesse releast / From matters of bondage, surely there's none can / Admit of, though but slightly they do scan / The cause..." (stanza [36]). Reminiscent of Favorinus's argument is stanza [37]:

If there be no self-motivation in mans soul,
That she nor this nor that way can propend
Of her own self, nor can no whit controll
Nor will of her own self, who can offend?
For no mans self (if you do well perpend)
Guiltie's of ought when nought doth from him flow.
Whither do learning, laws, grave speeches tend?

More striking and significant is More's use of the puppet analogy to make a point about God's creation that mirrors almost exactly Cudworth's remarks on the law of the spirit within. The text I have in mind comes from *A Collection of Aphorisms* (1704), which the editor (probably J. Downing, the publisher) describes as papers written in unknown circumstances, "though it having been the *Author's* custom, when any thing more than ordinarily affected him, to set down a *Memorandum* thereof, whilst the Sense continued strong and fresh upon his Mind; some are apt to believe, that the following Papers might be of this Stamp."[43]

Aphorism I of part 2 is a short meditation on a question discussed by the Stoic Chrysippus, as related by Gellius: were diseases too created by Nature, the source of all that is good? Only indirectly and unintentionally, argues Chrysippus. The creation of things that are good and useful inevitably brings with it – *per sequellas quasdam necessarias*, as Gellius glosses Chrysippus – other things that are harmful and bad. Disease was created at the same time as health, vices at the same time as virtues, and the delicate bone structure of the human head, which Nature found necessary for the higher functions, brought with it added susceptibility to injury.[44] More retails the example of the head's bone structure, adds a few more of his own, and concludes with the thought that "God would have made all things purely *Happy*, if the *Capability* of the Creature would have permitted."[45] At the beginning of the Aphorism, he advances the two truths which, if admitted, explain why in general the "deficiencies in the world" flow ineluctably from what God has created, not from God himself:

1st, that GOD looked not upon the *Universe*, when it was to be created, as one *Homogeneal* Lump, but seeing that *Heterogeneity* would admit of that Sweetness of *Subordination*, and comely Disposition of *different parts*, intended *Diversity of Essences*, one exceeding another in *Goodness* and *Participation* of the *First Essence*. *2ndly* That, whereby a more lively *Impression* of his own *Excellency*, who is altogether *Independent*, might be stamped upon the *Creatures*, He gave them a certain *Shadow* of his own *Independency*, that is, *inward Principles*, wherewith they might work; not being moved like your νευρόσπασ[τ]α, or *Puppits*, whose Motions are from without; but operating according to their own *inward Principles*; the *Power* of God concurring as an *universal* cause, not by *Determination* of every Action, but by affording them of his *Goodness and Wisdom*, such and such *Principles*.[46]

Knowing Christ, the most fundamental of the essentials of practical Christianity, is inseparable from obedience to His commandments, to the Law of the Gospel. The authentic Christian life is an inward and active love of Christ and His Law, not an outward show of seeming discipleship. As we reflect therefore on Cudworth's use of the puppet simile to convey this message, or on More's example of the galloping horse to show the presence of bestial soul in what appearance alone might suggest is only a puppet, or again on More's broader use of *neurospasta* to illustrate the presence of active principles within natural things, we see that since it is the mechanical nature of puppets that lends the simile its effectiveness, the humble neurospast promises us an unexpected link between the mechanical philosophy and latitudinarian spirituality. It is unlikely that the puppet simile was simply an apt yet adventitious choice for Cudworth to express the fervent convictions of March 31, 1647, or for More in his song of the soul within each of God's creatures, or again as an aid in explaining the manner of God's government of His creation.

For Cudworth and More, as perhaps for the generality of latitude-men, the Christian message takes precedence over philosophies of nature, or metaphysical systems. Our starting point must always be the fundamental Christian doctrines, among them being the reality of the living human soul, which fulfills its proper end only through obeying God's commandments, the Law of the Gospel within us. But that Law cannot be obeyed except through the exercise of the will, it does not operate outwardly, but only from within through our decision to allow God's grace to work in us, to allow Christ's message to work from within our being. The Law of the Gospel "is not merely a *Letter* without us, but a *quickning Spirit* within us" (above). Rejecting Calvinist predestination, the latitude-men insisted on man's freedom to choose or reject God's offer of salvation.

God is also the Creator of the natural world, and the natural philosophers' findings, provided their investigations be rightly conducted and interpreted, cannot therefore be at odds with the experience of the authentic Christian soul as part of God's creation. Largely through their explanatory and ontological inadequacies, the mechanical philosophies of the day had brought into focus problems concerning the causes of natural change, the solutions to which depended precisely on the issue of whether souls or spirits in some sense reside within the natural world. From Cudworth and More came solutions in terms of a plastic nature, or a spirit of nature, working in the world to make good what cannot flow from purely mechanical causes. The world too harbored therefore spirits acting according to principles within, just as the authentic Christian, obeying Christ's commandments, acts according to the law of the gospel within.

Pure mechanism was instantly discountable.[47] As Cudworth wrote, to hold "that all the Effects of Nature come to pass by *Material* and *Mechanical Necessity*, or the mere *Fortuitous Motion of Matter*, without any Guidance or Direction, is a thing no less Irrational than it is Impious and Atheistical."[48] Also discountable, on the other hand, was the claim that God's omnipotence enables Him to cause natural change directly, without the need for intermediaries like the Plastic Nature. That "would render Divine Providence Operose, Sollicitous and Distractious, and thereby make the Belief of it to be entertained with greater difficulty, and give advantage to Atheists."[49] On this view, in other words, were there no Plastic Nature in the World, it would be a vast *Neurospaston*, with God pulling the strings *immediatè* – an undecorous employment for the Creator.

God's creatures on earth too would be mere puppets, had they not the autokinetical bestial souls that More discovered move within them. And those who, though they possess an immortal rational soul, act only according to the external codes of the Christian life, who show only outward *mechanical* conformity to Christian discipline, are themselves like mere puppets, as far as their Christian witness is concerned. John Smith had warned against "a sort of *Mechanical* Christians in the world, that not finding *Religion* acting like a *living form* within them, satisfie themselves only to make an *Art* of it, and rather *inform* and actuate *it*, then are *informed by it*." True religion, Smith insisted, "is no Art, but an inward Nature that conteins all the laws and measures of its motion within it self. A Good man finds not his Religion *without* him, but as a living Principle *within* him." And Smith used the same metaphor of musical instruments that we found in Cudworth's House of Commons Sermon:

When God restores men to a new and divine life, he doth not make them like so many *dead Instruments*, stringing and fitting them, which yet are able to yield no sound of themselves; but he puts *a living Harmony within them*. That is but a *Mechanical religion* which moves no longer then some *External weights* and *Impulses* are upon it, whether those be (I think I may safely say) from some Worldly thing or from God himself, while he acts upon men from *without* them, and not from *within* them...[50]

For Cudworth and More, as for Smith, God's Law is truly universal. The Law of the Gospel acts within, if we allow it that freedom, and it does so unencumbered with the accoutrements and external constraints of custom or ceremony. The laws of nature are implemented within creation, through instruments such as the plastic nature or the spirit of nature, their external effects being the observational and experimental currency of the natural philosopher.

Cudworth's and More's *neurospaston* is therefore more than simply a figure of speech. It symbolizes the World as it would be were God to act the Puppeteer, doing "all the Meanest and Triflingest things himself Drudgingly, without making use of any Inferior and Subordinate Instruments" (Cudworth 1678). It symbolizes the would-be Christian who clings to external forms and systems of religion at the expense of the Law of the Gospel within. Perhaps it symbolizes therefore the closest and most significant link between the mechanical world of the new philosophy and the spiritual life of the latitude-men.

Notes

1 S. P. [Simon Patrick], *A Brief Account of the new Sect of Latitude-Men, Together with some reflections upon the New Philosophy. By S. P. of Cambridge. In answer to a Letter from his Friend at Oxford* (London, 1662), p. 14. T. A. Birrell (Los Angeles, 1963), p. 14.

2 Judging by some of the remarks in *A Brief Account*, it seems safe to infer that the nickname "latitude-men" originated during the Interregnum (1649–60), and probably more specifically during the Protectorate (1653–59): Patrick, *A Brief Account*, p. 5.

3 Patrick, *A Brief Account*, p. 5 (my italics).

4 Gilbert Burnet, *History of His Own Time*, ed. M. J. Routh, 2nd ed. enlarged, 6 vols. (Oxford, 1833), Vol. 1, p. 341.

5 F. B. Burnham, "The latitudinarian background to the Royal Society 1647–1667," (Ph.D. Dissertation, The Johns Hopkins University, 1970), pp. 17–18. It should not be inferred from this convenient categorization that the latitudinarian spirit appeared *ab ovo* among the Cambridge Platonists. The Arminian presence in early seventeenth-century England, the influence of the Tew Circle, and notably the ministry and teachings of Hales and Chillingworth, were also major factors in the development of latitudinarianism. Yet the Cambridge Platonists were the first identifiable group to be labelled as latitude-men by their contemporaries, so there is sufficient warrant for thinking of them as first-generation. On the early beginnings of latitudinarian ideals, see John Tulloch, *Rational Theology and Christian Philosophy in England in the Seventeenth Century*, 2nd ed., 2 vols. (Edinburgh and London, 1874), Vol. I, pp. 1–343; J. A. R. Marriott, *The Life and Times of Lucius Cary, Viscount Falkland* (London, 1908); W. K. Jordan, *The Development of Religious Toleration in England*, 4 vols. (London, 1932–40), Vol. II, pp. 315–421.

6 Patrick, *A Brief Account*, p. 20.

7 Patrick, *A Brief Account*, p. 22.

8 As might be expected, it is not always clear what latitudinarians or Cambridge Platonists took "reason" to be, assuming there was such a unitary concept available for them all to share, nor is it clear how far latitudinarian reason resembled the rational procedures that helped to produce the scientific advances of the day. See Lotte Mulligan, "'Reason,' 'right reason,' and 'revelation' in mid-seventeenth-century England," in Brian Vickers (ed.), *Occult and Scientific Mentalities in the Renaissance* (Cambridge, 1984), pp. 375–401; Sarah Hutton, "Reason and revelation in the Cambridge Platonists, and their reception of Spinoza," in Karlfried Gründer and Wilhelm

Schmidt-Biggemann (eds.), *Spinoza in der Frühzeit seiner religiösen Wirkung* (Heidelberg, 1984), pp. 181–200, especially pp. 184–89.

9 See Tulloch, *Rational Theology*, Vol. II, *passim*, especially pp. 13–31; Marjorie Nicolson, "Christ's College and the latitude-men," *Modern Philology* 27 (1929): 35–53, on 53; C. A. Patrides (ed.), *The Cambridge Platonists* (London, 1969), pp. 39–41 (specifically on the Cambridge Platonists); G. R. Cragg, *From Puritanism to The Age of Reason: A Study of Changes in Religious Thought within the Church of England 1660 to 1700* (Cambridge, 1966), pp. 61–86; Alan Gabbey, "Philosophia Cartesiana triumphata: Henry More (1646–1671)," in T. M. Lennon, J. M. Nicholas, J. W. Davis (eds.), *Problems of Cartesianism* (Kingston and Montreal, 1982), pp. 171–250, on pp. 225–28 (specifically on More).

10 Patrick, *A Brief Account*, p. 24.

11 Henry More, *The Apology of Dr. Henry More, Fellow of Christ's College in Cambridge; Wherein is contained as well A more General Account of the Manner and Scope of his Writings, as A Particular Explication of several Passages in his Grand Mystery of Godliness*. In his *A Modest Enquiry into the Mystery of Iniquity* (London, 1664), pp. 477–567, on p. 482.

12 Gabbey, "Philosophia Cartesiana triumphata"; Alan Gabbey, "Henry More and the limits of mechanism," in Sarah Hutton (ed.) and Robert Crocker (biog. and bibl.), *Henry More (1614–1687): Tercentenary Studies* (Dordrecht, 1990), pp. 19–35.

13 Henry More, *The Immortality of the Soul, So farre forth as it is demonstrable from the Knowledge of Nature and the Light of Reason. By Henry More D.D., Fellow of Christ's College in Cambridge* (London, 1659), in his *A Collection of Several Philosophical Writings of Dr. Henry More* (London, 1662), p. 193. See further John Henry, "Henry More versus Robert Boyle: the spirit of nature and the nature of providence," in Hutton (ed.), *Henry More*, pp. 55–76.

14 Ralph Cudworth, *The True Intellectual System of the Universe: the First Part; wherein, all the Reason and Philosophy of Atheism is Confuted; and its Impossibility Demonstrated* (London, 1678), in Patrides (ed.), *The Cambridge Platonists*, p. 293.

15 On this point see the sound comments in John Spurr, "Anglican apologetics and the Restoration Church" (D.Phil. thesis, University of Oxford, 1985), pp. 308–11.

16 Probably a reference to Edward Fowler, *Principles and Practices of certain Moderate Divines of the Church of England (greatly misunderstood)...in a Free Discourse between Two Intimate Friends* (London, 1670), or to the 1671 edition, where "abusively called latitudinarians" replaces "(greatly misunderstood)."

17 Christian Knorr von Rosenroth to Henry More, (1670–71), Sulzbach; More to von Rosenroth, (1671, Cambridge). "Commercium Epistolicum Knorrianum sive Litterae Domini Knorii à Rosenroth ad diversos Scriptae et à diversis accepta. Ex Mssptis. Jo. Chr. Knorr à Rosenroth, Bibliotheca Augusta à Jacobo Burckhardt donatis," Wolfenbüttel, Herzog August Bibliothek, Cod. Guelf. 30.4 Extravagantes Fol., ff. 27r–29v (von Rosenroth to More, draft), 23r–26v (More to von Rosenroth, copy), 54r–57v (More to von Rosenroth, signed autograph). The phrase from the Rosenroth letter appears on f. 27r, the

excerpt from More's reply on ff. 57r–v. The translations are my own. I wish to thank Prof. Dr. Wolfgang Milde, Leiter der Handschriftensammlung, Herzog August Bibliothek, for permission to quote from the Rosenroth-More letters, which I was able to consult during my tenure of a Gaststipendium at the HAB in 1986.

18 For a general survey of Toleration, see Jordan, *Development of Religious Toleration*; for a short account (post-1660), Cragg, *Puritanism to the Age of Reason*, pp. 190–224.

19 Benjamin Whichcote, *Select Sermons*, ed. [Anthony, Third Earl of Shaftesbury] (London, 1698), in Patrides (ed.), *Cambridge Platonists*, p. 43.

20 Gilbert Burnet, *History of His Own Time*, ed. O. Airy, 3 vols. (Oxford, 1897–1902), Vol. I, p. 335.

21 "Order in Parliament...That the committee for regulating the Universities of Oxford and Cambridge cause it [the Engagement] to be taken by all heads of houses, fellows, graduates, and officers, and that none be admitted to a degree without subscribing it...Order that the Council of State give direction for subscribing the said engagement, and return the names of subscribers, and of those who refuse or neglect to subscribe before 1 Jan." (*Calendar of State Papers, Domestic 1649–1650*: October 12, 1649, pp. 338–39). "Instructions to be observed in putting into execution the orders of Parliament of 12 Oct. inst., concerning the entering into the engagement:...4. You are to send one copy of the roll containing the said subscriptions, and also the names of those who neglect to appear or refuse to subscribe, both closely sealed, to Council, before 10 Dec. next, that they may then be transmitted to Parliament..." (*CSP, Domestic 1649–1650*, October 19, 1649, pp. 351–52). The "Act for subscribing the Engagement" applicable to all men of eighteen and over came on January 2, 1649/50: C. H. Firth and R. S. Rait (eds.), *Acts and Ordinances of the Interregnum 1642–1660*, 3 vols. (London, 1911), Vol. II, pp. 325–29. Being presumably unaware of the extant More–Hartlib letters, Nicolson believed that More never mentioned the Engagement: Nicolson, "Christ's College and the latitude-men," 38.

22 The first edition of *Considerations* is dated December 4, 1649, and there were three further editions by April 4, 1650. *A Case* saw three editions: March 29, 1649, 1650, and November 8, 1650. See John M. Wallace, "The engagement controversy 1649–1652: an annotated list of pamphlets," *Bulletin of the New York Public Library* 68 (1964): 384–405, on 393, 394–95. Dury argued that the ordinary individual should not meddle in state affairs, and that obedience, even to an illegitimate power, is required for peace and national unity. These ideas would have found favor with Henry More. For a general account of the Engagement controversy and arguments, see Perez Zagorin, *A History of Political Thought in the English Revolution* (London, 1954), pp. 62–77, 121–31.

23 Such would be the conscience of anyone who *refused* the Engagement, declared the Independent Dr. John Goodwin in a letter to William Heveningham, January 2, 1649/50: Davis Underdown, *Pride's Purge: Politics in the Puritan Revolution* (Oxford, 1971), p. 264.

24 Presumably an allusion to Rump legislation in religious matters, and more generally in the passage as a whole, to the revolutionary euphoria following Pride's Purge (6 December, 1648).

25 Henry More to Samuel Hartlib (London), Christ's College Cambridge, December 30 (*o.s.*) [1649]. University Library, Sheffield, Hartlib Papers, Bundle 18, 1 fol. The first quoted extract is *recto*, the second *recto verso*. In the original of the second quotation, after the words "in capitall letters, that" More continues to write in cursive characters, but in a slightly larger scale, which gradually returns to normal by the end of the sentence. In keeping with the spirit of the passage I have put the whole sentence in capitals, although in More's day "capital letters" did not necessarily mean capitalization in the modern sense. I am indebted to Michael A. Stewart for clarifying this point. I wish to thank the Librarian of the University of Sheffield for permission to quote from the Hartlib Papers, whose integral publication in electronic form is currently being prepared by the Hartlib Papers Project, University of Sheffield.

26 "The spirit of man is the candle of the Lord, searching all the inward parts of the belly" (Proverbs 20:27). See W. C. de Pauley, *The Candle of the Lord: Studies in the Cambridge Platonists* (London, 1937), also the excellent introduction to Patrides (ed.), *The Cambridge Platonists*, pp. 11–16.

27 Whichcote, *Select Sermons*, in Patrides, ed., *Cambridge Platonists*, p. 67.

28 H. R. Trevor-Roper, "The fast sermons of the Long Parliament," in H. R. Trevor-Roper (ed.), *Essays in British History, Presented to Sir Keith Feiling* (London, 1964), pp. 85–138, on pp. 102, 85.

29 George Yule, *Puritans in Politics: the Religious Legislation of the Long Parliament 1640–1647. Illustrative Texts from Contemporary Manuscript and Printed Sources: Fast Sermons, Speeches made in Parliament, Religious and Political Tracts, Letters and Petitions* (Appleford, 1981), pp. 107, 126.

30 Yule, *Puritans in Politics*, p. 126.

31 Trevor-Roper, "Fast sermons," p. 119.

32 Cudworth had friends in Cromwellian circles and was a confidential correspondent (in an advisory capacity) of John Thurloe, Secretary of State under both Cromwells, which would have been a sufficient condition for his invitation to preach to the House of Commons. When the Parliamentary Visitors ejected Dr. Thomas Paske from the Mastership of Clare Hall, Cudworth was the Parliamentary appointee (1645) in his place, without it seems showing much tenderness of conscience. Later, by Ordinance of 2 September 1654, Cudworth, Whichcote and John Worthington were appointed Commissioners for Visiting the University of Cambridge: Firth and Tait, *Acts and Ordinances*, Vol. II, pp. 1026–29. Cudworth was also Parliamentary appointee (1645) to the Chair of Hebrew in Cambridge, in succession to Robert Metcalfe of Trinity College. Shortly after the sermon of March 31, 1647, which was not well received in some quarters, Ralph Brownrigge, Bishop of Exeter, wrote to a friend in revealing terms: "'Tis said Mr Cudworth preacht to ye House of Commons last Fastday, and for his reward hath a grant of 150^{li} per annum out of ye revenues of ye Church of Ely to enable him to act ye M^r of Clare Hall more comfortably. He hath gott more at a fast then others can gett at a feast. He may take up ye boyes speech to his mother, Good mother, when shall we fast againe, having staid their stomachs with sweetmeats and juncketts. I doubt not but this large portion of his will quicken ye affection of ye other new masters to forrage for themselves, for why should they be

inferior to him, who love money as well as hee, and have as good right to it ":
Nicolson, "Christ's College and the latitude-men," p. 41, n. 2. Brownrigge's
claim is partly confirmed by the House of Commons Journal for March 31,
1647, the day of Cudworth's sermon. After the traditional expression of thanks
for their sermons to Cudworth and Robert Johnson, his co-preacher that day,
and the desire of the House that Cudworth print his sermon, the Journal
continues: "*Ordered*, That it be referred to the Committee for the University
of *Cambridge*, to settle the yearly Sum of an Hundred and Fifty Pounds, for
ever, upon the Mastership of *Clarehall* in the University of *Cambridge*": HCJ,
vol. V, p. 131. For more on Cudworth and his battles with his enemies, notably
Widdrington, see Nicolson, "Christ's College and the latitude-men," pp. 41–
47,. and H. L. Stewart, "Ralph Cudworth, the 'latitude-man'," *The Persona-
list* 32 (1951): 163–71.

33 *A Sermon Preached before the Honourable House of Commons, at Westminster,
    March 31, 1647, by R. Cudworth* (Cambridge, 1647). In Patrides (ed.),
    Cambridge Platonists, pp. 90–127, on p. 91.

34 The painting analogy turns up again in *A Collection of Aphorisms, in Two
    Parts. Written by the late Reverend and Learned Dr. Henry More, Fellow of
    Christ's College in Cambridge* (London, 1704), Part 1, Aphorism 34: "That
    which is *self-moving*, is *invisible*; and no Chymistry can unbare it to the eye:
    For that which is *visible* to the Eye, may be also describ'd by *Colours* and
    Pencil. But painted Fire burns not, neither doth painted Water sleek. But the
    inward Spirit in every thing is that which *operates all things*," p. 10.

35 Patrides (ed.), *Cambridge Platonists*, p. 92.

36 Ibid., p. 124.

37 *The Attic Nights of Aulus Gellius*, trans. John C. Rolfe, 3 vols. (London:
    Heinemann; Cambridge, Mass.: Harvard U.P., 1952), Vol. III, pp. 12–13.
    (Loeb Classical Library).

38 *Laws* 1, 644e et seq.

39 For example, Luis Vives uses the term *neurospaston* in his *De veritate fidei
    Christianae* (Basel, 1543). I am indebted for this information to Lenore
    Cooper, Department of History, University of Alabama, Tuscaloosa.

40 Henry More, *A Platonick Song of the Soul: Treating, Of The Life of the Soul,
    Her Immortalitie, The Sleep of the Soul, The Unitie of Souls, and Memorie after
    Death* (Cambridge, 1642). Second ed. in *Philosophicall Poems, by Henry More:
    Master of Arts, and Fellow of Christs Colledge in Cambridge* (Cambridge,
    1647).

41 More duly inserted the definition of the linguistic rarity in "The Interpretation
    Generall" that concludes the *Philosophicall Poems* of 1647: "Neurospast,
    νευρόσπαστον, a Puppet or any Machina that's mov'd by an unseen string or
    nerve," p. 430.

42 More, *Philosophicall Poems*, p. 88. In the 1647 ed. of this canto of
    Psychathanasia, stanzas 33 *et seq.* are misnumbered as 34 *et seq.*

43 More, *A Collection of Aphorisms*, "To the Reader."

44 Aulus Gellius, *Noctes Atticae* 7.1 7–13.

45 More, *A Collection of Aphorisms*, p. 14.

46 Ibid., p. 13.

47 Though it is not clear what "pure mechanism" meant for writers like

Cudworth and More. On this issue in More's thought, see Gabbey, "More and the limits of mechanism."

48 Cudworth, *True Intellectual System*, in Patrides (ed.), *Cambridge Platonists*, p. 289.

49 Ibid., p. 292.

50 John Smith, *Select Discourses ... by John Smith, late Fellow of Queen's College in Cambridge. As also a Sermon preached by Simon Patrick (then Fellow of the same College) at the Author's Funeral: with a brief Account of his Life and Death* (London, 1660), pp. 395, 470. (Facsimile ed., New York and London, 1978.) In *The Parable of the Pilgrim* (London, 1665; 1668), Simon Patrick alluded to Smith's attacks on "mechanical religion," which shows that the apologetic use of the mechanical analogy was not confined to Cudworth and More, and leads one to wonder if it originated with Smith, rather than with the two better-known Cambridge Platonists. Patrick described "religious puppets" and their "artificial religion," that "piece of work, which a good man now at *Jerusalem* was wont to call a Mechanical Religion," and which threatening the Pilgrim with spiritual pride keeps him from doing good to his brethren, under a pretence of love of God: "...let me tell you, that there is nothing in all the world can render you so divine and heavenly as to do much good. This puts us in the place of God to our poor Brethren to whom he sends relief and help by our hands. Is this not a very high honour? And is not that a very noble quality which so differences us from all others, that it makes us like to the Most High? The Mechanical Christian will here find himself to be dead and void of God; it being nothing but a Spirit of Life, and that very Divine too, which will carry us out of ourselves, and fill us with perpetual ardors of Love to others, and instigate us to be doing of good to all" (1668 ed., pp. 195, 204, 210).

6   Cudworth and Hobbes on Is and Ought[1]

Perez Zagorin

I

The towering stature of Thomas Hobbes in the intellectual history of the seventeenth century can be measured not only by the originality and importance of his contribution to philosophy, but also by the extent of the opposition his ideas provoked. It is of course true that Hobbes attracted a number of disciples and followers who absorbed some of his conceptions. Nevertheless, it is safe to say that no other English philosopher of the time was forced to encounter so many adversaries. In the controversies surrounding his work, moreover, it was largely his arguments that defined the terms of the discussion. These facts demonstrate the exceptional influence and even fascination Hobbes exerted upon the minds of his contemporaries; for such influence is manifested not only in assent and approval, but equally in the dissent and polemics of which he was so frequently the target. In a word, Hobbes's thought was an inescapable presence to contemporary thinkers, confronting them with a formidable challenge which many felt obliged to answer.

Of the seventeenth-century attacks on Hobbes, most possessed little intrinsic value and serve primarily to illustrate the scope of the reaction his ideas aroused. Others, however, were of a higher caliber and presented issues which remain of permanent interest. Among the works in this category are the writings of Ralph Cudworth.

Born in 1617 and associated for much of his life with Cambridge University, Cudworth's reputation is bound up with that of the Cambridge Platonists, of whom he was one of the principal representatives. Together with Henry More he was the leading philosopher of the group. More than any other writers, the Cambridge Platonists exemplified the latitudinarian trend which became a prominent feature of English religious thought in the latter part of the seventeenth century. Within the wider stream of latitudinarian principles they occupied a distinctive place as embodying and preserving the tradition of Christian humanism in relation to the momentous changes which were taking place in philosophy and science

128

during their time. As a philosopher Cudworth was probably the outstanding thinker of the Cambridge school. In his conceptions and values he fully reflected the rational, anti-dogmatic spirit, the rejection of Calvinism, and the emphasis on goodness and the moral life as the essence of Christianity, which the Cambridge Platonists strove to impress upon the religion and culture of the age. But beyond these concerns Cudworth was also greatly preoccupied with metaphysics and epistemology, the mind–body problem, and moral philosophy. The efforts he devoted to these subjects were contained in his most important book, *The True Intellectual System of The Universe*, published in 1678, as well as in other writings that were still unpublished at the time of his death ten years later.

His approach to philosophy was very different from that of the more famous men who effected the philosophic revolution of the seventeenth century. He did not reject tradition or strive to break with the past as they did. As a very learned scholar with a vast if somewhat uncritical knowledge of ancient philosophy and literature, he was convinced that many of the doctrines he opposed were merely a reincarnation of the erroneous opinions held by the philosophers of antiquity. In style of thought, as in his writing, he lacked the concision and terseness of Hobbes and Descartes or the plainness of Locke. While the latter seldom referred to other authors and disdained displays of erudition, Cudworth constantly discussed the views of earlier thinkers, weighed down his pages with quotations, and traced ideas back to their ancient sources.

Despite these habits of mind, however, he was far from being simply a conservative who looked for guidance only to the past. On the contrary, he was aware of and receptive to many of the new philosophical and scientific developments of his time. Thus he was highly critical of scholasticism and its doctrine of occult qualities, of which he wrote in a manner not dissimilar from Bacon. He was also familiar with the work of Descartes and in accord with some of his ideas. He likewise welcomed the newly revived theory of atomism, which he regarded as lending support to his spiritualistic conception of mind, his critique of materialism, and his dualistic conception of the universe.

Cudworth dedicated his life as a philosopher to the combat with atheism. For him atheism was comprised in materialism, mechanism, determinism, and the naturalistic ethics which he perceived as the core of contemporary irreligion and unbelief. He stated his objective clearly in the full title of his principal work, *The True Intellectual System of The Universe, Wherein All the Reason And Philosophy of Atheism is Confuted.*[2] The same aim is likewise present in his posthumously published *A Treatise Concerning Eternal And Immutable Morality* and *A Treatise On Free Will.*[3] In his eyes, Hobbes by his materialist, mechanist, and determinist principles stood as the foremost modern exponent of atheism. Although he never mentioned Hobbes directly in *The True Intellectual System of The Universe* or the treatise on immutable morality, he quoted him frequently and the allusions to him are unmistakeable. In *A Treatise On Free Will* he occasionally referred to Hobbes by name. A considerable part of his thought was thus concerned whether directly or indirectly with the refutation of Hobbes's ideas. As modern writers on Cudworth such as Tulloch and Passmore have pointed out, his opposition to Hobbes was perhaps the strongest intellectual motive in determining the direction of his interests as a philosopher. He might perhaps have never produced his chief works had Hobbes not first written *De Cive* and *Leviathan*.[4]

In this essay I wish to examine some of the differences between Cudworth and Hobbes in the domain of moral philosophy. These differences encompass several topics and will also involve a consideration of Hobbes's concept of the law of nature. Beside his achievement in attempting to create a thoroughgoing materialism, Hobbes made a fundamental break with tradition in his moral philosophy. Here his abandonment of older assumptions and certainties led him to base morals on a new foundation. A comparison between him and Cudworth in this respect will help to bring out the radicalism and, I dare say, the true modernity of Hobbes's moral theory.

II

Perhaps the primordial question in moral philosophy is the ground of moral standards which licenses our judgments of good and evil and right and wrong. One way of posing this question is in the form of the problem of is and ought. As far as I know, this problem was first explicitly pointed out by David Hume in a well known passage in *A Treatise of Human Nature* (1740). In that work Hume argued that moral distinctions are not among the objective properties of things nor perceived by reason. In a critical comment on the fallacies of moral philosophers, he noted the important logical truth that it is impossible for factual and non-moral premises to entail a moral or normative conclusion. The logical gap between is and ought, between propositions stating matters of fact and propositions stating values, has become one of the mainstays of ethical relativism in our time as well as a subject of widespread discussion in moral philosophy.[5]

Now Cudworth never saw any difference between facts and values. He ran them together in the conviction that values are an inherent and objective feature of the order of the world. This idea, a part of his teleological view of the creation, comprised his main thesis in regard to morals. For moral distinctions to be real and not merely arbitrary designations given to actions, he held that they must exist by nature as part of the immutable relations between things. Moral attributes for him were therefore identical with the other properties of things. A moral action, he contended, is moral by its own nature in the same way that things are white by their whiteness or alike by likeness. Hence that which is right and wrong, just and unjust, possesses this character as the eternal necessity of its nature and as a result of the disposition of divine reason.[6]

Cudworth affirmed this position against two separate opinions. One of them he ascribed to "divers modern theologers," by which he meant the Calvinists, although he traced it back to earlier thinkers such as William of Occam. This view stressed God's omnipotence and will and accordingly held, as Cudworth put it, that

nothing [is] absolutely, intrinsically and naturally good and evil, just, and unjust, antecedently to any positive command or prohibition of God; but that the arbitrary will and pleasure of God (that is, an omnipotent Being devoid of all essential and natural justice) by its commands and prohibitions is the first and only rule and measure thereof. Whence it follows unavoidably that nothing can be imagined so grossly wicked, or so foully unjust and dishonest, but if it were supposed to be commanded by this omnipotent deity, must needs upon that hypothesis forthwith become holy, just, and righteous.[7]

To be sure, in rejecting the conception of God as arbitrary will, Cudworth did not intend to impugn God's omnipotence. He contended rather that God's infinite and absolute power did not contradict his other attributes of supreme wisdom and goodness. God, he says, cannot "destroy or change the intelligible nature of things at pleasure," for if he could, this would mean that he could fool or baffle his own wisdom and understanding.[8] Thus God cannot make twice two equal five or devise a circle whose circumference is not everywhere equidistant from its center. Likewise, he cannot make that just which by its nature is unjust, because his will is ruled by justice, not justice by his will.[9]

The other view against which Cudworth's thesis was directed was the doctrine he attributed to "atheistic politicians" and a "late writer of Ethics and Politics," meaning of course Hobbes. This he describes as the opinion that nothing is just or unjust, good or evil, except what is defined as such by the positive law of every commonwealth. He further characterized it as holding that "justice is no nature, but a mere factitious and artificial thing, made only by men and civil laws."[10]

It is apparent in reflecting on Cudworth's formulation of the argument for a natural and immutable morality that it does not supply an answer to the basic question of why something is moral or immoral. Instead it is a confused attempt to resolve the problem of whether good exists by nature or convention and whether it is the same as being willed or commanded or is independent of them. As John Tulloch pointed out in his classic study of the Cambridge Platonists, Cudworth failed to realize that he was guilty of a tautology. All his position amounts to is the assertion that if something is moral, then it necessarily has the property of morality; in other words, what is moral is moral.[11] Although this was an empty claim, Cudworth's purpose is nonetheless evident. He wanted to defend the absolute and objective character of moral distinctions against the dangerous relativism he imputed to Hobbes. As we shall see, however, Hobbes was less of a relativist than he supposed.

Cudworth's moral philosophy was firmly rooted in Christian theism. He conceived the moral order as conforming to the providential disposition of divine wisdom and goodness. God's will, he said, "is the will of goodness, justice, and wisdom" and "the Ought itself." To believe in God is "to believe the existence of all possible good and perfection in the universe...and that the world is so well governed, as that the whole system thereof could not possibly have been better."[12] He disagreed profoundly with Hobbes's removal of God from the realm of philosophy. This referred to Hobbes's well known conception of philosophy as concerned exclusively with the properties of bodies and their generation, that is to say, with causes and effects. On this view, since God is eternal, uncaused, and incomprehensible, he cannot be a subject of philosophic inquiry.[13] Cudworth observed that Hobbes was willing to grant God whatever attributes the civil law of every country should appoint, since for him "the attributes of the Deity...signify neither true nor false, nor anything in nature, but only men's reverence and devotion towards the object of their fear: the manner of expressing which is by the civil law."[14]

In another significant criticism he argued that Hobbes's philosophy left no place for moral or political obligation. Hobbes had villainized human nature by picturing men in the state of nature as creatures of fear led only by their own appetite and utility, possessing a right to everything and free of all duty and obligation. If they were not under any obligation prior to the existence of the body politic, and if law and justice were merely the artificial creation of the commonwealth, then, according to Cudworth, they could never become obliged. He did not see how any obligation could derive from men's will and consent when they covenanted to form a body politic, since that which is based on will can also be undone by will.[15] For the same reason he held that it was not possible for the command of positive law as such to make something just or obligatory. Unless the authority of commanding were itself first established in natural justice or equity independent of mere will, it could not beget any duty or obligation to obedience.[16]

He went on to deny that Hobbes's conception of the law of nature provided a solution of this difficulty. According to Hobbes, the law of nature obliges men to stand to their covenants. Cudworth maintained, however, that Hobbes could not invoke the law of nature with any consistency. If it were true that nothing is naturally unjust or unlawful, then the law of nature would not exist. An obligation imposed by the law of nature, argued Cudworth, presupposes that "justice [is] already made by nature, or to be in nature," a conclusion he pronounced as contradicting Hobbes's fundamental principles.[17]

He advanced the further objection that Hobbes's notion of the law of nature was in any case "nothing but juggling equivocation, and a mere mockery." Hobbes had defined law as being exclusively the command of the sovereign. Consequently, as he acknowledged, the laws of nature were not properly laws but rather conclusions or theorems concerning what conduces to men's preservation or defense. They only become laws as the command of the sovereign.[18] For Cudworth this confirmed that the law of nature as Hobbes conceived it could not possibly be a source of obligation. He charged that the "atheistic politicians" simply reasoned in a circle. First they derived the obligation of the civil law from covenants, and next the obligation of covenants from the law of nature, and finally the obligation of the law of nature from the law and command of the civil sovereign.[19]

In contrast to Hobbes, Cudworth's own conception of obligation was a restatement of the traditional Christian theory of natural law. It presupposed the reality of a natural justice which constitutes a bond between human beings that enables them to be united in a body politic without either violence or the artificiality of covenants. It is this natural justice that obliges subjects to obey the lawful commands of sovereigns and likewise obliges sovereigns in commanding to seek the good and welfare of subjects. Cudworth describes it as "common and public ... in all rational beings" and as owing its origin to God. "Had not God and nature made [the] City," he said, and "were there not a natural conciliation of all rational creatures" in subjection to the deity, there would be "no ruling and being ruled, with their respective duty and obligation."[20]

In accord with this doctrine, Cudworth did not accept the sharp distinction Hobbes made between *lex* and *ius*, law and right. Hobbes had pointed out that authors who discuss the two constantly confuse them although they are directly contrary to each other. Law for him denoted restraint or obligation, while right signified liberty.[21] Cudworth refused to recognize this dissociation. His belief in a natural justice led him to regard law and liberty as inseparably intertwined in a reciprocal relationship in which each necessarily acknowledges its own true limits out of due respect for the other.[22]

There is an interesting and surprising correspondence between Cudworth's criticism of Hobbes and the modern interpretations of his moral philosophy in the well known studies by A. E. Taylor and Howard Warrender. Cudworth thought that Hobbes's moral theory was vitiated by its atheism, which rendered it incapable of providing for moral obligation. Without the recognition of a natural law and justice grounded in God's wise, good, and rational government of the world, no source of obligation could possibly exist. Taylor and Warrender have similarly held that Hobbes's moral philosophy is unworkable without God. But whereas Cudworth had no doubt that Hobbes left God out, Taylor and Warrender claimed that he brought God in. Both of them have tried to show that Hobbes's moral position requires that obligation, including the obligation imposed by the law of nature to abide by covenants, must ultimately derive from the law and command of God. They have argued furthermore that this was what Hobbes actually held and intended to say. Their thesis has failed to commend itself to most students of Hobbes's philosophy. If it is true, then obviously Cudworth gravely misunderstood Hobbes's ideas, as have nearly all his later readers. I do not think it is true, however. What seems to me to be the case, rather, is that Hobbes did establish a basis for obligation, but one that was independent of theistic presuppositions.[23]

Despite the fact that Cudworth identified Hobbes with atheism, it is noticeable that he never directly accused him of denying that there is a God. This charge would have been untenable, as Hobbes not only referred frequently to God's existence in his writings, but made other statements about God as well. Thus he allowed that philosophic reasoning could prove the existence of God as first cause, while also maintaining that God's nature was incomprehensible. Notwithstanding his opinion that we must be in ignorance of God, he nevertheless predicated certain attributes of him, such as that he is omnipotent and eternal. In particular he emphasized God's irresistible power. He also asserted that God is corporeal and would set up his kingdom on earth and raise men at the last judgment, that he actually governs the world, and that he works miracles. Whether or not Hobbes could consistently hold both that God exists and yet that nothing of his nature can be known, the two propositions were apparently basic to what he believed about God.[24]

What warrant, then, did Cudworth have to treat Hobbes as a philosopher of atheism? During the Renaissance and seventeenth century, the notion of atheism was used loosely in a variety of meanings. An "atheist" could be one who held any sort of heretical, heterodox, or scandalous doctrine or any belief that allegedly tended to immoral behavior. Cudworth wrote that those "are properly called atheists" who "derive all things from senseless matter... and deny that there is any conscious understanding being self-existent or unmade ... "; theists, on the other hand, affirm that a "perfect conscious understanding being (or mind) existing of itself from eternity, was the cause of all other things." He also noted that atheists commonly go disguised and "walk abroad in masquerade," oftentimes insinuating "their Atheism even then, when they most of all profess themselves Theists..." It was this disguised atheism that he detected in Hobbes. The proof of it was Hobbes's conviction that all things are corporeal or composed of body. Someone who adhered to this view, according to Cudworth, might pretend a belief in God, but would deserve no credence because his principles contradicted this belief.[25] Benjamin Whichcote, another of the Cambridge Platonists, made the same point when he commented that "the Foundation of Atheism [is] that all being is Body."[26]

Thus Hobbes had to be an atheist, in Cudworth's opinion, even though he professed the contrary, because his philosophical ideas were incompatible with theism. This was surely an arbitrary conclusion, however. It is much more in keeping with Hobbes's statements to regard him as a theist, although of a very unorthodox kind. His theism was obviously not the expression of a deep religious faith, but the result of deductions that seemed to necessitate at least the existence of God. His conception of God was assimilated to his comprehensive materialism and therefore contrary to the Christian understanding of God as a purely spiritual, all-good and loving creator. The scriptural interpretations of which Hobbes showed such ingenious mastery served him to defend his understanding of God as material and to refute the belief in souls or spirits as non-material entities. Some writers have suggested that his religion was a type of fideism which embraces religious truths as beyond all rational knowledge.[27] That there is an element of fideism in his religion is very likely, since apart from the existence and perhaps the omnipotence of God, all his other characterizations of God would have had to rest purely on faith. Christian fideism, however, has usually been closely associated with skepticism, as famous examples like Montaigne and Pascal show, and in Hobbes skepticism was far stronger than faith. His contemplation of the clash of irreconcilable religious opinions among Christians which helped to bring on civil war in England and elsewhere in Europe in the sixteenth and seventeenth centuries only reinforced his skepticism toward religion and its claims to truth. Convinced of the uncertainty and limitations of religious knowledge, Hobbes could not base his moral and civil philosophy on principles whose ultimate sanction is an unknowable God. While Cudworth was therefore wrong to condemn Hobbes as an atheist, he was right to hold that Hobbes's moral and political doctrines did not depend on the truth of Christianity or theism. Another way to put this is to say that even if

Hobbes had really been an atheist, the substance of his moral and political theory would have remained unaffected and been exactly the same.

III

Hobbes was a conscious innovator who deliberately set out to make a new departure in moral philosophy. To understand what he was about that distinguished his outlook so sharply from Cudworth's, it is necessary to consider his verdict on the deficiencies of traditional moral philosophy. He delivered some characteristic comments on this subject in his *De Cive*. In the dedication to this work, after pointing out how great had been the achievements in the science of geometry, he observed that

if the Morall Philosophers had as happily discharg'd their duty, I know not what could have been added by humane Industry to the completion of that happinesse, which is consistent with humane life. For were the nature of human Actions as distinctly knowne, as the nature of Quantity in Geometricall Figures, the strength of Avarice and Ambition, which is sustained by...erroneous opinions...touching the nature of Right and Wrong, would presently faint and languish; And Mankinde should enjoy such an Immortal Peace, that...there would hardly be left any pretence for war.

He also lamented that the "knowledge of the Law of Nature" had failed to progress, "not advancing a whit beyond its antient stature." He likewise criticized the wrangling of "the severall factions" of philosophers, some decrying the very same actions which were praised by others. This led him to conclude that "what hath been written by Morall Philosophers hath not made any progress in the knowledge of the Truth" nor given "any light to the Understanding."[28] Elsewhere he wrote that "they that have written of justice and policy, do all invade each other and themselves with contradiction." Repeating his criticism of previous philosophers' conception of the law of nature, he complained that they had built its foundations "in the air" and that it had "now become of all laws the most obscure..."[29]

This negative judgment on his predecessors provides a clear indication of Hobbes's own aims as a moral philosopher. He was convinced that moral philosophy needed to be given a new foundation in order to free it of interminable disputes and transform it into a science. On this foundation it would be possible to establish the doctrine of right and wrong with certainty and demonstrate conclusively what the law of nature is. His proposed method for achieving this ambitious program consisted of resolving or analyzing the matter of morality and justice into its constitutive causes which lay in human nature. It was also analogous to geometry, the science of constructing figures, in requiring that moral principles should be derived by evident connection in a strict process of deductive reasoning from prior truths.[30]

The material content of Hobbes's moral as well as political philosophy is accordingly supplied by human nature. Similarly, its primary postulates consist of truths and further deductions concerning human nature. As he concisely described his approach in *Leviathan*, " I ground the Civil Right of Soveraigns and the Duty and Liberty of Subjects upon the known naturall Inclinations of Mankind ... "[31] This means that Hobbes, while in some respects a great rationalist, claimed for his account of human nature an empirical justification. For in his famous analysis of human beings as self-centered, competitive creatures ceaselessly striving for dominance over one another in the race of life, he believed that the picture he presented could be confirmed by any one from personal observation and experience. This kind of doctrine, he declared, "admitteth no other Demonstration."[32]

In this connection he also made the striking comment that to reduce the notion of justice "to the rules and infallibility of reason, there is no way, but first to put such principles down for a foundation, as passion not mistrusting, may not seek to displace."[33] His attitude to human nature was thus completely naturalistic. He never blamed the passions or condemned human nature as evil despite its invincible self-centeredness. "The Desires, and other Passions of Man," he said, "are in themselves no Sin."[34] Hence the task of reason in his moral and political theory was not to suppress the passions but to instruct and direct them in attaining the good they actually seek, which is self-preservation.

The core concept and starting point of Hobbes's moral philosophy is the idea of natural right. He explains it as

The Liberty each man hath, to use his own power, as he will himself, for the preservation of his own Nature; that is to say, of his own Life; and consequently of doing any thing, which in his own Judgement, and Reason, he shall conceive to be the aptest means thereunto.[35]

This right of nature is related to the empirically ascertainable qualities of human beings as Hobbes portrays them. In a passage central to his entire argument, he says that every man desires what is good for himself and shuns what is evil,

but chiefly the chiefest of all naturall evils, which is Death; and this he doth, by a certain impulsion of nature, no lesse than that whereby a Stone moves downward: It is therefore neither absurd, nor reprehensible; neither against the dictates of true reason for a man to use all his endeavours to preserve and defend his Body, and the Members thereof from death and sorrowes; but that which is not contrary to right reason, that all men account to be done justly and with right; Neither by the word Right is anything else signified, than that liberty which every man hath to make use of his naturall faculties according to right reason: therefore the first foundation of naturall right is this, That every man as much as in him lies endeavour to protect his life and members.[36]

From this elemental fact that men naturally seek to preserve themselves from death, which he calls a natural right, Hobbes goes on to show the unlimited right that men necessarily possess in the state of nature when there is no government to protect them, how reason then teaches them an escape from the dangers of this state, and how they can gain security and peace by covenanting to renounce their total freedom and establish the commonwealth and sovereignty.

While Cudworth conceived moral principles as inherent in the divinely guided, rational world order, Hobbes perceived them as a human creation which he attempted to base on psychology and the observable characteristics of universal human nature. For him they are the way that human beings realize their natural right and subjective desire of survival and, beyond this, for the benefits of peace and civilized living which they likewise desire. This argument clearly raises the question of whether Hobbes was no less guilty than Cudworth of the error that Hume exposed of trying to deduce ought from is. It is one thing to demonstrate from an analysis of human nature how men actually behave; it is quite another to deduce from this analysis how they ought to behave. Was this not precisely what Hobbes did in claiming to derive normative statements of what men ought to and may rightfully do from empirical premises about human nature?

To this question two main answers have been given. One is to deny any necessary connection between Hobbes's psychology and ethics and to construe his moral philosophy as a deontology whose oughts are ultimately dependent on the command of God as given in the law of nature. This view, proposed, as I have noted earlier, by A. E. Taylor and Howard Warrender, is incompatible, however, not only with Hobbes's naturalism but with his own account of what he was doing. Since he laid such weight on the close dependence between his analysis of human nature and his treatment of morals, it is clearly unwarranted to dissociate them.[37]

The other answer, suggested alike by D. P. Gauthier and J. W. N. Watkins among others, holds that Hobbes's linkage between psychology and values means that his theory is in reality not a moral but a prudential doctrine which commends as good only such actions as reason proves to be in men's own interest. Thus instead of being a system of morality, it is more like a prescription relating means to ends, or like doctor's orders advising a patient to adopt a regimen which will be for his benefit. This sort of theory might perhaps allow for a concept of obligation based on rational prudence. It can have no room, though, for *moral* obligation, since the latter idea entails the possibility that there is something a person ought to do whether it is in his interest or not.[38]

The main objection to this interpretation is that Hobbes constantly employs the language of morality and conceives himself to be propounding a *moral* philosophy. The precepts he lays down are proffered by him as universal moral rules: for example, that men should seek peace and follow it, and that they should be contented with as much liberty against other men as they would allow others against themselves. Moreover, he holds that these precepts not only always oblige in conscience but are identical with the moral law of the gospel, "Whatsoever you require that others should do to you, that do ye to them."[39] The fact that Hobbes also believes that men so far as they are rational always have an adequate ground or incentive to observe these precepts because they are conducive to self-preservation and other desired goods, does not detract from their moral essence. In short, although reason teaches that the principles advanced by Hobbes are in men's interest, this need not make them something other than moral in character.

It might possibly be suggested, however, that in connecting propositions about human nature with certain ethical precepts, Hobbes was not asserting that there is a logical relationship between them but rather merely one of rational justification or rightness. That is to say, assuming the truth of his account of human nature, it would be justifiable to adopt as morally right the principles he recommends. This view would align Hobbes with those philosophers who believe that there can be good and compelling reasons, including facts, to prefer certain moral judgments and standards, even though they are not logically entailed by such reasons.

A scrutiny of Hobbes's statements, however, does not support this weaker interpretation of his position. His rigorous conception of philosophic method held that for an inquiry to qualify as science, its truths must be generated one from another in a logical process analogous to geometry. As I have pointed out, this is what he aimed to achieve in the realm of moral philosophy. His discussion leaves little doubt, moreover, that he sought to find in human nature the causes which give rise by a logical necessity to the commonwealth and its requisite moral and political rules as effects.

I do not think, therefore, that it is possible to exonerate Hobbes from the fallacy of attempting to deduce ought from is. To see more clearly, however, why he postulated this particular relation between fact and value and psychology and ethics, it is necessary to examine his concept of the law of nature, for it is here that he made his most radical breach with tradition and approached modernity most closely in his moral thought.

Hobbes formulated the basic normative precepts of his moral and political philosophy as the law of nature. In keeping with his emphatic distinction between law and right, the first denoting obligation, the second liberty to do or abstain, the law of nature consists of oughts. Generally, he defines it as a precept or rule devised by reason which forbids a man to do anything destructive of his life or to omit anything by which he thinks his life may be preserved. Reason, he explains,

is no less of the nature of man than passion, and is the same in all men, because all men agree in the will to be directed in the way to that which they desire to attain, namely, their own good, which is the work of reason. There can therefore be no other law of nature than reason, nor no other precepts of Natural Law, than those which declare unto us the ways of peace, and of defence where it may not.[40]

In *Leviathan*, he lists a number of laws of nature, the first of which he calls fundamental. This states that every man should seek peace and follow it. Correlative to it is the fundamental or supreme right of nature, which provides that if a man seeks and cannot obtain peace, then he may defend himself by all means. From the first law of nature is derived the second requiring that a man should be willing, when others are willing as well, to lay down his right to all things and be contented with as much liberty against others as he would allow them against himself. The third law of nature, a logical consequence of the second, ordains that men should perform the covenants they have made.[41] The remaining laws of nature follow from these in a deductive chain of reasoning.

Hobbes ascribes various characteristics to the laws of nature. Thus he notes that they oblige only to a constant, unfeigned effort to perform them and hence are easy to observe. He also declares that they are eternal and immutable. He comments further that the science of the law of nature is the only true moral philosophy, since the latter is nothing else than the science of what is good and evil in the relations between men. Because they lead to peace, he identifies the laws of nature as well with such virtues as justice, gratitude, modesty, equity, and mercy. But the crucial and most distinctive feature in his treatment of the law of nature is his denial that it is genuinely law. Hobbes remains consistently a legal positivist who defines law exclusively as the command of the sovereign power. He therefore holds that the dictates of reason which comprise the law of nature are improperly called laws. In reality, he says, "they are but Conclusions or Theoremes concerning what conduceth [to men's] conservation and defence of themselves..." Only if we should consider these same theorems as commands of God, he points out, could they be properly termed laws. They actually become laws, however, only when embodied in the civil law of the commonwealth as commands of the sovereign. Prior to this, they are "but qualities that dispose men to peace, and obedience."[42]

In conceiving norms in the form of the law of nature, Hobbes availed himself of a grand and venerable doctrine dating back to Cicero and the Stoics which persisted in several variations right down to the seventeenth century and beyond. In his own version, however, the concept of natural law was drained of its previous substance and infused with a new and radical meaning. In what did its novelty and radicalism consist?

First, Hobbes's conception effects a clear-cut separation between law and morality. For him law is determined by its positivity as a command with coercive sanctions, not by its moral content. The law of nature is accordingly deprived of the authentically legal essence which the traditional Christian doctrine of natural law had always ascribed to it. Its dictates are seen as rules pertaining purely to the moral domain, which does not possess the character of law. In taking this position, Hobbes came close to the modern critics of natural law theory who reject it partly because it represents a deep confusion between law and morality.[43]

Second, Hobbes detaches the law of nature from its grounding in a transcendental reality. It is not, as he conceives it, anchored in or revelatory of a divine source or order. An acute modern theorist has argued in defense of natural law that it does not logically entail the existence of God.[44] While this claim is, I think, justified, it remains historically true, nonetheless, that the traditional Christian theory of natural law was deeply rooted in theistic and teleological assumptions. Thus, in Aquinas's formulation, a *locus classicus* of the medieval doctrine, natural law is described as partaking in the eternal law which is the decree of divine providence for the government of rational creatures in the ends proper to them. Even Hobbes's eminent contemporary, Hugo Grotius, when he suggested in his famous discussion of natural law that its principles would remain valid even if God did not exist or concern himself with the affairs of men, immediately added that such a thought could not be conceded without the utmost wickedness.[45] Or we may likewise compare the view expressed by another contemporary of Hobbes, the Englishman Richard Cumberland in his treatise *De Legibus Naturae*, published in 1672. In this work as well, the precepts of the law of nature pertaining to the common good of mankind are traced to God as their cause, who has also annexed rewards and punishments to their observance and transgression.[46] The same position is also to be seen in the work on natural law by another of the Cambridge Platonists, Nathanael Culverwel's *A Discourse Of The Light Of Nature* (1652).[47]

In the case of Hobbes, however, the incomprehensible God whose being exceeds the compass of philosophic understanding cannot be the origin of the law of nature. The latter on his view possesses a purely autonomous status as the product of reason teaching every man the way to self-preservation. The good it prescribes is a purely individual good, although the result of attaining this good turns out to coincide with the good of all in making possible a life of peace and security in the commonwealth. Because Hobbes was addressing himself to the members of a Christian society, he conceded that the law of nature may also be regarded as properly law if it is taken to be the command of God. But this concession in no way altered the deeply secular and individualistic character of his version of natural law. Essentially, his moral and political theory is intended indifferently for all rational persons, whether they are believing Christians or not.[48]

In Hobbes's philosophy, neither God nor a teleologically ordered, value-inscribed universe underwrites the principles of morals. Men are bidden by him to look for these principles in their human nature and in their striving to live and to possess the fruits of civilization, which are ends they themselves desire and call good. Reason, which is also part of their nature, will then demonstrate to them the moral rules they should follow to attain these ends.

Moral obligation for Hobbes can therefore have no transcendental source or sanction, but is imposed by human beings upon themselves. It is the consequence of their rational recognition of the moral rules they must accept to obtain the goods they seek. Thus, when men covenant to renounce the unlimited liberty they possess by the right of nature in exchange for the benefits of peace and security, they thereby voluntarily become obliged. No ground of obligation other than their own consent is or could be available to them.[49]

By claiming to deduce values from human nature, Hobbes's moral philosophy reflects, as I have suggested, a confusion between is and ought. But perhaps we can also say that his naturalistic perspective strives to reduce the logically unbridgeable gap between is and ought to its smallest possible dimension. Because the divine realm of God is unknowable by his criterion of knowledge, it cannot be a source of moral truths either. He therefore had no recourse but to refer morals to the known needs and desires of men as submitted to the guidance of reason. While it is not possible to deduce values from facts, the facts on which Hobbes tried to establish moral principles were those which he presented as general truths of common experience accessible to anyone by the observation of himself and others.

In adopting this naturalistic type of solution, Hobbes seems to me to have been the first thinker to confront what was to become in the course of time the modern situation with regard to morals. It is the situation which emerges with the fading and loss of religious faith, as secular men increasingly cease to be able to conceive of God and eternal providence as the ultimate source and guarantor of their moral values. Left solitary in the universe, they are thrown back upon themselves and must turn to the needs of their own human nature and their common life to find therein the sole foundation of moral principles.

IV

To conclude this discussion, I want to consider briefly whether Hobbes's moral philosophy is flawed by relativism. As we recall, this was one of Cudworth's main charges against his teachings. According to Cudworth, by denying that good and evil, just and unjust, are among the natural, intrinsic properties of things, and by explaining them as products of human will and the law, Hobbes undermined the basis of moral distinctions and left them completely arbitrary. How far was this criticism justified?

As Hobbes develops his conception of the law of nature, it is at first purely moral. It consists of the rules discovered by reason to enable men to escape the continual fear and danger of death which is their natural condition in the absence of the commonwealth and a sovereign power to protect them. At this stage it still has no standing as law. With the existence of the political order, however, it becomes law through its embodiment in the commands of the sovereign as an expression of the latter's will. The sovereign power then establishes by its laws for its subjects the rules of property or mine and thine, of good and evil, and of just and unjust.[50] Hobbes also states that "The Law of Nature, and the Civill Law contain each other, and are of equall extent." This implies that they cannot be in contradiction, and indeed he goes so far as to assert that it is impossible "to command aught by the civil law, contrary to the laws of nature."[51]

The explanation of this claim that the law of nature and civil law are always in harmony is found in Hobbes's account of reason. On the one hand, he acknowledges that reason itself is always right reason and infallible. But on the other hand, however, he now points out that right reason does not exist in the nature of things, and because men are likely to disagree about what is reasonable and to mistake their passions for reason, they must accept the reason of some judge or arbitrator as right reason if they wish to end controversies and preserve peace. Such a judge or arbitrator is the sovereign, whose ordinances provide the standard of justice and moral virtue in the commonwealth.[52]

Hobbes's argument at this point reflects a strain of relativism which is hard to reconcile with the rationalistic side of his thought. To obviate conflicting moral understandings which might lead to rebellion and civil war, it reduces reason to a matter of convention by stipulating that it should be seen as identical with the laws of the sovereign. It thereby relativizes the law of nature so that it will never be at odds with the laws of any particular commonwealth. This seems a strange conclusion for a philosopher who was committed to the aims of demonstrative truth and certainty and claimed that he had made morals and politics into a science.

It is therefore noteworthy that he was unable to adhere consistently to this relativistic position. In spite of his equation of the law of nature with the positive laws of the sovereign, he made various statements that recognize the possibility of a contradiction between them. These appear especially in connection with his discussion of the duty or obligations of the sovereign. Thus in declaring that the latter "has...no other bounds, but such as are set out by the unwritten Law of Nature," Hobbes clearly implies that the sovereign could be guilty of transgressing this law. He also says that the sovereign must administer justice equitably, because equity is a precept of the law of nature "to which...a Soveraign is as much subject, as any of the meanest of his People."[53] In general, he comments that sovereigns "may diverse wayes transgresse against the Lawes of Nature, as by cruelty, iniquity, contumely, and other like vices..." He lays it down, moreover, that the sovereign should yield obedience to right reason as "the naturall, morall, and divine Law," thus acknowledging that the two need not be in harmony.[54]

The same inconsistency is evident in Hobbes's analysis of the liberty of subjects. This liberty consists in part of the rights which could not have been renounced or transferred by any covenant. Accordingly, the subject is not bound to obey a command that he kill or wound himself or abstain from food or anything else necessary for life. He may likewise refuse to serve in war provided he secures a substitute. And if he unjustly unites with other subjects to resist the sovereign, he nevertheless retains the right to persist in his resistance in order to preserve his life. These liberties are explainable as strict deductions from the natural right of self-preservation which leads men to consent to the commonwealth and sovereignty in the first place. But Hobbes goes well beyond them in also allowing that a subject may refuse obedience if a command "frustrates the End for which the Soveraignty was ordained..."[55] This is such a general exception to the duty of obedience that it makes no sense other than on the assumption that the sovereign's command may violate the law of nature.

Such concessions constitute an implicit admission that the precepts of reason and rules of morality are not completely swallowed up in the reason and commands of the sovereign. They also permit the law of nature to remain as an independent moral standard over against the law of the state. Hobbes cannot therefore ultimately be a relativist in morals, as Cudworth believed. It would appear, rather, that he is compelled by his own logic to grant to the normative dictates of the law of nature an objective character which obliges the sovereign as well as subjects. This view seems to me to be in accord with the basic premises of his moral theory. In both morals and politics Hobbes's philosophy expresses two different tendencies. On the one hand, in order to prevent the conflicting private judgments and opposing moral definitions which lead to anarchy and civil war he wished to oblige individuals as strongly as possible to submit to the civil laws of the sovereign. On the other hand, however, he built his moral and political theory on the pre-political human claim and natural right to life and the goods of civilized existence. Reason demonstrates the moral requirements instrumental to these ends, and the sole justification of the commonwealth and sovereignty is that they enable individuals to realize this natural right. This, I believe, represents the predominant tendency of his moral doctrine. The touchstone of morals for Hobbes is always natural right as founded in the common needs and desires of human nature, and this creates a standard of moral judgment which redeems his thought from relativism.

Notes

1 I wish to thank Professor Joel Kupperman of the University of Connecticut for his helpful comments on an earlier version of this paper.

2 I have used this work in the edition published in New York, 2v., 1838. It is cited hereafter as *TIS*.

3 *A Treatise Concerning Eternal And Immutable Morality* was first published in 1731. It is printed in Vol. II of *TIS* (New York, 1838), and cited below as *TCE*. *A Treatise of Free Will* first appeared in 1838. It is reprinted in D. Raphael, ed., *British Moralists 1650–1800*, 2 vols. (Oxford, 1969), Vol. I.

4 J. Tulloch, *Rational Theology And Christian Philosophy in England in The Seventeenth Century*, 2 vols. (Edinburgh, 1872), Vol. II, ch. 4; J. Passmore, *Ralph Cudworth* (Cambridge, 1951), pp. 11–12.

5 The text from Hume's *A Treatise of Human Nature*, Bk. III, pt. 1, sec. 1, p. 504, is reprinted in Raphael, Vol. II, p. 19; an analysis of Hume's argument and its possible interpretations is given in J. Harrison, *Hume's Moral Epistemology* (Oxford, 1976), ch. 5. On the debated question of deducing ought from is, see the penetrating analysis by W. K. Frankena, "The naturalistic fallacy," *Mind*, 48 (1939), reprinted in Philippa Foot, ed., *Theories of Ethics* (Oxford, 1967). My discussion in the text rests on my acceptance that ought statements cannot be deduced from statements of matters of fact. Among attempts to disprove this view, see J. R. Searle, "How to derive 'ought' from 'is'," *Philosophical Review* 73 (1964), reprinted in Foot. Searle's argument is effectively refuted by R. M. Hare, "The promising game," *Revue Internationale de Philosophie* 70 (1964), reprinted in Foot.

6 *TCE*, Vol. II, p. 373.

7 Ibid., Vol. II, p. 371.

8 *TIS*, Vol. II, p. 48.

9 *TCE*, Vol. II, p. 373; *TIS*, Vol. II, pp. 48, 358.

10 *TIS*, Vol. II, p. 350.

11 Tulloch, Vol. II, p. 285. Passmore, pp. 41–44, in a subsequent consideration of Cudworth's argument, brings out well what he was driving at and also tries to show that it may not have been tautologous, but is not convincing in this latter view.

12 *TIS*, Vol. II, pp. 348, 349.

13 T. Hobbes, *De Corpore, English Works*, ed. W. Molesworth, 11 vols. (London, 1839–45), Vol. I, p. 10.

14 *TIS*, Vol. II, p. 53.

15 Ibid., Vol. II, pp. 353–55.

16 *TCE*, Vol. II, p. 374–75.

17 *TIS*, Vol. II, p. 354.

18 T. Hobbes, *Leviathan*, reprinted from the 1651 ed. (Oxford, 1943), pp. 122–23.

19 *TIS*, Vol. II, p. 355.

20 Ibid., Vol. II, pp. 356–57.

21 *Leviathan*, p. 99.

22 *TIS*, Vol. II, p. 350.

23 A. E. Taylor, "The ethical doctrine of Hobbes," reprinted in K. C. Brown (ed.), *Hobbes Studies* (London, 1956); H. Warrender, *The Political Philosophy of Hobbes. His Theory of Obligation* (Oxford, 1957). For several critical discussions of the Taylor-Warrender interpretation, see S. Brown, "The Taylor thesis: some objections," in Brown; J. W. N. Watkins, *Hobbes's System of Ideas* (London, 1965), pp. 85–99; D. Gauthier, *The Logic of Leviathan* (Oxford, 1969), pp. 195–96 and *passim*.

24 See the survey of Hobbes's ideas on God by R. Hepburn, "Hobbes on the knowledge of God," in M. Cranston and R. Peters, eds., *Hobbes and Rousseau* (New York, 1972), which includes many citations; W. Glover, "God and Thomas Hobbes," in Brown; Gauthier, pp. 179–80.

25 *TIS*, Vol. I, pp. 122–23.

26 Cited in C. Patrides, ed., *The Cambridge Platonists* (Cambridge, 1970), p. 26.

27 See Hepburn and Glover for a consideration of this view.

28 T. Hobbes, *De Cive*, English version, ed. H. Warrender (Oxford, 1983), pp. 25–26.

29 T. Hobbes, *The Elements of Law*, ed. F. Tönnies (Cambridge, 1928), pp. 57, xvii; *Leviathan*, p. 212.

30 *De Cive*, pp. 32, 37.

31 *Leviathan*, p. 554.

32 Ibid., pp. 9–10, 97.

33 *Elements of Law*, p. xvii.

34 *Leviathan*, p. 97.

35 Ibid., p. 99.

36 *De Cive*, p. 47.

37 See above, n. 23.

38 Gauthier, pp. 89–98; Watkins, pp. 76–7.

39 *Leviathan*, pp. 100, 121.

40 *Elements of Law*, pp. 57–58.

41 *Leviathan*, pp. 99. 100, 110.

42 Ibid., pp. 122–23, 205.

43 See the discussion in H. Kelsen, *The Pure Theory of Law* (Berkeley, 1967), ch. 2, pp. 217–21, and the review of the problem of natural law by H. L. A. Hart, *The Concept of Law*, 10th impression (Oxford, 1979), ch. 9.

44 J. Finnis, *Natural Law and Natural Rights* (Oxford, 1980), ch. 2; see also the discussion by S. M. Brown, Jr., "Huntsman, what quarry?," in S. Hook, ed., *Law And Philosophy* (New York, 1964), p. 179. A number of papers in this volume are concerned with the viability of the theory of natural law, including an illuminating discussion by W. Frankena, "On defining and defending natural law."

45 Thomas Aquinas, *Summa Theologiae*, Prima secundae, qu. 91, art. 2; H. Grotius, *De Jure Belli Ac Pacis Libri Tres*, 1625, Prolegomena, n. 11.
46 See the passages from this work printed in Raphael, Vol. I, pp. 81, 91, 93–94.
47 Printed in E. Campagnac, ed., *The Cambridge Platonists* (Oxford, 1901).
48 *Leviathan*, p. 123; cf. the comments of Gauthier, p. 178.
49 See Gauthier, pp. 41–42.
50 *Leviathan*, p. 137; *De Cive*, p. 95.
51 *De Cive*, p. 173.
52 *Leviathan*, pp. 33, 137–38, 205.
53 Ibid., pp. 173, 265.
54 *De Cive*, pp. 112–13, 157.
55 *Leviathan*, p. 167.

Part II

The Restoration settlement

7   Latitudinarianism and toleration: historical myth versus political history

Richard Ashcraft

In this essay, I wish to discuss one of the problems which, *en ensemble*, constitute the grand controversy among historians, sociologists, and political theorists concerning the relationship between science, religion, economic change, and politics in seventeenth-century England, and the significance that relationship has for an understanding of the origins and meaning of Western capitalist society. The specific political problem to be considered is the toleration of dissent from the legally established Anglican Church, a problem with far more profound implications than might at first glance appear evident. Indeed, for seventeenth-century Englishmen, "the toleration controversy...called into question the whole structure of society."[1] That is, viewed in terms of a religious–political struggle between Anglicans and dissenters, the problem of toleration claims a structural significance for an understanding of social life in Restoration England.

From another standpoint, recently revived by a new generation of historians, the toleration of religious dissent was the outcome of the triumph of rationalism, the new experimental science, and the development of a latitudinarian perspective within Anglican theology during this period.[2] According to this view, it is the historical tide of enlightenment – the power of ideas – rather than the tawdry clash of politically organized groups that provides the explanatory force in the historical account of the emergence of toleration.

Unfortunately, the passage of the Toleration Act of 1689 supplies virtually no empirical support for this viewpoint. While it is true that some details relating to this event are still shrouded in mystery, what is clear is that the passage of the Toleration Act cannot be explained in terms of the general acceptance by either the laity or the Anglican clergy of the reasonableness of toleration as a political policy. "I do not understand the mystery of it," Roger Maurice wrote in his diary, "nor the true reason why the Lords Spiritual, and those Lords and Commoners of their sentiments did pass that bill."[3] As one contemporary observed, "[Anglican] Churchmen are for penal laws, and there is no reasoning with" them on this issue.[4] Nor do appeals to the authority of science figure prominently in the writings of advocates of religious toleration. Not only is it true that "no one ardently welcomed the Toleration Act," but also, some of the supporters of the parliamentary bill immediately regretted their decision to do so, realizing that they had allowed themselves to be tactically outmaneuvered in responding to political exigencies of the moment.[5] Toleration, in short, was in its realization less the fulfillment of a tendency towards cultural rationalism than the product of deep-rooted fears and prejudices directed against Catholicism which, momentarily, produced a political alliance between Anglicans and dissenters in their common struggle against James II's attempt to reclaim the throne following the Glorious Revolution.

As is well known, a bill for comprehension was introduced into the House of Lords simultaneously with a bill granting toleration, with the design that the two bills should pass through the legislative process together. The general objective was to incorporate most, if not all, presbyterians into the established church through comprehension, leaving a relatively small number of sectarian dissenters outside its boundaries, isolated from their nonconformist brethren. Toleration was viewed by many as a temporary expedient to be adopted during a period of transition, and necessary as a means of gaining support for the more important Comprehension Bill from presbyterian sympathizers who were unwilling to leave independents and others with no guarantees against persecution. In the event, the Comprehension Bill was derailed in mid-journey, while the Toleration Bill completed its legislative course.[6] The overwhelming consensus among political historians, however, is that this outcome in no way signalled a parliamentary – let alone, a popular – recognition of the "rights" of dissenters. The Toleration Act of 1689 came into existence prefaced by no doctrine of tolerance, accompanied by no paeans to the enlightenment of a rationalistic age, and with no supporting claims that it reflected the application of a scientific attitude to religious issues. Rather, the Act was "reactionary in tone and content, and fell far short of contemporary ideals." Some of the harsher measures of the Clarendon Code were retained as statutes, and, technically, nonconformity remained an illegal activity.[7] As several scholars have noted, for contemporaries, the meaning of the Toleration Act remained in doubt.[8]

Against the grandiose claims advanced by intellectual historians on behalf of an enlightened cultural consciousness of seventeenth-century Englishmen, therefore, must be set the fears, prejudices, miscalculations, political exigencies, and unintended consequences on the part of the historical actors who actually secured the political enactment of religious toleration. To say that politicians "are invariably behind the times in their political philosophy" simply will not suffice as an explanation for this historical disjuncture. Rather, the latter ought to serve as a warning to historians who have paid too little attention to the dimensions of political conflict to reconsider their presuppositions concerning the process of social change.[9] It is with this admonitory precept in mind that I propose in this essay to reexamine the relationship between latitudinarianism and the role of reason in religion in Restoration England.

Let me begin by observing that in the secondary literature latitudinarianism is most often identified with a set of philosophical beliefs, or more vaguely, with a religious attitude.[10] This is not surprising, considering the historical influence of the Cambridge Platonists upon the development of latitudinarianism, and the fact that the latitudinarians themselves attempted to draw a definitional line separating fundamental from non-fundamental elements of protestant theology. The idea was to formulate in broad philosophical terms a consensus on the essentials of religious doctrine, thereby avoiding fractionating conflict focused upon the marginal elements of protestantism. Without minimizing the difficulties to be surmounted by this strategy, it is fair to say, and especially with regard to the presbyterians, that the real problem was not the construction of a theoretical consensus of beliefs, but rather, how this consensus could be practically implemented through collective action. That is, how, in practice, would the church be structured and how would political and economic power (through clerical appointments) be distributed?[11] Theoretically, and certainly from the standpoint of religious doctrine, these questions were non-fundamental, or indifferent. But then, by what ecclesiastical authority could certain forms of religious worship be made necessary to church membership? From time to time, when challenged on this point, Anglicans responded by providing a scriptural defense of episcopacy, equating the latter with "the primitive Christian church." For the most part, however, they simply conceded that Anglicanism was a political church, i.e., a religion whose practice depended upon the civil magistrate's authority to enforce compliance with the law.[12]

In other words, a doctrinal consensus did not preclude political controversy; it merely shifted the focus of debate to questions concerning the magistrate's role with respect to religious matters, or to questions about the origins of religious and political authority, and the nature of the obligations attached to religious worship. If then, one simply identifies latitudinarianism with a set of shared philosophical beliefs or a religious doctrine consensually accepted, how can one account for the role actually played by the latitudinarians in the political conflict between Anglicans and dissenters which, for the most part, was fought out on other ground?[13]

Let me rephrase the issue by returning to comprehension, which was a practical policy designed to implement a doctrinal consensus, and with which virtually all of the latitudinarians were associated. Did adherence to comprehension indicate a willingness on the part of the Anglican clergy to accept a broad definition of a church, permitting variant ceremonial practices in its local congregations? Did it mean the elimination of those particular indifferent features of Anglican worship which dissenters found objectionable? Did it mean that religious latitude implied a political latitude, in the sense that legal penalties against the nonconformists might be eliminated? All of these matters were discussed from time to time by those who supported the policy of comprehension, but, viewing the period from 1660 to 1689 as a whole, it would be difficult to make the case that comprehension implied an affirmative answer to any of these questions. On the contrary, what comprehension most often meant was simply conformity to the existing practices of the Anglican Church; that is, the abandonment of religious dissent.[14]

Not only is there plenty of evidence to show that many dissenters saw that comprehension really meant religious conformity, but they also had good reasons for their suspicions that some of the advocates of comprehension used that policy as a means of fostering distrust amongst the dissenters, hoping to disunite presbyterians, independents, baptists, and other sectarians, thereby strengthening the power of the established church against its opponents.[15] These machiavellian motives aside, the fact is, the hierarchy of the Anglican Church – and especially the latitudinarians – consistently underestimated the opposition of Restoration dissenters to any policy of comprehension.[16] As we previously mentioned, the latter would have left independents and others subject to persecution under the penal laws, and by 1660, or shortly thereafter, the vast majority of presbyterians had resolved not to abandon their fellow nonconformists to that fate. They had decided not to accept comprehension for themselves without an agreement to extend toleration to those who remained beyond the pale of Anglicanism.[17] Thus, with a few exceptions, it can be said that the dissenters were united on a policy of toleration and that comprehension was only meaningful to them in the context of an endorsement of that policy, while Anglicans rejected toleration in favor of the persecution of nonconformity and comprehension was only acceptable to them in *that* context. In other words, within the framework of Restoration politics, a policy of comprehension advanced by Anglicans functioned as part of an attempt to defeat the policy of toleration, while legitimating the prosecution of religious dissent.[18]

From a political perspective, therefore, emphasis upon a doctrinal consensus amongst Anglicans and certain nonconformists necessarily obscures the meaning of that consensus as a proposed solution to the religious/political conflict between the two groups. More specifically, such an approach makes it virtually impossible to understand the ideological role played by latitudinarianism (and biographically, the political role played by individual latitudinarians) in Restoration England. Latitudinarianism is not a moderate middle ground between contending extremes; it is, rather, *part* of one of the extremes.[19] It is the acceptable face of the persecution of religious dissent.

I will return to a consideration of this political characterization of latitudinarianism in a moment. Thus far, I have argued that the secondary literature on latitudinarianism seriously underestimates or ignores entirely the political dimensions of that movement in a way that not only obscures the meaning of latitudinarianism, but which also makes it difficult to appreciate what the political struggle over the most important problem – toleration of religious dissent – in Restoration England was all about. If this is the weakest aspect of the secondary literature, I now want to examine what is supposedly its strongest feature; namely, its portrayal of latitudinarianism as the embodiment of rational theology. Surely the claims advanced by historians that latitudinarianism represented a *via media* between superstitious and irrational religious beliefs, between the idolatrous practices of Catholicism and the fanatical enthusiasm of sectarians, must be accepted, whatever adjustments in this picture one insists must be made to allow for its neglected political aspects. However, since this is also what the latitudinarians wanted their contemporaries to believe, in light of what has already been said, one ought to proceed with some caution before conceding the latitudinarians the theological middle ground and accepting their claims at face value.[20] To my critique of the willingness of historians to do so because it inhibits our understanding of Restoration political life, I now want to add that it also misrepresents some very crucial developments in the cultural thought of that period. If latitudinarianism is made synonymous with rational theology, in other words, the consequence will be a distortion or neglect of some significant aspects of the cultural consciousness of Restoration England. For, as I will show, there was not one but two "rational theologies" propounded during this period; one by the latitudinarians, and the other by the dissenters.

Naturally, I believe these two dimensions of my critique of the secondary literature on latitudinarianism are interrelated, and that, more generally, different religious world views were implicated in the political conflict between Anglicans and dissenters over seemingly indifferent and relatively minor practical matters. Methodologically, what I want to insist upon is that it would never occur to a historian sensitive to the importance of political conflict to the assessment of cultural values or their development to adopt the viewpoint that the institutionalization of toleration was merely the technical implementation of a set of consensually held cultural beliefs. To put it another way, beginning on the ground of political conflict, as articulated by the historical actors themselves, allows one to *investigate* the importance of differences in meaning which contemporaries attached to the same word or phrases in a particular social context. Instead of an arbitrary assumption by the interpreter that the actors must have meant x, where "x" is a relatively abstract and timeless definition (of "rational," for example), what is required is empirical evidence which attempts to establish the connections between the use of a specific linguistic terminology and the social actions executed by its users, thereby minimizing one's reliance upon "free-floating" ideas in one's analysis of the cultural life of a particular society. As we shall see, this is a point of some importance when one is dealing with such elusive terms as "reason" or "natural law."

To ask whether the religious life of Restoration England can be adequately understood within a framework that identifies Catholicism with idolatry and superstition, Anglicanism with rational theology, and nonconformity with irrationality and fanaticism should, in its very posing, give warning to historians to avoid the danger of oversimplification in their interpretive reconstructions of the cultural consciousness of that period. Indeed, even to recognize the latitudinarians as a specific group of rational theologians requires that some distinction be drawn separating them from other Anglicans who were not committed to their principles or to their conception of the relationship between reason and religion. But is this not also possible with respect to the dissenters? Were not significant numbers of presbyterians, independents, and other nonconformists committed to a "rational theology," a conception which *they* employed in order to distinguish themselves from superstitious Catholics and en-thusiastic sectarians? If the answer to this question is yes – and I shall argue that it is – then, clearly, the claim of the latitudinarians that their position is identified with rational theology is not only ideologically self-serving in terms of their political interests, but also, its acceptance leaves us with no possibility of understanding what non-latitudinarian rational theology could possibly have meant in Restoration England.

Whatever the precise historical origins of the theological framework that assigned Anglicans the reasonable middle ground between Catholic and nonconformist extremists, its intellectual antecedents certainly extend at least as far back as Richard Hooker. The political efficaciousness of this viewpoint in the seventeenth century was immeasurably increased through references to the miseries of the English Civil War. In both its general

theological formulation and its specifically political employment, therefore, this perspective clearly antedates Restoration latitudinarianism,
which is the focus of my discussion. Still, it is fair to say that Restoration
latitudinarians displayed an especially keen appreciation of the hegemonic
power of the concept of "reason."[21]

Simon Patrick's *A Brief Account of the New Sect of Latitude-Men*,
published in 1662, seems designed to reassure orthodox Anglicans of the
loyalty of latitudinarians. "They cordially love and obey" the Anglican
Church and, notwithstanding their emphasis upon reason, Patrick insists
that they are staunch defenders of episcopal authority.[22] By the time his
A Friendly Debate Between a Conformist and a Non-Conformist appeared,
seven years later, this point is simply taken for granted, and the emphasis
has shifted toward demonstrating the irrationality of nonconformity. The
conformist has reason on his side; the nonconformist is contemptuous of
"rational discourses." Conformist ministers preach sermons with the
intent of convincing their auditors through appeals to reason and a "sober
consideration" of the meaning of religion, while the nonconformist,
according to Patrick, appeals to the passions, indulges in excessive
rhetoric and "pretty similitudes," and employs other "mad fanatic
tricks" to deceive the multitude.[23] Edward Fowler, in *The Principles of
Practices of Certain Moderate Divines of the Church of England...Fairly
Represented and Defended* (1670), likewise defends latitudinarians as
"obedient sons of the Church of England" while declaiming against the
"violent and boisterous passions" exhibited by nonconformists.[24]
Dissenters may not be fairly characterized as heretics, Fowler admits, but
since he believes that only "unreasonable, ill-minded, and wild-headed
men" could possibly refuse to accept communion in the Anglican Church,
this is small consolation from their point of view.[25] In his essay, "The
agreement of reason and religion," Joseph Glanvill maintains that "the
enemies of our church and government" – namely, all nonconformists –
are notably lacking in the possession of reason. Indeed, if reason were
accepted as a standard by mankind, Glanvill remarks, dissenters would
cease to exist, leaving, in Glanvill's view, the established institutions of
church and state exactly as they were. Since "reason" and "dissent"
cannot peaceably co-exist in Glanvill's theological vocabulary, he
concludes that, as a practical matter, "it will be impossible for sober men
to have any success in their endeavors to convince them."[26]

In his "sober answer" to Patrick on behalf of the nonconformists,
Samuel Rolle responded to what he conceived was less than "a friendly
debate." In fact, Rolle accused Patrick of engaging in slanderous and
shameful abuse of the dissenters. The purpose of Patrick's book, he
asserted, was "to excite rulers to persecute them."[27] Not only was Patrick

insensitive to the imprisonment of hundreds of individuals and the starvation of their families, but also, Rolle charged that the "poisoning" of men's minds "with vile prejudice against good men" through his writings was, in itself, a form of "persecuting the nonconformists with your pen."[28]

Glanvill's devotion to reasonableness, moderation, peace, and all the other virtues of latitudinarianism did not prevent him from attacking the dissenters as hypocritical fanatics and advocates of tyranny.[29] In *The Zealous and Impartial Protestant* – more zealous than impartial – Glanvill launched a furious assault against the claims for religious toleration. On the contrary, he argued, the existing penal laws should be "put in punctual, vigorous execution" against the dissenters. What they required was not greater leniency and moderation, but to be more "restrained by the exacting of the penalties" than they heretofore have been. "Penalties duly exacted" through prosecution, Glanvill observed, will serve as a "warning" to others and "force" nonconformists to return to the established church. Glanvill lamented the fact that the Conventicle Act had not been more "briskly executed" when it was first enacted, for if it had been rigorously enforced, he thought, "it would have done the business" of eliminating nonconformity long ago. In any event, "that method" (i.e., persecution) should now be revived and applied with "firm resolution" to the dissenters.[30]

Samuel Parker, whom some have identified with the latitudinarians, authored one of the severest attacks upon Restoration dissenters.[31] Throughout the nearly one thousand pages of his *Discourse of Ecclesiastical Polity*, Parker relentlessly heaps abuse upon their characters and their ideas. He refers to dissenters as "wild and savage" individuals "unalterably resolved never to be convinced" of the "truths" of Anglican doctrine. Since there was no way "to pierce their thick and inveterate prejudices," Parker concluded, like Glanvill, that there was no point in engaging in debate with them. He candidly admitted that the objective of the *Discourse* was not to reason with the nonconformists, but to "silence them." Hence, he believed that the state ought to "punish them with the severest inflictions."[32] It must "root up" the principles espoused by the dissenters, Parker insisted, "and brand and punish all persons that publicly profess them."[33] To characterize nonconformists as "enemies and outlaws to human society" and then to suggest that the nation's welfare might be best promoted "by cutting off such persons as are pests and enemies to it" pointed towards a final solution to the problem of dissent that, in the dissenters' eyes, hardly amounted to a moderate proposal or reflected a "reasonable" temper of mind.[34] Rather, what they perceived in Parker's *Discourse* was a book filled with "dogmatical assertions" which served as an ideological defense of persecution.[35]

The sermon of another latitudinarian, Edward Stillingfleet's "The mischief of separation," provoked a tremendous outcry from the dissenters, and drew replies from John Owen, Richard Baxter, John Humfrey, and John Howe, to mention just a few. Stillingfleet's lengthy reply to his critics in *The Unreasonableness of Separation* unleashed a new spate of critical responses to what was, as the titles of Stillingfleet's works suggest, an assault upon the dissenters as treacherous and unreasonable enemies to church and state.[36] Even John Tillotson preached a notorious sermon accusing nonconformists of "gross hypocrisy" and justifying the application of penalties to them, equating religious dissent with the "prejudices [of] partial and inconsiderate men."[37] Indeed, in other sermons, Tillotson defended the right of the magistrate to "restrain and punish" these "perverse and disobedient" individuals for the sake of "the peace and unity of the church." For "those who neglect this Sacrament" of the Anglican Church, Tillotson declared, "there is hardly any thing left to restrain them ... and to give a check to them in their evil course; nothing but the penalty of human laws."[38]

It should not be surprising, therefore, that the latitudinarians did not always or necessarily appear to the dissenters as the tolerant moderate representatives of sweetness and light they have become through the laying on of hands of later historians. In his reply to Stillingfleet's sermon, John Howe expressed his bitterness towards the "mean narrow spirit" and "intemperate heat" displayed by "one of such avowed latitude." Stillingfleet, Howe wrote, had decided to compensate for "the defect of reason" in his argument by employing the "sharpness" of invective against the nonconformists.[39] Similarly, Baxter attacked Glanvill as "a most triumphant conformist," referring to the "shame of his persecuting counsel," and he criticized the hypocrisy of Stillingfleet's rhetoric on behalf of peace and moderation in religious disputes while, at the same time, "urging magistrates to execute the laws against us."[40] In his replies to Stillingfleet, Humfrey remarked caustically that some Anglican churchmen are "resolved to revive Laud's design" in the apparent belief that strict enforcement of the penal laws is "a sure way of uniting us."[41] For Humfrey, there was no evidence of a "generous" or latitudinarian disposition in Patrick's *Friendly Debate*, Parker's *Discourse*, or Stillingfleet's *Unreasonableness of Separation*, which he grouped together.[42] Rather, from the perspective of the dissenters, what these works shared in common was their sanctioning, on behalf of the established church, of the use of "military methods of converting the dissenters."[43] What is the difference, another nonconformist asked, between those individuals, such as Tillotson, who attack dissenters, condemning them "to the pit of Hell," and the more orthodox divines of the Anglican Church who have not yet thought up a worse fate for them?[44]

For those caught up in the political conflict of Restoration England, the meaning of the words used by the latitudinarians had to be understood in relation to their actions. John Owen reflected that in the midst of a period of persecution of dissenters, he came upon a sermon entitled, "Moderation stated," which he began to read with great pleasure. The first part of the sermon extols the virtues of meekness and patience, advising individuals to decide religious controversies with a "calm, cool, gentle temper" and "to take the most amicable way in the accommodating of differences." The author then proceeds to characterize those who advocate toleration as "knaves"; he attacks the Quakers for having "degenerated" from the truth of Christianity; he labels all nonconformists "false and treacherous" vipers; and he summarily dismisses their complaints about suffering under the penal laws, whose sturdy enforcement he recommends. The sermon concludes with the declaration that "nothing less than … a constant and close conformity" to Anglicanism will suffice, and, on this issue, "there is no room for equity and moderation."[45] It is incredible, Owen remarks, that the same individual who wrote the first doctrinal part of the sermon could have written the second part, where the application of these principles is considered. Nevertheless, he observes, it allows us to "see what manner of men" the Anglican Church believes "moderate men to be."[46] The point is not only that, notwithstanding their doctrinal pleas for moderation and reasonableness, latitudinarians, by stirring up animosities and hatred with their epithets and invectives directed against dissenters, often served as the shock troops of persecution in the war against nonconformity, but also that contemporaries naturally took these actions into account in forming some assessment of what the latitudinarians meant when they used words such as "reason" or "moderation" in the context of their discussion of religion.

I said earlier that dissenters did not accept the claim that rational theology could be identified with latitudinarianism. This denial was premised not merely upon the disparity they perceived between the principles and the actions of the latitudinarians, but also upon the positive claims advanced by the nonconformists that *they* – and not the latitudinarians – were the true defenders of rational theology. To assert that nonconformists are devoid of reason or that they are its opponents in matters of religion, Rolle argued in his reply to Patrick's *Friendly Debate*, is simply absurd. On the contrary, "they love and esteem a rational discourse as much as you can do." He ridiculed the latitudinarians, "high pretensions to reason above other men" and their attempt "to appropriate to yourselves the name of rational divines … that you should pretend to be the only men of reason."[47] Similarly, in his defense of the nonconformist position, Robert Ferguson charged that the efforts of a few Anglican churchmen to "monopolize to themselves the name of rational divines" was nothing more than an act of overblown pride.[48] Baxter and many other dissenters wrote tracts addressed to this "church-troubling controversy," namely, the role of reason in religion. More specifically, they sought to demonstrate the falsity of the "deep accusations" of "unreasonableness" which were levelled against them by the Anglican clergy.[49] In writing *The Interest of Reason in Religion*, Ferguson explained, his objective was "to vindicate the Non-Conformists from the aspersions lately cast upon them; as if they were *defamers* of reason, disclaiming it from all concern in religion."[50] In addition to Ferguson's book, the titles of some of these works suggest both the direction and the seriousness of the dissenters' argument: *The Judgment of Non-Conformists, of the Interest of Reason in Matters of Religion*, signed by Baxter and ten other nonconformist ministers; Charles Wolseley's *The Reasonableness of Scripture-Belief*; Ferguson's other contribution, *A Sober Enquiry into the Nature, Measure, and Principle of Moral Virtue*; John Owen's *The Reason of Faith*; and another collective work by Baxter and others, *The Judgment of Non-Conformists About the Difference Between Grace and Morality*.

In these writings, nonconformists argue that "there neither is nor can be anything in Divine Revelation that overthrows the rational faculty or crosses it in its regular and due exercise." Hence, "there is no conviction begot by the Holy Ghost in the hearts of men, otherwise than by rational evidence satisfying our understandings."[51] They maintain that it is through "an industrious exercise of reason," through appeals to "rational proofs" and the engagement in the same kind of scientific investigation that one applies to the study of nature, that one will discover "the evidence, and true reasons of all things in religion."[52] Indeed, for reasons that will become clearer in a moment, these nonconformists insisted much more strenuously than did the latitudinarians upon the importance of viewing religion from the standpoint of "a rational free agent, whose will must be guided by the light of his understanding."[53] "Whatever men do as men," Ferguson declared, "it is upon arguments and reasons that prevail with them."[54] Thus, in assessing the testimony of prophets or divine revelation, or in considering "miracles," the nonconformists defended the importance of relying upon reason and the probability of the evidence relating to these and other religious matters. Individuals, Owen argued, must "use and exercise the best of their rational abilities" in determining their religious position. The alternative, he believed, was either atheism or reliance upon some authority, and the latter was closely identified in the minds of the dissenters with Catholicism. For Owen, and for many other Nonconformists, therefore, the choice was between "assent" to "the sole authority of [the] church," whether Catholic or Anglican, and "rational arguments" grounded on evidence.[55]

In other words, if space permitted, an examination of the various religious issues to be considered in relation to the exercise of human reason would show that *none* of the arguments or defenses of reason with respect to religion to be found in the works of the latitudinarians are exclusive or peculiar to them; they also appear in the writings of numerous nonconformists.[56] Moreover, like the latitudinarians, the nonconformists position themselves between "the great ills of idolatry and superstition" of the Catholics "and all sorts of enthusiasts" who rely upon "pretended inspiration" rather than reasoned arguments to support their conceptions of Christianity. Not only do the dissenters repudiate any attempt to equate the evangelical aspects of Christian doctrine with "enthusiasm," they also expose this tactic as nothing more than "a pretence to discard all rational arguments" and to discount the importance of reason to religion.[57]

What, then, are the specific points of contention between nonconformists and latitudinarians on the subject of reason and religion? The answer to this question is not easy to state in the form of particular propositions, for reasons already alluded to above; rather, what must be grasped is a difference in the way in which these propositions are structured into an argument, one defending religious dissent. Briefly stated, the argument is as follows. For nonconformists, "rational theology" meant that the linkage between divine reason and human reason is an essential precept of religion. That is, God as the Author of reason, has given mankind the Law of Nature as a law of reason and has created individuals with those faculties and powers of reason that enable them to understand and to fulfill the moral obligations laid upon them by natural law. In fact, the industrious use of reason is itself an imperative, the violation of which by man constitutes an affront to the purposive intentions of his Creator. In short, "being a rational creature," man "must owe God a rational subjection," which "necessarily follows from the constitution of his nature." This "reasonable subjection" to God means for the nonconformists that religion itself must depend upon "a rational choice" on the part of the individual.[58] For what, Owen asked, "is their reason given unto them...unless it be to use it in those things which are of the greatest importance to them?"[59] The "method of [God's] government over reasonable creatures," Howe declared, is not "to overpower them into that obedience" which they owe to Him, but rather, to rely upon "pleadings and expostulations," that is, upon persuasion and rational argument.[60] Obviously, this perspective ruled out the use of force in matters of religion; swords are not arguments, as the nonconformists reminded their persecutors. Religious persecution, they maintained, is "contrary to the principles of the Law of Nature," and violators of natural law were no better than a wild and savage beast.[61]

Nonconformists argued that "we are under the obligation of the divine law to worship God," but there was no specific revelation or natural law defining the ceremonies or rituals to be performed in executing that obligation. Hence, the scriptures provided no unequivocal endorsement of a particular institutional form of religious worship, a point frequently conceded by Anglicans.[62] It is within this context that the notion of "rational choice" assumes considerable importance. For, according to the dissenters, in the fulfillment of *all* his natural law duties, the individual must rely upon his own judgment, for which he alone is held morally accountable. Even if this were not the essential ingredient of protestantism nonconformists believed that it was, they asserted, as an operative rule of reason, that in all matters of doubtful or probable evidence, the individual's exercise of reason was the best guide for making a decision.[63] Why, then, Owen asked, should individuals allow the decision as to the form of divine worship they practice to be made by those who "can neither give evidence to their propositions, nor warrant to their authority in their impositions in spiritual things?"[64] To resign ourselves to the command of "superiors" simply on the basis of their appeal to authority, nonconformists argued, "is to say that God would have us lay aside our reason, which he has given us for a guide." It was nothing less than an atheistical or papist belief "that in religion, inferiors must believe all that their superiors assert, and do all that they shall command...without using their own reason to discern...whether it be agreeable or contrary to the Laws of God."[65]

These remarks express both a theological and a political view of the world. That every individual is endowed with reason and free will and is presumed capable of acting morally, according to his private judgment, was for the nonconformists not so much an empirical description of human behavior as it was a reflection of their image of the Deity. Not only is God possessed of reason and free will, but, in creating man in His image, He purposely structured the world so that there would be a harmonious relationship between the subjective and the objective dimensions of rationality.[66] Anglicans – including latitudinarians – denied that individuals were rational in the sense of acting according to their consciences. Reliance upon individual conscience, they asserted, meant that individuals would "follow the wild enthusiasms of their own brains." The result would be chaos and anarchy, a point relentlessly hammered home by Parker in his *Discourse*, and seconded by Glanvill, Fowler, Stillingfleet, Sprat, and other latitudinarians in their writings.[67] That Anglicans displayed a prudential fear of the "giddy multitude" or "wild enthusiasts" is not at all surprising. But in generalizing that fear as part of an argument against subjective reason, they severed the link between the individual as a rational agent and natural law. If individuals could not be trusted to rely upon their reason or to choose their form of worship, Owen asked, how could they be supposed rational enough to fulfill any of the other commands of the Law of Nature? To deny the rationality of individuals, he argued, was to "disturb the whole harmony of divine Providence ... and break the first link of that great chain whereon all religion and government in the world do depend."[68] Anglicanism interposed the arbitrary will of the magistrate between the individual's subjective reason and the dictates of natural law relating to his obligation to worship God, and, I am arguing, in their definition of "rational theology," nonconformists could not reconcile this interposition with their image of the Deity, their definition of "conscience," or their ontological view of a rationally structured universe. Moreover, the nonconformists uniformly identified this viewpoint with a Hobbesian position.[69]

Without entering into a consideration of the influence of Hobbes's ideas in Restoration England, a subject too complex to be treated here, the last reference does raise the question of how the latitudinarians and the nonconformists defined the parameters of political authority, especially in relation to the individual's use of reason. There are statements in the writings of the latitudinarians which sound like the propositions advanced by the nonconformists in their defense of the "rational" exercise of political authority. But, as with "moderation," one must consider the context within which such concepts or statements were used. Simon Patrick, for example, criticizes the view that individuals should "give up" their reason to clerical authority. "By what means," he asks, "do we trust others to choose our religion for us?" Why should we not use our reason to judge for ourselves? And if we were to surrender our reason to clerical authority in one matter, why not in all matters? Patrick is using these arguments to criticize the view of authority he associates with Catholicism. He then proceeds, unquestioningly, to defend a reliance upon the authority of the Anglican clergy because they "know better" how "to guide you aright" through their "use of the most impartial and unbiased reason," as if these same questions could not be put, as they were by the dissenters, to the Anglican clergy.[70] According to both reason and Christianity, Tillotson asserted, individuals possess a liberty "to judge for themselves in matters of religion." But, he insisted, this liberty was meaningful only in the context of a "great submission and deference to our spiritual rulers and guides, whom God hath appointed in his church." To use one's liberty to depart from communion in the Anglican Church, Tillotson declared, was a factious act of "pride" and "self-conceit."[71] Other instances could be cited, but the fact is, whenever latitudinarians were forced to consider matters where the conjuncture of "reason" and "authority" was a relevant issue, they invariably *assumed* the "reason-ableness" of the hierarchy of the Anglican Church. In other words, even when Anglican clerics departed from a general denial that mankind was rational or that individuals could be trusted to choose rationally, their most favorable comments on individual rationality occurred within a context in which there was an unquestioned "presumption" that existing civil and religious authorities were "more competent judges" of what ought to be done than were those without authority.[72]

By contrast, when nonconformists extolled the virtues of rational judgment, they meant that every individual was capable of making a rational decision with respect to his/her religious duties. Since God has not "given any man authority to make laws" for mankind with respect to religion, Howe declared, no individual can entrust the welfare of his soul to another "representative."[73] "When all is done," George Care wrote, "We must choose for ourselves, and not [according to] the political reason" of others, "or else we shall believe upon authority."[74] As Locke expressed the nonconformist viewpoint in the *Letter Concerning Toleration*: "those things that every man ought sincerely to inquire into himself, and by meditation, study, search, and his own endeavors to attain the knowledge of, cannot be looked upon as the peculiar possession of any sort of men...The care, therefore, of every man's soul belongs unto himself, and is to be left unto himself." It does not belong to any individual, "whether prince or subject," Locke argued, "to prescribe to him what faith or worship he shall embrace," for "every man...has the supreme and absolute authority of judging for himself" with respect to matters of religious worship.[75]

Neither "judging for oneself" nor "liberty of conscience," the nonconformists argued, was merely an internal state of consciousness or mental act. Rather, they maintained that such liberty is a "determination of the practical understanding...an act of the will," which manifests itself through social action.[76] We do not need the latitudinarians to preach that we have a liberty of conscience, dissenters declared, if all they mean by that phrase is that we have the freedom to believe whatever we want so long as we do not *act* upon such beliefs by preaching or publishing them, or by expressing them through church services, since no civil magistrate or ecclesiastical authority can command an individual's consciousness.[77] Hence, what liberty of conscience means must be assessed in the context of practical action; that is, how individuals collectively organize themselves as a religious society. For the nonconformists, a church was a voluntary society constituted by "the consent of every man in particular" who joined it.[78] Individuals must consent to church authority, the dissenters argued, because no other explanation for the origins of authority in either church or state is consistent with the exercise of human reason.[79]

Those who attacked a reliance upon individual conscience as a guide to rational action equated "conscience" with the "self-interest" of the individual. Anything, they argued, might be justified by appealing to conscience, since they assumed that individuals were guided by subjective desires and passions which, if unchecked by authority, would produce a Hobbesian war of all against all.[80] Latitudinarians were thus able to employ the concept of self-interest as a weapon against the nonconformists' appeal to conscience and individual rationality. The latter countered this ideological attack by associating conscience with the Law of Nature and by supposing that all individuals were members of a natural moral community. Humfrey, for example, spoke of "a community" as "a company of persons, who have no power one over another." He could easily imagine, therefore, the existence of "a community of Christians" without any government over them, subject only to the dictates of natural law.[81] Similarly, Owen referred to "the state of nature" as that pre-political (but not pre-social) condition where individuals were governed by the Law of Nature.[82] Individuals in a state of nature, Locke wrote, are members of a natural moral community who enforce the precepts of natural law in order to secure the preservation and common good of mankind.[83] Living within that state of nature, Ferguson argued, individuals could claim a natural right to toleration, a right, that is, that was a pre-political entitlement rooted in the moral life of the invisible church of protestant Christianity.[84] It need hardly be stressed that Locke developed and defended this perspective in both his *Two Treatises of Government* and in the *Letter Concerning Toleration*.[85]

Nonconformists assumed that individuals could act rationally because they conceived of individuals as constituting a moral community in nature under the governance of natural law. The latter embodied those precepts which, taken together, comprised the meaning of the "common good." Hence, from the dissenters' standpoint, to act rationally was to act for the common good. Since political power was constrained in its exercise by its effectiveness as a means for the realization of the common good, the nonconformists attempted to provide a theory which linked subjective (individual) and objective reason (natural law) within the framework of a natural community out of which the institutions of church and state emerged through the consent of those who created them. Thus, the employment of force or coercion by any political authority against the individual's natural right to liberty of conscience and freedom of religious worship was, *ipso facto*, a violation of the "law of reason."[86] The issue, the nonconformists argued, is not simply whether dissenters are guilty of disobeying a lawful authority – the civil magistrate – but rather, whether the latter *has* a lawful authority to punish individuals for not worshiping as he does. Since, in their view, such an action contravened the law of nature, and was, therefore, "without authority," nonconformists, they maintained, could not be accused of displaying any "contempt of authority."[87] In short, no defense of religious persecution could be reconciled with "rational theology," whatever the rhetorical claims of the latitudinarians.

What I have tried to show is that "rational theology" meant a great deal more to nonconformists than simply a general exhortation in favor of a positive role for reason in religion. It meant a willingness to *rely* upon the judgment of the individual as a rational free agent. For nonconformists, the term represented an appeal to the rational character of the Deity, and the conception of a church as a collective rational activity. These views were, and were perceived to be, a challenge to the traditionalist, arbitrary, and elitist conceptions of authority defended by the "rational divines," the latitudinarians. And, if space permitted, many other aspects of the differential meanings of rational theology, ranging from deontological notions of divine providence to the social significance of the "new science," relative to the political conflict between Anglicans and dissenters in Restoration England could be added to this discussion. Yet, extension of the discussion to these issues will accomplish little if the importance of this conflict is not recognized.

A cultural history approach that brackets political and social conflict in order to assume a homogeneous cultural consciousness or in order to consider certain topics as part of a "given" smorgasbord of issues laid out for the historian to select according to his/her taste, or which tries to compartmentalize ideas into separable disciplinary channels or "traditions" will never succeed in understanding the meaning of ideas for historical actors with a far more acute sense of the interrelatedness and structure of the social life-world and the significance of the struggle to realize group-defined practical objectives than that displayed by the historian. Latitudinarianism was an important phenomenon in the cultural life of late seventeenth-century England, but neither its meaning nor its relationship to other aspects of Restoration culture will ever be adequately conceptualized or accurately portrayed by historians until a prominent role is assigned to political conflict as an interpretive foundation of historiography, and the long-standing divorcement between intellectual and political history is finally ended.

Notes

1 J. A. W. Gunn, *Politics and the Public Interest in the Seventeenth Century* (London, 1969), p. 153.

2 Barbara J. Shapiro, *Probability and Certainty in Seventeenth-Century England* (Princeton, 1983); *John Wilkins: An Intellectual Biography, 1614–72* (Berkeley, 1969); "Latitudinarianism and science in seventeenth-century England," *Past and Present* (1968), reprinted in Charles Webster, ed., *The Intellectual Revolution of the Seventeenth Century* (London, 1974), pp. 286–316; Richard S. Westfall, *Science and Religion in Seventeenth-Century England* (New Haven, 1958). For the older version of this thesis, see John Tulloch, *Rational Theology and Christian Philosophy in the Seventeenth Century*, 2 vols. 2nd ed. (London, 1874); A. A. Seaton, *The Theory of Toleration under the Later Stuarts* (Cambridge, 1911); C. E. Whiting, *Studies in English Puritanism from the Restoration to the Revolution, 1660–1688*, (New York, 1931) p. 477.

3 Cited in Douglas R. Lacey, *Dissent and Parliamentary Politics in England, 1661–1689* (New Brunswick, 1969), p. 237. "The sudden revival of the toleration bill in mid-May [1689] is not easy to explain." Henry Horowitz, *Parliament, Policy and Politics in the Reign of William III* (Manchester, 1977), p. 29.

4 Lacey, *Dissent*, p. 193.

5 Charles F. Mullet, "Toleration and persecution in England, 1660–89," *Church History* 18 (March 1949): 42; Roger Thomas, "Comprehension and indulgence," in *From Uniformity to Unity, 1662–1962*, eds. Geoffrey F. Nuttall and Owen Chadwick (London, 1962), p. 251; Horowitz, *Parliament*, p. 29; Lacey, *Dissent*, p. 237; Seaton, *Theory of Toleration*, pp. 233, 325.

6 On the attempt to limit toleration to a period of seven years, and the threats by dissenters to refuse to lend money to the king if the toleration bill did not pass, see Lacey, *Dissent*, p. 237; Horowitz, *Parliament*, p. 29; Raymond C. Mensing, Jr., *Toleration and Parliament 1660–1719* (Washington, D.C., 1979), p. 95. For accounts of the political maneuvering to secure passage of both bills, see G. V. Bennett, "Conflict in the Church," in *Britain after the Glorious Revolution, 1689–1714*, ed. Geoffrey Holmes (London, 1969), pp. 161–62; Thomas, "Comprehension," pp. 246–51; F. G. James, "The bishops in politics, 1688–1714," in *Conflict in Stuart England: Essays in Honour of Wallace Notestein* (London, 1960), pp. 227–57; Mullet, "Toleration and persecution," pp. 18–43.

7 Henry Kamen, *The Rise of Toleration* (New York, 1967), p. 211; Seaton,

Theory of Toleration, pp. 233, 325; Mensing, *Toleration and Parliament*, pp. 95–98; Mullet, "Toleration and persecution," p. 42; Horowitz, *Parliament*, pp. 22–29; Lacey, *Dissent*, pp. 234–38.

8 Bennett, "Conflict," p. 162. As Lacey points out, the Toleration Act came into existence amidst threats by its supporters to repeal it forthwith if the dissenters misbehaved. *Dissent*, p. 238. One contemporary who explicitly attempted to explain the meaning of the law confessed that "it is an Act...of a mixed complexion," which, in his view, accounted for the widespread divisions amongst both Anglicans and nonconformists as to its merits. James Fraser, *King William's Toleration: Being an Explanation of that Liberty of Religion, which May be Expected from His Majesty's Declaration...* (London, 1689), p. 4.

9 Kamen, *Rise of Toleration*, p. 216. Indeed, the presupposition ought to be reversed, for the survival of religious toleration as a feature of social life can be more easily explained in terms of the institutional practise of toleration and the unintended consequences produced by the passage of the Toleration Act than it can as a consciously intended act of will executed by some "rational" cultural or political elite. Mensing, *Toleration and Parliament*, p. 99; Mullet, "Toleration and persecution," p. 42.

10 Shapiro, *Probability*, p. 10; G. R. Cragg, *From Puritanism to the Age of Reason* (Cambridge, 1966), p. 81.

11 "The fundamental difference between the Churchman and the Nonconformist lay in their conception of Church government." Whiting, *Studies*, p. 17. John Humfrey, for example, had suggested that if a policy of comprehension were adopted, the appointments and pluralities under the control of deans and bishops could be distributed to "the laboring ministry," i.e., reclaimed nonconformists. *A Case of Conscience* (London, 1669), pp. 13–14.

12 Fowler, for example, made an attempt to identify episcopal organization with the institutional structure of "the primitive church," but Sprat and Glanvill were more inclined simply to admit that the Church of England was a state-religion, and to defend its authority and practises in terms of their relationship to "the stability of our civil government." Edward Fowler, *The Principles and Practices of Certain Moderate Divines of the Church of England...Truly Represented and Defended* (London, 1670), pp. 323ff.; Thomas Sprat, *Sermon* (January 29, 1682), (London, 1682), pp. 40–41; Joseph Glanvill, *The Zealous and Impartial Protestant* (London, 1681). The dilemma of this unresolved position is acutely exposed in the dissenters' replies to Edward Stillingfleet's *The Unreasonableness of Separation* (London, 1681) – and especially in John Humfrey's critique – discussed below.

13 Latitudinarianism tends to be defined so broadly that it only serves to obscure or conceal the political differences between Anglicans and dissenters. Michael Hunter, *Science and Society in Restoration England* (Cambridge, 1981), p. 115; Lotte Mulligan, "Anglicanism, latitudinarianism and science in seventeenth-century England," *Annals of Science* 30 (June 1973): 213–19; J. R. Jacob and M. C. Jacob, "Scientists and Society: The Saints Preserved," *Journal of European Studies* 1 (March 1971): pp. 87–92.

14 Mensing, *Toleration and Parliament*, pp. 5–10, and *passim*; Mullett, "Toleration and persecution"; Seaton, *Theory of Toleration*, pp. 89, 199, 219, 233,

325; Thomas, "Comprehension and indulgence." It should not be forgotten that comprehension was a policy favored by some High Churchmen, including Archbishop Sancroft, and that it was frequently defended as a political expedient, especially in periods of political instability. Bennett, "Conflict in the Church," p. 158; Geoffrey Nuttall, introduction, in Nuttall and Chadwick, *From Uniformity to Unity*, p. 9; Henry Horowitz, "Protestant reconciliation in the exclusion crisis," *Journal of Ecclesiastical History* 15 (October 1964): 201–17.

15 Thomas, "Comprehension and indulgence," p. 220; Bennett, "Conflict in the Church," p. 158. For an example of this strategy, see Thomas Tomkins, *The Modern Pleas for Comprehension, Toleration … Considered and Discussed* (London, 1675), pp. 79–92. And for the Dissenters' recognition of how they had been deceived on numerous occasions by the Anglicans' promises of comprehension, see Richard Baxter, *A Second True Defence of the Meer Nonconformists* (London, 1681). This is, by the way, Baxter's reply to both Glanvill and Stillingfleet.

16 Horowitz, "Protestant reconciliation," p. 212.

17 Lacey, *Dissent*, pp. 45–9, 64; Horowitz, "Protestant reconciliation," p. 208; Thomas, "Comprehension and indulgence," pp. 204ff.; Mullett, "Toleration and persecution," pp. 39ff. Baxter was, perhaps, one of the exceptions, though not consistently for the entire period of the Restoration. See the letter from William Penn to Baxter complaining about the latter's willingness to abandon his nonconformist brethren for the sake of comprehension. Cited in William M. Lamont, *Richard Baxter and the Millennium*, (Totowa, N.J., 1979), p. 240. But see also Lamont's discussion of a post-Restoration merging of presbyterian and independent ideas and the alliances formed by several sectarian groups in the face of Anglican persecution. Ibid., p. 211. John Humfrey, whose considerable influence with Baxter helped to maintain this alliance, strongly insisted upon both comprehension and toleration in his writings. *Case of Conscience*, pp. 13–14; *An Answer to Dr. Stillingfleet's Sermon by Some Nonconformists* (London, 1680), pp. 26–27; cf. John Corbet, *A Second Discourse of the Religion of England* (London, 1668).

18 Indeed, as one scholar has remarked, the degree of organic unity of church and state which the Anglicans sought during the Restoration could only be realized in a context which necessarily included persecution and the employment of force. Seaton, *Theory of Toleration*, p. 199; cf. T. Lyon, *The Theory of Religious Liberty in England, 1603–39* (Cambridge, 1937), pp. 5ff., 145; Bennett, "Conflict," p. 158; Cragg, *Puritanism*, pp. 200, 203. Contemporaries had a rather clear understanding of the Dissenters' unity on toleration and opposition to comprehension without the former. cf. Fraser, *King William's Toleration*, p. 4.

19 Shapiro's writings – and, I would argue, the historiographical approach she adopts – consistently obscure just this point. *Probability*, pp. 109–11; "Latitudinarianism and science." To characterize the philosophical endorsement of tolerance by the latitudinarians and their defense of political persecution as simply a "curious equivocation" in their attitudes trivializes the pain and suffering experienced by the victims of that persecution to a degree of political insensitivity that I find objectionable. Kamen, *Rise of Toleration*, p. 203; cf.

Seaton, *Theory of Toleration*, pp. 89, 123–25. The dissenters certainly found it so. "How easy is it for them that are at ease," Vincent Alsop wrote in reply to Stillingfleet, "to read lectures of patience to those in misery!" *The Mischief of Impositions*, 2nd ed. (London, 1680), p. 100. Latitudinarians, Rolle declared in his reply to Patrick's *A Friendly Debate*, were like ostriches who stuck their heads in the sand in the face of religious persecution. Samuel Rolle, *A Sober Answer to the Friendly Debate Betwixt a Conformist and a Nonconformist* (London, 1669), p. 247. However, while I believe notions of philosophical inconsistency or attitudinal confusion on the part of the latitudinarians are inadequate conceptualizations through which to convey the meaning of latitudinarian ideas in the context of the social practise of religious persecution – and I have, therefore, stressed the ideological role played by these ideas – it is neither necessary, nor historically accurate, to deny that some of these individuals personally intervened on various occasions to protect individual nonconformists.

20 As Brian Vickers warns in an essay discussing science and religion in Restoration England, whether one is examining Sprat's *History of the Royal Society* or various defenses of the Anglican Church's claim to a monopoly on "rational theology," "it is exceedingly naive to take such claims at face value." "The Royal Society and English prose style: a reassessment," in *Rhetoric and the Pursuit of Truth* (Los Angeles, 1985), pp. 24, 41–2.

21 Indeed the powerful appeal of the contrast between "reason" and "fanaticism," rested not only upon a historically formed consciousness of the miseries of the English Civil War, which could be more or less accurately stated, but also upon the consciously intended mischaracterization of Restoration nonconformists which applied the labels, categories, and beliefs associated with the Civil War to individuals for whom such labels and categories were not accurate representations of their perspective. Whatever their interest in or commitments to science or "reason," therefore, the latitudinarians (e.g., Sprat, Glanvill, Patrick) were as oblivious to the changes of circumstance and ideas with respect to Restoration dissenters in their reliance upon these categories vis-a-vis the evidence and the arguments adduced by the nonconformists which demonstrated their inappropriateness as were their non-scientifically minded political contemporaries.

22 Simon Patrick, *A Brief Account of the New Sect of Latitude-Men* (London, 1662), (reprint Los Angeles, 1963), pp. 11, 13.

23 Simon Patrick, *A Friendly Debate Between a Conformist and a Non-Conformist* (London, 1669), (6th ed., 1684), pp. 4–5, 13, 55.

24 Edward Fowler, *The Principles and Practices of Certain Moderate Divines of the Church of England...Truly Represented and Defended* (London, 1670), p. 340; cf. Epistle to the Reader.

25 Ibid., pp. 310–11, 334.

26 Joseph Glanvill, *Essays on Several Important Subjects in Philosophy and Religion* (London, 1676), p. 28; cf., *The Zealous and Impartial Protestant* (London, 1681), pp. 33–34.

27 Samuel Rolle, *A Sober Answer to the Friendly Debate Betwixt a Conformist and a Nonconformist* (London, 1669), preface, p. 254. This was not a far-fetched allegation. Patrick's *Friendly Debate* was published in the midst of a vigorous

campaign against the nonconformists launched by Archbishop Sheldon, which laid the groundwork for the passage of the Second Conventicle Act of 1670. I do not know what degree of approval, if any, Sheldon conferred on Patrick's work prior to its publication, but he certainly extended his appreciation to Patrick after its appearance in print. Simon Patrick, *The Autobiography of Simon Patrick, Bishop of Ely* (Oxford, 1839), pp. 59ff. (I owe this reference to Professor J. van den Berg. See his paper, "Between platonism and enlightenment: Simon Patrick (1625–1707) and his place in the latitudinarian movement," presented at a conference on latitudinarianism held at the William Andrews Clark Library, UCLA, April 1987.) See also Whiting, *Studies*, p. 499. Samuel Parker, one of Sheldon's chaplains, was more forthright in declaring that his purpose in writing *Discourse of Ecclesiastical Polity*, as part of Sheldon's campaign, was indeed not to argue with but to silence the dissenters and to encourage magistrates to enforce the penal laws against them. *Discourse of Ecclesiastical Polity* (London, 1670), pp. ix–xii, 18. Parker was also rewarded by Sheldon for his efforts. For a further discussion of this campaign of persecution of the nonconformists and their response to it, see my *Revolutionary Politics and Locke's Two Treatises of Government* (Princeton, 1986), pp. 23–25, 39–74.

28 Rolle, *Sober Answer*, pp. 109, 247, 250.

29 Glanvill, *Zealous*, pp. 5–6.

30 Ibid., pp. 33–34.

31 I would not myself classify Parker as a latitudinarian, but he is included in this group by Shapiro, "Latitudinarianism and science," p. 307; *Probability*, p. 113. Yet, Patrick was a friend of Parker, Fowler recommended Parker's book, and Glanvill came to Parker's defense, threatening to kill Andrew Marvell for having written against the *Discourse of Ecclesiastical Polity*. A J. Mason, *The Church of England and Episcopacy* (Cambridge, 1914), p. 251; John Marshall, "The ecclesiology of the latitude-men 1660–1689: Stillingfleet, Tillotson and 'Hobbism'," *Journal of Ecclesiastical History* 36 (July 1985): 427; Jackson I. Cope, *Joseph Glanvill, Anglican Apologist* (St. Louis, Mo., 1956), p. 34. And many nonconformists identified the position of the latitudinarians with that of Parker. See John Humfrey, *A Case of Conscience* (London, 1669); *An Answer to Dr. Stillingfleet's Book of the Unreasonableness of Separation* (London, 1682), p. 38; and the writings of Robert Ferguson, cited below.

32 Parker, *Discourse*, pp. ix–xii, 19.

33 Samuel Parker, *A Defence and Continuation of the Ecclesiastical Polity* (London, 1671), p. 541.

34 Parker, *Discourse*, pp. vi, 221.

35 John Owen, *Truth and Innocency Vindicated: In a Survey of a Discourse Concerning Ecclesiastical Polity* (London, 1669), pp. 2–3, 9, 11, 61.

36 Edward Stillingfleet, *The Unreasonableness of Separation* (London, 1681). For a list of some of the replies to Stillingfleet, see William Orme, *Memoirs of the Life, Writings, and Religious Connections of John Owen* (London, 1820), pp. 414–17, and Whiting, *Studies*, p. 524. There is a brief discussion of Stillingfleet's sermon and its critics in Gerald R. Cragg, *Puritanism in the Period of the Great Persecution, 1660–1688* (Cambridge, 1957), pp. 233–36. I

have discussed Locke's manuscript reply to Stillingfleet's *Unreasonableness* – which defends the nonconformists' position on toleration – in my *Revolutionary Politics* (pp. 490–96), though I am now persuaded that John Marshall is correct in attributing the sole authorship of that manuscript to Locke, rather than viewing it as a jointly-authored (with James Tyrrell) work. (See Marshall's contribution to this volume.)

37 John Tillotson, *Works* (London, 1696), pp. 311–12.

38 Ibid., pp. 230, 277.

39 John Howe, *A Letter Written Out of the Country to a Person of Quality in the City* (London, 1680), pp. 43, 46. The author of *A Rational Defense of Nonconformity* also attacked Stillingfleet's alleged reputation for "moderation," complaining that he had displayed a "contempt and severity" towards the nonconformists "that was not expected from a man of his worth." Cited in Robert Todd Carroll, *The Common-Sense Philosophy of Religion of Bishop Edward Stillingfleet, 1635–1699* (The Hague, 1975), p. 29.

40 Richard Baxter, *A Second True Defence of the Meer Nonconformists* (London, 1681), preface, pp. 174, 176.

41 John Humfrey and Stephen Lobb, *A Reply to the Defence of Dr. Stillingfleet* (London, 1682), preface, p. 2.

42 Humfrey, *Answer to Stillingfleet*, p. 38.

43 Seaton, *Theory of Toleration*, p. 201. For the evidence relating to this persecuting activity, including the use of the militia against the dissenters, see G. Lyon Turner, *Original Records of Early Nonconformity under Persecution and Indulgence*, 3 vols. (London, 1911); Mullett, "Toleration and persecution; Ashcraft, *Revolutionary Politics*, pp. 24–8.

44 John Collinges, *Short Animadversions upon a Sermon Lately Preached by the Reverend Dr. Tillotson* (London, 1680), p. 20.

45 John Evans, *Moderation Stated* (London, 1682), pp. 2, 4–8, 28, 38, 40ff.

46 John Owen, *Moderation a Virtue* (London, 1683), epistle dedicatory.

47 Rolle, *Sober Answer*, preface, pp. 16–17, 31, 168.

48 Robert Ferguson, *The Interest of Reason in Religion* (London, 1675), p. 273.

49 Richard Baxter (signed by ten Nonconformist ministers), *The Judgment of Non-Conformists of the Interest of Reason in Matters of Religion* (London, 1676), p. 1.

50 Ferguson, *Interest*, pp. 62, 272.

51 Ibid., pp. 20–21, 56–58, 171, 234; John Owen, *The Reason of Faith* (London, 1677), pp. 4, 25, 93; Baxter, *Judgment*, pp. 10, 12.

52 Charles Wolseley, *The Reasonableness of Scripture-Belief* (London, 1672), p. 73; Robert Ferguson, *A Sober Enquiry into the Nature, Measure, and Principle of Moral Virtue* (London, 1673), p. 59 (Ferguson's work is dedicated to Wolseley); *Interest*, p. 24.

53 Baxter, *Judgment*, p. 14; *The Second Part of the Nonconformists Plea for Peace* (London, 1680), p. 45; Wolseley, *Scripture-Belief*, p. 68.

54 Ferguson, *Sober Enquiry*, p. 273.

55 Owen, *Reason of Faith*, pp. 4, 25, 93; *Truth*, pp. 157–58, 372–74; Ferguson, *Sober Enquiry*, p. 273; Baxter, *Second Part*, p. 45; *Judgment*, pp. 12, 14, 18; Thomas Carter, *Non-Conformists No Schismaticks, No Rebels* (London, 1670), pp. 14–15; Vincent Alsop, *The Mischief of Impositions*, 2nd ed. (London,

1680), epistle dedicatory, p. 27; Wolseley, *Scripture-Belief*, epistle dedicatory, pp. 68, 73.

56 It is simply not true that "the latitudinarians were peculiarly concerned with the development of rational proofs in the realm of religion," which is Shapiro's explanation for excluding from her work all evidence relating to the nonconformists' views on the subject. *Probability*, p. 14.

57 Ferguson, *Interest*, pp. 56–58; Owen, *Reason of Faith*, pp. 4, 90; Wolseley, *Scripture-Belief*, epistle dedicatory.

58 Ferguson, *Sober Enquiry*, epistle dedicatory, pp. 51, 57, 59–60, 168; *Interest*, p. 234; Owen, *Reason of Faith*, pp. 4, 25; *Truth*, p. 188; Baxter, *Judgment*, p. 14; *Second Part*, pp. 10, 15, 45; *Second True Defence*, p. 88; *The Judgment of Non-Conformists about the Difference Between Grace and Morality* (London, 1676), p. 7; Humfrey, *Case of Conscience*, p. 5; *The Authority of the Magistrate about Religion Discussed* (London, 1672), p. 72; John Howe, *The Reconcileableness of God's Prescience of the Sins of Men with the Wisdom and Sincerity of His Counsels...* (London, 1677), pp. 94–95.

59 Owen, *Reason of Faith*, p. 93; *Truth*, pp. 372–4.

60 Howe, *Reconcileableness*, pp. 94–95.

61 Carter, *No Schismaticks*, p. 17; John Owen, *Indulgence and Toleration Considered* (London, 1667), pp. 12, 22; William Penn, *The Reasonableness of Toleration and the Unreasonableness of Penal Laws and Tests* (London, 1687), pp. 3, 9–10, 12; *The Great Case of Liberty of Conscience* (1670), in *The Select Works of William Penn*, 4th ed., 3 vols. (London, 1825), Vol. II, p. 140; Humfrey, *Authority*, pp. 72, 91; Baxter, *Second Part*, p. 53; Robert Ferguson, *A Representation of the Threatening Dangers, Impending over Protestants in Great Britain* (n.p. 1688), p. 36. For Locke's statement of this position in the *Letter Concerning Toleration*, and a discussion of the relationship of that work to the dissenters' arguments, see John Locke, *The Works of John Locke*, 12th ed. 9 vols. (London, 1824), Vol. V, pp. 9, 21–29, 41–44, 47–48, 53; Ashcraft, *Revolutionary Politics*, pp. 467–520.

62 Howe, *Letter*, p. 22; Owen, *Truth*, pp. 100–1, 313; Ferguson, *Sober Enquiry*, pp. 175–76; Humfrey, *Answer to Stillingfleet*, pp. 14–15; Humfrey and Lobb, *Reply to Defence*, p. 78.

63 Owen, *Reason of Faith*, pp. 4, 70–78, 163–64; *Truth*, p. 113; Baxter, *Judgment*, pp. 12, 14; Alsop, *Mischief*, epistle dedicatory, p. 47.

64 Owen, *Indulgence*, p. 16. If one allows the clergy "to propose to the people what they ought to believe" simply because "they are invested with authority and jurisdiction," and, moreover, to identify their proposed beliefs with "reason," then, a contemporary warned his readers, you may as well suppose that you are only a Christian "because the Church (meaning the clergy) tells you so." *The Reformed Papist, or High-Church Man* (London, 1681), p. 3.

65 Carter, *No Schismaticks*, p. 14; Baxter, *Judgment*, p. 18; Owen, *Truth*, pp. 253ff.

66 Ferguson, *Sober Enquiry*, pp. 56–58, 60, 94, 276; Owen, *Truth*, pp. 188, 253–57; Humfrey, *Authority*, pp. 72, 117; Howe, *Reconcileableness*, pp. 94–5; cf. *Postscript*, pp. 40–42 (separately paginated).

67 Parker, *Discourse*, pp. 6–7, 28, 262–65, 300–1, 312–13, 318; Glanvill, *Zealous*, pp. 27–29; Fowler, *Principles*, p. 330; Thomas Sprat, *Sermon* (January 29, 1682), (London, 1682); cf. Marshall, "Ecclesiology," p. 409.

68 Owen, *Truth*, p. 70.
69 Humfrey, *Authority*, pp. 44, 67–70; Ferguson, *Interest*, p. 433. On the charges of Hobbism directed against Stillingfleet and Tillotson, and generally on the relationship between Hobbes's ideas and those of the latitudinarians, see Marshall, "Ecclesiology," pp. 407–27.
70 Simon Patrick, *Sermon* (London, 1686), pp. 26–27, 36.
71 Tillotson, *Works*, p. 220 (mispaginated).
72 Parker, *Discourse*, p. 280; Edward Stillingfleet, *The Unreasonableness of Separation* (London, 1681), pp. 309, 330–31; cf. Thomas Pittis, *An Old Way of Ending New Controversies* (London, 1682), pp. 38–40; William Sherlock, *A Vindication of the Rights of Ecclesiastical Authority* (London, 1685), pp. 137, 151–53; Thomas Long, *The Character of a Separatist* (London, 1677), epistle dedicatory. "There is no principle of the Reformation more undoubted than" that the people ought to follow the direction of their pastors, viz, those persons "appointed to be their instructors and guides." Thus, in place of a reliance upon the individual's private judgment, "the order, disposition, form, and manner" of religious worship must be "determined by the wisdom of the governors of the church." Simon Patrick, *Sermon* (December 22, 1680), (London, 1680), pp. 67–69, 100–3.
73 John Howe, *The Case of the Protestant Dissenters, Represented and Argued* (London, 1689), pp. 2–3. "I affirm that it is out of the power of any man to make another a representative for himself in matters of religion, much less can another make one for him, since nobody can give another man authority to determine in what way he should worship God Almighty." Locke MS c. 34, fol. 122. This is a direct reply by Locke to Stillingfleet's argument in *The Unreasonableness of Separation*.
74 George Care, *A Reply to the Answer of the Man of No Name* (London, 1685), p. 15; Penn, *Liberty of Conscience*, p. 141.
75 Locke, *Works*, Vol. V, p. 25; cf. pp. 10–11; Penn, *Reasonableness*, p. 9.
76 By liberty of conscience, Penn wrote, "we understand not only a mere liberty of the mind, in believing or disbelieving this or that principle or doctrine; but the exercise of ourselves in a visible way of worship." *Liberty of Conscience*, p. 134. "It is vain," Owen declared, "to pretend that conscience is not concerned in the practice of the worship of God." *Indulgence*, pp. 4, 13; cf. Owen, *Truth*, pp. 251–53, 256–57; Ferguson, *Sober Enquiry*, p. 170; Carter, *No Schismaticks*, p. 14.
77 George Care, *Liberty of Conscience Asserted and Vindicated* (London, 1689), p. 20; Humfrey, *Case of Conscience*, pp. 5, 10; Owen, *Truth*, p. 118. As Glanvill observed, "liberty of practice" is "the thing in dispute," and the crucial element of any legitimization of religious toleration, which he, and most other latitudinarians opposed. *Zealous*, pp. 26–27. Stillingfleet was equally careful to insist that "I would not be mistaken, it is the liberty of judgment I plead for, and not of practice." Edward Stillingfleet, *The Reformation Justified* (London, 1674), pp. 26–27; cf. Tillotson, *Works*, p. 311; Parker, *Discourse*, pp. 91–92, 95, 316–18; William Assheton, *Toleration Disapproved and Condemned* (Oxford, 1670), p. 20; Seaton, *Theory of Toleration*, pp. 90–91.
78 Humfrey, *Answer to Stillingfleet*, p. 21.
79 Viewing the entire spectrum of dissent and the period, 1660–89, as a whole, the

political positions adopted by nonconformists were more heterogeneous than this statement suggests. The controversy generated by Stillingfleet in the 1680s, however, helped to unite the Dissenters on this issue. In *The Unreasonableness of Separation*, Stillingfleet attempted to rest his defense of established authority in church and state on the notion of "general consent," without tying his argument to "a democratical form" of the church or to any idea of popular sovereignty that allowed "the people to resume the liberty of elections," according to some theory of natural right (pp. 135, 309, 328). In their replies, Baxter, Humfrey, Alsop, and others emphasized the confused status of "consent" in relation to religious and political authority in Stillingfleet's argument, which, in turn, I am arguing, reinforced the consistency in their employment of that concept, as I have indicated in the text. See Baxter, *Second True Defence*, Alsop, *Mischief*, and especially, Humfrey, *Answer to Stillingfleet*.

80 Parker, *Discourse*, pp. 6–7, 28–29, 114, 262–65; Glanvill, *Zealous*, pp. 28–29; Patrick, *Sermon*, pp. 67–69, 100–3; Fowler, *Principles*, p. 330; Tomkins, *Modern Pleas*, p. 151.

81 Humfrey, *Answer to Stillingfleet*, pp. 15, 19. See Locke's discussion in the *Letter Concerning Toleration* of the natural fellowship of Christian charity obtaining amongst individuals and churches where no superior/inferior relationship exists. *Works*, Vol. V, pp. 18ff.

82 Owen, *Moderation a Virtue*, p. 60.

83 John Locke, *Two Treatises of Government*, ed. Peter Laslett (Cambridge: Cambridge Univ. Press, 1967), *Second Treatise*, par. 128.

84 Ferguson, *Representation*, p. 36; Owen, *Truth*, pp. 258–60; William Penn, *Some Free Reflections upon the Occasion of the Public Discourse about Liberty of Conscience* (London, 1687), pp. 10, 20. Individuals in the state of nature have a "natural and evangelical right" to freedom of religious worship and toleration of their differences in the practise of that worship. Locke MS c. 34, fol. 101; Locke, *Works*, Vol. V, pp. 53–54, 212.

85 Although, given the tendency of some cultural historians (e.g., Westfall, *Science and Religion*, Shapiro, *Probability*) to view Locke as the spokesman for the intellectual synthesis of science, religion, and political theory they attribute to latitudinarianism, what does need to be emphasized is Locke's defense of the political perspective of the nonconformists on the issue of toleration. But, as I have suggested, this represents more than a minor disagreement about the application of commonly shared opinions. It is true, as Marshall remarks in his contribution to this volume, that Locke owned the works of the latitudinarians, that some of them (Tillotson) were his friends, and that their writings (especially those of earlier latitudinarians, such as Chillingworth) exercised an influence on his intellectual development. What is also true is that Locke's library contained many more works by nonconformists, that many of them (Howe, Ferguson, Owen, William Kiffin, John Collins) were his close friends, and that he wrote or defended himself against the position adopted by such latitudinarians as Stillingfleet (in the manuscript reply to the *Unreasonableness* and the controversy over the *Essay Concerning Human Understanding*) and John Norris (*The Reasonableness of Christianity*). The fact is, as Marshall recognizes, there is nothing in the writings of the latitudinarians that matches Locke's radical anti-clericalism in his political and religious writings, his

doctrinal reduction of Christianity to a simple belief in *The Reasonableness of Christianity*, or his defense of revolutionary political action in the *Two Treatises of Government* (cf. Cragg, *Puritanism*, p. 126, and my *Revolutionary Politics, passim*). Yet, *all* of these important elements of Locke's thought appear in the writings of the nonconformists during the Restoration. If, in addition, as I have suggested, the arguments relating to epistemology, science, and rational theology contained in those writings were examined with some care, then we might have a reasonable picture of Locke's place with respect to the development of the cultural and political consciousness of Restoration England. This will never be possible, however, if this evidence is ignored or excluded simply in order to fit Locke into the latitudinarianism, science, toleration hypothesis.

86 Humfrey, *Authority*, p. 91; Owen, *Indulgence*, p. 12; Penn, *Liberty of Conscience*, p. 140; *Reasonableness*, pp. 3, 10, 12, 35–36.

87 Carter, *No Schismaticks*, p. 18; Penn, *Reasonableness*, pp. 33–36; Howe, *Protestant Dissenters*, pp. 1–2; Baxter, *Second Part*, pp. 15, 53; cf. Lacey, *Dissent*, p. 184. For the political implications of this exercise of "force without authority," see Ashcraft, *Revolutionary Politics*, ch. 10.

8   The intellectual sources of Robert Boyle's
      philosophy of nature: Gassendi's
      voluntarism and Boyle's physico-theological
      project

Margaret J. Osler

Robert Boyle (1627–91), an influential proponent of the new science in seventeenth-century England, articulated a philosophy of nature which has come to be the focus of considerable scholarly attention.[1] Boyle's corpuscularianism, his voluntarism, empiricism, and latitudinarianism,[2] as well as his considerable contemporary reputation, have made his work a convenient locus for the examination of questions about the relationships among natural philosophy, religion, and society in the turbulent period of English history and intellectual life during which he lived. Historians have variously sought the roots of Boyle's ideas in Calvinist theology, medieval voluntarism and nominalism, Old Testament imagery, and the Hermetic tradition.[3] James R. Jacob, in a number of extended discussions, has argued that Boyle's philosophy of nature, his latitudinarianism, and the theological and philosophical underpinnings of these views resulted from his response to the ideological conflicts present in seventeenth-century English society.[4] While all of these factors may have influenced Boyle's thought to one degree or another, the most central fact about Boyle is that he was a natural philosopher whose primary concerns were the defense of the mechanical philosophy against philosophical and theological detractors and its extension to encompass chemistry within its domain.[5]

As a second generation mechanical philosopher, Boyle derived many of his ideas from the founding fathers of this philosophy of nature, René Descartes (1596–1650) and Pierre Gassendi (1592–1655). Many of the issues that troubled Boyle and many of the ways he conceptualized his version of the mechanical philosophy bear the mark of the debates and conflicts that surrounded the development of the mechanical philosophy earlier in the century. In particular, it is clear that a number of Boyle's claims about the theological and epistemological ramifications of his corpuscularianism are remarkably similar to Gassendi's views on these questions. The fact that Boyle's ideas had deep historical roots weakens Jacob's claim that particular ideological concerns played a primary role in the formation of Boyle's thought. Boyle may well have written various treatises in response to political conflicts of his day, and his providential

178

corpuscularianism may have been utilized, by himself and others, to support a particular ideological position. His philosophy of nature, however, was formulated for different ends, ends dictated by intellectual and theological concerns which characterized debates about the mechanical philosophy from the time of its first enunciation. Boyle adapted ideas articulated earlier in the century in a different country and a vastly different political climate to his own purposes. In particular, Boyle shared many of Gassendi's concerns about the mechanical philosophy, and he adopted many of the same concepts and formulations in articulating his own version of this philosophy of nature. Whether Boyle's corpuscularianism derived from his direct reading of Gassendi or whether Gassendi's ideas were widely disseminated in mid-seventeenth-century English thought and thus "in the air" and available for Boyle's use, the marked similarity between Boyle's corpuscularianism and Gassendi's version of the mechanical philosophy coupled with the documented fact that Boyle was directly familiar with Gassendi's project to Christianize Epicureanism lend credence to the claim that Boyle drew heavily on Gassendi's ideas in formulating his own philosophy of nature.

Gassendi is best known for producing a Christianized version of Epicurean philosophy in order to provide metaphysical foundations for the new science. He thereby introduced the physics and ethics of this Greek atomist into the mainstream of European thought.[6] Epicurus (341–270 B.C.) had articulated his atomism in the context of his ethical hedonism. Arguing that the proper aim of life is to maximize pleasure and to minimize pain and that the greatest sources of mental pain are fear of the gods and fear of punishment in life after death, Epicurus created a philosophy of nature in which the gods play no role and according to which the soul is material and mortal. Accordingly, nature consists of an infinite number of uncreated and indestructible atoms moving in infinite void space. The world and the objects composing it are the result of chance collisions between moving atoms; and the human soul, consisting of the swiftest and subtlest of the atoms, dissipates at death.[7] The eternal duration of atoms and the unending sequence of worlds, infinite in both directions of time, violated the Christian doctrine of creation. The role of chance and the random swerve or *clinamen* which Epicurus ascribed to atoms in order to account for their collisions denied the possibility of any providential understanding of nature and human history. And the corporeality and mortality of the soul violated a most fundamental Christian doctrine.[8] Consequently, the Epicurean philosophy had suffered an eclipse in Christian Europe. Gassendi, a Catholic priest, wished to adopt Epicurean atomism in order to provide foundations for the new science; but he perceived the need to expunge it of its heterodox assertions. He denied the Epicurean doctrines of the eternity of the world, the infinitude of atoms, and the existence of the *clinamen* random swerve of the atoms.[9] He also took great pains to emphasize God's providential relationship to the creation and to argue for the immortality of the human soul.[10] This baptized version of Epicureanism provided a mechanical view of nature according to which all phenomena (excluding those involving the human soul) could be explained in terms of matter and motion.

A central feature of Gassendi's philosophy is his voluntarist theology. Voluntarism derives from an emphasis on God's free will and omnipotence in contrast to his intellect and omniscience. According to this view, God's will is absolute, and nothing can impede it. God created the world absolutely freely, and it continues to exist contingent on his will. Consequently, the created world contains no element of necessity. He can create regularities – laws of nature – and he can alter them at will. There can be no rational order independent of God: such entities as Platonic forms or Cartesian eternal truths world limit God's freedom by entailing a certain necessity in the creation. Lack of necessity in the world implies that *a priori*, demonstrative knowledge of the creation is not possible. Thus a nominalist ontology and an empiricist epistemology are regular concomitants of voluntarist theology. This cluster of ideas had a long history in the middle ages; for the history of science, it began in important ways with the condemnations of 1277.[11]

Gassendi held a voluntarist understanding of God's relationship to the creation, and this theological view formed the basis for his epistemological and ontological foundations for science.[12] Gassendi believed that God created the world and that he continues to rule it with "general providence and also special providence for humanity."[13] His emphasis on providence and divine freedom led him to argue frequently and vigorously against the Epicurean doctrine of chance and the Stoic doctrine of fate.[14] God is free from any restrictions in his relationship to the creation: "there is nothing in the universe which God cannot destroy, nothing which he cannot produce; nothing which he cannot change, even into its opposite qualities."[15] Hence there can be nothing like fate capable of limiting God in the free exercise of his will. God is free to do anything he wants except violate the law of non-contradiction.[16]

God's omnipotence finds expression not only in his freedom to act but also in his providential relationship to the creation. An important expression of divine providence, according to Gassendi, is design in the world. In objecting to Descartes' use of the ontological argument, Gassendi spoke warmly of

the royal road, smooth and easy to follow, by which one comes to recognize the existence of God, his power, his wisdom, his goodness, and his other attributes, which is nothing other than the marvelous working of the universe, which proclaims its author by its grandeur, its divisions, its variety, its order, its beauty, its constancy, and its other particularities.[17]

Gassendi's attraction to the argument from design is manifest from the frequent references to the design and order of nature scattered throughout the *Syntagma Philosophicum*.

Gassendi's appeal to the argument from design led him to argue in favor of admitting final causes in natural philosophy. He thought that we need to consider them in order to recognize God as creator and governor of the universe. Without admitting final causes, we might be tempted to regard the universe as the product of chance.[18] God's ends are frequently knowable to us, a conclusion Gassendi reached from the consideration of many features of human anatomy and physiology.[19] It is even the case that final causes are sometimes easier to know than efficient causes, as for example the valves of the heart: their purpose is clear, but their manner of formation is not readily known.[20] For Gassendi, there was no inconsistency between his claim that final causes find a place in natural philosophy and his empirical approach to knowledge. They both derive from the theological exigencies within which his mechanical philosophy was framed.

For the voluntarist, the argument from design had the advantage that it was consistent with his empiricist approach to scientific knowledge: it is, in essence, an empirical argument, based on empirical evidence; and it encourages the practice of science in the name of religion. These themes found a prominent place in Boyle's thought.

Gassendi was not a deist, and he did not restrict God's power and concerns to the act of creation. The world does not run on immanent principles of any kind, but depends on God absolutely for its continued existence.[21] Although God does make use of second causes in running the world, they have no real autonomy and ultimately depend on his will. God established the laws of nature, but he is not bound by them and can violate them at will.[22]

Consonant with his voluntarism, Gassendi was a nominalist and an empiricist. He believed that all our ideas come from experience. "All the ideas which are contained in the mind derive their origin from the senses ... The intellect or mind is a *tabula rasa* in which nothing is engraved or represented [prior to sensation]."[23] Because his nominalism precludes the existence of essences or natures, natural philosophy becomes a "science of appearances."[24]

It is thus that the all-powerful good Lord seems to have established the creation and left it to our use. It is in fact all that is necessary for us to know about each thing: he has revealed it to us, giving properties to things, permitting us to recognize them, and diverse senses by which we apprehend them and an interior faculty permitting us to judge them. But as for that which is the interior nature, ... since that is the thing which is not necessary to know, he wished that it would be hidden from us; and when we presumptuously pretend to know it, we bear the pain in full measure.[25]

Gassendi acknowledged the human yearning for deeper knowledge of essences, but he also recognized the futility of such a quest: " ... not that it does not appear beautiful and desirable to know that, but that is the same manner in which it is good and desirable for us ... to have wings or to remain forever young."[26]

This science of appearances leads to knowledge that is at best highly probable. Gassendi walked a middle road between what he perceived as the prejudice of the skeptics, who would deny the possibility of any knowledge, and the dogma of the Aristotelians who claimed certainty as the product of their science.[27] Voluntarism, nominalism, and empiricism formed the main themes of Gassendi's philosophy and were decisive factors in the formation of his atomic view of nature.[28]

Although Gassendi was not the only advocate of a mechanical philosophy of nature, his thought was very influential on English natural philosophers and particularly on Robert Boyle.[29] Gassendi's writings were transmitted to the English speaking world largely through the paraphrases of Walter Charleton, which were published in the 1650s. Charleton's *Physiologia Epicuro-Gassendo-Charltoniana* (London, 1654) is a very close paraphrase of Gassendi's short resumé of Epicurean philosophy, *Philosophiae Epicuri Syntagma* (1649). His *Darkness of Atheism Dispelled by the Light of Nature: A Physico-Theological Treatise* (London, 1652) is a thorough elaboration of Gassendi's voluntarist understanding of divine providence. And Charleton's *The Immortality of the Soul* (1657) is an accurate rendering of Gassendi's views on this subject. Boyle was familiar both with Gassendi's own works and with Charleton's rendition of them.[30] There are numerous references to Gassendi scattered throughout Boyle's writings. Many of them are to Gassendi's scientific work, especially in astronomy. But many of them refer to details of his mechanical explanations of particular phenomena. He refers to Gassendi as the "best interpreter" of Epicurus' works.[31] Kargon argues, on the basis of close comparison of texts, that Boyle acquired his knowledge of Gassendi from Charleton.[32] It is interesting to note, however, that whereas Boyle directly cited Gassendi's writings over fifty times throughout his *Works*, the only direct citations to Charleton in Boyle's *Works* are in letters other people wrote to Boyle. Although Boyle was not a slavish follower of Gassendi and, in fact, took many ideas from Descartes and refused to judge between the two founding fathers on the metaphysical questions of the existence of the void and the infinite divisibility of matter,[33] his familiarity with Gassendi's ideas is clearly demonstrable.

Boyle's writings, as a whole, can be best understood in the context of the seventeenth-century quest for a philosophy of nature to replace the Aristotelianism that had lost credibility in the wake of the Copernican Revolution, the skeptical crisis,[34] the protestant Reformation, and the humanist revival of alternative ancient philosophies of nature. By the middle of the seventeenth century, there was an active competition among several of these philosophies of nature. The mechanical philosophers, influenced by Descartes and Gassendi, advocated a mechanical analogy to explicate the phenomena of nature. Followers of Paracelsus espoused a chemical philosophy, which endeavored to account for natural phenomena in terms of a more or less occult, holistic, chemical metaphor.[35] And, of course, despite the successes of the new science, there remained firmly entrenched Aristotelians. Although the mechanical philosophy eventually came to dominate scientific thinking, in the middle of the seventeenth century, the outcome of this competition was far from clear.[36] The points of contention were as much theological as they were scientific; and, as Jacob argues, they frequently involved political ideology as well.[37]

From his earliest writings on natural philosophy (1649–53), Boyle favored the mechanical philosophy.[38] Drawing on both Gassendi's Christianized version of Epicurean atomism and Descartes' mechanical philosophy and departing from each in certain crucial ways, Boyle elaborated his own "corpuscular hypothesis" to explain the phenomena of the physical – and most especially chemical – world. The bulk of his scientific writings have a dual thrust: to provide empirical and experimental support for his corpuscularianism[39] and to render chemistry as respectable as her sister sciences, astronomy, mechanics, and optics, which had been so successfully wedded to mechanical principles. This latter task was complex and difficult because of the occult alchemical and Paracelsian associations that chemical thinking had acquired historically.[40]

The basic tenets of Boyle's corpuscular philosophy are well known. *The Origin of Forms and Qualities* (1666) contains his most succinct and coherent account of his position. The most fundamental assertion of his – and every other – version of the mechanical philosophy is that all physical (that is, not spiritual) phenomena can be explained in terms of matter and motion. All the different kinds of matter encountered in the world can be reduced to "one catholick or universal matter common to all bodies, by which I mean substance, extended, divisible, impenetrable."[41] Since matter is inactive, it cannot be the source of diversity and change. Another principle, motion, is needed.[42] With the two ontological components of the physical universe, matter and motion, in hand, Boyle proceeded to describe the manner in which matter is formed into the substances we daily encounter. Bypassing the metaphysical question of whether indivisible, Epicurean atoms exist, Boyle described the microscopic structure of the material world. Matter is composed of tiny particles which lie below the threshold of sense and which, though divisible in principle, are hardly ever divided. These he called *minima naturalia*. The *minima naturalia* form clusters which combine to form macroscopic bodies. The shape, size, and motions of the clusters and their constituent *minima* cause the qualities and changes observed in material objects.[43] Different kinds of substances are formed by different arrangements of the particles composing the clusters that unite to form bodies. And changes in bodies occur when the composition or arrangement of the clusters changes.

He then proceeded to demonstrate how the Aristotelian accounts of form, substantial forms, and generation and corruption could be recast in corpuscular terms or eliminated altogether in accounting for the physical world.[44] Given the ontological framework of the mechanical world, Boyle then sought a theoretical account of the chemical substances and processes which he understood from his laboratory experience.

While Boyle's scientific writings were largely devoted to providing support for his corpuscularianism and for applying it to chemical phenomena, like almost all the other seventeenth-century mechanical philosophers, Boyle found himself having to defend his views against charges that natural philosophy in general would become a serious distraction from religion and that the mechanical philosophy in particular would lead to atheism and materialism. Most of his theological writings can be understood as his defense of his corpuscularianism against these charges. Examination of his extensive writings on theological topics illustrates this point repeatedly. In *Some Considerations Touching the Usefulness of Experimental Natural Philosophy* (1663),[45] Boyle argued against the charge that the pursuit of natural philosophy turns men into "enemies of the being and providence of God."[46] Far from fostering atheism, the study of nature reveals God's aims in the creation, and it renders visible the divine attributes, God's power, wisdom, and goodness.[47] Moreover, it discloses so much evidence for design in nature, that it simultaneously leads to admiration for the designer[48] and refutes those Epicureans who would ascribe everything in nature to chance.[49] These ideas are developed further in his late treatise, *The Christian Virtuoso: Shewing, That, by being addicted to Experimental Philosophy, a man is rather assisted than indisposed to be a good Christian* (1690).[50]

Boyle elaborated this theme in *The Excellency of Theology, Compared to Natural Philosophy (As Both are Objects of Men's Study)* (1674).[51] In this work he argued that although natural philosophy leads inevitably to the knowledge of God, knowledge thus acquired is not complete but must be supplemented by revelation (as provided by scripture) which contains a more thorough account of the attributes of God and the history of his actions.[52] Furthermore, certain tenets of religion – the existence of angels and human souls, the creation and resurrection of man, and the end of the world – can only be known by revelation. In this way, Boyle denied that natural philosophy can stand alone and supplant religion. In several treatises, Boyle addressed the question of the relationship between reason and religion.[53] Claiming that reason can lead to awareness of its own limits, he argued that any conflict between reason and revelation can be avoided by frank acknowledgement of which conclusions can be derived from natural reason without revelation and which lie beyond reason.[54]

In addressing the major tasks of articulating his corpuscularian philosophy and defending it against charges of materialism and atheism, Boyle developed a complex position that provided philosophical and theological foundations for his philosophy of nature. These foundations consisted of a voluntarist understanding of God's relationship to the creation and of providence, a nominalist ontology, and an empiricist approach to scientific knowledge.

Central to Boyle's theology, metaphysics, and natural philosophy was his solidly voluntarist conception of God's relationship to the creation. Accordingly, the laws of nature are what they are because God created them so; it is not the case that he created them because they are true; and he can alter them at will. Miracles are evidence of his acting freely, since nothing, not even the laws of nature, can obstruct God from exercising his will freely:

if we consider God as the author of the universe, and the free establisher of the laws of motion, whose general concourse is necessary to the conservation and efficacy of every particular physical agent, we cannot but acknowledge, that, by with-holding his concourse, or changing these laws of motion, which depend perfectly upon his will, he may invalidate most, if not all the axioms and theorems of natural philosophy: there supposing the course of nature, and especially the established laws of motion among the parts of the universal matter, as those upon which all the phenomena depend. It is a rule in natural philosophy, that *causae necessariae semper agunt quantum possunt*; but it will not follow from thence, that the fire must necessarily burn *Daniel's* three companions ... when the author of nature was pleased to withdraw his concourse to the operation of the flames, or supernaturally to defend against them the bodies, that were exposed to them ... though it be unreasonable to believe a miraculous effect, when attributed only to a mere physical agent; yet the same thing may reasonably be believed, when ascribed to God, or to agents assisted with his absolute or supernatural power.[55]

Time and again, throughout his works, Boyle alluded to God's freedom in creating the world and to his power over the laws of nature:[56] " the laws of nature, as they were at first arbitrarily instituted by God, so, in reference to him, they are but arbitrary still."[57]

Consistent in his voluntarism Boyle was a nominalist, and his nominalism directly informed both his philosophy of nature and his scientific method. Boyle's major treatise, *A Free Inquiry Into the Vulgarly Received Notion of Nature* (1685/6),[58] articulated and defended his corpuscularianism in the context of his voluntarist understanding of God's relationship to the creation.[59] He argued that the alternative philosophies of nature associated with Aristotelians, Platonists, Hermeticists, Paracelsians do not allow enough scope for divine will. The "vulgarly received notion of nature" offended Boyle's voluntarist sensibilities precisely because it interposed another order of being between God and his creation.[60] Denying the existence of or the need for any agents mediating between God and the individuals he created, Boyle was quite explicit in his nominalism:

for aught I can clearly discern, whatsoever is performed in the merely material world, is really done by particular bodies, acting according to the laws of motion, rest, &c. that are settled and maintained by God among things corporeal[61]

Among the agents intermediate between God and the material world which Boyle explicitly rejected were the Chance of the Epicureans and the Fate of the Stoics. His grounds for rejecting each of these were that they interfered with the free exercise of divine will and that they presupposed the existence of some kind of intermediate agent. Boyle considered chance to be a poor substitute for providence, which he regarded as one manifestation of divine wisdom and power.[62] Similarly, fate was an illegitimately reified notion; simply expressing the causal nexus of the created world.[63]

Boyle's nominalistic rejection of the "vulgarly received notion of nature" was in keeping with his rejection of substantial forms and real qualities in the context of his corpuscularian chemistry. In his most abstract presentation of his corpuscularian philosophy, *The Origin of Forms and Qualities*, Boyle devoted twelve pages to "An Examen of the Origin and Doctrine of Substantial Forms." Arguing that all of the properties of material objects can be explained in terms of the properties of matter, Boyle stated that substantial forms, like the "vulgarly received notion of nature" would be entities above and beyond the matter and motion, out of which Boyle believed that God created the universe. He found them useless, unintelligible, and physically incomprehensible.[64] In fact, he argued, working chemists, of whatever philosophical persuasion, actually employed a nominalistic method when dealing with the problem of classifying chemical substances.

And if you ask men, what they mean by a ruby, or nitre, or a pearl, they will still make you such answers, that you may perceive, that whatever men talk in theory of substantial forms, yet that, upon whose account they really distinguish any one body from others, and refer it to this or that species of bodies, is nothing but an aggregate or convention of such accidents as most men do by a kind of agreement (for the thing is more arbitrary than we are aware of) think necessary or sufficient to make a portion of the universal matter belong to this or that determinate genus or species of natural bodies.[65]

Boyle's nominalism extended beyond theory into chemical practice. Rejecting the Aristotelian elements and Paracelsian principles as being as useless as substantial forms,[66] Boyle employed laboratory experiments to determine the particular set of accidents that defined each sort of matter.[67] His procedure for classifying substances was an entirely nominalist enterprise.

And since to every determinate species of bodies there doth belong more than one quality, and for the most part a concurrence of many is so essential to that sort of bodies, that the want of any one of them is sufficient to exclude it from belonging to that species; as the chymists' *Luna fixa*, which they tell us wants not the weight, the malleableness, nor the fixedness of gold, nor any other property of gold, except the yellowness (which makes them call it white gold) would by reason of that want of colour be easily known from true gold.[68]

In short, the nominalism which informed Boyle's philosophy of nature generally and which derived directly from his voluntarist theology was entirely compatible with his approach to chemistry. As McGuire has noted, Boyle started writing *The Notion of Nature* in 1666 at the same time that he wrote *The Origin of Forms and Qualities*, and Boyle saw the two enterprises as thoroughly consistent.[69] I would take the argument a step further and say that *The Notion of Nature* provided the theological and philosophical underpinnings for the corpuscular philosophy that lay at the heart of all of Boyle's work in natural philosophy.

If nominalism is the usual ontological concomitant of voluntarist theology, then empiricism is its epistemological consequent. In this respect, Boyle's thought fit perfectly into the tradition. In an early, unpublished manuscript which deals with questions of method in natural philosophy, Boyle emphasized that the grounds for evaluating scientific statements are intelligibility, simplicity, explanatory scope, and predictive power and success.[70] Moreover, the degree to which a theory is confirmed can be measured by the number of different kinds of observed facts it successfully explains.[71] These are the grounds of a thoroughly empiricist thinker.

Boyle acknowledged that an empirically based natural philosophy could not attain certainty; and he classified different kinds of knowledge according to the degree of certainty they reached.[72]

as a moral certainty (such as we may attain about the fundamentals of religion) is enough in many cases for a wise man, and even a philosopher to acquiesce in; so that physical certainty, which is pretended for the truths demonstrated by naturalists, is, or even when it is rightfully claimed, but an inferior kind or degree of certainty, (that is, a certainty upon a supposition, that the principles of physick be true), not a metaphysical certainty, (wherein it is absolutely impossible, that the thing believed should be other than true).[73]

The results of natural philosophy could attain, at best "physical certainty," that is to say, a high degree of probability. In this conclusion, Boyle was at one with Gassendi. He also shared Gassendi's anti-rationalist conclusion that there is no necessary connection between the ideas in our minds and the external world.

I see no necessity, that intelligibility to a human understanding should be necessary to the truth or existence of a thing, any more than that visibility to a human eye should be necessary to the existence of an atom, or of a corpuscle of air, or of the effluviums of a loadstone... I might here observe, that even by the same sense, some creatures may discern things, that may not be perceptible to others[74]

Although Boyle never spelled out his epistemology in a systematic way, the bits and pieces that we can piece together form a fabric which is close in every detail to Gassendi's and which seems to derive from a similar theological basis.[75]

Boyle carried his empiricism into all areas of knowledge including religion. Thus he regarded revelation as a special form of empirical knowledge, though empirical nonetheless.

I do not in this discourse take experience in the strictest sense of all, but in a greater latitude, for the knowledge we have of any matter of fact, which, without owing it to ratiocination, either we acquire by the immediate testimony of our own senses and other faculties, or accrues to us by the communicated testimony of others... Since... learned men, as well as the common use, confine not the appearance of the word experience to that which is personal, but employ it in a far greater latitude, I see not, why that, which I call theological experience, may not be admitted; since the revelations, that God makes concerning what he has done, or purposes to do, so far forth as they are merely revelations, cannot be known by reasoning, but by testimony: whose being divine, and relating to theological subjects, does not alter its nature, though it give it a peculiar and supereminent authority.[76]

Boyle thought there were two grounds for knowledge of God's attributes, "the contemplation of his works, and the study of his word."[77]

Since contemplation of God's works is the study of natural philosophy and since his word consists of testimony of God's revelation to others, both sources of religious knowledge are empirical. It should be noted that Boyle did not think man could attain complete knowledge of God's attributes in this manner,

since the divine attributes which the creatures point at, are those whereof themselves have some, though but imperfect, participation, or resemblance; and since the foecundity...of the divine nature is such, that its excellencies may be participated or represented in I know not how many ways; how can we be sure, that so perfect and exuberant a Being may not have excellencies, that it hath not expressed or adumbrated in the visible world, or any parts of it, that are known to us?[78]

Nevertheless, what we can know of God's attributes, and consequently of religious doctrine, is known through experience of one kind or another.

Not surprisingly, Boyle placed a heavy emphasis on the argument from design.[79] Indeed, the promise of discovering design in the natural world was one of Boyle's chief stated motives for pursuing natural philosophy.

God has couched so many things in his visible works, that, the clearer light a man has, the more he may discover of their unobvious exquisiteness, and the more clearly and distinctly he may discern those qualities, that lie more obvious. And the more wonderful things he discovers in the works of nature, the more auxiliary proofs he meets with to establish and enforce the argument, drawn from the universe and its parts, to evince that there is a God: which is a proposition of that vast weight and importance, that it ought to endear every thing to us, that is able to confirm it, and afford us new motives to acknowledge and adore the divine Author of things.[80]

Like Gassendi, Boyle saw design everywhere in nature; and knowledge of this design was a fundamental component in his providential under-standing of nature and of human life; and like Gassendi, Boyle found support for his argument from design in the possibility of knowing at least some final causes.[81] For this reason, coupled with Boyle's interpretation of revelation as a form of empirical knowledge, religious belief was, for him, an empirical and rational enterprise.

Although Boyle unambiguously recognized the limits of reason,[82] nevertheless reason played a central role in his account of religious knowledge. Indeed, he believed all of "the fundamental and necessary articles of religion to be both evident, and capable of moral dem-onstration."

And if there be any articles of religion, for which a rational and cogent proof cannot be brought, I shall for that very reason conclude, that such articles are not absolutely necessary to be believed, since it seems no way reasonable to imagine, that God having been pleased to send not only his prophets and apostles, but his only son into the world, to promulgate to mankind the Christian religion, and both to cause it to be consigned to writing, that it may be known, and to alter the course of nature by numerous miracles, that it might be believed; it seems not reasonable, I say, to imagine that he should not propose those truths, which he in so wonderful and so solemn a manner recommended, with at least so much clearness, as that studious and well-disposed readers may certainly understand such as are necessary for them to believe.[83]

This emphasis on rationality gave a prominent place to natural religion in Boyle's analysis of religious knowledge. He considered natural religion to be necessary, though not sufficient, for belief in Christianity, "as it were the stock upon which Christianity must be grafted."[84] In this spirit he rejected the Roman Catholic doctrines of transubstantiation and the infallibility of the Church on the grounds that the one contradicted sensory experience and the other demanded the abandonment of rationality.[85] "I do not think, that a Christian, to be truly so, is obliged to forego his reason; either by denying the dictates of right reason, or by laying aside the use of it."[86]

Boyle's rational and empirical understanding of religion provided the foundations for his latitudinarian sentiments. He was not wedded to the doctrinal niceties of any particular sect, but rather to truths of faith which he thought to be based on scripture interpreted in light of right reason.

it is one thing to contradict the articles or sentiments of this or that church, and (*a fortiori*) of this or that school, or particular divine; and another thing to contradict an article of faith, really delivered in the scripture ... there is not any thing in the Christian religion, that does really contradict any principle of right reason; if the principle be found, and the article rightly proposed, and duly grounded on scripture, well interpreted.[87]

Thus there is a profound consonance within Boyle's thought, a harmony among his ideas about theology, philosophy, knowledge, and religion, a harmony which is most clearly disclosed if we understand the importance of voluntarist theology as the foundations for all his views.

Boyle's ideas on these matters place him in a long tradition of philosophers and theologians, contemplating God's relationship to the creation and the influence of that relationship on the kind of knowledge of the world that it is possible for us to attain. I have argued that one important source for Boyle's views was Gassendi's version of the mechanical philosophy, with which Boyle was thoroughly acquainted. Although Jacob may be right in claiming that Boyle chose to publish particular works in response to ideologically laden political events of his day, I do not think that this explanation gives an adequate account of the sources of Boyle's ideas. Boyle created a coherent account of nature, understood on mechanical principles, and a providential interpretation of God's role in it. This view was deeply compatible with his latitudinarian sentiments, which may well have had political motives. But the political motives are not sufficient to account for Boyle's entire philosophy of nature which has deep roots in the history of the mechanical philosophy.

Notes

1 I am grateful to Betty Jo Teeter Dobbs, Barbara J. Shapiro, Martin S. Staum, J. J. MacIntosh, J'nan Morse Sellery, and Betty Flagler for providing encouragement and helpful suggestions.

2 I follow Barbara Shapiro in my definition of "latitudinarianism." According to her account, "The chief characteristics of this group, many of whom were involved in or sympathetic to natural science, were their emphasis on morality and ethics as opposed to theology, and the distinction they made between fundamentals and nonfundamentals of religion. They identified the nonfundamentals of religion with 'opinion,' and this identification led them not only to discussions of the nature of opinion but to considerations of how to construct a single church in a society where opinion was diverse... The fundamentals of religion were few: the principles of natural religion and the essentials of Christianity... Nonessentials, which included not only ceremonies, vestments, and forms of prayer but most theological doctrines, were easy to identify since substantial disagreement about a practise or proposition indicated that it was unlikely to be a fundamental... In philosophical terms... the latitudinarians attempted to take a position somewhere between skepticism and dogmatism. They rejected the skeptical position which denied the possibility of any knowledge. They also rejected a zealous dogmatism which was overly confident in opinions which, given the opportunity, would impose its opinions on others." I agree with Shapiro in her claim that the latitudinarians shared a theory of knowledge with the English natural philosophers. Barbara J. Shapiro, *Probability and Certainty in Seventeenth-century England* (Princeton, 1983), pp. 104–14.

3 See, for example, J. E. McGuire, "Boyle's Conception of Nature," *Journal of the History of Ideas* 63 (1972): 523–42; Eugene M. Klaaren, *Religious Origins of Modern Science: Belief in Creation in Seventeenth-century Thought* (Grand Rapids, Mich., 1977); Edward B. Davis, Jr., "Creation, Contingency, and Early Modern Science: The Impact of Voluntaristic Theology on Seventeenth Century Natural Philosophy" (Ph.D. Dissertation, Indiana University, 1984); Harold Fisch, *Jerusalem and Albion: The Hebraic Factor in Seventeenth-Century Literature* (London, 1964); Harold Fisch, "The scientist as priest: a note on Robert Boyle's natural theology," *Isis* 44 (1953): 252–65.

4 "For Boyle, the question of a conflict between his science and his faith scarcely arose because the latter bred the former and the grounds for both were a common social matrix and his responses to it. Where he did see conflict between faith and science, it was not between *his* faith and *his* science but

between *his* faith and *other* faiths or between *his* faith and *another* kind of science which for him was not as valid as his own ... These other faiths and this other science were also in part generated by the conditions of revolution; they represented other responses to events, responses produced by social situations in the revolution very different from Boyle's own ... He read the same meanings into nature that he learned from the revolution. Such were the dictates of the assumption of providential order in terms of which he thought. By interpreting nature in light of the lessons of experience, he arrived at a new comprehension of divine providence, God's acting in the world, the harmony of nature and history." James R. Jacob, *Robert Boyle and the English Revolution: A Study in Social and Intellectual Change* (New York, 1977), pp. 4, 6; James R. Jacob, "The ideological origins of Robert Boyle's natural philosophy," *Journal of European Studies* 2 (1972): 1–21; James R. Jacob, "Robert Boyle and subversive religion in the early Restoration," *Albion* 6 (1974): 275–93; James R. Jacob, "Boyle's circle in the protectorate: revelation, politics, and the millennium," *Journal of the History of Ideas* 38 (1977): 131–40; James R. Jacob, "Boyle's atomism and the Restoration assault on pagan naturalism," *Social Studies of Science* 8 (1978): 211–33. Jacob's thesis about the ideological origins of Boyle's philosophy of nature is part of a larger project in which he and Margaret C. Jacob are arguing "(1) that there was a territory in the debates between natural philosophers in revolutionary and post-revolutionary England in which conflicts between ideas of nature reflected ideological differences, and (2) that these conflicts, at once philosophical and ideological, created a tension and a dialectic which contributed to the origins of modern science." James R. Jacob, *Henry Stubbe, Radical Protestantism, and the Early Enlightenment* (Cambridge, 1983), p. 173. See also, James R. Jacob and Margaret C. Jacob, "The Anglican origins of modern science: the metaphysical foundations of the Whig constitution," *Isis* 71 (1980): 251–67.

5 Margaret J. Osler, "John Locke and Some Philosophical Problems in the Science of Boyle and Newton" (Ph.D. Dissertation, Indiana University, 1968).

6 For Gassendi's treatment of Epicurus' ethics and political philosophy, see L. T. Sarasohn, "The ethical and political philosophy of Pierre Gassendi," *Journal of the History of Philosophy* 20 (1982): 239–60; Lisa T. Sarasohn, "Motion and morality: Pierre Gassendi, Thomas Hobbes, and the mechanical world-view," *Journal of the History of Ideas* 46 (1985): 363–80.

7 See J. M. Rist, *Epicurus: An Introduction* (Cambridge, 1972); and Whitney J. Oates, ed., *The Stoic and Epicurean Philosophers* (New York, 1940).

8 It is interesting to note that Aristotle's philosophy also argued that the world is eternal and that the soul is mortal. It was not until Thomas Aquinas Christianized Aristotelianism that it became an acceptable philosophy in Europe; and that process was surrounded by much controversy. See Gordon Leff, *Paris and Oxford Universities in the Thirteenth and Fourteenth Centuries* (New York, 1968).

9 Pierre Gassendi, *Syntagma Philosophicum*, Pt. II, Sec. III, Bks. III, IV, V. In *Opera Omnia*, 6 vols. (Lyons, 1658; reprinted Stuttgart-/Bad Canstatt, 1964), Vol. II. All quotations from Gassendi's works are my translation, unless otherwise noted.

10 See Margaret J. Osler, "Providence and divine will in Gassendi's views on

scientific knowledge," *Journal of the History of Ideas* 44 (1983): 549–60; and Margaret J. Osler, "Baptizing Epicurean atomism: Pierre Gassendi on the immortality of the soul," in *Religion, Science, and Worldview: Essays in Honor of Richard S. Westfall*, ed. by Margaret J. Osler and Paul Lawrence Farber (Cambridge, 1985), pp. 163–84. To sum up Gassendi's argument for immortality in a few words, he claimed that the soul is not material, therefore it is immortal.

11 See Francis Oakley, *Omnipotence, Covenant, and Order: An Excursion in the History of Ideas from Abelard to Leibniz* (Ithaca, 1984); Edward Grant, "The condemnation of 1277, God's absolute power, and physical thought in the late Middle Ages," *Viator* 10 (1979): 211–44.

12 For a detailed account of Gassendi's voluntarism, see Margaret J. Osler, "Providence and divine will in Gassendi's views on scientific knowledge."

13 Pierre Gassendi, *Syntagma Philosophicum*, in *Opera Omnia*, Vol. I, p. 311.

14 Ibid., Vol. II, pp. 821–60.

15 Ibid., pp. 296–97.

16 Ibid., p. 309.

17 Pierre Gassendi, *Disquisitio Metaphysica seu Dubitationes et Instantiae adversus Renati Cartesii Metaphysicam et Responsa*, ed. and trans. into French by Bernard Rochot (Paris, 1962), pp. 302–3. My translation.

18 Ibid., pp. 406–7.

19 Ibid., pp. 408–11.

20 Ibid., pp. 410–11.

21 Pierre Gassendi, *Syntagma Philosophicum*, in *Opera Omnia*, Vol. I, p. 323.

22 Ibid., p. 309.

23 Ibid., p. 93.

24 Pierre Gassendi *Dissertations en forme de paradoxes contres les Aristotéliciens*, trans. by Bernard Rochot (Paris, 1959), p. 504. My translation.

25 Gassendi, *Disquisitio Metaphysica*, pp. 186–89.

26 Ibid., pp. 188–89.

27 Richard H. Popkin, *The History of Scepticism from Erasmus to Spinoza*, rev. ed. (Berkeley, 1979), pp. 99–109.

28 See Olivier René Bloch, *La philosophie de Gassendi: nominalisme, matérialisme, et métaphysique* (The Hague, 1971).

29 Robert Hugh Kargon, *Atomism in England from Hariot to Newton* (Oxford, 1966).

30 Kargon, ch. 8. My colleague J. J. MacIntosh has kindly shared with me an index of names he compiled from Boyle's *Works*.

31 Robert Boyle, *The Excellency of Theology, Compared with Natural Philosophy ... To Which are Annexed Some Occasional Thoughts about the Excellency and Grounds of the Mechanical Hypothesis* (1674), in *The Works of the Honourable Robert Boyle*, a new edition, edited by Thomas Birch, 6 vols. (London, 1672; reprinted Hildesheim, 1966), Vol. IV, p. 30.

32 Kargon, pp. 97–98.

33 "I have forborn to imploy arguments, that are either grounded on, or suppose indivisible corpuscles called *atoms*, or any innate motion belonging to them; or that the essence of body consists in extension, or that a vacuum is impossible; or that there are such *globulae coelestes*, or such a *materia subtilis*, as the

Cartesians imploy to extricate most of the phaenomena of nature. For these and divers other notions, I (who write rather for the Corpuscularians in general, than any party of them) thought it improper needlessly to take in..." *The Origin of Forms and Qualities* (1666), in *Works*, Vol. III, p. 7.

34 See Richard H. Popkin, *History of Scepticism*.

35 Allen G. Debus, *The Chemical Philosophy: Paracelsian Science and Medicine in the Sixteenth and Seventeenth Centuries*, 2 vols. (New York, 1977); *The English Paracelsians* (New York, 1965).

36 For two examples of just how active and complex this competition was, see Allen G. Debus, *Science and Education in the Seventeenth Century: The Webster-Ward Debate* (New York, 1970) and Thomas Harmon Jobe, "The devil in Restoration science: The Glanvill-Webster witchcraft debate," *Isis* 72 (1981): 343–56. See also, Charles Webster, *From Paracelsus to Newton: Magic and the Making of Modern Science* (Cambridge, 1982).

37 The chemical philosophy of the Paracelsians had a certain currency among the radical sects during the revolution, for example. The innate activity of matter and immanentism of this view seemed to provide support for some of the radically democratic ideologies of these groups. See Christopher Hill, *The World Turned Upside Down* (London, 1972). One must be careful, however, to distinguish between the use made of various philosophies by political groups and the reasons why philosophers formulate these views in the first place.

38 Richard S. Westfall, "Unpublished Boyle papers relating to scientific method," *Annals of Science* 12 (1956): 63–73 and 103–17.

39 In fact, it should be noted, that the mechanical philosophy, in any of its versions, is not really susceptible to empirical proof. It acts as a conceptual framework within which empirically testable theories are couched; but since it defines the ultimate terms of explanation for science, it must have an epistemological status different from that of a testable, scientific theory.

40 The standard account of Boyle's chemical work is Marie Boas, *Robert Boyle and Seventeenth-century Chemistry* (Cambridge, 1958).

41 Robert Boyle, *The Origin of Forms and Qualities, According to the Corpuscular Philosophy*, in *Works*, Vol. III, p. 15.

42 Ibid., p. 15.

43 Ibid., pp. 29–30.

44 Ibid., pp. 27–54. Boyle explicitly excluded the human soul from the physical world.

45 Boyle, *Works*, Vol. II, pp. 1–246.

46 Ibid., p. 2.

47 Ibid., pp. 15–30.

48 Ibid., p. 40. This theme was prominent in the thinking of the seventeenth-century virtuosi. See Richard S. Westfall, *Science and Religion in Seventeenth-century England* (New Haven, 1958). Harold Fisch develops this idea from a slightly different standpoint in *Jerusalem in Albion*, cited above.

49 *Some Considerations Touching the Usefulness of Experimental Natural Philosophy*, in *Works*, Vol. II, pp. 42–46.

50 Boyle, *Works*, Vol. V, pp. 508–40; Vol. VI, pp. 673–796.

51 Boyle, *Works*, Vol. IV, pp. 1–66.

52 Ibid., p. 7.

53 *Some Considerations About the Reconcileableness of Reason and Religion ... To which is annexed ... A Discourse of Mr. Boyle about the Possibility of Resurrection* (1675), in *Works*, Vol. IV, pp. 151–202; *A Discourse of Things Above Reason. Inquiring whether a Philosopher should admit there are any such. To which are Annexed by the Publisher ... some Advices about judging things, said to transcend Reason* (1681), in *Works*, Vol. IV, pp. 406–69; *Of the High Veneration Man's Intellect owes to God, Peculiarly for his Wisdom and Power* (1688), *Works*, Vol. V, pp. 130–57; *Reflections Upon a Theological Distinction. According to Which it is said, That some Articles of Faith are above Reason, but not against Reason*, in *Works*, Vol. V, pp. 541–49.

54 Boyle, *Reconcileableness of Reason and Religion*, in *Works*, Vol. IV, pp. 155–159.

55 *Reconcileableness*, in *Works*, Vol. IV, pp. 161–62. It is illuminating to compare Boyle's account of God's omnipotence and free will with Gassendi's: the two accounts are strikingly similar. See Pierre Gassendi, *Syntagma Philosophicum*, in *Opera Omnia*, Vol. I, pp. 308–11.

56 See, for example, *Notion of Nature*, in *Works*, Vol. V, p. 179.

57 *The Christian Virtuoso*, in *Works*, Vol. VI, p. 714.

58 Boyle, *Works*, Vol. V, pp. 158–254.

59 Boyle's *Notion of Nature* has been the focus of a considerable amount of scholarly debate. Jacob argues that, although Boyle wrote the treatise in 1665 or 1666, he published it in the mid-1680s, at which time it spoke directly to particular ideological issues of the day. See James R. Jacob, *Robert Boyle and the English Revolution*, ch. 4; and James R. Jacob, "Robert Boyle and subversive religion in the early Restoration," *Albion* 6 (1974): 275–93. Steneck rejects Jacob's ascription of ideological motives to Boyle, arguing instead that Boyle's treatise is addressing the neoplatonism of Henry More and the Cambridge Platonists. See Nicholas Steneck, "Greatrakes the Stroker: the interpretation of historians," *Isis* 73 (1982): 161–77. Jacob replies to Steneck's criticisms in his recent book *Henry Stubbe, Radical Protestantism, and the Early Enlightenment*, pp. 161–74. J. E. McGuire, "Boyle's conception of nature" argues, and I agree, that Boyle's *Notion of Nature* develops a conception of the laws of nature built on voluntarist theology and nominalist ontology.

60 Boyle, *Notion of Nature*, in *Works*, Vol. V, p. 162.

61 Ibid., p. 218.

62 Ibid., p. 202.

63 Ibid., pp. 220–21. Compare Boyle's rejection of Fate and Chance to Gassendi's: "it is true that the almighty God is not, as Jupiter of the fable is to the fates, subjected to things created by him, but can, by virtue of his absolute power, destroy all that he has established." *Disquisitio Metaphysica*, pp. 480–81.

64 Boyle, *The Origin of Forms and Qualities*, in *Works*, Vol. III, p. 38.

65 Ibid., p. 27.

66 Boyle, *The Sceptical Chymist*, in *Works*, Vol. I, pp. 458–651.

67 See Boas, *Robert Boyle*, ch. 7.

68 Boyle, *Origin of Forms and Qualities*, in *Works*, Vol. III, p. 28.

69 McGuire, "Boyle's conception of nature," p. 528.

70 Richard S. Westfall, "Unpublished Boyle papers relating to scientific method," *Annals of Science* 12 (1956): 116–17.

71 Boyle, *Experiments, Notes, &c. About the Mechanical Origin or Production of Divers Particular Qualities*, in *Works*, Vol. IV, p. 234. For a detailed discussion of Boyle's uses of experiment, see Steven Shapin and Simon Schaffer, *Leviathan and the Air-Pump: Hobbes, Boyle, and the Experimental Life* (Princeton, 1985).

72 For background on the question of certainty, see Henry G. van Leeuwen, *The Problem of Certainty in English Thought, 1630–1690* (The Hague, 1963). To see how these ideas were applied in many areas of seventeenth-century thought, see Barbara J. Shapiro, *Probability and Certainty in Seventeenth-Century England*.

73 Boyle, *The Excellency of Theology*, in *Works*, Vol. IV, pp. 41–42.

74 Boyle, *Advices in Judging of Things Said to Transcend Reason* (1681), in *Works*, Vol. IV, p. 450. See similar statements in *The Usefulness of Experimental Natural Philosophy*, in *Works*, Vol. III, pp. 46, 47; and *The Christian Virtuoso*, in *Works*, Vol. VI, p. 694.

75 Peter Alexander, *Ideas, Qualities, and Corpuscles: Locke and Boyle on the External World* (Cambridge, 1985) works out many of the details in Boyle's philosophical thought. Alexander, justly, finds a close resemblance between Boyle's ideas and Locke's. I would argue, further, that Gassendi was the ultimate source on which both of these thinkers relied.

76 Boyle, *The Christian Virtuoso*, in *Works*, Vol. V, p. 525. Two older works deal with Boyle's religious views in considerable detail, although neither of them deals with the kinds of issues with which this paper is primarily concerned. See, Mitchell Salem Fisher, *Robert Boyle, Devout Naturalist: A Study in Science and Religion in the Seventeenth Century* (Philadelphia: 1945) and Richard McMasters Hunt, *The Place of Religion in the Science of Robert Boyle* (Pittsburgh, 1955).

77 Boyle, *Of the High Veneration Man's Intellect owes to God, Peculiarly for his Wisdom and Power* (1688), in *Works*, Vol. V, p. 131.

78 Ibid., p. 131.

79 Boyle did not rely exclusively on the argument from design. In at least one passage, he seems to have accepted the soundness of the ontological argument. See *Advices in Judging of Things Said to Transcend Reason*, in *Works*, Vol. IV, pp, 460–62. I am grateful to Thomas M. Lennon for bringing this passage to my attention.

80 Boyle, *The Christian Virtuoso*, in *Works*, Vol. V, p. 516.

81 Robert Boyle, *A Disquisition about the Final Causes of Natural Things: Wherein it is Inquired, Whether, and (if at all) with what Cautions, a Naturalist should admit them?* (1688), in *Works*, Vol. V, p. 410.

82 Boyle, *Some Considerations About the Reconcileableness of Reason and Religion* and *A Discourse of Things above Reason*, in *Works*, Vol. IV.

83 Boyle, *The Excellency of Theology*, in *Works*, Vol. IV, p. 41.

84 Boyle, *The Christian Virtuoso*, in *Works*, Vol. VI, p. 718.

85 Robert Boyle. *Reasons Why A Protestant Should Not Turn Papist: Or, Protestant Prejudices Against the Roman Catholic Religion; proposed in a*

Letter to A Roman Priest, by a person of quality (London, 1687), pp. 17–18, 30.

86 Boyle, *Some Considerations About the Reconcileableness of Reason and Religion* (1675), in *Works*, Vol. IV, p. 157.

87 Boyle, *The Christian Virtuoso*, in *Works*, Vol. VI, p. 712. See also, *Some Considerations about the Reconcileableness of Reason and Religion*, in *Works*, Vol. IV, p. 158.

Latitudinarianism and the "ideology" of the early Royal Society: Thomas Sprat's *History of the Royal Society* (1667) reconsidered

Michael Hunter

In this chapter I intend to take a fresh look at one of the most famous texts of the scientific movement in seventeenth-century England, which, it has been said, "should also be read as a latitudinarian manifesto."[1] In part I want to consider what light is thrown on Thomas Sprat's *History of the Royal Society* by some new manuscript evidence concerning its genesis and reception which I have found, including a draft by Henry Oldenburg for the passage in which Sprat attempted to deal with problems about the repeatability of experiments noted by no less a figure than Robert Boyle,[2] and some gleanings from the manuscript remains of another prominent Fellow of the Society, John Evelyn. Of the latter, the most significant are some hints to be derived from Evelyn's correspondence with the Somerset virtuoso, John Beale, now preserved in the Evelyn Collection at Christ Church, Oxford; but the most poignant are perhaps my own notes on Evelyn's markings in his copy of Sprat's *History*, made when the book was on show at a London auction house in 1978. For the volume was stolen before the sale, and my notes may now constitute the only record of these annotations. I have therefore appended a record of them to this essay, together with a transcript of the paper by Oldenburg.

More important, however, I want to use this and other evidence to reconsider the context of Sprat's book, and especially the relationship of the views that it expresses to the opinions of the members of the Society on whose behalf it was published. A number of authors, notably Margery Purver and J. R. Jacob, have acclaimed the book as the Society's "official manifesto," representing, if not the Society's "official ideology," then at least its "public stance." They have seen the book as written "under the watchful care of the Society" and Miss Purver, in particular, has reacted strongly against the alternative view that Sprat's book was "an expression of his own or John Wilkins's private opinion."[3]

I am not going to argue that either of these positions is unreservedly true. In fact, as will become apparent in the course of this paper, I am

This chapter was first published in Michael Hunter's *Establishing the New Science: The Experience of the Early Royal Society* (Woodbridge, 1989).

199

going to suggest that the truth lies somewhere between them: that the book was commissioned by the Society, but that it was not very closely supervised. It is my contention, however, that this ambivalence has a significance in itself which has hitherto been overlooked, accounting for many of the difficulties which the Society experienced about the book at the time and which historians studying it have encountered since.

Moreover this raises a still broader issue, and this is that, in so far as the book has been taken to be – and, indeed, may have been intended to be – a statement of the Society's "ideology," it raises the question of the extent to which the Society actually *had* a corporate "ideology," and, if it did, just how coherent this was, how accurately it represented the views of the Society's members, and how indispensable it was to their view of their scientific work and its implications. Indeed, I would argue that the men who founded the Royal Society had a rather hazier view of the broad public role of science than has sometimes been thought, and that, though they tried to formulate a kind of "ideology," they found this a much more difficult task than they expected or than many modern scholars have presumed.[4]

Not the least of the implications of this concern the debate between scholars as to what kind of position the Society adopted. Was it, as J. R. Jacob has argued in an influential and widely distributed paper, an essentially positive rather than negative stance, one which not only "forestalled those who said at the time science is injurious to religion" but also gave science "an ideological edge"? Is it true that "the leading Fellows who preached a social message in the Society's name did so with a view to building a particular kind of kingdom that would serve particular ends," consciously promulgating a stance with fairly precise resonances in the political and religious thought of the day?[5]

Alternatively, is there truth in the position which Jacob has sought to modify if not to refute – namely the view classically expounded by Barbara Shapiro that the Society's position was intended as one of altruism and withdrawal, that "latitudinarian science and moderation, far from being ideological, represented the end of ideology"?[6] To us in retrospect this position may seem a naive one, but that is no reason why it should not have been genuinely held at the time. Moreover, if this was indeed the stance of those associated with the new science it would give a different and more diffuse meaning to the "latitudinarianism" of the Society than would the view adopted by Jacob, and this, in turn, may assist us in understanding the true place of the new science in contemporary society.

The Royal Society was founded in 1660 with the aim of reforming knowledge by experiment, and it is wrong to underestimate the single-minded devotion to this intellectual enterprise as the motive force behind the Society's early activities. "It aimes at the improvement of all usefull Sciences and Arts, not by meer speculations, but by exact and faithfull Observations and Experiments," as Oldenburg explained in a letter to an overseas correspondent in 1668, thereby echoing the sentiments of the Society's charter, which stated that its "studies are to be imployed for the promoting of the knowledge of natural things, and useful Arts by Experiments. To the glory of God, and the good of mankind."[7]

But although this was always the centre of the Society's perception of itself, there was also a sense at the time that the Society needed what might be called an "ideology" or public stance. In other words, there was a feeling – not least because of the sheer grandeur of the ultimate outcome that the new scientists predicted for their endeavours – that they needed to spell out the non-scientific implications of what they were doing.

For this, I think that there were three reasons. One was connected with the granting of the charter that I have already referred to, which gave the Society a constitutional structure and a permanence which differentiated it from earlier, less formal groups devoted to natural philosophy. By acquiring a charter and joining the ranks of the legally incorporated institutions, the Society gained a degree of public visibility which raised questions about natural philosophy's public import which otherwise might never have surfaced. Much in evidence in Sprat's *History* is a feeling that as a public body as the Society had thus become *needed* some kind of position statement as to its role.

Related to this is another factor, which comes across strongly from the pages of Sprat and other sources concerning the Society in its early years, and this is that the infant institution had numerous critics. These attacked the Society's enterprise from a number of viewpoints and in a number of ways – from the sermons of High Churchmen like Robert South to the lampoons of the wits. It was in response to the "Objections and Cavils" of "the Detractors of so noble an Institution" that Sprat's book was explicitly written.[8] It is thus hard to accept Barbara Shapiro's claim that "there was no serious opposition to the new philosophy" except for "a tiny group of critics" – even if apathy may have been as great an enemy as outright hostility – for there is no mistaking the defensiveness that the new philosophers felt about their enterprise.[9]

Thirdly, I believe that the Society's organizers were anxious to spell out the broader implications of what they were doing because of a genuine – if naive – belief that the enterprise of the Royal Society *was* innocuous and reconciling, and that, if this were expounded, the suspicions that people harboured towards it could be swiftly overcome and many others enrolled in support of a worthwhile activity in which the Society's members often felt themselves to be embattled pioneers. We may be in danger of making the early Royal Society seem too Machiavellian in its motives, except that this did go with a hope to attract potential patrons for the design. In the words of John Evelyn – urging the poet Cowley to complete his verses for Sprat's book in 1667 – what was needed was a way to "bespeak it some veneration in the world" and "to raise us up benefactors."[10]

The most rudimentary attempt to "place" the Society in this way is to be seen in the deliberate enrollment of the socially eminent to its ranks, and the advertisement of this fact through the publication of printed lists of the Society's members, of which the first appeared in 1663, to be followed by annual publication thereafter. Though in part intended as ballot papers for the annual elections of officers to the Society, these were clearly widely distributed, doing much to spread esteem for the Society, not least due to the distinction of many of the rather nominal Fellows whose names appeared on them.[11]

Indeed, in a status-conscious age, it is striking how often the *eminence* of the membership was advanced as an argument for the respectability and innocuousness of the Society's enterprise. Reviewing Sprat's *History* in the *Philosophical Transactions*, Henry Oldenburg went to the trouble to compute that the Society included in its ranks not only "three of the Greatest Princes of *Europe*," but two archbishops, four bishops, twenty-nine dukes, marquesses, earls, viscounts and barons, thirty-five knights, fourteen D.D.s and B.D.s, and so on. This had been still more graphically expressed by a manuscript membership list dated November 20, 1663 which survives in a volume of Royal Society papers in the British Library and which actually divides up the membership by social rank, each being given a separate section.[12]

Clearly, however, there was a limit to the potential of lists like these as a defense of a novel intellectual enterprise. It was for this reason that, in June 1662, we hear of the appointment of a committee of various leading Fellows "to draw up a paper concerning the design of the society," while, writing to Christiaan Huygens in May 1663, Sir Robert Moray spoke of plans to publish "a little treatise, by which you can learn all that concerns the Society."[13] Possibly Moray was already referring to a putative work by Sprat, who had been elected to the Society in April that year, presumably with the intention that he should write such a book, since his composition of the *History* represents virtually his only known participation in the Society's affairs. Sometime in 1663, he evidently embarked on the work we have.[14]

I need not say much about Sprat, who, as is well-known, was a young graduate of Wadham College, Oxford, and a protégé of its former Warden, John Wilkins, but I wish to stress one point to which in my view inadequate attention has been paid, and this is that Sprat was a self-conscious writer, brought in to serve a specific literary function. As J. I. Cope and H. W. Jones put it, Sprat was part of "the circle of Buckingham, Rochester, Clifford, Cowley, Dryden – the Court Wits and witlings who set the tone for restoration literature."[15] An awareness that Sprat was a polished author is much in evidence in the comments of the Society's supporters concerning his book when it appeared. The virtuoso, Nathaniel Fairfax, described Sprat as "a Gent. who has enough of the knack of fair speaking"; others spoke highly of his "elegant prose"; while many of the passages which John Evelyn marked in his copy of the work appear to be *obiter dicta* which he intended to copy out into his commonplace book for reuse at a later date.[16]

It is interesting that a "professional" like Sprat was chosen in preference to Fellows with literary pretensions such as Evelyn, who had already promoted the Society in print, and whose *Public Employment and an Active Life prefer'd to Solitude*, published in 1667, suggests that he could perfectly well have purveyed some of the sentiments that Sprat was to express.[17] Clearly stylistic excellence was at a premium in compiling the Society's apologia, and there is almost an element of the *prima donna* in Sprat's relationship with the Society. In deference to Sprat's skill as an author, he was evidently given considerable initiative as to exactly what he wrote and how he expressed it, though within agreed parameters and subject to close supervision concerning the book's account of the Society's constitutional status and its scientific work. There is also evidence of a certain remoteness in Sprat's relations with the Society, about which anxious remarks are to be found among the Society's organizers at different stages during the progress of the project.[18]

At this point it is worth briefly expounding what is known about the making of Sprat's book, not least since this provides such hard evidence as there is on the issue of its status as an official statement by the Society.[19] Having begun the work in 1663, Sprat had made considerable progress with it by the end of the following year, since in a letter to Boyle of November 24, 1664, Oldenburg wrote: "Mr Spratt intends to begin next week to print the History of our Institution." He added that the book had been perused by the President, William, Viscount Brouncker, and by such prominent members as Sir Robert Moray, John Wilkins, John Evelyn "and others," though he regretted that Boyle himself was not going to be able to see it before publication. He then gave an exposition of the work's structure and content which tallies almost exactly with what Sprat says about his book at the start of the published version.[20]

Whether Charles Webster is right to presume from this that the book as we now have it was already written, however, is dubious.[21] Oldenburg's correspondence in the mid 1660s is sprinkled with over-optimistic hopes for the impending appearance of the work, and against his implication that the entire book was complete late in 1664 we have to balance Sprat's own statement on page 120 of the published version that "thus far I was come in my intended *work*, when my *hand* was stop'd and my *mind* disturb'd" by, first, the Great Plague of 1665 and then the Fire of London in 1666. In his "Advertisement to the Reader" he states "That much of this Discours was Written and Printed above two years before the rest." This suggests that by late 1664 he had completed Part I – which gives "a short view of the *Ancient*, and *Modern* Philosophy; and of the most Famous Attempts, that have been made for its *Advancement*" – together with at least the first seventy pages or so of Part II, which comprises a narrative of the Society's origins, foundation, aims, methods and composition.[22]

But Sprat's apology that, because of the gap in the writing of the book, the reader "may chance to find some Expressions that by reason of the difference of time may seem not well to agree with the last" in its first two parts makes it clear that, even if already drafted, Part III as we have it was substantially composed at a later date. Moreover, that work continued even on Part II after the date of Oldenburg's letter to Boyle is shown by the fact that in December and January 1664–65, references in the Society's minutes show that efforts were being made to strengthen up what Oldenburg had singled out as the weakest part of the book: as he put it, "I know not whether there be enough said of particulars, or, to speake more truly, whether there are performances enough, for a R. Society, that hath been at work so considerable a time." A further committee to "review" Sprat's efforts was appointed in May 1665, whose work was presumably still in progress when the plague struck in the summer of that year.[23]

There is also evidence that Sprat was increasingly dilatory in his task even before the suspension of the work due to the catastrophes that struck London in 1665 and 1666, evidently due to other preoccupations, including the attack on Samuel Sorbière which he composed at this time.[24] Indeed, John Beale in Somerset seems to have presumed that Sprat's book would never appear, thereupon preparing a substitute of his own, and the fact that he was encouraged by prominent members of the Society suggests that they may have had their doubts too.[25]

Possibly in connection with this, Beale seems to have been shown the section of Sprat's text that had been set in type in 1664. For, retrospectively, Beale was to mention an opinion he had formed about the book "before many sheets were printed off," which must therefore have been at this stage. He claimed to have had reservations about the book's apologetic, as against its purely descriptive, functions, and he took particular exception to a specific passage on page 34, in which Sprat half-implied that God was likelier to bestow an "extraordinary Light in Nature" on virtuosi than on others. Though Beale "did at first sight desire" that this be suppressed, in fact nothing was done about it, which suggests that, at this stage, Beale was unusual in his sensitivity about the precise message that Sprat was putting across in the more discursive passages of his book: this is a point to the significance of which we will return.[26]

After the gap caused by the Plague and Fire, by 1667 Sprat had returned to work on the project. Moreover it is clear that the bulk of Part II as well as Part III of his book was substantially remodelled at this stage, even if drafted earlier, for references in the minutes show that the question of the "instances" of the Society's scientific work that Sprat should include was again taken up, as also of what he should extract for his work from the Society's journal book and its statutes. At this stage, the person who was authorized to take the initiative on these specific matters was John Wilkins, who already before the Plague: had had more to do with supervising Sprat's work than any other Fellow: indeed, Sprat had flatteringly referred to Wilkins' role in a passage of the book which was already in print by this time. But – since considerable stress has been laid on the part played by Wilkins – it is worth pointing out that it was specified that Wilkins' decisions should be ratified by the Council and by the President, Lord Brouncker, while on at least one point (concerning the statutes) Wilkins' supervision was supplemented by that of a committee.[27]

This is virtually all that we know of the book's preparation in its later stages: the evidence relates exclusively to the extracts from the Society's statutes and scientific work, and nothing is said about the supervision of Part III of the *History* by John Wilkins or anyone else. The only other clue is the hitherto unpublished paper by Oldenburg printed here, which, though never before noted, is clearly the source for pages 243 to 245 of Sprat's text. This demonstrates that on one key issue Sprat was working from a draft prepared by a leading figure in the Society: whether this was unique is unclear, but it is quite likely that it was, in view of the delicacy of the topic that the paper deals with – the skeptical critique of experiment made a few years earlier by one of the Society's most eminent members, Robert Boyle.[28] Interestingly, this, like the scientific papers and statutes, was a section of Part II.

Collation of Sprat's text with this draft and with the originals of the scientific papers and constitutional documents that he included shows that various alterations were made, particularly to the former. Sprat virtually rewrote Oldenburg's notes on the Society's experimental policy, mainly making stylistic embellishments, but in one case slightly obscuring the point of Oldenburg's argument. The papers illustrating the Society's work that he included were subjected to more minor emendations, while his version of the statutes comprises a workmanlike epitome.[29] The latter almost certainly *was* supervised, in view of the solicitousness over legal matters that the Society showed throughout its early years, and it is possible that the other changes were also made by Wilkins or other prominent Fellows rather than by Sprat. But the fact that the "instances" had still not been finally selected by May 23, 1667, whereas the book was published later that same summer, makes it equally likely that Sprat was given a free hand in modifying such passages, and highly probable that the supervision that the book received once written was cursory in the extreme. The controversial Part III, especially, in which Sprat defended the new science at length, may well not have been read by anyone, and certainly not by a committee, before it went to press, though the fact that Sprat was working from an agenda that he had been given is suggested by the accuracy of the brief summary of the burden of this part of the work that Oldenburg could already give in 1664.[30]

The special solicitude that was shown regarding the exact content of the scientific and constitutional sections of Sprat's book suggests that it was about these that the Society felt most anxiety. On the other hand, the relative lack of evidence of supervision of the part of the work in which Sprat dealt with the broader implications of the new science suggests that only a rather generalized concern was felt about this – as if all that was required were a few soothing platitudes on a range of agreed themes, which Sprat could be left to express in his superlative prose. Indeed, it may well be that – aside from their concern to demonstrate the viability of the Society's constitution – what the Society's organizers visualized was something more similar to the *Saggi di Naturali Esperienze* published by the Accademia del Cimento in the same year as Sprat's book, which virtually eschews broader material and concentrates on the scientific work of the group.[31] Moreover it may be noted in passing that, as far as the Society's international readership was concerned, it was precisely these scientific sections which were eagerly read and absorbed, while the rest of the content was apparently virtually ignored.[32]

This brings us to the nature of the message that Sprat was putting across in the course of his book, and the relationship of this to the collective views of the members of the Society. The way in which Sprat's presentation even of the Society's scientific work was affected by his apologetic intention has been ably indicated by Paul Wood, and I do not need to go into it here.[33] As Wood has shown, Sprat misrepresented the real nature of the Society's activity in the interests of proffering an uncontentious and undemanding range of activities to potential supporters. In particular, he failed to do justice to the role of hypothesis in the work of the Society's leading researchers, and upgraded the role of the pure accumulation of data.

In addition, it is clear that Sprat was inspired by ulterior motives to set up a somewhat artificial polarization between science and magic, between the clarity of the aims and method of the new empirical science and the obscurity of alchemists and others.[34] Insofar as, in the course of this, Sprat gave the impression that members of the Royal Society wholly eschewed a concern with magical phenomena like apparitions or with alchemical investigations, he again dispensed a misleading view of the actual state of affairs, in which a more mixed position was the norm. After all, one member, Joseph Glanvill, had in the previous year published a "Philosophical Endeavour towards the Defence" of witches and apparitions in which he was prominently identified on the title-page as "A Member of the Royal Society."[35] Evidently on such matters Sprat adopted a line which he saw as publicly prudent, something which says more about his own views than about the preoccupations of the heterogeneous body of virtuosi which the Society comprised, and such passages have to be treated with the greatest of caution as a "public statement" by the Society.

What, however, about Sprat's more general comments about the place of the new science in contemporary society, particularly those in the lengthy Part III of his work? These are widely read and cited concerning the aspirations and affiliations of the new philosophy, but what significance should be attached to them and to the message that they purvey?

The passages in question may be briefly summarized. Already, in Part I, Sprat had included a certain amount of such material, including some forty-five pages on the history of learning, from the ancients to the "*Modern Dogmatists*," and an exposition of the Society's position in relation to this. In Part II, there is also some material which goes beyond an account of the Society's constitutional structure and scientific method, as in Sprat's narrative of the Society's origins in the aftermath of the Civil War and his description of the width of its support in religious, social and national terms. But in Part III such material burgeons, with a twenty-page defense of the experimental philosophy in educational terms, both in its own right and in relation to "the usual wayes of *Education*" and their content, together with a three-and-a-half page annexe on the value of science "*for the cure of mens minds.*" This is followed by what Sprat describes as "the weightiest, and most solemn part of my whole *undertaking*," the justification of the Royal Society and the new science in religious terms, which occupies thirty-three pages. There are then twenty-five pages on the advantageousness of experiments to the manual arts, followed by nine and a half pages justifying experiments as "*a proper Study for the Gentlemen of our Nation*," six pages recommending them to the wits, and twelve arguing for the advantageousness of science to the national interest more generally, before a List of the Fellows of the Society and a concluding peroration.[36]

If, as I have stated elsewhere, Sprat's book is to be seen as "a summation of polemical attempts to define the role of science in the atmosphere of the mid seventeenth century,"[37] what can be said about its antecedents and context? One response to the problem of dealing with science's relationship with broader issues which went back at least to the mid 1640s in England and earlier still on the continent was to deny that there was one. Thus the Accademia dei Lincei in Rome in the early years of the seventeenth century had explicitly avoided political discussion, and this was echoed by John Wallis in his famous account of the 1645 London group: "Our business was (precluding matters of Theology and State Affairs) to discours and consider of *Philosophical Enquiries*, and such as related thereunto."[38]

A similar attitude is in evidence in the early years of the Royal Society in an anonymous memorandum, usually, but I believe erroneously, attributed to Hooke on the basis of an unsubstantiated claim by C. R. Weld, who first published the text in the early nineteenth century (all that can in fact be said about it is that it is certainly of late seventeenth-century date). This defines the "business and design" of the Royal Society as "To improve the knowledge of naturall things, and all useful Arts, Manufactures, Mechanick practises, Engynes and Inventions by Experiments – (not meddling with Divinity, Metaphysics, Moralls, Politicks, Grammar, Rhetorick, or Logick)."[39] The sense that the Royal Society should eschew religious matters is found later, as, for instance, when it refused to license a book for publication in 1696 on the grounds that its subject was "Theologicall" and hence "not within the Cognizance of the Society."[40]

At some points in his book, Sprat echoes this kind of line, arguing that the Fellows of the Royal Society "meddle no otherwise with *Divine things*, than onely as the *Power*, and *Wisdom*, and *Goodness* of the *Creator*, is display'd in the admirable order, and workman-ship of the Creatures," seeing experiments as "*calm*, and *indifferent* things," above the hubbub of politics.[41] Elsewhere, however, he juxtaposes this with a more positive view of science's role not only as appealing to all men, but as a useful form of intellectual exercise which, through its methods and attitudes, could form the intellectual underpinning for the revived Anglican Church of his day. This juxtaposition might seem uneasy, but it is arguably symptomatic of the rather naive – even inept – presumption of the protagonists of the new science that what they were doing was not only harmful to no one, but somehow might at the same time be positively appealing.[42]

For the same reason, there was also a proclivity to try to align the new science with the status quo, a fairly obvious strategy for a society which was ill-established and the subject of hostility. Thus Sprat was fullsome in his profession of loyalty to the King and he stressed again and again how well the new science was suited to the "present prevailing *Genius* of the *English* Nation."[43] In this, it seems to me, Sprat's aim was simply to align the new science with as many consensus values as possible, his specifics as to what was excluded mainly comprising elaborations of the enmity towards "fanaticism" whose wide support among divers sections of the political nation was what had made the Restoration of the Stuarts possible a few years earlier.

Can one, however, be more precise, and, in particular, is it convincing to see Sprat's book, as J. R. Jacob has, as a statement of a fairly specific ideological position, echoing views expressed by Robert Boyle and his circle at the time of the Restoration? According to this view, Sprat was doing more than voicing bland commonplaces: his message included not only "religious moderation...civil obedience, private enterprise, and profit," but also "ecclesiastical comprehension." He thus took up ideas advocating a broad church, liberty of conscience and perhaps even limited episcopacy which Boyle and his friends had outlined and which are central to the latitudinarianism which Professor Jacob sees the Royal Society as exemplifying.[44]

In assessing such claims, it seems to me crucial to try to distinguish between sentiments which could have been expected to appeal to a very wide range of people in Restoration England, and ones which had a more limited cachet. Until we have evidence that non-latitudinarians *did not* believe in overseas trade and empire, it is not very helpful to describe these as latitudinarian, as against commonplace, views, and the indications do not look promising on this front: even if some contemporary commentators were more enthusiastic about commerce than others, a growing acceptance is to be found among all.[45] But I think that there is one, crucial part of Jacob's case which *did* have precise resonances at the time and which, if proven, would therefore show the Royal Society to have been latitudinarian in a positive and precise sense rather than a negative and broad one, and this relates to the issue of comprehension. For ideas of comprehension were notoriously controversial in Restoration England, and hence were party-political in a way that many of Boyle's and his friends' notions were not.[46] Is it true, then, that the Royal Society, and Sprat, can be claimed to have adhered to this more exactly defined viewpoint?

Now it is true that on the face of it there appears to be some support in Sprat for such a view, since he repeatedly trumpets the virtue of sober, collaborative research involving people from a wide range of backgrounds. In the most generalized sense, Sprat was perhaps thus claiming that intellectual enterprise offered "a model for the nation as a whole." But is Jacob right to paraphrase Sprat as meaning that "the Royal Society might serve then as the basis of *ecclesiastical comprehension*," and, by way of background to this, what evidence is there that such a party-political view – even if expressed by Sprat – was generally shared within the Royal Society?[47]

Bishop Wilkins, as is well-known, was a keen advocate of comprehension, who was associated with attempts to introduce legislation along these lines at much the time that Sprat's book appeared.[48] But, perhaps because he suits perfectly certain views about the affiliations of the new science in this period, we have arguably heard too much about Wilkins in connection with the Society's public stance in its early years. If one looks more broadly, one comes up with a more varied pattern which makes it hard to credit even the Society's central core with anything approaching unanimity on this crucial issue.

Of those who took a leading role in directing the Society's affairs in its early years, one, Sir Robert Moray, was certainly a protagonist of moderate episcopacy, as was shown by his activities both at the time of the Restoration and in Scottish affairs thereafter.[49] But what about another figure who had a role matching Moray's in the Society's early administration, Seth Ward, Bishop of Salisbury? It was Ward whose open opposition proved fatal to Wilkins' comprehension scheme in 1668, and throughout these years Ward was active in the "Sheldonian" wing which opposed moves towards broadening the basis of the church championed by those of Wilkins' ilk.[50]

There are hints of a similar attitude on the part of the figure who was arguably more important than anyone else in directing the Society's affairs during these years, the President, Lord Brouncker, despite the fact that Brouncker's political views are on the whole rather shadowy, like those of many prominent members of the Society. For in his diary, Brouncker's colleague at the Navy Office, Samuel Pepys, recorded that on August 21, 1665 he heard Brouncker "speak of some presbyter-people that he caused to be apprehended yesterday at a private meeting in Covent garden, which he would have released upon paying £5 per man to the poor; but it was answered they would not pay anything, so he ordered them to another prison from the guard [i.e., the Guard-House at Whitehall]." One cannot draw absolutely definite conclusions about Brouncker's churchmanship from such persecution, since latitudinarians as well as High Churchmen were to be found advocating that those who refused to join the state church should suffer for it: but the fact that Brouncker was a layman, and that he carried out this policy during the Great Plague, when others in London suspended the persecution of nonconformists, suggests a zealous High Church attitude on his part.[51]

Looking slightly more widely at the Society's active membership, we find at least two regular attenders of Council meetings in the late 1660s, who, as Members of Parliament, were committed defenders of the established church who were actively involved in promoting the new Conventicles Act passed in 1670, Wilkins' implacable opposition to which earned him the King's disfavor. Thus the former royalist exile, Sir Gilbert Talbot, assisted the passing of the measure by reading out in the Commons a letter denouncing nonconformist insolence, while Sir John Lowther, the great improver of Whitehaven in Cumberland, was another "firm Anglican" who played an active role in the making of the Act.[52] If such men belonged to the active core on which the Society's work depended, it is also worth pointing out that the Society's more nominal supporters included churchmen who were certainly not latitudinarians, such as Gilbert Sheldon and John Pearson in the 1660s and Henry Paman in the 1670s, while among lay members on the periphery of the Society were some extreme supporters of the Anglican reaction, including Sir John Berkenhead, Sir Winston Churchill and Sir Nicholas Stewart.[53]

If, in the light of this, one goes back to Sprat's text to see if he advocates comprehension in any sense that has resonances in the political atmosphere in Restoration England, the answer is that he does not. In other words, he was saying something about intellectual activity which was only intended to be extrapolated in a negative rather than a positive sense to the political realm. This is seen especially clearly in what he says – and, indeed, in what the early Royal Society exemplified – on the question of attitudes to Roman Catholics. Thus Boyle and his friends would have no truck with tolerance for Catholics in their state church.[54] But Sprat states categorically that the Royal Society numbered Catholics among its Fellows, and this was indeed the case: active Catholic Fellows included Sir Kenelm Digby as well as Charles Howard of Deepdene and his brother, Henry Howard, later sixth Duke of Norfolk.[55]

Moreover, lest one suspect that the Society was made up only of figures inhabiting a spectrum from latitudinarian Anglicans towards the "right," it is worth pointing out that these Catholics can be matched by a practicing nonconformist, Nehemiah Grew, elevated to the Secretaryship in 1677 after researching under the Society's auspices in the 1670s, while there was no objection to electing the Quaker, William Penn, to the Society in 1681. The dangers of trying to discern an undue degree of consensus in the Society is also shown by the presence among its activists of figures tainted with religious heterodoxy, including the highly Erastian Sir William Petty: even Moray is perhaps to be placed in this category in the light of Charles II's opinion that "I believe he is head of his own church."[56]

This is not, of course, to say that the Society was moving towards a position of "complete indifference to religion," as Lotte Mulligan has claimed:[57] on the contrary, its members would have been shocked by this, as they repeatedly and quite genuinely exclaimed. But they *were* moving towards a religious pluralism, reflecting the fact that all the evidence now suggests that the motivation to scientific activity in this period was convergent rather than specific – in other words, it was not inspired by any single religious position but by a range of religious or secular stimuli, which brought people together in pursuit of shared goals which were largely defined by the internal dynamic of scientific enterprise.

This is also borne out by what we know of contemporary impressions of the Royal Society's political and religious stance. For in these the Society often seems to have taken on a veritably chameleon-like character which tells us more about the sentiments of the commentators than about the actual position of the Society. Thus while the University orator at Oxford, Robert South, indulged in "Satyrical Invectives, against Cromwell, Fanaticks, the Royal Society, & New Philosophy," John Beale reported a completely different attitude among certain of his gentry neighbours in Somerset, who "were fallen out with God & the King, & could not endure to heare well of any Royall Act, or Royall Society."[58] Such accusations arguably cancel one another out, their chief significance being to illustrate the range of parties from which hostility might be expected. Moreover, as already noted, this was precisely the reason why Sprat's book had seemed necessary in the first place.

It is in this context – as an apologia for a heterogeneous body widely regarded with suspicion – that Sprat's message makes sense. On the one hand, he *was* trying to say that science was above religious and political distinctions. This was not, however, exclusive of a complementary attempt to invest the Royal Society with a generalized, uncontroversial role in Restoration society, taking advantage of areas where he thought a positive point could be made of the Society's aspirations without entailing divisive overtones, but avoiding any very precise statement of position, especially of a party-political kind. This was, after all, essential for a society whose active core contained people from a range of ecclesiastical positions and which managed to attract and retain at least the nominal support of churchmen and others with a wide range of opinions. Indeed, one might go further and argue that, when allowance is made for the rather unfavorable environment in which the institution subsisted in its early years, it would have been difficult for the Society to have been as party-political as commentators such as Jacob have implied. The whole object of the exercise was to placate potential critics rather than to risk making new enemies.

Turning to the reception of Sprat's book, such evidence as we have suggests that it was Sprat's generalized attempt to appeal to everybody and antagonize nobody that impressed supporters of the new science when they read the work in the immediate aftermath of its appearance. John Evelyn's annotations to his copy, for instance, seem predominantly to show an approval of Sprat's well-turned phrases in praise of the new philosophy and of the eirenic commonplaces that he purveyed.[59] John Beale forgot his earlier anxieties and itemized the parties whom Sprat had courted, "besides what he hath done in the whole for the Soc[iety]" – academics, lawyers, parliamentarians, merchants and so on – concluding: "I make no doubt but it will prove an Invincible Light to all the world, & for all ages." Nathaniel Fairfax expostulated: "the Hist[ory] of the R.S. I have read, admird & lov'd. & I am hugely pleased to se a busines of that importance, intrusted with a penman, so well fitted for the work," thereupon going on to praise Sprat for capturing "the life & soul" of the Society and its potential in terms which Oldenburg subsequently echoed himself when expatiating on the book to John Winthrop in Connecticut.[60]

Those who believed that Sprat had written a winning book, however, were quickly outnumbered by those with qualms about it. A consideration of these reservations will return us to the theme of the general difficulty of writing a statement of the "ideology" of a corporate body like the Royal Society to which allusion was made at the start of this paper, and the specific problems that stemmed from the lack of supervision that Sprat had evidently received in writing a book to which the Society officially put its name.

In spite of the efforts made to improve the scientific content of the book while Sprat was writing it, Oldenburg remained concerned about this facet of the work, encouraging Joseph Glanvill to publish his *Plus Ultra* (1668) as a supplement to Sprat in illustrating the solid achievements of the new philosophy.[61] Indeed, Oldenburg's dissatisfaction with the *History* from this point of view is clearly in evidence in the review of it that he wrote for *Philosophical Transactions*. For he extrapolated from Sprat's text to give actual *numbers* of the Society's "most remarkable particulars," which Sprat had omitted, to show how "the *Particulars* upon which *Heads* are more numerous, and of greater moment and variety, than perhaps Detractors and Cavillers imagine or expect: they exceed indeed the number of 700; of which the *Experiments* and *Observations* both together amount to above 350; the *Relations*, to about 150; the *Queries, Directions, Recommendations*, and *Proposals*, to above 80; the *Instruments*, to about 60; the *Histories* of *Nature* and *Art*, to above 50; and the *Theories* and *Discourses*, to as many."[62]

Despite his lack of satisfaction on this point, it is worth observing that there is no evidence that Oldenburg dissented from the general view of the proper method of science that Sprat presented, however little it represented the actual practice of scientists: to this extent the special degree of supervision that this part of the book had received arguably paid off. Yet even here the book had its deficiencies. One of these was Sprat's defense of experiments against reservations "rais'd by the *Experimenters* themselves" – in the person of Boyle – which, as we have already seen, Sprat based on a draft by Oldenburg. Paul Wood, who did not know this, describes Sprat's handling of the matter as "inept." So it is, but the ineptness was largely that of Oldenburg, whose argument Sprat closely followed. It thus cannot be put down to lack of scientific expertise on Sprat's part, but evidently to the difficulty of constructing a readily comprehensible justification of the new science which tried to do justice to its complexities. The fact that Oldenburg's manuscript draft, and especially his "Answer" to the "Objection," is rather hesitant and repetitious – traits which Sprat's version tended to iron out – is perhaps symptomatic of the trouble he had in trying to devise an appropriate public stance.[63]

If this was true of the scientific component of the book, it was much truer of its religious and political facets. By 1670, John Beale had reverted to his earlier dissatisfaction with the book from this point of view, observing how "I was alwayes of [opin]ion, that the His[tory] of R.S. should be purely narrative & [suitable] alike for all Climates, of Rome, Spaine, New England." He now reiterated how he had felt all along "that the Defensive & Apologetical part should be quite sever'd from the History; & confin'd to a peculiar Treatise," largely because of the difficulty of doing justice to the religious policy of an institution "which admitted of all partyes into their Membership."[64]

Comparable anxieties may help to explain what might otherwise seem an anomaly in the coverage that Oldenburg gave to Part III of the book when he reviewed it in *Philosophical Transactions*. Oldenburg devoted almost a whole page to Sprat's arguments concerning the innocuousness and potential of the new science in relation to education and nearly as much to its value to the manual arts. On the other hand, he dismissed the religious arguments which took up more space than any other in this section of Sprat's work in a mere five lines, summing up Sprat's verdict on the new science as "not at all dangerous," and thus suggesting that he was either embarrassed or not particularly impressed by this section.[65]

In the wider public arena, it may be argued that Sprat's book, so far from being "immediately successful," as some authors have claimed,[66] was little short of a disaster, at least as far as its domestic reception was concerned, though (as already noted) it may have fared better overseas. In 1668, the Cambridge don, John Worthington told Henry More that he considered Sprat "perfect Hylobares" – an allusion to the figure of the materialist in More's *Divine Dialogues* – criticizing him as devoted to "nothing but what gratifies externall sense, or what sense doth reach."[67] Worse was to follow, for over the next three years Sprat's *History* – together with Glanvill's *Plus Ultra* – was to stimulate the two most serious attacks on the new science to be published during the period, those of Meric Casaubon and Henry Stubbe. Casaubon's *Letter... to Peter du Moulin* (1669) was a searching critique of *Natural experimental Philosophie, and some books lately set out about it*, while one of Stubbe's books was actually entitled *A Censure upon Certaine Passages Contained in the History of the Royal Society, As being Destructive to the Established Religion and Church of England* (1670). Moreover it comprised just that, taking a series of what he saw as questionable and dangerous statements in Sprat's book and subjecting them to detailed and effective scrutiny: significantly, all but one of these came from Part III of the work.[68]

The effect was devastating, especially since Sprat's book *had* been officially commissioned by the Society, even if, as we have seen, it had apparently not been closely supervised. The dilemma in which this placed the Society is shown by the reaction of Sir Robert Moray to Stubbe's threatened assault, which Stubbe reports in one of his later books. "When the first *brute* of my designing to write against the R.S. did reach *London*, Sir *R.M.* writ to the Lady *E.P.* to inform them of my intentions; adding, That there was nothing in which the R.S. as a Body, could be concern'd, excepting this *History*: and if I would civilly represent unto them any defaults therein, they would take it kindly, and amend them." Stubbe therefore wrote to him concerning both Sprat's *History* and Glanvill's *Plus Ultra*, "and DEMANDED that the R.S. should disclaim *both of them by some authentick Declaration*." Revealingly, however, the Society felt obliged to stick by the *History* as an "official" statement, although embarrassed by the reaction it had inspired, while finding it easy to disown Glanvill on the grounds that "He was a Private Person, and that the *sense of the R.S.* was not to be collected from the Writings of every *single Member*."[69] The problem was that, while it could not be denied that the *History was* an authorized statement, its blunt printed statements of policy provided hostages to fortune which need not otherwise have existed.

Clearly the Society's supporters were particularly shocked precisely because they had not thought that they were saying anything controversial. Indeed, they would have been relieved to learn of the subversively radical motives which we have recently been encouraged to see in Stubbe, which might have reassured them that they were on the side of the angels: as it was, they were worried by Stubbe precisely because he seemed to be appealing to commonplace anxieties of the day.[70]

Telling evidence in this respect comes from a letter written by John Evelyn to John Beale in the aftermath of Stubbe's attack. After a lengthy tirade against the "petulant Scribbles" of "this angry monster," which bears evident testimony to his shock at Stubbe's onslaught, Evelyn explained how: "For my part I have read & seriously ponder'd both Dr. *Sprat* and *Glanvil*, and can find nothing which a sober person can take just Exceptions at." He went on to assert the kind of "safe," "apolitical" role for science which, as I have suggested, had always been at the back of the minds of the virtuosi, even when they had tried to argue that it was possible to be above politics and yet solve the problems of politics at the same time. Sprat and Glanvill, he claimed, "have said nothing but what is justifiable for the bespeaking the favour and Civilities of honest and learned men" to the Society, whose activities he proceeded to characterize in a revealingly low-key manner, consoling himself by noting with satisfaction how even the hitherto apathetic universities were beginning to take an interest in the studies which the Society had pioneered, in addition to reverting to further bitter recriminations against Stubbe.[71]

What is clear is that, by trying to give an account of science's broader role which they hoped would offend no one, the Society's organizers found that they had stirred up a hornet's nest of hostility, illustrating that some of the religious, intellectual and political implications of the new science *were* potentially more controversial than they seem to have appreciated, especially in the context of commonplace attitudes of the late seventeenth century. Moreover the problem was exacerbated by the choice of author, for Sprat was almost *too* glib in his ability to make the best showing of every facet of the Society's activities, and the notions of the brash young graduate were less mainstream in the context of the 1660s than he perhaps thought, or than many of his modern readers have realized. As it was, there was much to shock susceptible contemporaries, including Sprat's rather "Hobbist" sentiments on various points, his iconoclastic attitude towards the existing educational curriculum, his disdain for the ancients, and perhaps above all his rationalistic and anti-intellectualist religious views.[72]

The fact that this difficulty had apparently not even been foreseen by the Society's organizers, who would otherwise surely have ordered that the text should be carefully read before it was sent to press, suggests to me that the reaction to Sprat awakened them from a considerable state of naivety concerning the difficulties involved in composing a public statement of this kind. Indeed, in these circumstances, the apparent lack of supervision of the book's controversial later sections is astonishing, though it would not have surprised Stubbe: he thought it highly likely that the Fellows "had not patience to read it, or *any Book* of *that bulk*; but, as in other cases, gave their *assent* and *applauds* upon *trust*." He reiterated, however, "that the R.S. did own it, any man knows that was in *London* at its publication, not to mention the character which Mr. *Glanvill* and the Transactor fix on it."[73]

The result was that the effort to define science's broader role represented by Sprat's book was quietly abandoned. In 1668, there was talk of a proposed second edition with additions which might have helped to rectify the book's shortcomings from the scientific point of view: but, although the book soon became scarce, no revision or even reprint occurred during the rest of the seventeenth century.[74] There are hints that a further defense of the new science was planned early in 1678, this time by Thomas Smith, a divine who had just been elected to the Society and may have been recruited specifically for this purpose.[75] But, if so, nothing materialized, and the nearest approach to a follow-up to Sprat's apologia for the Society comprised some remarks "to *vindicate* that *Assembly*" that John Evelyn included in the preface to the third edition of his *Sylva: or a Discourse of Forest-Trees* in 1679.

Moreover these are interesting precisely because their burden is so internalist: it was for its contribution to the task of improving knowledge about the natural world, not its religious, political or social potential, that Evelyn defended the Royal Society. His comments on the broad implications of the new science were defensive, and were virtually limited to saying that, so far from the King and kingdom being diminished in reputation by such activities, the adulation of foreigners had accrued to national esteem.[76] And, though claims have been made for an "ideology" for the Royal Society in the period of the Exclusion Crisis, the evidence is very limited by comparison with the open attempt at a public statement on major issues made by Sprat.[77]

Only in the eighteenth century was Sprat's *History* reprinted, first in 1702, and then again in 1722 and 1734, and I think that this may itself be significant. For one thing, shifts in attitudes meant that religious and intellectual positions which had seemed controversial in the 1660s were by this time becoming increasingly commonplace.[78] In addition, the new science was by now much more "established" than it had been in the pioneering days of the early Restoration, due to the increase of fashionable participation in it, to the rise of public lectures and demonstrations, and to the inclusion of experimental philosophy in the university curriculum.[79] By this time, assisted by the acclaim that Newton received for his

Principia, the new science had "arrived" in a way that it had not half a century earlier, acquiring a superior prestige to which appeal was frequently made, and Sprat now seemed almost prophetic in his claim as to how science represented the country's "present prevailing *Genius*."[80]

This, however, has important negative implications for the late seventeenth century, when it is easy to overrate the popularity that the new science enjoyed. In fact, at this stage the new science was a marginal and widely unappreciated activity, which was susceptible to hostility because of the extent to which it could be deemed to offend against crucial religious and learned preoccupations of the day.[81] It was for this reason that the new scientists were so often on the defensive in these formative years. Not only does this explain why they had to work so hard to distinguish themselves from thinkers with overlapping concerns who were commonly perceived as pernicious, such as Hobbes.[82] It also accounts for the fact that Sprat's apologia seemed necessary in the first place, and, if this is forgotten, the message that Sprat attempted to purvey in his book is easily misunderstood.

But the aftermath to the publication of the *History* illustrates the difficulty of constructing a satisfactory apologia in such circumstances and shows that, even if a statement of the religious and political implications of the new science seemed in theory desirable, it was in practice dispensable. Moreover the investigation of the context of Sprat's *History* given here should indicate how unwise it is to take the views expressed in that book as reflecting a "party line" on the Society's part. In my view, even the book's broad message about science's compatibility with rational religion and with national prosperity and harmony – in a word, its "latitudinarianism" – is to be read negatively rather than positively. In his *History*, Sprat was not aligning the Royal Society with the ecclesiastical policy of Bishop Wilkins. The object was to find a generalized creed which would enjoy at least the tacit support of people from a wide range of positions, which would disarm criticism and might also enlist support. This is the true, if facile, message of an apologia which in fact proved much more problematic than either its author or his sponsors expected.

Documents

(1) OLDENBURG'S DRAFT FOR PP. 243–45 OF SPRAT'S
HISTORY

This item survives as Royal Society Classified Papers XXIV, item 42. It is in the hand of Henry Oldenburg throughout, but it is clear that it was written in two stages: after the first two paragraphs, which set out the problem, the concluding two paragraphs which give an "Answ[er]" to it are written in a different, darker ink, as if added later, perhaps after consultations with others. There are numerous deletions and insertions reflecting Oldenburg's hesitations and second thoughts in drafting the paper: these are recorded in footnotes. A few editorial insertions have been made to clarify the sense; contractions have been expanded throughout.

OBJECTION

AGAINST THE EXPERIMENTAL WAY

OF PHILOSOPHY;

THOUGHT NECESSARY TO BE ANSWERED IN M. SPRATS HISTORY.

There is a great nicety and difficulty in the making of many Experiments: The success of very many is[1] various[,] inconstant, and differing, not only in the hands of different, but even[2] the self same Experimenters, upon the account 1. Of the more or lesse skill, care, patience; 2. of the diversity of the materials, whereof some are genuine, some sophisticated; some simple, some mixed; some fresh and vigorous, some old and effete: And particularly in Chymical Trials, many dissolvents are well, many ill prepared; some Spirits[3] too litle, some too much purified, etc. 3. Of some circumstances, which are either constantly unobvious, or at least scarce discernable, till the Tryall be past: which makes the[4] Experiments very obnoxious to contingencies.

Upon these and the like considerations, it is to be feared that, though the R[oyal] Society should take due care of having their Experiments and Observations made[5] skillfully,[6] and with care, and recorded with[7] faithfulnesse, yet other Companies both of this present Age, and of future times, will meet with successes much differing from theirs, and yet pretend to as much skill and caution, as possibly they can doe. And if there be no agreement in Experiments, at least in many such, as are important to determine truth by /verso/[8] there appears small hopes of ever raising a Systeme of solid Philosophy, etc.

Answ[er]. All circumstances concurring in the making of the Experiments,[9] will render[10] the effects to be constantly the same.[11] If the effects differ, it will put men upon investigating[12] the causes of that difference, which must needs discover a great many considerable and luciferous things.

It is presumed that the present[13] R[oyal] Society, which is to lay the foundation of this work, and to give an Example to their successors[14] will[15] make use of very expert, carefull,[16] diligent and circumspect men in the making of Experiments, and in the recording[17] the proces and all the circumstances of it with all possible exactnes.

(2) JOHN EVELYN'S ANNOTATIONS TO HIS COPY OF THOMAS SPRAT'S *HISTORY OF THE ROYAL SOCIETY* (1667)

The information which follows was derived from Evelyn's copy of this work, which was stolen from Christies when sent for auction there in 1978. Since the present whereabouts of this volume is unknown – if it survives at all – it seems worth preserving here what may constitute a unique record. Details of the book are given in the Christies sale catalogue, *The Evelyn Library*, *Part 3*, *M–S*, March 15–16, 1978, lot 1405 and plate 24. Line numbers have been taken from the modern edition of Sprat's text by J. I. Cope and H. W. Jones. All notes were in the margin unless otherwise stated. "1." denotes a vertical stroke beside the lines of text specified. If more than one line is given (e.g. 21/22), this is because it is not clear whether the marking was supposed to be adjacent to the upper or the lower of the two.

        p. 4, line 32: "new?".

        p. 8, line 31: "–".

        p. 12, lines 25–26: "strongster" altered to "stronger" in text.

        p. 26, line 24: "of" underlined in text and "or?" inserted in margin.

        p. 27, line 29: "ich" deleted in "which" in text, and "le/" added in margin.

        p. 61, lines 10–11: 1.

        p. 67, line 10: "Author" in text underlined, and the following written in margin: "Mr *Graunt* a Bodice-maker in Birchin-lane, a man of extraordinary natural parts & solid judgement."

        p. 69, lines 6–8: 1.

        p. 75, lines 19–20, 25–26: 1.

p. 89, in margin at top of page: "Lipsius/ Scaliger/ Salmosius/ De Cartes."

p. 90, lines 3/4–5: l.

p. 91, lines 5–6, 7–8: l.

p. 93, lines 11–13: l.

p. 94, line 16/17: "Dr. Wilkins" [i.e., referring to lines 14–15].

p. 97, lines 27–28: l.

p. 98, lines 28–30: l.

p. 100, lines 13–14: l.

p. 101, lines 34–35: l.

p. 107, lines 5–6: l.

p. 110, lines 18–end: l.

p. 111, lines 1–9: l.

p. 112, lines 18–20: l.

p. 127, lines 4–6: diagonal stroke.

p. 163, line 18: "sheds" in text altered to "opens."

p. 164, lines 27–30: l.

p. 165, lines 3–4, 24–25, 31–32: l.

p. 200, title: after "Receiv'd," the words "by Mr. Evelyn" have been inserted in the text, not in Evelyn's hand.

p. 208, line 29: cross above line in text between "spungy" and "Stone," and note in adjacent margin: "of which I have one."

p. 213, lines 17–18, 19–20: l.

p. 277, line 20: horizontal line "—".

p. 313, line 32: "r" in "more" deleted in text and "v/" added in margin.

p. 314, line 20: "s" deleted in "diamets" in text and "er/" added in margin.

p. 350, lines 6–8, 12–16: l.

p. 352, lines 17–18: l.

p. 355, lines 9–11, 18–22: l.

p. 360, lines 10/11–15: l.

p. 364, lines 10–12: l.

p. 367, lines 12–16: l., with an extra l. to lines 12–13.

p. 370: above page number: "mispag. 362"; lines 20–29: l.

p. 371: above page number: "mispag. 363."

p. 382, lines 15–18, 19–21/2, 25–28: l., with "nb" beside latter.

p. 386, lines 14–16: l.

p. 388, line 16: "East" deleted in text and "so" [sic] in margin.

p. 391, lines 14–16: l.

p. 393, lines 2–5, 32–35: l.

p. 397, lines 5–7, 29–31: l.

p. 398, lines 28/9–31: l.

p. 400, line 3: horizontal line "—".

p. 401, lines 16–18: l.

p. 402, lines 17–19, 21–22: l.

p. 404, lines 1–3, 8–9, 31–32: l.

p. 407, lines 7–8: l., and "nb" [?].

p. 412, lines 4–5, 15–16, 22–24: l.

p. 429, lines 9–14: l.

p. 438: at end of text: "perlegi" and mark #.

p. [439]: after the title "ERRATA," "correcta – " inserted in scribal hand.

Back fly-leaf: "Art of shooting flying p. 277."

Notes

I am grateful to the following for their comments on a draft of this paper: Mark Goldie, John Henry, J. E. McGuire, Steven Shapin and Paul B. Wood. I also benefited from the discussion that followed my presentation of a shortened version of it at the conference, "Latitudinarianism, science and society" held at the William Andrews Clark Memorial Library, Los Angeles, in April 1987. Material in the Evelyn Collection at Christ Church, Oxford, is quoted by kind permission of the Trustees of the Will of Major Peter George Evelyn.

1 J. R. Jacob, *Robert Boyle and the English Revolution* (New York, 1977), p. 155.
2 This text is printed on pp. 219–220. On its background, see Paul B. Wood, "Methodology and apologetics: Thomas Sprat's *History of the Royal Society*," *British Journal for the History of Science* 13 (1980): 6–7. My general indebtedness to Wood's important article will become apparent in the course of this chapter.
3 Margery Purver, *The Royal Society: Concept and Creation* (London, 1967), p. 9 and *passim*; J. R. Jacob, "Restoration, Reformation and the origins of the Royal Society," *History of Science* 13 (1975): 169; J. R. Jacob, "Restoration ideologies and the Royal Society," *History of Science* 18 (1980): 25; J. R. and M. C. Jacob, "The Anglican origins of modern science: the metaphysical foundations of the Whig constitution," *Isis* 71 (1980): 258. For an important critique of the views of Purver, see Charles Webster, "The origins of the Royal Society," *History of Science* 6 (1967): 106–28.
4 I have deliberately placed the word "ideology" in inverted commas throughout this paper, since it is not clear to me whether the public stance that I wish to argue that the Royal Society adopted is properly so described. The scholar who has been mainly responsible for the use of the term in the context is J. R. Jacob, but I have been unable to find a definition of it in his writings. For further discussion of this concept and its meanings see, in a historical context, Morris Berman, *Social Change and Scientific Organisation* (London, 1978), pp. xxiiff., and, more generally, Raymond Williams, *Keywords* (revised ed., London, 1983), pp. 153ff.
5 Jacob, "Restoration" (n. 3), 155, 169 and *passim* (this article has achieved wide circulation by being included in the Open University reader, *Seventeenth-century England: A Changing Culture. Volume 2: Modern Studies*, ed. W. R. Owens [London, 1980], pp. 241–52). See also Jacob, *Robert Boyle* (n. 1), pp. 153ff.; "Restoration ideologies" (n. 3), 25–28; "Anglican origins" (n. 3), 258–59.

6 J. R. and M. C. Jacob, "Scientists and society: the saints preserved," *Journal of European Studies* 1 (1971): 88, and see Barbara Shapiro, "Latitudinarianism and science in seventeenth-century England," *Past and present* 40 (1968): 16–41; *John Wilkins, 1614–72: an Intellectual Biography* (Berkeley and Los Angeles, 1969), ch. 8.

7 Oldenburg to Norwood, February 10, 1668, in A. R. and M. B. Hall, eds., *The Correspondence of Henry Oldenburg* (Madison and London, 1965–86), Vol. IV, p. 168; Thomas Sprat, *The History of the Royal Society of London*, ed. J. I. Cope and H. W. Jones (London, 1959), p. 134 (I have preferred Sprat's translation of the second charter to more modern ones).

8 Sprat, *History* (n. 7), sig. B4v and *passim*. Cf. Wood, "Methodology" (n. 2), 2, and Michael Hunter, *Science and Society in Restoration England* (Cambridge, 1981), esp. chs. 6–7.

9 Barbara Shapiro, *Probability and Certainty in Seventeenth-century England* (Princeton, 1983), p. 73. On apathy, see Hunter, *Science and Society* (n. 8), pp. 83–84, 196–97.

10 Evelyn to Cowley, March 12, 1667, in John Evelyn, *Diary and Correspondence*, ed. William Bray and John Forster (London, 1852), Vol. III, pp. 194–95. Cf. Thomas Birch, *The History of the Royal Society of London* (London, 1756–57), Vol. I, p. 84.

11 See Michael Hunter, *The Royal Society and its Fellows, 1660–1700* (Chalfont St. Giles, 1982), pp. 9–10, 55.

12 *Philosophical Transactions* 2 (1667): 508; British Library Additional MS 4441, fol. 79 (dated November 20, 1663).

13 Birch, *History* (n. 10), Vol. I, pp. 84–85; Sprat, *History* (n. 7), p. xiii.

14 Sprat, *History*. Cf. Hunter, *Royal Society* (n. 11), catalogue entry 132.

15 Sprat, *History* (n. 7), p. xxv. On Sprat as a stylist, see Robert Cluett, "Style, precept, personality: a test case (Thomas Sprat, 1635–1713)," *Computers and the Humanities* 5 (1971): 257–77.

16 Fairfax to Oldenburg, September 28, 1667, *Oldenburg* (n. 7), Vol. III, pp. 491–92; Beale to Evelyn, September 11, 1667, Evelyn Collection, Christ Church, Oxford, Correspondence (bound volumes), no. 64. See also *Phil. Trans* 2 (1667): 503; Oldenburg to Boyle, November 24, 1664, *Oldenburg* (n. 7), Vol. II, p. 321; Webster, "Origins" (n. 3), 115. For Evelyn's markings, see below.

17 John Evelyn, trans. G. Naudé, *Instructions Concerning Erecting of a Library* (London, 1661), sigs. A2–7: cf. also *A Panegyric to Charles the Second* (London, 1661), p. 14. Evelyn's *Public Employment* has recently been reprinted in Brian Vickers, ed., *Public and Private Life in the Seventeenth Century: the MacKenzie-Evelyn Debate* (New York, 1986). For an interesting insight into the relationship between Sprat and Evelyn, see a letter from Evelyn to Sprat of November 12, 1667 in Evelyn's Letterbook, Evelyn Collection MS 39, no. 297: this accompanied verses which Evelyn had written on the death of Cowley, which he deprecatingly considered would seem a "crude paper" to "great Witts" like Sprat and other *litterateurs*.

18 For a full account, see Wood "Methodology" (n. 2), 4.

19 For earlier accounts, see Sprat, *History* (n. 7), pp. xiiiff.; Purver, *Royal Society* (n. 3), ch. 1; Hans Aarsleff, "Thomas Sprat," in C. C. Gillispie, ed., *Dictionary*

of Scientific Biography (New York, 1970–80), Vol. XII, pp. 582, 584; Webster, "Origins" (n. 3), 111ff.; and, above all, Wood, "Methodology" (n. 2), 3ff.

20 *Oldenburg* (n. 7), Vol. II, pp. 320–21; Sprat, *History* (n. 7), p. 4.

21 Webster, "Origins" (n. 3), 112–13.

22 *Oldenburg* (n. 7), Vol. II, pp. 288, 301, 399, 632; Vol. III, p. 73. Sprat, *History* (n. 7), sig. B4, pp. 4, 120, Cf. Aarsleff, "Sprat" (n. 19), 582.

23 *Oldenburg* (n. 7), Vol. II, p. 321; Birch, *History* (n. 10), Vol. I, p. 507; Vol. II, pp. 3, 6–7, 47. Cf. ibid., Vol. II, p. 51, for the wish to vet Sprat's passage concerning the Society's imprimatur.

24 For accounts of this episode see Sprat, *History* (n. 7), pp. xvi–xvii; Aarsleff, "Sprat" (n. 19), 584–85. See also Evelyn to Sprat, October 31, 1664, in Evelyn, *Diary and Correspondence* (n. 10), Vol. III, pp. 144–47.

25 Hunter, *Science and Society* (n. 8), pp. 194–97.

26 Beale to Evelyn, June 11, 1670, Evelyn Collection, Correspondence, no. 96.

27 Birch, *History* (no. 10), Vol. II, pp. 138, 161, 163, 169, 171, 176; see also the passages cited in notes 13 and 23; Sprat, *History* (n. 7), p. 94. In addition, Robert Hooke, the Society's Curator of Experiments, was ordered to assist Wilkins. It seems to me that, in reacting against the views of Purver, Wood, "Methodology" (n. 2), 2–4, downplays the extent to which others shared responsibility with Wilkins at this point.

28 See above, n. 2.

29 See the text above and compare Sprat, *History* (n. 7), pp. 243–45, particularly his treatment of the second part of the penultimate paragraph of the draft; note also his omission of the passage about "more or lesse skill, care, patience" in the first paragraph. On the alterations made to the papers from the Society's archives, see ibid., pp. x–xi. For the statutes, see *The Record of the Royal Society* (4th ed., London, 1940), pp. 287–301. I am not inclined to attach significance to any of Sprat's omissions, but one might draw attention to his interpolation on p. 146 of a note to the effect that the Vice-President should take the President's powers in his absence, which had not appeared in the statutes, but which evidently reflects a concern on the part of the Society at this time which was to be taken up in its 1669 charter: see Michael Hunter, *Establishing the New Science: the Experience of the Early Royal Society* (Woodbridge, 1989), p. 21.

30 See above, n. 20. On the date of publication, see Sprat, *History* (n. 7), p. ix, and Beale to Evelyn, September 11, 1667, Evelyn Collection, Correspondence, no. 64: Beale, living in Somerset, had received his copy by that date.

31 See W. E. K. Middleton, *The Experimenters: A Study of the Accademia del Cimento* (Baltimore, 1971). For another possible model which is almost equally descriptive, Paul Péllison-Fontanier's *Relation Contenant l'Histoire de l'Académie Françoise* (1653), see Sprat, *History* (n. 7), p. xv.

32 *Oldenburg* (n. 7), e.g. Vol. IV, p. 63, Vol. V, p. 126, Vol. VI, p. 487.

33 Wood, "Methodology" (n. 2), *passim*. See also Webster, "Origins" (n. 3), 114ff.

34 Wood, "Methodology" (n. 2), 16ff.; Brian Vickers, "The Royal Society and English prose style: a reassessment," in Brian Vickers and N. S. Struever, *Rhetoric and the Pursuit of Truth: Language Change in the Seventeenth and Eighteenth Centuries* (Los Angeles, 1985), pp. 41ff.

35 Sprat, *History* (n. 7), pp. x, 37–38, 97, 340. See Charles Webster, *From Paracelsus to Newton: Magic and the Making of Modern Science* (Cambridge, 1982), pp. 93–96; K. T. Hoppen, "The nature of the early Royal Society," *British Journal for the History of Science* 9 (1976): 1–24, 243–73.

36 Sprat, *History* (n. 7), pp. 28, 323, 342, 345, 403 and *passim*.

37 Hunter, *Science and Society* (n. 8), p. 29.

38 Stillman Drake, trans., *Discoveries and Opinions and Galileo* (New York, 1957), p. 78; C. J. Scriba, "The autobiography of John Wallis," *Notes and Records of the Royal Society* 25 (1970): 40.

39 C. R. Weld, *A History of the Royal Society* (London, 1848), Vol. I, p. 146. On the attribution see Michael Hunter and Paul B. Wood, "Towards Solomon's house: rival strategies for reforming the early Royal Society," *History of Science* 29 (1986): 107 n. 211.

40 Royal Society Council Minutes, Vol. II (1682–1727), p. 93. Cf. also Glanvill to Oldenburg, December 17, 1669, *Oldenburg* (n. 7), Vol. VI, p. 372.

41 Sprat, *History* (n. 7), pp. 82, 426.

42 Ibid., Part III, *passim*. For a different reading of this juxtaposition, see Steven Shapin and Simon Schaffer, *Leviathan and the Air Pump: Hobbes, Boyle, and the Experimental Life* (Princeton, 1985), pp. 306–7.

43 Sprat, *History* (n. 7), Ep. Ded., p. 78 and *passim*.

44 Jacob, *Robert Boyle* (n. 1), pp. 155–56 and ch. 4, *passim*; "Restoration" (n. 3), 169 and *passim*.

45 See R. B. Schlatter, *The Social Ideas of Religious Leaders, 1660–88* (London, 1940), esp. ch. 5.

46 See G. F. Nuttall and Owen Chadwick, eds., *From Uniformity to Unity, 1662–1962* (London, 1962); W. G. Simon, "Comprehension in the age of Charles II," *Church History* 31 (1962): 440–48; D. R. Lacey, *Dissent and Parliamentary Politics in England, 1661–89* (New Brunswick, 1969); R. A. Beddard, "The Restoration Church" in J. R. Jones, ed., *The Restored Monarchy, 1660–88* (London, 1979), pp. 155–75.

47 Jacob, *Robert Boyle* (n. 1), p. 156; Jacob, "Restoration" (n. 3), pp. 169, 170 (my italics).

48 Shapiro, *John Wilkins* (n. 6), ch. 6. See also the works cited in n. 46.

49 Alexander Robertson, *The Life of Sir Robert Moray* (London, 1922), pp. 105ff.; see also 170ff. and *passim*, and David Stevenson, "Masonry, symbolism and ethics in the life of Sir Robert Moray, F. R. S.," *Proceedings of the Society of Antiquaries of Scotland* 114 (1984): 405–31, esp. 426ff.

50 Simon, "Comprehension" (n. 46), 443–45 and 447 n. 27; Lacey, *Dissent* (n. 46), pp. 57–58. See also Walter Pope, *The Life of Seth*, ed. J. B. Bamborough (Oxford, 1961), pp. 71–74. On the significant role of Ward (and Moray) in the Society, see especially Michael Hunter, "Reconstructing Restoration science: problems and pitfalls in institutional history," *Social Studies of Science* 12 (1982): 453–4.

51 Pepys, *Diary*, ed. R. C. Latham and William Matthews (London, 1970–83), Vol. VI, p. 199. For latitudinarian advocacy of intolerance, see, e.g., J. I. Cope, *Joseph Glanvill, Anglican Apologist* (St. Louis, 1956), pp. 79ff., and, on the suspension of persecution during the plague, Shapiro, *John Wilkins* (n. 6), p. 170. On Brouncker's importance, see particularly Hunter, "Reconstructing Restoration science" (n. 50), 453.

52 B. D. Henning, *The House of Commons, 1660–90* (London, 1983), Vol. II, p. 770, Vol. III, p. 524, and Hunter, *Royal Society* (n. 11), catalogue entries 71, 157. On Wilkins and this Act, see Shapiro, *John Wilkins* (n. 6), pp. 188–89.

53 Hunter, *Royal Society* (n. 11), catalogue entries 190, 222, 354 (for churchmen), 138, 178, 238 (for laymen). Cf. Henning, *House of Commons* (n. 52), Vol. I, pp. 635–36, Vol. II, p. 72, Vol. III, p. 485. On the Society's active core, see Hunter, *Royal Society*, pp. 30, 119–20.

54 Jacob, "Restoration" (no. 3), 157; *Robert Boyle* (n. 1), p. 135.

55 Sprat, *History* (n. 7), 427. Cf. Ibid., pp. 62–63. For these Fellows, see Hunter, *Royal Society* (n. 11), catalogue entries 24, 123, 218.

56 Stevenson, "Sir Robert Moray" (n. 49), 426. See also Hunter, *Royal Society* (n. 11), catalogue entries 8, 209, 387.

57 "Debate: science, politics and religion," *Past and Present* 66 (1975): 142.

58 Wallis to Oldenburg, July 16, 1669, *Oldenburg*, Vol. VI, p. 129; Beale to Evelyn, May 24, 1666, Evelyn Collection, Correspondence, no. 52.

59 See above. In addition, some evidently note factual references.

60 Beale to Evelyn, September 11, 1667, Evelyn Collection, Correspondence, no. 64; Fairfax to Oldenburg, *Oldenburg* (n. 7), Vol. III, pp. 491–92. Cf. Oldenburg to Winthrop, October 13, 1667, ibid., Vol. III, pp. 525–26.

61 Oldenburg to Boyle, October 1, 1667, ibid., Vol. III, p. 503.

62 *Phil. Trans.* 2 (1667): 505. Cf. Sprat, *History* (n. 7), p. 155. It is interesting that Evelyn marked this paragraph in his copy of the journal, now British Library Eve.a.149: the only other point he marked was that at which Oldenburg referred to the book's dedication to the King (p. 503).

63 Wood, "Methodology" (n. 2), 7. See also below and Sprat, *History* (n. 7), pp. 243–45.

64 Beale to Evelyn, March 14, 1670, preserved among a folder of loose letters in a box of "Evelyn period" papers in the Evelyn Collection (it is severely damaged by damp, and I have supplied the bracketed words); Beale to Evelyn, June 11, 1670, Evelyn Collection, Correspondence, no. 96.

65 *Phil. Trans.* 2 (1667): 506–8.

66 Webster, "Origins" (n. 3), 115. Cf. p. 118, and, e.g., Purver, *Royal Society* (n. 3), *passim*. For an estimate more similar to that given here, see Aarsleff, "Sprat" (n. 19), 581.

67 Worthington to More, February 5, 1668, in John Worthington, *Diary and Correspondence*, ed. R. C. Christie, Vol. II, part 2 (Chetham Society, 1886), p. 265.

68 A number of extracts from Stubbe's attacks are printed in the "Notes" to Sprat, *History* (n. 7). See also ibid., Appendix B. For modern accounts of these attacks, see esp. Hunter, *Science and Society* (n. 8), ch. 6 and the references cited on pp. 212–13. Two works there referred to as forthcoming have now appeared: M. R. G. Spiller, "*Concerning Experimental Natural Philosophie*": *Meric Casaubon and the Royal Society* (The Hague, 1980) (see also Michael Hunter, "Ancients, moderns, philologists and scientists," *Annals of Science* 39 (1982): 187–92) and J. R. Jacob, *Henry Stubbe, Radical Protestantism and the Early Enlightenment* (Cambridge, 1983).

69 Stubbe, *A Reply unto the Letter written to Mr. Henry Stubbe* (Oxford, 1671), pp. 19–20. Lady E. P. was evidently Lady Puckering: cf. Stubbe to Moray, May 27, 1667, Royal Society Early Letters S.1.89. Cf. ibid., no. 91. For a

slightly different view on the issue of the Society's authorization, see *A Letter to Mr. Henry Stubs* (London, 1670), p. 3.

70 See Jacob, *Stubbe* (n. 68), *passim*. For a caveat, see Hunter, *Science and Society* (n. 8), pp. 139–40.

71 Evelyn to Beale, July 27, 1670, Evelyn Collection MS 39, no. 329. Evelyn's characterization of the Society is quoted in Hunter, *Science and Society* (n. 8), p. 44, and his comment on Oxford in ibid., pp. 146–47.

72 See Hunter, *Science and Society* (n. 8), ch. 6. For "Hobbist" sentiments, see Sprat, *History* (n. 7), e.g. pp. 33, 379.

73 Stubbe, *A Reply* (n. 69), p. 19.

74 Birch, *History* (n. 19), Vol. II, p. 266; Oldenburg to Beckman, March 30, 1668, *Oldenburg* (n. 7), Vol. IV, p. 278; Beale to Evelyn, June 11, 1670, Evelyn Collection, Correspondence, no. 96. It is perhaps worth noting here a defense of the Royal Society published in 1670 as *A Letter to Mr. Henry Stubs* (see above, n. 69): but this is almost wholly devoted to the refutation of specific accusations by Stubbe (see Oldenburg to Williamson, March 14, 1675, *Oldenburg*, Vol. XI, p. 226, for what is apparently a later reference to it). For a reference in 1681 to the "right of copies" if Sprat "and other works" were to be reprinted, see Birch, *History*, Vol. IV, p. 82.

75 Robert Hooke, *Diary, 1672–80*, ed. H. W. Robinson and H. W. Adams (London, 1935), pp. 342, 345. On Smith, see Hunter, *Royal Society* (n. 11), catalogue entry 333.

76 John Evelyn, *Sylva* (3rd ed., London, 1679), sigs. A1–4, a1. On the background to this material see Hunter, *Science and Society* (n. 8), pp. 177–78. Quotations from this preface are included in the notes to Sprat, *History* (n. 7): see especially that to p. 78, line 31 (though it is there wrongly stated that the material first appeared in the 1670 edition).

77 Jacob, "Restoration ideologies" (n. 3). It should also be noted that it is far from clear that any of the writings of this period cited in this article were intended to represent the corporate views of the Royal Society.

78 Hunter, *Science and Society* (n. 8), esp. p. 159.

79 Ibid., esp. pp. 84–85, 191–92; A. E. Musson and Eric Robinson, *Science and Technology in the Industrial Revolution* (Manchester, 1969), ch. 1; John Gascoigne, "Politics, patronage and Newtonianism: the Cambridge example," *Historical Journal* 27 (1984): 1–24, esp. pp. 14ff.

80 Sprat, *History* (n. 7), p. 78.

81 See above, notes 8–9.

82 I would thus place a somewhat different construction from Shapin and Schaffer on the evidence they adduce in *Leviathan and the Air Pump* (n. 42): it seems to me that they underestimate the *defensiveness* of the posture of Boyle and his colleagues. Cf. Hunter, *Science and Society* (n. 8), pp. 172–73, 178–79.

NOTES TO DOCUMENTS

1 After "is," "so" has been deleted. In the next line, "differing" has been altered from "different."

2 "even" replaces "also", deleted.

3 After "Spirits", "etc." has been deleted.

4 "the" replaces "such," deleted.

5 After "made", "and recorded carefull" has been deleted.

6 After "skillfully", "car" has been deleted.

7 "recorded with" is inserted above the line.

8 Before "there", "it seems" has been deleted.

9 Before "will", "though by severa" has been deleted.

10 Replacing "make", deleted.

11 After "same", a comma has been replaced by a full-stop and "though i" has been deleted.

12 After "investigating", "and discovering" has been deleted.

13 "present" is inserted above the line, as is "to" in the next line.

14 "their successors" replaces "posterity", deleted.

15 After "will", "use" has been deleted.

16 After "carefull", "and ci" has been deleted.

17 This was replaced by a word which was then deleted and is now illegible.

10   Locke and the latitude-men: ignorance as a ground of toleration

G. A. J. Rogers

Pope's confident line "God said 'Let Newton be!' And all was light," whilst no doubt reflecting the eighteenth-century English view of Newton's achievement, masks the far from certain intellectual steps that preceded and surrounded the birth of the *Principia*. That Newton's great work was seen as so illuminating, even though it was almost unintelligible to most of the educated public, perhaps suggests the degree of darkness which had so recently prevailed. Indeed, Pope had indicated as much in the first line of his intended epitaph for Newton, the couplet reading as follows:

> Nature and Nature's Laws lay hid in Night.
> God said, *Let Newton be*! and All was *Light*.

The seventeenth century was not uniformly an age of intellectual confidence, despite its unprecedented intellectual achievements. Indeed the latter were often a source for the anxieties and uncertainties so characteristic of the age. Other obvious and powerful factors were the numerous religious conflicts, the implications of the new natural philosophy, and the plethora of speculative philosophies, new and old, which were canvassed in the century.

In England political disagreement, fired by religious and other differences, combined with these other forces to provide an environment from which emerged arguments for individual liberty and toleration which were to become incorporated into the political and legal framework of the liberal state.

In this chapter I wish to explore aspects of the development in the second half of the seventeenth century of just one of the arguments for toleration – though I suspect that it is a very important one. It was an argument that found its fullest expression in the writings of Locke, but which had been nudging towards the surface at least since the 1630s. It is an argument familiar enough to scholars of the period. I shall call it the Argument from Ignorance.

The argument is at first sight deceptively simple. It is, simply, that unless you know that you know what the truth is on some matter then you have no business attempting to force others to accept your opinion or of

230

suppressing those who propound a view contrary to one's own. The argument was applied particularly to matters of religion. But it clearly has wider implications, and because it is a principle which has general application it allows for the possibility of drawing analogies from disputes outside of the religious sphere to those within. The difficult questions, of course, are deciding which issues are ones on which it is impossible to know that we know.

Our inability to settle a knowledge claim may arise in three ways. It may be that our ignorance is merely contingent and at some future date we may discover the truth. Or it may be that our ignorance is inherent in our nature. Or, thirdly, we may be mistaken in believing that there is a fact of the matter of which we are ignorant.[1] Notoriously, our inability to settle a knowledge claim is not always self-evident either in particular or in general. Unjustified and unjustifiable claims to knowledge are constantly made with complete sincerity.

If we are not merely to acquiesce in skepticism we must allow that some knowledge claims are justified. In the seventeenth century precisely which ones these were and what their mark should be was, of course, at the center of the theological debate. Equally obviously, and almost as closely related, was the issue of who had the authority to decide on the matter. For English thinkers of the mid-seventeenth century the problem was of course a real one affecting the livelihood and even possibly the lives of those involved.

Central to the theological debate, too, was the place of conscience. If conscience was indeed an infallible guide to moral truth, then the Argument from Ignorance could not be deployed against it. But, apart from the obvious circularity in an appeal to conscience – how can we know it is infallible? – the advocates of conscience as a direct source of moral knowledge had to come to terms with the apparently embarrassing fact that conscience did not speak with the same voice to all. Should all claims to conscience be allowed? Or were there to be limits? And if so, where should they be drawn, and by whom? As Ireton put it, was "any thinge that any man would call religion" to be accepted?[2]

That there was a problem as to how the truth could be known was acknowledged. In 1646 it was explained thus: although the state should not permit the dissemination of opinions which contravene the laws of nature and the light of religious truth, we unfortunately possess no certain and infallible means for determining between truth and error.[3]

The epistemological problem of the Argument from Ignorance, then, was well in the arena by the 1640s, and there were many articulate advocates of the view that neither the State nor the Church had an infallible source of religious truth.[4]

The issue of infallibility

By the time that we reach the Restoration Cambridge was being seen as the center for a new group of advocates of religious toleration and Simon Patrick's little pamphlet (if indeed he was the author) on "the new sect of latitude-men"[5] gives important insight into the Cambridge movement. We learn of their commitment to the Church of England and to the primacy of reason in man's judgment, and we learn too of their sympathy for "the Platonick Philosophy"[6] and for the new atomical philosophy, and their opposition to Aristotle and the schoolmen. But of their detailed epistemology we learn very little directly, and there is good reason why we should not, for one of the points which Patrick makes about the movement is that it provides for a liberty of intellectual position incompatible with a detailed orthodoxy on the finer issues of philosophy. In fine, Patrick offers us the characterization of a viewpoint rather than a justification of it. But the picture is sufficiently clear for us to be able to discern a strong liberal current (in their attitude to liturgy, for example) and a rejection of dogma. The position is well illustrated by his account of reason:

Reason is that faculty whereby a man must judge of every thing, nor can a man believe any thing except he hath some reason for it, whether that reason be a deduction from the light of nature, and those principles which are the candle of the Lord, set up in the soul of every man that hath not wilfully extinguished it; or a branch of Divine revelation in the oracles of holy Scripture; or the general interpretation of genuine antiquity, or the proposal of our own Church consentaneous thereto, or lastly the result of some or all of these: for he that will rightly make use of his Reason, must take all that is reasonable into consideration.[7]

Whilst it would be wrong to read too deeply into this passage (to attempt to extract from it an account of the limits of reason, for example), there are some points of note. First it may be observed that Patrick does not make clear whether he is concerned with knowledge or belief. Although he talks in the passage of belief the passage concludes with a discussion of truth to which the proper use of reason leads, combined with a gesture towards the *prisca theologia*: "Nor is there any point in Divinity, where that which is most ancient doth not prove the most rational, and the most rational the ancientist; for there is an eternal consanguinity between all verity."[8] The implication is that the coherence of the various sources of enlightenment increases their probability, but it would be quite out of keeping with the tone of Patrick's document to make strong claims for certainty from the method which he advocates. Not surprisingly he was here at one with the great figures of the Cambridge school, Whichcote,

Smith, Cudworth and More, about whom we shall have more to say in a while.

On the great issue of liberty of conscience Patrick's position is again one characterized by lack of dogma. The latitude-men, he tells us, are for it, but within bounds. There must be an agreed liturgy and ceremonies – "a Church cannot be without Unity and Uniformity" – but it is important not to try to impose too much as an over protective mother that "would have all things bound up and nothing free."[9]

One implication is of the need for one broad church – there is no suggestion here of allowing the nonconformity that Locke was to advocate against Stillingfleet in the 1680s.[10] But Patrick does not spell out the justifications for the school's position: the theory had already been given form in a series of works by the school. The school itself may be both narrowly and broadly conceived. Narrowly conceived the latitudinarians are limited to those whose views coincided with Patrick's characterization. More widely it includes those thinkers who shared the liberal outlook of the Cambridge men and their commitment to the new learning, but who did not necessarily share their sympathy for neoplatonism.

Of the many non-platonists – Falkland, Hales, Chillingworth, Taylor, Stillingfleet are just the most famous – I shall take only one, Chillingworth, to illustrate the issue which was seen as central by many to the argument for toleration, the Catholic claim to papal infallibility.

The Religion of Protestants of 1638 embodies the full emotional and intellectual response that Chillingworth generated to his earlier conversion to Catholicism. In it and in his unpublished manuscripts we find as clear an account of the limits of certainty as was to appear in England in the first half of the seventeenth century. This pre-Cartesian work is largely untroubled by the skeptical worries to appear in later thinkers, but it draws distinctions to appear again in the writings of such as Glanvill, Boyle and Locke.

For Chillingworth the crucial argument is always that the certainty of a conclusion can never exceed the certainty of its premises. Granted that the premises of most arguments, including all arguments establishing religious truths, begin from premises that are only probable, then the conclusions too can be only probable. Thus, to the Catholic church's claim to known infallibility Chillingworth replies:

But if there be no other ground of certainty but your church's infallibility, upon what certain ground do you know your church is infallible? Upon what certain ground do you know all those things which must be known before you can know that your church is infallible? as, that there is a God; that God has promised his assistance to your church in all her decrees; that the Scripture wherein this promise is extant is the word of God; that those texts of Scripture which you allege for your infallibility are uncorrupted; that that which you pretend is the true sense of them! When you have produced certain grounds for all these things, I doubt not but that it will appear, that we also may have grounds certain enough to believe our whole religion, which is nothing else but the Bible, without dependence on the church's infallibility.[11]

Chillingworth's argument would seem conclusive. All possible arguments for infallibility must rest on premises which may only be judged probable at best and are therefore unable to support their conclusion.

Whether Chillingworth had only the Church of Rome in mind, or whether his argument was intended also for some of his fellow protestants I shall not now speculate. But it is to be noted that the argument is generalizable to other claims to certain knowledge in matters of religion and the age was hardly one of diffidence in the expression of religious positions.

Chillingworth's philosophical argument was spelt out more fully in his manuscripts. The kinds of certainty possible and their sources are identified clearly:

The schools distinguish of two kinds of certainty; Metaphysical, whereby we know that a thing is so, and cannot be otherwise; and Moral, whereby we are assured a thing is so and cannot be otherwise, though there is no absolute impossibility nor contradiction but that it may be, Metaphysical and absolute certainty must proceed either from sense, or demonstration, or revelation. For by all these means and no more we may know, that a thing is so, and cannot be otherwise.

Chillingworth's acceptance of sense experience as a basis for absolute certainty reflects his debts to Aristotle and reveals that the rising tide of skepticism in European thought had not eroded his confidence in experience as a source of knowledge.

He goes on to spell out what the implications are for revelation:

I say by divine revelation, because there is no doubt that God can make me know anything immediately without the interposing of sense or reason, as he did the prophets; but then to make me undoubtedly certain thereof, it is requisite, not only that God reveal the truth, but also assure me, that it was his revelation, and no fancy nor illusion.

And he then explains moral certainty:

Moral certainty is begott in us, by presumption and probabilities, which either by their strength ... or by their multitude, make up a moral demonstration, to which being well considered ... no prudent and sober man can possibly refuse to yield a firm, certain, undoubting, reasonable assent and adherence.[12]

The introduction of talk of probabilities is a reminder that the assessment of evidence and argument in such terms was new, even rare, in the 1630s.[13] It reminds us, too, that introduction of such assessment was as relevant to theological debates as to those in the natural sciences.

To admit talk of moral certainty, to deny infallibility, was also to admit the possibility of disagreement. Chillingworth was happy to accept the implications: "There is no danger to any state from any man's opinion, unless it be such an opinion by which disobedience to authority or impiety is taught or licensed," he wrote in *The Religion of Protestants*,[14] and without dwelling on the subject at length he was clearly committed to liberty of conscience: "if Protestants did offer violence to other men's consciences, and compel them to embrace their Reformation, I excuse them not."[15]

The Cambridge Platonists

It is appropriate now to move back from Great Tew to Cambridge, for as the Civil War extinguished activities at the one place there arose in the other the most powerful philosophical movement to reach fruition in a European university in the seventeenth century. I refer, of course, to the Cambridge Platonists.

Burnet's account of the school at Cambridge contains a series of remarks which provide an appropriate introduction to the themes of this chapter. He begins by contrasting them favorably with the bulk of Anglican clergy who had acceded to the Act of Conformity of 1662 and had thereby swelled their purses and forgotten their intellectual and pastoral duties. The new set of men "of another stamp" were "generally of Cambridge... the chief of whom were Drs. Whichcot[e], Cudworth, Wilkins, More and Worthington."[16] Whichcote, he tells us, was for much liberty of conscience and elevated the religious consciousness of his pupils through the study of the classical platonists, a policy in which he was followed by More and Cudworth who joined battle against the rising tide of atheism, sullied as men were by the "hypocrisy of some, and the fantastical conceits of the more sincere enthusiasts" together with the seductive powers of the corrupting Hobbes.[17] Their moderation and toleration was widely recognized: "They loved the constitution of the church, and the liturgy, and could well live under them; but they did not think it unlawful to live under another form. They wished that things might have been carried with more moderation, and they continued to keep a good correspondence with those who had differed from them in opinion, and allowed a great freedom both in philosophy and in divinity from whence they were called men of latitude."[18]

Undoubtedly a major reason for the tolerance urged by the Cambridge Platonists was irenic. As Whichcote urged, "The Spirit of Religion is a

Reconciling Spirit."[19] But there was also argument that many questions were not capable of final knowledge by mortals. Their favorite text, already cited by Patrick, that "The spirit of man is the candle of the Lord,"[20] was an indication not only that the mind of man could reach truth but also, since a candle gives little illumination, that the truths reached are likely to be limited.

Whichcote wrote no major work of philosophy. But Smith, Cudworth, and above all More were more prolific. Even Whichcote, in his aphorisms, indicates the rationale of the liberal position. Central to man's nature is reason. "We are not" he wrote, "to submit our Understanding to the belief of those things, that are *contrary* to our Understanding. We must have a Reason, for that which we believe *above* our Reason."[21] Over-enthusiasm for one's cause was a sign of insincerity: "The more *False* any one is in his Religion, the more *Fierce* and furious in Maintaining it."[22] Our own spirits, finite and fallible, may yet be directed by a "Spirit Infinite and Infallible," but the process of obtaining such guidance is not immediate or guaranteed. And again, "Our Fallibility and the Shortness of our Knowledge should make us peaceable and gentle: because I *may* be Mistaken, I *must* not be dogmatical and confident, peremptory and imperious. I *will* not break the certain Laws of Charity, for a doubtful Doctrine or of uncertain Truth."[23]

Similar cautions were urged by Henry More, even though More's enthusiasm to condemn Enthusiasm, Atheism, or in later days, Cartesianism, often led to an outspokenness he criticized in others. His confrontation with Thomas Vaughan in the 1650s well illustrates both points. Both men, hiding behind pseudonyms, denounced each other with a verbal ferocity indicated by some of their titles: Vaughan assailed More in 1650 with *A Man Mouse Taken in a Trap*, to which More replied with *The Second Lash of Alazonomastix*, with Vaughan's counter: *The Man-Mouse taken in a Trap, and Tortur'd to death for gnawing the margins of Eugenius Philalethes* (the latter being Vaughan's pseudonym). But through all the rhetoric, some differences in intellectual approach are discernible. Thus, Vaughan's claim to have independent empirical evidence of the existence of a "first matter" apart from its manifestation in any particular form is dismissed by More on the powerful ground that such first matter could only be observed in some form or other.[24]

More's most systematic attack on Enthusiasm, *Enthusiasmus Triumphatus, or a Discourse of the Nature, Kinds and Cure, of Enthusiasm* (1656) well illustrates his commitment to the faculty of reason, and his concern to reject unfounded claims in religion, politics and natural philosophy. It is also important as an attack on the imagination as a source of knowledge, echoing the low place allocated that faculty by

Bacon, a position it was in general to retain until the end of the eighteenth century.

Enthusiasm, More says, is "a full, but false, persuasion in a Man that he is inspir'd."[25] It is, he surprisingly says, akin to atheism, for both are born of "an overbearing *Phancy*" to which men respond rather than to "the calm and cautious insinuations of free *Reason*."[26] And an overbearing fancy or imagination is substantially the product of physical causes such as diet or the humors, particularly melancholy.

Physically caused illusions, then, are the cause of Enthusiasm, and often emerge as a conviction of communication with God:

Whence it is a strong temptation with the *Melancholist*, when he feels a storm of devotion or zeal come upon him like a mighty wind, his heart being full of affection, his head pregnant with clear and sensible representations, and his mouth flowing and streaming with fit and powerful expressions, such as would astonish an ordinary Auditory to hear, it is, I say, a shrewd temptation to him to think that it is the very *Spirit of God*, that *then moves* supernaturally in him; whenas all that excess of zeal, and affection, and fluency of words is most palpably to be resolved into the power of *Melancholy*, which is a kind of *natural inebriation*.[27]

Enthusiasm, then, is a kind of flatulence which "rises out of the *Hypochondriacal* humour upon some occasional heat."[28]

More's explanation of "religious inspiration" would have done credit to the hard-headed Hobbes to whom he was so strongly opposed. It was also generalizable in the sense that Enthusiasm could manifest itself not only in religion but also in politics or speculative and natural philosophy. Chemists and theosophists exhibited the disease and More saw Paracelsus as a prime, perhaps *the* prime, example.

More's antipathy to the Enthusiasts is mirrored in his cautious approach to claims to proof and knowledge. In a work which he undoubtedly regarded as one of his major achievements, *An Antidote against Atheism* (1652), he placed a caution over the idea that he might offer a demonstration of the existence of God: he does not pretend, he says, to be able to show "that it is impossible to be otherwise than as I have concluded."[29] He thinks there is probably no such demonstration, for even "*Mathematical Evidence* it self may be but a constant undiscoverable Delusion, [to] which our Nature is necessarily and perpetually Obnoxious."[30] His arguments, then, will not always be so strong that the reader will be forced to confess it must be so; "For I conceive that we may give *full Assent* to that which notwithstanding may possibly be otherwise."[31] From what follows it is clear that he particularly has in mind the Argument from Design which occupies a very substantial part of the work. In similar vein, and reminding us of arguments to be presented in detail by Locke, but in marked contrast to the philosophies of his acknowledged mentors Plato and Descartes, More holds out no hope of our reaching knowledge of the essence of substances. His remarks on this subject are brief but his position is clear enough: if we subtract from our idea of a subject, he says, all aptitudes, operations, properties and modifications, then what we are left with is merely undifferentiated substance so that one substance is not then distinguishable from another.[32] He spells out the argument in a note to the chapter. It is for him an important issue as on it he rests his dualism. He writes: "we can have no full or distinct Idea of any specifick Substance...all its properties set aside." However, where a "contrariety of Properties is found, and this permanent and essential, there must be a distinct Essence for the Ground of those Properties; tho' we are not able to form any distinct Idea of that Subject of them."[33] Since penetrability and impenetrability are two such contrary properties they must belong, More held, to the essence of different substances.

No doubt there are difficulties in More's account. He requires that we know the essential properties of substances but offers us no route from our ideas of the substances to the substances themselves. But our present purpose is not to assess these arguments of More, nor even to set them in his whole philosophy. Rather it is to note his recognition of limits to the intellectual enquiry and his rejection of unwarranted claims to certainty.

Since we only know substances by their properties the next question is how do we come to know those properties? More here distinguishes between immediate attributes and others. Immediate attributes may only be known directly. They can never be demonstrated "otherwise they would not be immediate."[34] Thus, as an example, the substance, matter, might have been penetrable or impenetrable, but is actually the latter, and we do not know why because we can discern no necessary connection between being a three-dimensional substance and being impenetrable. However, once we know some of the immediate properties of substances we may demonstrate others.

More's *An Explanation of the Grand Mystery of Godliness* (1660), even by the standard of More's works, is not much read these days, as for the most part it rehearses arguments familiar from his earlier works. But it contains a discussion on liberty of conscience which takes us into the wider implications of More's thought. It is, he says, the right of nations and persons to examine their religion, to hear the religion of strangers, and, if they are convinced, to change their own. The liberty of religion is the common and natural right of all nations and persons, and the truth of the Christian religion is fostered by its recognition.[35] Rather than damning infidels, and we should remember that two-thirds of the known world is pagan, we should look to see if there is anything wrong with our propagation of the Christian message, because it is so clear in principle that it should immediately carry conviction if it is explained properly. The failure suggests corruption in the Christian church itself of which a chief cause is the "obtrusion of ceremonies... For while the Heart goes a whoring after those outward shows, and an over-value be put upon them, the inward life of Godliness will easily be extinguished."[36] He attacks "that highly-esteemed knowledge called *Orthodoxness* or *Rightness of Opinion*"[37] and reminds us that whilst "Knowledge puffeth up... charity edifieth."[38] Again the emphasis is on the fallibility of our intellects. We must be wary of "affixing any of our own Inventions or Interpretations of Scripture for Christian Truths."[39] They come from "a fallible and doubtful hand,"[40] and should not be forced on those who did not readily accept them. The date of publication of *The Grand Mystery of Godliness*, 1660, is possibly significant. Whether it was aimed at the new king I do not know, but the message is clear.

More places much emphasis on conscience as a source of knowledge. But he is careful to circumscribe its authority. Whilst conscience must be obeyed as a way in which God promulgates his law, it is also subject to reason's authority. Our conviction, then, must be monitored by our rational faculty, "for I speak of such as are in their wits, not mad-men and Fanaticks, nor yet such as embrace for Religious Precepts contrary to the *Light and Law of Nature*, which is the highest and most incontrovertible law of God, as being not Topical but Universal."[41] In those cases where the light of nature is not obvious and people are convinced by their conscience, then God must indeed be speaking to them. However, this does not rule out different people receiving different commands from God, and More sees no difficulties in this. In fact he thinks it is obvious that it happens, for he accepts that such differing commands are received via conscience by, say, Turks, Jews and Christians. However, he never doubts but that conscience is the word of God.

Any account of the Cambridge Platonists must place much emphasis on the role of reason within their scheme of things. But we would be wrong to place a narrow conception on their understanding of it. They were hostile to any attempt to impose *a priori* solutions on problems which they saw as empirical and to seek demonstrations where none might be obtained was, to them, itself a mark of irrationality. More's proofs of the existence of God well illustrate this commitment. His *Antidote against Atheism* and its long Appendix offer several arguments for a deity, including the Ontological Argument. But by far the most space is devoted to the Argument from Design, an argument based on empirical evidence. And More gives the distinct impression that it is the empirical evidence which he personally finds the most convincing. It is relevant, too, that

Cudworth, in *The True Intellectual System of the Universe* (1678) strongly supports the Argument from Design and rejects Descartes' repudiation of final causes. Both More and Cudworth became Fellows of the Royal Society and its emphasis on observation and experiment, whilst apparently standing in contrast with the spirit of platonism, was far from uncongenial to their outlook.

Enough has now been said to justify my claim that within the Cambridge movement there was recognition of the limits of human enquiry and to indicate connections between this and a commitment to toleration. But we may also note that the plea for toleration was substantially untranslated into any political program or policy on legislation. The cultivation of toleration within the framework set by ignorance did not result in a campaign with specific goals. And here we may underline the difference between these earlier thinkers and John Locke, who, at the end of the century was arguing, albeit mainly anonymously, for a new political program of toleration, which he saw as justified by his own philosophical argument. Nor did the earlier thinkers attempt to spell out the philosophical implications for a theory of action that the ignorance thesis might with justice be seen as implying. In marked contrast, Locke's *Essay* set standards for rational belief – in contrast to knowledge – in terms of probability, which in Book IV of the *Essay* he examined in considerable detail and not a little originality.[42]

However, before we turn to look in more detail at Locke's place in all of this we must surely recognize that of Glanvill who, in the early decades of the Royal Society articulated a unity of position, founded on modest skepticism and toleration, from within the community of the Anglican church and the Royal Society.

Glanvill's liberal stance is manifest in many of his works, but I shall confine my attention to just one of his essays which well conveys his commitments on the major areas of intellectual dispute in the 1670s. In "Anti-fanatical religion and free philosophy. In a continuation of the New Atlantis" (1676) Glanvill makes use of Bacon's imaginary land as a literary device to explain his own position on philosophy and religion. The tone of the work is precisely what any one familiar with Glanvill would expect. It is a rejection of enthusiasts in religion, of Aristotle in philosophy, and a plea for a recognition of the mediocrity of man's intellect, whilst rejecting a paralyzing skepticism in human enquiry.

Glanvill gives us a detailed account of the education of the young academicians of New Atlantis. University studies required the study of the ancient philosophers "that were before the days of Aristotle."[43] But they "did not think themselves perfect, as soon as they were acquainted with the knowledge contain'd in *Systems*." They considered their principles only as hypotheses, without passing judgment on their truth or falsehood. And thus they studied Plato "much," and Aristotle's own works (which were much better than the commentators, especially the more recent), and were well instructed in all the great classical thinkers. But this concern with the Ancients did not result in contempt for the Moderns, and they read "all sorts of late Improvements in *Anatomy, Mathematicks, Natural History*, and *Mechanicks* … and the *Experimental Philosophy of Solomon's House* … so that they rendered themselves more capable of judging of the *Truth*, or *likelyhood* of any propos'd *Hypothesis*."[44] A comparable program of education was followed in Divinity.

Fundamental to the education was a rejection of the blind acceptance of authority, the assertion of a liberty of enquiry, and a determination not to prejudge contentious issues. They considered man's understandings to be at best very weak, and the search for truth difficult, so that

we are very likely to be imposed on by our Complexions, Imaginations, Interests and Affections. That whole Ages, and great Kingdoms, and Christian Churches, and Learned Counsels, have joyn'd in Common Errors; and have obtruded false and absurd Conceits upon the World with great severity, and flaming Zeal; That much Folly and great Non-sense have … been held for certain … that all Mankind are … bafled in the … most *obvious* things; In the *Objects* of *Sense*, and *Motions* of our own Souls: That (in earnest) we cannot tell, *How we speak a Word*, or *move a Finger: How the Soul is united to the Body*; or the *Parts of Bodies to one another*: how our *own* were *framed* at first; or how afterwards they are nourish'd; that these *nearest* things, and a thousand more, are hid from our deepest Enquiries.[45]

Such reserve and modesty, Glanvill argues, allowed for a liberty in matters of religion where they labored "to *demonstrate* the *Truth* and *Reasonableness* of the *Christian Religion*."[46] He thus recognized that there was no set and right model of worship laid down in the scriptures. This did not, however, allow Glanvill to take the further step of toleration for all patterns of public worship. For whilst there was no set form which must be adhered to timelessly, if the endless animosities of recent times were to be avoided then "the *Form*, and *Circumstances* of *Government*, was to be left to the *Ruling Powers* in the Church."[47] Thus Glanvill, whilst appearing to side so often with the liberal view, uses a liberal argument to justify the imposition of an orthodoxy, but an orthodoxy which might itself change in the light of discussion and debate. The political and social realities which lie behind Glanvill's position have been well explained by Jackson Cope. There was first of all the belief that episcopacy was central to the English constitution, and second there was the fear of Popery, with a king whose Roman sympathies were manifested regularly.[48] To express this more critically we may say that Glanvill, no more than the Cambridge Platonists and others in the latitudinarian movement, never seems to have entertained the possibility of allowing either for a multitude of churches within the one kingdom, or a separation of roles between church and state, and removing the power of the civil magistrate from the arena of religion altogether. It was just such possibilities that needed to be considered before the debate on toleration may be said to have reached maturity. It is only with Locke that this more radical stage of the implications of the arguments from ignorance is reached.

Glanvill's essay concludes with an account of the other branches of learning taught in New Atlantis, in which, once again, he lays much emphasis on the "shallowness of our deepest enquiries."[49] No account of nature was taken for anything more than hypothesis or probable conjecture, though special study was to be given to the atomic philosophy of Gassendi and the system of Descartes.[50]

For all his prolificacy Glanvill never reaches above moderate profundity in his philosophic works, and the constant message coming from the latitudinarians that the human intellect is both weak and fallible and yet may reach truth in important select areas had still to be given firm philosophical foundations. It was Locke's works, and especially the *Essay Concerning Human Understanding*, which were to do this and it is to him that we should now turn.

Locke and the argument from ignorance

"To come therefore to what we have in hand; if you would have your son *Reason well*, let him read *Chillingworth*."[51] Thus Locke advised his friend Edward Clarke. Locke was undoubtedly impressed both by the form and content of *The Religion of Protestants*. He was also in agreement with the assault that Chillingworth had launched on the papal claim to infallibility for similar arguments appear in Locke's little tract on the subject.[52] The papal claim, Locke holds, is defeated by, among others, the Argument from Ignorance. But at this relatively early stage of Locke's political thought – the tract was written in 1661 – Locke emerges as more conservative in matters of toleration than he was later to be, adopting a position close to that which we have already seen advocated by Glanvill.[53] And it is as well to remember that it was not only the pope who was seen as a threat by Locke at the time of the Restoration. He expressed his fears in letters to his father in the uncertain days before the return of Charles. In the land, he said, "Divisions are as wide, factions as violent and designes as pernicious as ever and those woven soe intricately, that there are few know what probably to hope or desire."[54] Like Descartes before him, he even contemplated joining the army, though we cannot take his conjecture very seriously for he continues "Armes is the last and worst of refuges, and 'tis great misery of this shatterd and giddy nation that warrs have produced noething but warrs." He goes on to hope that his father will not "venture [his] rest, health or estate for ingratefull men as all ambitious are, nor deceitfull, as religious pretenders are, nor tyrants such as are the promisers of liberty."[55] It is perhaps not surprising that in such a clime it was caution rather than the libertarian spirit that emerged in his writings. "Tis not without reason," he wrote in *The First Tract on Government*, "that *tyranny* and *anarchy* are judged the smartest scourages can fall upon mankind, the plea of *authority* usually backing the one and of *liberty* inducing the other: and it is between these two it is, that human affairs are perpetually kept tumbling."[56]

The political pressures, then, favored caution. But our concern is with those of the argument. And the argument for toleration applied constant and increasingly sophisticated intellectual force on the unacceptability of compelling others to accept opinions in matters of religion where those applying the force could not, as a matter of logic, know that they were in the right. The claims to papal infallibility of the Romans and the Enthusiasts' claims of the inner light were consistently rejected. It is an argument to be found in all his major and many of his minor writings on toleration and on epistemology.

The "Essay on Infallibility" takes it as agreed by all parties that the scriptures are God's word. The question is whether anybody may justly claim to have infallible knowledge of their correct interpretation. Locke says that the conflict of interpretation within the church of Rome is itself conclusive evidence of fallibility. But he goes on to advance the argument we have already seen deployed by Chillingworth – "Even granting that some infallible interpreter...be given, he will still not be able...to contribute anything to the solution of problems of faith...unless he can infallibly show that he is infallible. Since he cannot prove this about himself, for nobody's testimony about himself is acceptable, and since the Scripture is silent, I cannot easily discover how he can be recognized."[57]

In this brief work Locke makes no attempt to offer a detailed justification of these claims, but in his many writings which touch on the subject we consistently find his insistence on the ignorance of the law makers, because they are merely men, on matters of religious practice. Often, too, he contrasts the actual state of man's ignorance with the claims of the papists to have an infallible source of knowledge. (See, for example, his letter to Henry Stubbe in 1659, and his early "Essay concerning toleration" of 1667.)[58] But his own developing thoughts on toleration were taking shape in the following decades at the very time that he was composing his great account of the limits of knowledge, which, famously, arose from conversations in 1671 about morality and revealed religion.[59]

The strong connections between Locke's advocacy of toleration and his account of the real limits of human knowledge, that much of his argument for toleration is a version of the Argument from Ignorance, has been well noticed by several recent commentators.[60] I shall not, therefore, enter into the matter in great detail. I do, however, need to spend some time on the issue for my final purpose. For I wish to underline the way in which Locke's argument was misinterpreted. My major example will be Jonas Proast. But, in a rather different way, Leibniz too rejected the Argument from Ignorance, reflecting, I would suggest, a difference of intellectual position of some importance. The failure to grasp the force of Locke's case suggests that it was an argument not well understood by men of undoubted intelligence in his own day, and the most likely sources of their incomprehension lie partly in the novelty of the argument and partly, perhaps, in a strong inner resistance to the conclusion. Toleration only became self-evidently a virtue after a major intellectual struggle, a struggle far from over.

In Chapter XVIII of Book IV of *An Essay Concerning Human Understanding*, "Of Faith and Reason and their distinct Provinces," Locke commits himself firmly to the primacy of reason in matters of religion, entirely in line with the earlier latitudinarians already noticed, and sets the boundaries of religious knowledge.

The chapter begins with a rehearsal of the grounds of ignorance. We lack knowledge, Locke says, where we lack ideas, or where we lack proof, or where we do not have determinate specific ideas. Further, where we lack either personal knowledge or the testimony of others we lack even probable reasons.

Failure to draw the boundaries between faith and reason has been the cause of great disputes: "For till it be resolved, how far we are to be guided by Reason, and how far by Faith, we shall in vain dispute, and endeavour to convince one another in matters of Religion."[61] Reason, for Locke in this context, is the discovery of the certainty or probability of propositions made by deductions from ideas obtained by experience. Faith, in contrast, is the assent to any proposition on the basis of revelation. Locke then points out that a man inspired by God cannot convey to another any new simple idea (because, as he had shown in Book II, simple ideas may only enter the mind by experience). Reason can enable us to know many truths which are self-evident or demonstrable, and for these revelation is unnecessary. Putative revelation can only be accepted as genuine if it does not contradict our "clear and distinct Knowledge... For *Faith* can never convince us of any Thing that contradicts our Knowledge."[62] Thus it is, for Locke, a matter of logic that the evidence of revelation can never be more certain than conclusions founded on the principles of reason, and therefore "*Nothing that is contrary to, and inconsistent with the clear and self-evident Dictates of*

Reason, has a Right to be urged, or assented to, as a matter of Faith, wherein Reason hath nothing to do."[63] Failure to acknowledge this has resulted in almost all religions being filled with superstition, with the consequence that religious belief, far from being the high-point of man's endeavors, has too often revealed man at his most irrational.

In the *Essay* Locke does not enter into debate about any disputed article of the Christian religion but it is clear enough how his approach would translate into the assessment of specific disputes. In *Epistola de Tolerantia*, written concurrently with the *Essay*,[64] Locke offers several different arguments for toleration, and the Argument from Ignorance is often central. Thus he reminds us that disputes between two churches "about the truth of their doctrines and the purity of their worship, is on both sides equal; nor is there any judge...upon earth, by whose sentence it can be determined,"[65] so neither has authority to suppress the other. Further, of those things about which all men ought to attempt to gain knowledge (and Locke thought religion one of these), that knowledge so obtained "cannot be looked upon as the peculiar possession of any sort of men," princes in this matter being no whit superior to any other, for "neither the right nor the art of ruling does necessarily carry along with it the certain knowledge of other things, and least of all of true religion,"[66] as religious conflict well testifies. Princes have other matters to concern them, for "the business of laws is not to provide for the truth of opinions, but for the safety and security of the commonwealth."[67] He held, he said, for liberty in "speculative opinions," which are such that they do not impinge on the lives of others, thereby implicitly drawing Mill's distinction between self- and other-regarding actions.

Locke emphasized the same points in his correspondence with the leading divine among the Dutch Remonstrants, Philip van Limborch. In October 1698 he wrote from London explaining why he was an "Evangelical Christian," who contrasted with the papists: "the latter those who, as if infallible, arrogate to themselves dominion over the conscience of others; the former those who, seeking truth alone, desire themselves and others to be convinced of it only by proofs and reasons; they are gentle to the errors of others, being not unmindful of their own weakness; forgiving human frailty and ignorance, and seeking forgiveness in turn."[68]

Before this, in 1690, Jonas Proast had, on reading Popple's translation of the *Epistola* immediately set out to refute it. The aspect on which I wish to concentrate, the issue of knowledge, did not clearly emerge until Locke's *A Third Letter for Toleration* (1692). Proast had argued that the magistrate by the law of nature had power to restrain false and corrupt religion.[69] To this Locke replied that magistrates only had a power to do what they were capable of doing. But Proast, Locke said, was claiming that they had a duty to restrain false religion, and this implied that they had at least some knowledge of the true one. However, "if the Magistrates of the World cannot know, certainly know the true Religion to be the true Religion; but it can be of a Nature to exercise their Faith, (for where Vision, Knowledge and Certainty is, there Faith is done away) then that which gives them the last Determination herein, must be their own Belief, their own Persuasion."[70] Of course, Locke continues, he and Proast accept the Christian religion as the true one. But the question is can they demonstrate that it is? Assurance to the highest degree is not knowledge. The fundamental articles of the Christian religion cannot be demonstrated, for "such remote Matters of Fact" are too distant to be the objects of knowledge. Locke's use of the term "demonstration" is the precise sense he had given it in the *Essay* where he had explained it as "the shewing the Agreement, or Disagreement of two *Ideas* by the intervention of one or more Proofs, which have a constant and immutable and visible connexion one with another."[71] In the case of historical testimony no such demonstration is possible and one's conviction rests on faith and persuasion, not knowledge and certainty.

Locke's distinction is here bearing a lot of weight. The line between knowledge and faith is fundamental to his whole account of religion and his justification of toleration. We can know that there is a God, we can know the moral law, at least in part. But the particular doctrines of the church were a matter of faith, and faith itself was ground for salvation. He was certain that this was the human condition and happy to have it so and he rams the point home: "This is the highest the Nature of the Thing will permit us to go in Matters of revealed Religion...'Tis all God requires in the Gospel for Men to be saved."[72]

Either Proast missed Locke's epistemic argument or chose to ignore it. His reply was long delayed, and appeared only in 1704, months before Locke's death. In it he claims that every magistrate who "upon just and sufficient grounds believes his Religion to be true, is obliged to use some moderate Penalties...to bring men to his Religion."[73]

Locke, in his last weeks – his reply was unfinished at his death – responded again, and again he returns to the crucial distinction. The crux is who is to decide that the grounds are just and sufficient. Everybody who believes his religion, Locke points out, believes he has just and sufficient grounds for his belief. But what is needed is an independent standard and this Proast does not supply.[74]

Locke himself did believe he had provided the requisite standard. It was that set out in the *Essay Concerning Human Understanding*, and by this criterion the doctrines of the Christian church, other than knowledge of a deity, did not meet the required standards to justify any attempt to impose an orthodoxy. But the fact that according to Locke knowledge of God's existence was possible suggests that toleration of the atheist was not required, a position consistent with his remark in the *Essay* that atheists, without the notion of a law giver, have no notion of a law and therefore no obligation to obey it.[75]

Locke, then, held to this position. The Magistrate was under no obligation to enforce a religion he did not know was the true one. Indeed, he was under the obligation not to interfere with the religions of individuals because he did not know that they were wrong in their faith. The implication is obvious. If that was the position then non-conformist churches must also be allowed, since they are merely collections of individuals following their own religious persuasions. The argument from ignorance is thus seen by Locke as providing a powerful justification for diverse churches within one state. The old idea of even the liberal thinkers of the previous generation that there needed to be just one church, albeit "of wide swallow" was rejected. It was a position that was to take some time in finding wide favor, but few would wish to deny the importance of its conclusion for the modern liberal state.

Along with Locke's rejection of the need or even the desirability of one central church there went a skeptical regard of the nature of conscience. More, as we have seen, had allowed God to speak via conscience in different ways to different people, but nevertheless continued to regard it as genuine divine guidance. Locke went further. Conscience, he said in the *Essay Concerning Human Understanding*, is "nothing else, but our own Opinion or Judgment of the Moral Rectitude or Pravity of our own Actions."[76] Conscience was too easily the justification of the Enthusiast and Locke was quite unprepared to allow it as a special source of moral knowledge. It was only a source of opinion and thus only a matter of belief.

Finally, we turn briefly to another thinker, many rungs above Proast on the intellectual ladder, but who shared with him a rejection of Locke's picture of the limits of knowledge. For Proast's failure to appreciate Locke's version of the Argument from Ignorance has echoes in Leibniz's response to Locke's *Essay*. It would, however, at least in the case of Leibniz, be presumptuous to suppose he had not understood Locke's argument. It would seem, rather, that Leibniz was already committed to an account of the origins and nature of knowledge which did not have the epistemic implications of Locke's philosophy. As he wrote in a letter, "Locke did not adequately appreciate the dignity of our mind, nor did he adequately understand that the principles of necessary truths are latent in it; nor did he adequately distinguish these from other truths; and in general he serves more to confirm common opinions than to establish sound judgements."[77] Leibniz's whole approach to Locke was colored by his view that Locke was a skeptic whose skepticism could be defeated by deep rational argument. As Jolley aptly remarks, Leibniz believed that Locke "fails to recognize both the nature and extent of [the mind's] capacity for *a priori* knowledge of necessary truths."[78] Whereas, for example, Locke saw it as possible, *for all we know*, for matter to think, Leibniz believed that he could establish on *a priori* principles that matter was incapable of such activity.[79]

It is not my intention to adjudicate between these two positions. But perhaps enough has been said to suggest that Leibniz is likely to be less sympathetic to the Argument from Ignorance than is Locke, for the import of his philosophy is that we can, if we dig deep enough, answer many questions which we at first might believe impossible of resolution, and there can be little doubt that he saw this as one of the tasks of the philosopher. Locke, in contrast, as we have seen, emphasized the contrary position, and each saw as the major threat to religion contrasting positions. For Leibniz it was the Socinians and for Locke it was the Enthusiasts.

In the opening paragraphs of his correspondence with Clarke Leibniz launches an attack on both Newton and Locke, not to mention Hobbes. In England natural religion is decaying, Locke wonders whether the soul is material and perishable whilst the implications of Newton's philosophy were antithetical to religion.[80] Leibniz would never have accepted Pope's verdict on Newton from which we began. And in some respects Leibniz was correct. For no matter how they viewed themselves, there can be little doubt that the new liberal theology which we have seen developing at least partly through deployment of the argument from ignorance, combined with the mechanical philosophy, was in the eighteenth century to provide an environment in which the opponents of established Christianity could flourish. It was an environment, too, in which free debate blossomed as it had never done before.[81]

Notes

1 There is a possible fourth category. It may be that some things *in their nature* cannot be known. Pi might be such an object.

2 Quoted in W. K. Jordan, *The Development of Religious Toleration in England*, Vol. III (Cambridge, Mass., 1938), p. 123. For discussion of "The great debate on the question of toleration, December 1648–January 1649" see pp. 119–31. Jordan's four-volume work remains the classic text on the rise of toleration in seventeenth-century England, though, if the argument of this paper is correct, we may not wholly agree with his judgment that "[t]he theory of religious toleration stood substantially complete in 1660."

3 *Tolleration justified, and persecution condemn'd, in an answer or-examination, of the London-ministers letter...* (London, 1646), p. 3. Cited in Jordan, Vol. III, p. 439.

4 Important figures holding the position included John Goodwin, Richard Baxter, Jeremiah Burroughs, Henry Burton, John Owen, and John Milton. What exactly its practical implications were was another matter.

5 *A Brief Account of the new Sect of Latitude-Men Together with some reflections on the New Philosophy*, By S. P. of Cambridge. In answer to a letter from his friend at Oxford. (London 1662), 244pp. T. A. Birrell, ed. (Los Angeles, 1963).

6 Ibid., p. 24.

7 Ibid., p. 10.

8 Ibid., pp. 10–11.

9 Ibid., p. 11.

10 Cf. Bodleian Library MS John Locke c. 34 which is a set of critical notes by James Tyrrell and Locke on Stillingfleet's *The Mischief of Separation* (1680) and *Unreasonableness of Separation* (1681). Extracts are printed in Lord King, *The Life and Letters of John Locke, with Extracts from His Journals and Common-place Books* (London, 1884), pp. 346–58.

11 *Religion of Protestants, A Safe Way to Salvation*, with his *Ten Tracts Against Popery*. Edited and published in 1687 at the request of the London clergy, by the Rev. John Patrick D.D., Master of the Charter-House. A new edition (London, 1845), p. 449.

12 Wharton MSS. 943, f. 871. Lambeth Palace Library. Quoted in Robert R. Orr, *Reason and Authority, The Thought of William Chillingworth* (Oxford, 1967), p. 51. For a discussion of Chillingworth see Henry G. Van Leeuwen, *The Problem of Certainty in English Thought 1630–1690,* second ed. (The Hague, 1970), pp. 15–31.

13 On this see especially Ian Hacking, *The Emergence of Probability* (Cambridge, 1975), *passim*, though Hacking does not discuss Chillingworth specifically, Barbara J. Shapiro, *Probability and Certainty in Seventeenth-Century England* (Princeton, 1983), and G. A. J. Rogers, "The basis of belief. philosophy, science and religion in seventeenth-century England," *History of European Ideas* (1985): 19–39.

14 Chapter 5, p. 96; Chillingworth, *The Religion of Protestants*, p. 382.

15 Ibid., p. 382.

16 Gilbert Burnet, *Bishop Burnet's History of his Own Time*, new ed. (London, 1850), p. 127.

17 Ibid., p. 128.

18 Ibid., pp. 128–29.

19 *Moral and Religious Aphorisms, Collected from the Manuscript Papers of the Reverend and Learned Doctor Whichcote*, republished by Samuel Salter (London, 1753), Aphorism 712.

20 Proverbs XX.27.

21 Salter, Aphorism 771.

22 Ibid.

23 Ibid., Aphorism 130.

24 *The Second Lash of Alazonomastix: Conteining a Solid and Serious Reply to a very uncivill Answer to Certain Observations upon Anthroposophia Theomagica, And Anima Magica Abscondita* (London, 1655), Sections IX and X (pp. 255 and 276). This edition was published as an addition to More's *Enthusiasmus Triumphatus or a Discourse of the Nature, Causes, Kinds and Cure of Enthusiasme* (London, 1656). For a recent account of this dispute see Arlene Miller Guinsburg: "Henry More, Thomas Vaughan and the late renaissance magical tradition," *Ambix* 27, pt. 1 (March 1980): 36–58.

25 In *A Collection of Several Philosophical Writings of Dr. Henry More, Fellow of Christ's College in Cambridge*, Fourth ed., (London, 1712), p. 2.

26 Ibid., p. 1. Sarah Hutton has pointed out to me that More's fellow Cambridge Platonist, John Smith, in "Of prophesy" (*Select Discourses*, 1660) was more sympathetic to the imagination.

27 Ibid., p. 12.

28 Ibid., p. 12.

29 In *A Collection of Writings of Dr. Henry More*, p. 10.

30 Ibid.

31 Ibid.

32 *The Immortality of the Soul*, Bk. I, Ch. II, Axiom VIII, in *A Collection of Writings of Dr. Henry More*.

33 Ibid., p. 7.

34 Ibid., p. 5.

35 *An Explanation of the Grand Mystery of Godliness* (London, 1660), Bk. X.

36 Ibid., p. 493.

37 Ibid., p. 494.

38 Ibid., p. 494.

39 Ibid., p. 499.

40 Ibid., p. 500.

41 Ibid., p. 517.

42 There was *some* politics in the Cambridge movement: see, for example, G. A.

J. Rogers: "More, Locke, and the issue of liberty," in S. Hutton, ed., *Henry More (1614–1687)* (Dordrecht, 1989), pp. 189–200. Locke's place in the development of the theory of evidence and probability has yet to be properly charted.

43 In *Essays on Several Important Subjects in Philosophy and Religion* (London, 1676), p. 8. The Essay is Essay VII. Each is separately paginated.

44 Ibid., p. 9.

45 Ibid., p. 13.

46 Ibid., p. 19.

47 Ibid., p. 41.

48 See Jackson I. Cope *Joseph Glanvill, Anglican Apologist* (St. Louis, 1956), p. 79.

49 Cope, *Joseph Glanvill*, p. 48.

50 Ibid., p. 50.

51 *Some Thoughts Concerning Education*, edited with an Introduction, Notes and Critical Apparatus by John W. and Jean S. Yolton, *The Clarendon Edition of the Works of John Locke* (Oxford, 1989), p. 240. In his original letter to Clarke on the subject (March 1686) Chillingworth is not mentioned, rather it is Bacon who is recommended for his logic, and apparently only after reflection, for the name of Bacon is inserted into the manuscript by Locke at a later date. Cf. *The Correspondence of John Locke*, edited by E. S. de Beer in eight vols. (Oxford, 1976–), Vol. II, p. 785, note. Locke, however, soon had further thoughts on the matter for in his letter to Clarke in May he wished Chillingworth to replace Bacon. Cf. *Correspondence*, Vol. III, p. 3.

52 John C. Biddle, "John Locke's essay on infallibility: introduction, text and translation," *Journal of Church and State* 19 (1977): 301–27.

53 Locke's early conservatism has been the subject of considerable research. See especially Philip Abrams' Introduction to *John Locke: Two Tracts on Government* (Cambridge, 1967).

54 *Correspondence*, Vol. I, p. 136.

55 Ibid., p. 137.

56 In Abrams, n. 48, p. 119.

57 Biddle, p. 321.

58 *Correspondence*, Vol. I, Letter No. 75, p. 111, and H. R. Fox Bourne *The Life of John Locke*, 2 vols., (London, 1876), Vol. I, p. 188.

59 Or so James Tyrrell tells us in the margin of his copy of the *Essay Concerning Human Understanding*, now in the British Library.

60 See especially Biddle, esp. pp. 310–11; Abrams, esp. pp. 98–107; Richard Ashcraft, "Faith and knowledge in Locke's philosophy," in John W. Yolton, ed., *John Locke, Problems and Perspectives* (Cambridge, 1969), pp. 194–223.

61 *An Essay Concerning Human Understanding*, ed. P. H. Nidditch (Oxford, 1975), Bk. IV, Ch. XVIII, Section 1. Cited hereafter by book, chapter and section number.

62 IV, VIII, 5.

63 IV, XVIII, 10.

64 According to Le Clerc in his *Eloge Historique de feu Mr. Locke*, the *Epistola* was written in Amsterdam between early November and mid-December 1685. Throughout the year Locke was redrafting the *Essay*.

65 Mario Montuori, ed., *John Locke On Toleration and the Unity of God*

(Amsterdam, 1983), which contains the Latin and English editions of *Tolerantia*. The cited passage is on p. 35.

66 Ibid., p. 49.

67 Ibid., p. 79.

68 *Correspondence* VI, no. 2498, pp. 495–96.

69 Cf. Proast *A Third Letter Concerning Toleration: In Defense of the Argument of the Letter Concerning Toleration, briefly Consider'd and Answer'd* (Oxford, 1691), p. 31. This and Proast's two other related works have been conveniently reprinted under the title *Letters Concerning Toleration* in the series published by Garland as *The Philosophy of John Locke* (New York and London, 1984). The series is edited by Peter A. Schouls.

70 Locke *Works*, second ed. (London, 1722), Vol. II, p. 296.

71 *Essay*, IV, XV, 1.

72 *Essay*, n. 70, p. 296.

73 *A Second Letter to the Author of the three Letters for Toleration* (Oxford, 1704), pp. 4–5, n. 69.

74 "A fourth letter for toleration," *Works*, n. 70, Vol. III, p. 460.

75 *Essay* I, IV, 8. As comment on the context of Locke's position it can be noted that the Atheism and Blasphemy Bill of 1678 proposed the death penalty for atheism, with no reprieve possible. Passed by the Lords, it was laid aside by the Commons. The death penalty for atheism was normal in most European countries.

76 *Essay* I, III, 8.

77 Leibniz to Bierling, October 1709, quoted in Nicholas Jolley, *Leibniz and Locke, A Study of the 'New Essays on Human Understanding'* (Oxford, 1984), p. 164.

78 Ibid., p. 164–65.

79 Cf. Jolley, *passim*, esp. p. 18ff. and Ch. 6.

80 Cf. *The Leibniz Clarke Correspondence*, edited by H. G. Alexander (Manchester, 1956), p. 11ff. Leibniz's first letter was written in November 1715.

81 I am grateful for comments made at the conference at the William Andrews Clark Library, Los Angeles in 1987 where an earlier version of this chapter was given, and to an anonymous reader who encouraged me to develop my thoughts further about Locke and toleration.

11   John Locke and latitudinarianism[1]

John Marshall

I

Between the late 1650s and the early 1680s John Locke came to know many of the leading latitudinarians. He was almost certainly a member of Benjamin Whichcote's congregation at St. Lawrence Jewry. He was probably one of the circle of intellectuals, including several latitudinarians, who gathered at the house of the Anglican unitarian Thomas Firmin. He also met latitudinarians in Oxford colleges, in London society, and at meetings of the Royal Society.[2] He became friends with John Mapletoft and Thomas Grigg, describing Grigg privately in 1670 as "vir optimus." Isaac Barrow's death in 1677 Locke lamented as robbing him of a "very considerable" friend. He was close to Edward Fowler, who visited him during his final illness in 1704, and in 1678 Locke sent his regards through Mapletoft to "our friends" Whichcote and Fowler. He was especially close to Robert Boyle, his greatly admired correspondent for thirty years on religious and scientific matters, and to John Tillotson, the "great and candid searcher after truth" whose death in 1694 Locke mourned as leaving him virtually no one he could consult on "doubtful points of divinity." From about 1681 Locke also became very close to Damaris Cudworth, daughter of the Cambridge Platonist Ralph Cudworth; it was in her house that Locke lived for most of the last fourteen years of his life.[3]

By the time of his death in 1704 Locke's personal library collection included over a hundred separate works by contemporary latitudinarians, and many more by their Tew Circle and Cambridge Platonist forefathers, such as Chillingworth, Hales, More and Smith.[4] Although his tireless promotion of individual enquiry caused him to refer to other authors only rarely in his works,[5] Locke recommended and cited from several latitudinarian works, especially those of Tillotson and Chillingworth.[6] Locke's extensive manuscript collection and annotated library books now in the Bodleian Library indicate much personal consultation of many latitudinarian works. Notebooks show that Locke was reading works by Hales, Falkland, Chillingworth, and Boyle in the late 1650s and early

1660s. An unspecified number of works listed by Locke simply as "latitudinarians" were taken into the country by Locke and Shaftesbury in the mid-1670s. Locke arranged for several of Stillingfleet's works to be sent to him while he was in France in the late 1670s. In the early 1680s his reading included works by Cudworth, Stillingfleet, Smith, Hales, Croft, Burnet, and Chillingworth. Locke's journals, notebooks, and perhaps more importantly his theological manuscripts and interleaved bibles of the 1690s and early 1700s tell a similar tale. Works by Fowler, Hales, Tillotson, Stillingfleet, Barrow, Whichcote, Lloyd, Burnet and Patrick were the source of many notes.[7]

II

Locke was baptized into the Church of England in 1632.[8] In many different writings into the 1690s he identified himself as a member of the Church of England.[9] He considered but rejected an Anglican clerical career in the 1660s and probably for this purpose had his conduct, character and orthodoxy certified by John Fell, high church Dean of Christ Church, Oxford, and others in 1666.[10] From 1672 to 1674 Locke was in charge of clerical appointments in the King's patronage when Shaftesbury appointed him "Secretary of Presentations." He used the position in an unsuccessful attempt to advance the career of John Highmore, rector of Shaftesbury's country-home parish of Wimborne St. Giles, and more successfully in advancing Nathaniel Hodges, Shaftesbury's chaplain, John Williams, later latitudinarian bishop of Chichester and defender of the reputations of Burnet and Tillotson, and John Spencer, learned Hebraist and friend of Thomas Tenison and Isaac Newton.[11] Locke was still attempting to obtain positions in "our church" for Jean Le Clerc in the 1690s. He died and was buried in Anglican communion in 1704, having received the Sacrament at home in his final months.[12]

Locke's first extensive writings, now published as the *Two Tracts on Government*, were composed between 1660 and 1662 largely as a defense of the re-establishment of the Church of England. They praised the laws that had established in England before the Civil War "the purest church of the latter age." Locke asserted repeatedly that the magistrate had the authority to impose indifferent matters in religious worship. He could enforce an "outward conformity," enjoining ceremonies that he judged to be decent and orderly. The ideal of men permitting one another "to go to heaven every one his...way" was briefly paraded, but declared to be currently completely unfeasible. Although giving little detailed indication of the desirable ceremonial form of the re-established church, Locke seems to have viewed much indulgence as undesirable. Depicting the multitude as "beasts" in need of restraint who were always "craving" to destroy established forms, Locke suggested that it was good to have "outward fences" imposed in worship because "they may be with least danger assaulted and shaken and…there may be always something…to be parted with…without injuring the indispensable and more sacred parts of religion when their fury and impatience shall make such an indulgence necessary."[13]

By 1667 at the latest Locke's attitude towards the desirability of indulgence had changed.[14] From 1667 until his exile to Holland in 1683, and even to a lesser degree after 1683, an important desire of Locke was for a comprehensive Anglican church, broadened enough to host the vast majority of English protestants. In 1667 he composed a slim "Essay on toleration." This "Essay" ended with a list of "particulars to be handled" at a later date. It would have been necessary to show "that toleration conduces no otherwise to the settlement of a government than as it makes the majority of one mind, and encourages virtue in all, which is done by making and executing strict laws concerning virtue and vice, but by making the terms of communion as large as may be; i.e. that your articles in speculative opinions be few and large, and ceremonies in worship be few and easy, which is latitudinism." It would also have been desirable to show whether "toleration and latitudinism" would have prevented the many "factions, wars and disturbances" which had been caused by Christian contentions.[15]

Locke and Shaftesbury's *Letter from a Person of Quality* of 1675 combined condemnation of "high episcopal men" and their Laudian claims to *jure divino* authority for episcopal church government with intimated desire for a broadened Anglican church. The 1662 ejection of a "very great number of worthy, learned, pious, and orthodox divines" and the "narrow bottom" upon which the Church rested were condemned. Against the proposal of an oath recognizing as unalterable the severely defined episcopal church government established in 1662, the *Letter* noted that "prudence" and "compassion" might make alteration of the form of church government desirable. The *Letter* suggested that the liturgy might be altered and attacked the requirement that all Anglican ministers had to be episcopally ordained.[16]

In his still unpublished 167-page "Critical notes upon Edward Stillingfleet's mischief and unreasonableness of separation," largely composed in early 1681, Locke frequently identified himself as a member of the Church of England. He declared that he believed that the "lives as well as sermons" of the "many excellent preachers we have in the Church of England" were "the most seriously Christian that are now in the World, or have been at any time in the Church." Stillingfleet's *Unreasonableness of Separation* had advocated removal of "those bars" to non-conformist communion with the Church of England that could easily be achieved, including the vexed issues of use of the sign of the cross in baptism and enforced kneeling at the sacrament. Locke lauded these proposals with "great admiration" of Stillingfleet's "ingenuity, temper and candour" and praise for his "Christian largeness of mind." He repeatedly advocated the union of dissenters and Anglicans in which "both sides" would "remit something and ... meet in an amicable yielding to each other." "I believe it is the apprehension of many sober Protestants of the Church of England" he wrote "that the setting up of all these outward formalities ... and narrowing the Terms of Communion" in 1662 had contributed more to the recent Roman Catholic advances against protestantism than the "miscarriages of our dissenters, who I will not deny to have had their share in it." Had ceremonies which most Anglicans argued were indifferent "been lessened, and the borders of ... the Church of England" enlarged, it would have had "more Partisans and less contentions."[17]

Locke noted that ceremonies had been retained at the Reformation to gain converts at a time when people had been brought up to think that ceremonies were "almost the total of religion." By the Restoration, however, most people thought Anglican ceremonial injunctions too stringent. Since "dissenters may be gained, and the Church enlarged by parting with a few things," it would be wise to remove "as many as is possible of our present ceremonies." The church should "remit, or leave at liberty some not necessary modes of worship" which would "give admittance and quiet the minds, and certainly stop the mouths of so many dissenters."[18]

Although we will see later that the attitudes of Locke and the latitudinarians towards toleration outside the church differed significantly, Locke's desire in these years for a broadened Anglicanism, willing to yield or to compromise on many disputed ceremonial and sacramental issues in order to gain protestant dissenters, ran parallel to the desires of many latitudinarians at many points in the Restoration. Edward Stillingfleet's *Irenicum* of 1660 eloquently voiced this sentiment, its title page bearing the biblical motto "Let your moderation be known unto all men." It praised Charles II's promise in his Declaration of Breda of "liberty for tender consciences." Stillingfleet pointed out the incongruity of men being "tied up to such things which they may do or let alone, and yet be very good Christians still." He suggested that "were we so happy but to take off things granted unnecessary by all, and suspected by many, and judged unlawful by some; and to make nothing the bonds of our communion, but what Christ hath done ... allowing a liberty for matters of indifferency ... we might indeed be restored to a true, primitive lustre far sooner, than by furnishing up some antiquated ceremonies, which can derive their pedigree no higher than from some ancient custom and tradition."[19]

Edward Fowler's 1670 catalogue of latitudinarian attitudes, *The Principles and Practices of Certain Moderate Divines*, took the same text as Stillingfleet's work for its motto, and displayed a similar desire for Anglican moderation. Fowler declared it "extremely desirable" that "the terms of communion with the Church of England and likewise of exercising the ministerial function therein, may be so enlarged, as to take in all that are of any reason, sobriety and moderation." He would be "very glad," he wrote in concluding the work, "if our Church Doors were set wider open." John Wilkins reputedly voiced similar sentiments to the high church Anglican John Cosin at Wilkins' consecration to the see of Chester in 1668. He declared that he opposed the maintenance of a narrow church by severe penal codes "which set up the Church as a top on the toe, it will not spin or stand longer than as it is whipped by penal laws; I would have it stand on the broad basis, and then it will stand without whipping." In early 1668 Wilkins discussed with some of the moderate bishops his desire to determine "what might be yielded without damage to...our worship to effect an understanding among all moderate Protestants."[20]

John Tillotson frequently pleaded for the church "not to insist upon little things, but to yield them up," writing of the "plausible exceptions of those, who differ from us." Gilbert Burnet summed up Tillotson's attitude in his funeral sermon: Tillotson thought that "the less the communion of the church was clogged with disputable opinions or practices, the world would be the happier, consciences the freer, and the church the quieter." Surveying the attitudes of the Restoration latitudinarians in 1696, Richard Baxter wrote that they abhorred "the imposition of...little things." Burnet summed up the sentiments of his fellow latitudinarians similarly, writing that while they "loved the constitution of the Church and the liturgy, and could well live under them" they "did not think it unlawful to live under another form" and "wished that things might have been carried with more moderation."[21]

These sentiments led to several attempts by some of the latitudinarians to secure a comprehension. Wilkins, Tillotson, Stillingfleet and Thomas Barlow joined forces in 1667 and 1668 in drawing up proposals for a comprehension which would have "left indifferent or wholly omitted" many disputed ceremonial issues, such as the wearing of surplices and kneeling at receipt of the Lord's Supper. The liturgy would have been reviewed. Equally importantly, ministers who had been ordained by presbyterians would not have had to be reordained in order to minister in the Church of England. The resulting 1668 bill for comprehension foundered on the rocks of parliamentary opposition, with the implacable churchmanship of the Cavalier Parliament reinforced by an energetic campaign against comprehension orchestrated by Archbishop Sheldon. Stillingfleet and Tillotson, however, continued to meet with nonconformists and support plans for comprehension later in the Restoration, in 1674, 1680 and 1688. They supported comprehension again in 1689 in the immediate aftermath of the Revolution of 1689. All of these attempts withered on the vine.[22]

III

The latitudinarians de-emphasis of sacramental and ceremonial issues owed much to their stress upon moral behavior as the key element of Christianity. Simon Patrick's *Brief Account of the New Sect of Latitude-Men* voiced the sentiment of many latitudinarians in declaring that "I shall always think him the most conscientious who leads the most unblameable life, though he be not greatly scrupulous about the externals of religion." They often suggested that concentration upon the external parts of religion deflected attention away from morality. As Tillotson put it, "whenever the external part of religion is principally regarded, and men are more careful to worship God with outward pomp and ceremony, than in 'spirit and in truth'...men embrace the shadow of religion and let go the substance."[23] The substance of religion was moral reformation. "The grand design of the Gospel," Fowler wrote in the *Principles and Practices*, was "to make men good...to reform men's lives." Burnet's summary of Tillotson's views agreed: "the great design of the Gospel was the reforming men's natures."[24]

Many latitudinarians depicted revelation as largely the restatement of the precepts of natural law. "Excepting a very few particulars" wrote Tillotson "they enjoin the very same things." Christianity was "as to the practical part of it...nothing else but the religion of nature, or pure morality, save only praying...and...the two Sacraments." The central purpose of Christianity was to "restore and reinforce the practice of the natural law." The precepts of natural law were accessible by unaided reason, but they had been promulgated in revelation more clearly and backed by stronger incentives for obedience. As Fowler commented, the gospel "enforceth its precepts with infinitely stronger, and more persuasive Motives and Arguments, than were ever before made known." Particularly heavy emphasis was placed upon God's rewards for the dutiful in the works of Wilkins and Tillotson. Man was depicted as motivated by desire for happiness, "our chief end," and moral behavior was commended as a form of enlightened self-interest. According to Tillotson, "religion and happiness, our duty and our interest, are really but one and the same thing considered under several notions." Prudential appeals were seen as "effective" or "practical" preaching; one of Tillotson's most famous sermons was entitled *The Wisdom of Being Religious*.[25]

Emphasis upon the importance of morality pervaded many of the latitudinarians' treatments of justification by faith. Fowler's *Principles* noted that the latitudinarians were frequently known as the "Moral Preachers" because of their opposition to the Calvinist doctrine that Christ's righteousness was imputed to the individual, having been apprehended by faith. They taught instead that the individual's faith was itself counted for righteousness by God. Fowler declared, a little too synoptically, that the latitudinarians were "very careful so to handle the Doctrine of Justifying Faith, as not only to make obedience to follow it, but likewise to include a hearty willingness to submit to all Christ's precepts in the nature of it." Often holding that sanctification preceded justification, many latitudinarians ranged the Apostle James's emphasis upon the necessity of works alongside Paul's assertion that faith alone justified. They held that justifying faith could not be divorced from works, assaulting "idle, ineffectual faith" and extolling "working faith." On this issue they often cited Titus 3:14, which spoke of Christ desiring a people "zealous of good works," and Galatians 5:6, which spoke, Fowler declared, of justification by a "faith that worketh by love; which takes in the whole of obedience." Patrick concurred with Fowler that justifying faith was "not an idle ineffectual faith... but that which works by love." Tillotson agreed, with Galatians 5:6 again prominent: the "condition of our Justification" was "such an effectual belief as expresseth itself in suitable acts of Obedience and Holiness, such as the Apostle calls... a Faith which worketh by Love." According to Glanvill, "Faith that is said to justify... takes in an Holy Life." Burnet was a little more cautious: justifying faith was "such a believing as exerted itself in good works." Faith could not be divorced from a holy life on the point of justification, but it was a speculation "of very little consequence" whether a holy life was a "condition of justification, or... the certain distinction and constant effect of that faith which justifies."[26]

Exhortation to the strenuous endeavours of a working faith was combined with continual battle against antinomian explications of grace. The grace of God was given to those who exerted themselves. The Holy Spirit was "ever ready to assist those who comply with his blessed Motions, and do vigorously put forth their own endeavours." Most men had free will. They could resist or fall from God's grace. Election for these men involved acceptance of the Gospel, not an irresistible decree. Conceit that one had been elected, particularly if it led to condemnation of others, was roundly condemned.[27]

Many latitudinarians held that Christ's death was of universal intent, attacking the doctrine of absolute reprobation. In his autobiography

Patrick noted that he had "presumed ... in my sermons" that "God would really have all men to be saved." At many points in the *Principles and Practices* Fowler depicted the latitudinarians as not believing in eternal reprobation. This disbelief was often tied to a picture of God which emphasized his goodness and mercy. Many of the latitudinarians opposed the "sour and dismal opinions" of God which stressed his will rather than his goodness. Assertion of God's love was enough, Glanvill argued, to overthrow the "fierce and churlish reprobatarian doctrines." "I am as sure," Tillotson declared of eternal reprobation, "that this doctrine cannot be of God as I am that God is good and just." Magnifying God's mercy and the importance of moral behavior, many latitudinarians were unwilling to say that virtuous heathens had not been saved. Baxter noted that the latitudinarians generally had "more charitable thoughts than others about the salvation of heathens." Fowler even went so far as to suggest that he thought that virtuous pagans were probably saved.[28]

Although Locke composed many manuscripts and filled several journals and notebooks with notes on a very wide variety of subjects before his 1683 exile to Holland, by which time he was fifty-one, there is remarkably little evidence of theological enquiry in these years. Indeed there is little to indicate the character of his theological commitments.[29] He was probably brought up a moderate Calvinist, but there is almost no evidence of Calvinist sentiment in any of his writings.[30] Only one piece of extended evidence that may indicate the complexion of Locke's soteriological views in these years survives. This is part of a draft of a sermon, dated January 1667,[31] in a hand that is at the least very similar to Locke's hand, but which has some letters formed in a manner in which Locke occasionally but not usually wrote these letters. It is therefore not possible to be even close to certain that this draft was composed by Locke. Because he apparently kept this draft to the end of his life, through the many moves of his papers, it would, however, appear likely that even if it was not by him he was sufficiently interested by it to think that it probably represented his own broad views. Its subject was the text of Galatians 5:6, on faith "which worketh by love."[32]

Paralleling the latitudinarians' contention that faith itself was counted for righteousness, this sermon declared that "faith shall be imputed" to the individual "for righteousness." Like the latitudinarians' writings, the sermon stressed a working faith. The sermon seemed to assert that this working faith was necessary for justification, although the evidence is too sketchy to be certain that this is what was meant. It was by faith, it argued, that the individual would live: "by this he shall be justified, by this he shall be saved, without circumcision, and without the works of the law... without the precepts of Moses, but not without the works of the Gospel, not without the precepts of Christ, not without obedience and charity for tis faith working, working by love, and that alone, which thus avails." Faith could not avail "except it work; nor if it work, except it work by love."[33]

According to the sermon, this need for a working faith "cut off" much of the faith "abounding in the world." Rejected first was "idle unactive faith." Faith was "In its own nature...active and busy." An idle faith was "like a talent hid in a napkin, or buried under ground, and he that hath it is a slothful servant, whose wages is punishment." Also condemned was the faith which worked by pride. This was the faith of those "who confining the favour of God unto a very few, and supposing him to reprobate, for his pleasure only, the greatest part of men, strongly conceit themselves...to be of the elected handful." A similar fate attended the faith which worked "by hatred...by love to those who are of our way, our sect, or party, but by enmity to all dissenters." Finally condemned at great length was the faith of those who "joyfully listen to the mistaken explications of free grace, and are glad to hear it said that God justifies the ungodly, that we are saved freely by the alone faith in Christ without works." These antinomians believed that Christ "died to save sinners...and apply his righteousness to their souls." James had said that faith without works could never save, and Paul's statements on faith without works excluded "only...works of the law of Moses."[34]

During the last twenty years of Locke's life, starting almost immediately upon his exile to Holland, theological enquiries were the major subject of his assiduous and meticulous notetaking. In these years composition of theological manuscripts occupied Locke at least as much as work on his more famous epistemological writings. During this period Locke found much to admire in the latitudinarians' theological views. In 1703 he wrote to the Reverend Richard King that for a "larger view of the parts of morality, I know not where you will find them so well explained and so strongly enforced, as in the practical divines of the Church of England. The sermons of Dr. Barrow, Archbishop Tillotson and Dr. Whichcote are masterpieces in this kind." Many of Locke's extensive notes in his annotated bibles taken in the 1690s and early 1700s came from latitudinarian works. Such was Locke's succinct note on Romans from Whichcote: "The reforming our lives is the way to believe the Gospel."[35]

In Locke's works from the late 1680s to his death the central role played by moral behaviour in achieving salvation can hardly be overstated. It was a key theme of his 1695 *Reasonableness of Christianity*, his two *Vindications* of the *Reasonableness*, and his posthumously published *Paraphrase Upon the Epistles of St. Paul*. Morality was stressed in the *Letters Concerning Toleration*, and constructing a sufficient defense of man's ability to know the duties that he was required to perform was a fundamental reason for composition of the *Essay Concerning Human Understanding*.

Several of these works stressed the importance of a working faith and made it necessary to justification. The *Reasonableness* put the case straightforwardly. Faith was counted for righteousness rather than Christ's righteousness being applied to the individual by faith. Repentance was as necessary as faith. Although Paul had often put faith "for the whole duty of a Christian" in his epistles "yet the tenour of the Gospel is what Christ declares... 'unless ye repent, ye shall all likewise perish.'" Joining together the biblical texts favored by the latitudinarians, Locke wrote that Christ had come to "purify unto himself a peculiar people zealous of good works... And therefore St. Paul tells the Galatians, That that which availeth is faith but faith working by love. And that faith without works... is not sufficient for our justification, St. James shows." The *Second Vindication* of the *Reasonableness* repeated the argument, with Galatians 5:6 again prominent: "the faith for which God justifieth, is not an empty speculation, but a faith joined with repentance, and working by love." The *Letter Concerning Toleration* cited Galatians 5:6 on its opening page.[36]

Paralleling the argument of many of the latitudinarians, Locke suggested in the *Reasonableness* that Christ's mission was largely to republish natural law more clearly and backed by stronger incentives. Moral philosophers had mistakenly focused upon the beauty of virtue. Christianity focused instead on the incentives provided by God's rewards and punishments, making moral behavior "visibly" the "best bargain." Man was motivated by desire to achieve happiness and to avoid pain; moral behavior was enlightened self-interest. For Locke, as for the latitudinarians, God was good and merciful. He had not eternally reprobated anyone, and there was an obvious answer to those who questioned the salvation of virtuous heathens. God would judge such men for their sincere attempts to obey natural law.[37]

IV

The latitudinarians' focus upon the moral requirements of Christianity de-emphasized its doctrinal requirements as well as its ceremonial injunctions. Indeed, according to Burnet it was largely from their allowance of "great freedom both in philosophy and in divinity" that the latitudinarians derived their name. Latitudinarian support of enquiry in philosophy and theology owed much to a shared vision of the limits of men's understandings and emphasis upon the extent of men's ignorance. Developing the moderate skepticism inherited from debates over the rule of faith in the sixteenth and early seventeenth centuries, the latitudinarians argued that man was not capable of attaining metaphysical certainty in physical science. He was to be content instead with the acceptance of probability. They assailed on the one hand the claims to knowledge and useless questions of scholasticism, and on the other any paralyzing skepticism that discouraged enquiry simply because much could not be known.[38]

Religious knowledge was significantly limited by the mediocrity of men's understandings. Many latitudinarians iterated and reiterated that man was fallible and therefore ought not to seek to impose his own views on others. As Whichcote put it in his *Moral and Religious Aphorisms*, "our Fallibility and the Shortness of our Knowledge should make us peaceable and gentle; because I may be mistaken." They were suspicious of religious systems and often opposed the dogmatism of much religious sectarianism. They indicted many of the Interregnum sects of claiming infallibility and of desiring to impose their own views on others, and composed much polemic against Roman Catholic claims to infallibility. This allowed them to depict the Anglican church as the most tolerant of differing opinions in practice.[39]

The latitudinarians declared that the essential doctrines of scripture were few and plain. These were therefore "generally acknowledged among Christians" and did not need an infallible interpreter. They were, however, "not at all forward to give a Catalogue of Fundamentals." Men were free to disagree about doctrines that were not fundamental, and such disagreement was inevitable because of the different constitutions of men's minds, tempers and educations. The latitudinarians therefore extolled a unity of spirit, not an unattainable uniformity of opinion, in scriptural interpretation. Fowler described the latitudinarians as seeking to bring together in affection those differing in opinion. Burnet suggested that the latitudinarians "continued to keep a good correspondence with those who had differed from them in opinion." Tillotson argued that he had made it a cardinal principle of his life "never to abate anything of humanity or charity" from any man "for his difference from him in opinion."[40]

Following the lead of Wilkins and Tillotson, latitudinarian preaching largely eschewed mystery and allegory and adopted instead a plain prose style focused upon moral injunctions and prudential appeals. Their works attempted to avoid most theological controversies and to focus instead upon those doctrines to which all Christians subscribed and upon the actual words of scripture. They were often concerned to demonstrate that religion could commend itself by its reasonableness. In scriptural interpretation they emphasized literalism and a commonsense exegetical style which clearly displayed the train of reasoning behind the acceptance of beliefs. They disapproved of appeals to faith against reason, although they maintained that many propositions in Christianity were to be believed as "above reason." Claims for the belief of doctrines because of individual inspiration were generally rejected as "enthusiasm."[41]

At their most eirenic, perhaps represented more by Fowler and Tillotson than by the other Restoration latitudinarians, these attitudes were combined with hostility to almost all credal requirements and with suggestions that heresy was an act of the will rather than of the understanding. It was argued that the sincere search for the truth of scripture would prevent any errors of interpretation from proving fatal. The works of Hales, Falkland, and especially Chillingworth, were important influences here, and were frequently cited and praised by many of the latitudinarians. Fowler declared that Chillingworth would have been called a latitudinarian had he lived until the Restoration. Citing Chillingworth, Fowler argued that industry in the search for truth removed culpability from error. It was "sufficient for any man's Salvation, that he assent to the truth of the Holy Scriptures, that he carefully endeavour to understand their true meaning," and that he lived accordingly.[42]

Many of Locke's epistemological writings, including the *Essay Concerning Human Understanding*, were in large part sophisticated statements of arguments contained in latitudinarian works. The *Essay* stressed the mediocrity of men's understandings and lauded scientific investigation while arguing that its result could only be probability and not certainty. As early as 1661 or 1662 Locke had assaulted Roman Catholic claims to infallibility, and he continued to direct his fire at these papal claims throughout his career. Locke's 1667 "Essay on toleration" assaulted the "pride or overweeningness of my own opinion and a secret conceit of my own infallibility" that led me to use "force and compell others to be of my mind, or censure and malign them if they be not." The draft sermon of 1667 attacked the faith that worked by "hatred...and uncharitableness...by love to those who are of our way, our sect, or party, but by enmity to all dissenters" and identified this as the faith of those who "forget their fallible and imperfect nature" and proposed "their own or others interpretations of Scripture and conjectures as necessary articles of belief." Many of Locke's later works reprised this theme and attacked the presumption of infallibility underlying much religious sectarianism. He continually pressed the need for friendly persuasion and the maintenance of charity and humanity among differing opinions.[43]

Locke argued that the fundamental doctrines of scripture were few and plainly stated. Paralleling the most eirenic of the latitudinarians, he deemphasized heresy and suggested that industrious search for the truth of scripture prevented sinful errors. He defended at great length the use of reason in the interpretation of scripture and assaulted those who cried up faith against reason. He argued that belief of doctrines because of a claimed individual inspiration generally involved "enthusiasm" and inserted a chapter in the later editions of the *Essay* against this extravagance.[44]

Locke commended John Worthington's *Scripture Catechism* for its avoidance of theological controversy and reliance upon the "precise words of Scripture, a thing of good Example." Tillotson's clear and plain prose came in for praise on several occasions. Proposing the teaching of the usage of clear language in *Some Thoughts Concerning Education* Locke recommended "an author excellent in this faculty, as well as several others... Dr. Tillotson... in all that is published of his." It was, however, Chillingworth's *Religion of Protestants* that came in for more praise than any contemporary latitudinarian work. In *Some Thoughts Concerning Education* Locke wrote that "if you would have your son reason well, let him read Chillingworth." Praising the *Religion of Protestants* as the pattern of "good temper, and clear and strong arguing" in 1703, in 1701 he declared that "I know not a better book that you can give... than Chillingworth."[45]

V

There were, then, important personal and intellectual threads linking Locke to at least the most eirenic strands of latitudinarianism. Focus upon the parallels between Locke and the latitudinarians, however, obscures many areas of very significant disagreement. The latitudinarian supporters of the 1667–68 plans for comprehension desired to join comprehension with toleration, and many of the latitudinarians condemned the Restoration persecution of dissenters. Generally, however, the latitudinarians emphasized comprehension, or toleration within the church, much more than toleration outside of its boundaries. Stillingfleet's *Unreasonableness of Separation* combined support for comprehension with hostility to all but the most limited of tolerations, and was far from enthusiastic about even that possibility.[46]

Behind Stillingfleet's position was a strong bias towards uniformity of worship that was shared by most of the latitudinarians. Stillingfleet accused the 1672 Declaration of Indulgence of setting up a "Presbyterian Separation." Patrick's *Brief Account* stated the need for the church to be a generous mother who did not impose too much, but also stressed the need for unity and uniformity of worship and a settled liturgy. This desire for uniformity was often combined with emphasis upon the role of the Church of England as the national religion "established by law."

Tillotson suggested many times that only a national, established religion could withstand the threat of Roman Catholicism. On one notorious occasion he even preached a sermon suggesting that only an extraordinary commission could justify preaching against the law.[47]

The latitudinarians generally defended at length "the power of the governors of the Church to compose Forms of Prayer... and such Rites as they in their Wisdom shall conceive most proper." Often focusing upon the Church "as incorporated into the civil state," they declared that the Civil Magistrate had the authority to impose forms and circumstances of worship which were indifferent. As Fowler put it in the *Principles*, they believed "the Civil Magistrate to have a Power, both Legislative and Judiciary, as well in Sacred, as in Civil Affairs." Although it might be wise and charitable for these church governors or the magistrate to lessen ceremonial injunctions, as Stillingfleet and Tillotson suggested in promoting comprehension, it was clearly the "duty of all under their authority to submit." Stillingfleet's *Unreasonableness* suggested that "prudent submission" was the mean between endless separations and tyranny over conscience. In this context, latitudinarian support for "liberty of conscience" could involve support only of "liberty of judgement." This was the position, for instance, of Stillingfleet's *Irenicum* and *Unreasonableness of Separation*. Emphasis upon the duty of submission to the church governors and to the law of the land even helped to lead some of the latitudinarians to condemn the "insolence" and "silly superstition" of the dissenters and to declare comprehension unnecessary. This was the position of Patrick's *Friendly Debate* and of Glanvill's "Anti-fanatical religion and free philosophy."[48]

In contrast, from 1667 Locke supported toleration, with comprehension only one form of such toleration. The "Essay on toleration," especially in the last of its four drafts, advocated toleration of separate protestant churches as well as "latitudinism." Locke declared that purely "speculative opinions and divine worship" had an "absolute and universal right to toleration." Men had a "perfect and uncontrollable liberty" in choosing the forms of their worship and in holding speculative opinions. Reversing the position he had adopted in the *Two Tracts*, Locke declared that in religious worship nothing was indifferent unless the individual believed it to be indifferent. Every individual had to judge that his worship was "acceptable" to God. It would be good, Locke suggested, if dissenters could be persuaded to join with the Church of England, but if that were not possible then they should be made "friends to the state, though they are not sons of the church."[49]

In early 1674 Locke argued in a manuscript entitled "Excommuni-cation" that church membership was "perfectly voluntary, and may end whenever any one pleases without any prejudice to himself." The *Letter from a Person of Quality* a year later mentioned broadened Anglicanism only in passing, and defended the toleration allowed by the 1672 Declaration of Indulgence. In the 1681 "Critical notes" Locke declared that men had a "natural and evangelical right of taking care of their own salvation." It was the "true Liberty of the Gospel" for a man to be "guided by his own Conscience in things of Faith and worship." Nothing was indifferent in worship that the individual was not fully satisfied was indifferent. A church, he repeatedly suggested, was "nothing but a voluntary union of men for exercising and propagating the worship of God." Men were at liberty to join whatever church they thought best served their own edification and were free to leave any church for another at any time. Against Stillingfleet's desire for one church, Locke proposed the unity of charity among different churches. The "peace, and unity of the Christian church may...be as well preserved in distinct churches" he argued "as the peace of a parish in distinct families." It was sufficient "for the union of...Protestants that they keep up a Friendship under different forms, and modes of worship."[50]

From 1667 Locke consistently sought to distinguish the separate natures of church and state and opposed Erastian conceptions of church power. In the 1667 "Essay on toleration" he argued that the magistrate's power was limited to securing peace and the preservation of men in society. Religious worship and speculative opinions had a "clear title" to toleration, Locke asserted, because they did not concern "government and society at all" and gave "no bias to my conversation with men." This theme was reiterated in many later writings, from the 1674 "Excommunication" and the "Critical notes" to the *Letters Concerning Toleration*. Religion, Locke suggested in the "Critical notes," was the name for actions "referred wholly to the pleasing or displeasing God without any concerning at all my neighbour, civil society, or my own preservation in this life. For my praying to God in this or that fashion...or speculative opinions...entrenches not at all upon...any... right of my neighbour." Religion was therefore "not within the civil magistrate's inspection." Stillingfleet had seemed to make the law of the land part of the obligation to be of the Church of England but "it can never be judged to be a sin not to obey the law of the land commanding me to join in communion with the Church of England, till it be proved that the Civil Magistrate hath a power to command and determine...what church I shall be of."[51]

Locke's 1683 exile only reinforced this commitment to toleration. He still noted in passing his desire for broadened Anglican communion. His central concern, however, was with the broader principle of religious toleration and with its application in Europe as well as in England. William Popple's preface to the English edition of the *Letter Concerning Toleration*, probably composed with Locke's knowledge, called comprehension insufficient and demanded "Absolute Liberty...Equal and Impartial Liberty" of peaceful religious worship. Repeating the themes of his earlier manuscripts, the *Letter* declared churches voluntary societies which men were free to join or leave as they judged best, and sought to "distinguish exactly the Business of Civil Government from that of Religion." The Civil Magistrate was empowered only to seek civil interests and had no power to establish "any Articles of Faith, or Forms of Worship, by the force of his Laws." Locke wrote to Van Limborch in 1689 that he could not "feel any hopes" for ecclesiastical peace from comprehension. "Men" he wrote "will always differ on religious questions and rival parties will continue to quarrel and wage war on each other unless the establishment of religious liberty for all provides a bond of mutual charity by which all men may be brought together into one body."[52]

In many of Locke's works this support for toleration was underpinned in part by a considerable lay anticlericalism that was not characteristic of the latitudinarians. Locke's anticlericalism had started early, before his commitment to toleration. In the *Two Tracts* he had focused on the radical protestant clerics, lambasting the "crafty men" who had ignited Civil War with "coals from the altar." In the 1661–62 "Essay on infallibility" his fire was turned on the "sharp-sighted" priests of Roman Catholicism who desired control over consciences. From the *Letter from a Person of Quality* his venom was directed at high church Anglicans who preached that both monarchy and clergy had *jure divino* authority in order that "priest and prince may, like Castor and Pollux, be worshipped together as divine in the same temple, by us poor lay subjects." In a journal entry, also of 1675, he suggested more generally of the clergy that they had "found a Mistress, called the Preast Power that pays them much better than truth can."[53]

The "Critical notes" was the most strident of Locke's writings in its anticlerical assault. "Churchmen of all sorts with power" he wrote "are very apt to persecute and misuse those that will not pen in their fold." This, he suggested, might "sometime open the Laity's eyes, and make them consider that those men, who pretended a commission to teach them the truths of God, have made little other use of that authority, but to make slaves of those that submitted to them, and miserable those that dissented." Locke declared that "if there were no more power...annexed to the being guides to the new Jerusalem, than there is to any other place" then clerics would "as little obtrude themselves with authority or require us to travel by their Charts as other guides do." When Christians were frequently called sheep it was "no wonder they should contend for the largeness of their flocks since they have the more to milk and shear and have often the selling of them." No denomination was immune from clerical ambition. The example of New England showed that protestant persecution was little short of Catholic persecution "only Rome being the elder." Even Independent pastors made their churches "like bird cages, with...free admittance to all birds...but when they are once in, they are to be kept there."[54]

In the 1690s this view of clerical motivation underpinned Locke's use of the term "priestcraft," then becoming the fashionable term of abuse of clerics' interest in lay ignorance. Close friends such as the Quaker Benjamin Furly wrote to assure Locke that "Priest-craft will fall." Christ had come, Locke suggested in the *Reasonableness*, in order to dissipate the darkness spread by priests who had attempted to secure their empire by excluding reason from religion. In "Of the conduct of the understanding" Locke described theology as the best science "where it is not by corruption narrowed into a trade or faction, for mean or ill ends, and secular interests." Repeating the theme of the *Letter from a Person of Quality* and the "Critical notes," in 1698 Locke argued that the preaching of monarchy and episcopacy to be *jure divino* was undertaken to keep the sheep in their folds to be jointly "shorn" by priests and princes.[55]

VI

The latitudinarians magnified the role of reason in religion, stressed Christ's prophetic rather than priestly office, and were in some cases reluctant to use extended trinitarian language. They were therefore often accused of Socinianism. Their soteriology was, however, much closer to Arminianism than to any of the other major contemporary theological systems, and often closer to Calvinism than to Socinianism. Baxter called many of the latitudinarians "Arminians with some additions." Burnet noted that they "read Episcopius much." Many of the latitudinarians greatly admired Grotius, and several corresponded with contemporary Dutch Arminians such as Philipp Van Limborch. Fowler's *Principles* depicted the latitudinarians as attempting to mediate between Arminianism and Calvinism, agreeing with the Arminians in denial of eternal reprobation and in holding that most men could resist grace, but agreeing with the Calvinists against the Arminians that some men were converted irresistibly and that others had sufficient grace offered to them but in many cases rejected the offer. This *via media* was described by Tillotson as the view "most agreeable" to scripture and reason. Burnet similarly attempted to depict the advantages of both Arminianism and Calvinism in his popular *Exposition of the Thirty-Nine Articles*. Burnet himself believed that Christ's death had not been of universal intent; some had been eternally reprobated. It was an early attack on Burnet's sermons that he sought to combine inconsistent elements of Arminianism and Calvinism.[56]

Unlike the Socinians, all of the latitudinarians stressed at many points in their sermons the enormous effects of original sin. Stillingfleet put the case most strongly, suggesting that those who magnified men's free will "in this degenerate state seem to consider them only in theory and speculation." There was very little free will left amongst mankind's corrupt inclinations and evil dispositions. Burnet's exposition of the Ninth Article declared that corruption from Adam's sin had clearly "over run our whole Kind." Even Tillotson, the latitudinarian who wrote the least about original sin, wrote repeatedly of mankind's "degenerate and depraved" condition. By Adam's transgression, he wrote, "all Mankind suffers, and our Natures are extremely corrupted and depraved."[57]

The latitudinarians preached at length of the sacrifice and satisfaction of Christ. Again Stillingfleet was perhaps the most ardent on this subject, writing repeatedly throughout his career of the foundation of reconciliation in Christ's sacrifice. Burnet's *Exposition* made clear his agreement, with the propitiatory sacrifice of Christ defended against the Socinian view that Christ's death was most important in offering testimony to his mission, the teaching of morality. Tillotson, again the latitudinarian who wrote the least on this issue, argued many times in his writings that the force of Christ's intercession was located in his ransom and propitiation; only he that "paid the price" could be intercessor for man. Christ had satisfied for man's sins.[58]

Although some of the latitudinarians disliked the damnatory Athanasian creed, all of the latitudinarians were trinitarians. Patrick's *Brief Account* declared of the latitudinarians that "whatsoever may be privately whispered to the contrary they do devoutly adore the blessed Trinity in the Litany, and make solemn profession of the orthodox faith, both concerning it and other points, in the three creeds, not excepting therefore the Athanasian." Edward Fowler defended the Trinity from Socinianism in *Twenty-Eight Propositions by which the Doctrine of the Trinity is...explained*, later republished as the *Certain Propositions*. Burnet defended the Trinity at length in *Four Discourses*, and came to oppose Socinianism with some vehemence in the 1690s.[59]

Stillingfleet was perhaps the stoutest advocate for trinitarianism among the latitudinarians. He was chosen in the 1660s to persuade William Penn that Penn had erred in being anti-trinitarian. In many works across the following thirty years Stillingfleet defended the Trinity. Even Tillotson was a strong defender of the Trinity in his *Sermons Concerning the Divinity and Incarnation of our Blessed Saviour*, and at many other points in his works. He unequivocally declared Christ God "by participation of the divine nature." He contended that there were "three differences in the Deity, which the Scripture speaks of by the Names of Father, Son and Holy Ghost, and every where speaks of them as we use to do of three distinct Persons: And therefore I see no reason why in this Argument we should nicely abstain from using the word person."[60]

In Locke's early "Essay on infallibility" he argued that the union of divine and human natures in Christ was something to be believed as above but not contrary to reason. His 1676 translation of three of Pierre Nicole's *Essais de Morale* spoke of "God himself dying for them." There is very little evidence in any of Locke's manuscripts that he had any serious doubts about the Trinity before his exile to Holland. Locke's translation of the *Essais* also set out a bleakly Augustinian view of sinful men, and gave a strong emphasis to the need for God's grace. Nicole combined this, however, with an opposition to Calvinist assurance and strict predestination, and supported instead men's free will and need to cooperate with grace. The resulting combination was similar to Arminian thought.[61] Locke's theology in these years was probably therefore broadly similar to latitudinarian and Arminian views, combining trinitarianism with a very broad "moral theology" and significant stress upon men's fallen nature. Philipp Van Limborch, the Remonstrant Professor who became a very close friend of Locke, recorded that upon his introduction to Locke in 1683 they had discussed religion and Locke had acknowledged "how closely" the Arminians "agreed with many of his own opinions."[62]

In 1684–85, Locke began to purchase Socinian works avidly and started taking many notes on the Trinity.[63] He may have begun to have doubts about the Trinity at this time, and he developed close friendships with antitrinitarians like Newton and Popple in the late 1680s and early 1690s. In the Bodleian Library there is a lengthy unpublished manuscript of the mid-1690s, probably from late 1695 or 1696, and very probably by Locke, that sets out a Socinian view of Christ. A central text for trinitarians was John 1:1, "In the beginning was the word, and the word was with God, and the word was God." Trinitarians argued that the purpose of this passage, and John's intent in writing his entire Gospel, was to make clear that Christ, the word, was a coeternal, consubstantial and coequal person of the Godhead. Locke's manuscript, entitled "Some general reflections upon the beginning of St. John's Gospel" set out "to clear" this "shield of the Trinitarians."[64]

According to Locke, St. John had "not writ his Gospel to make us believe that Jesus is the Supreme God, or an eternal spirit of the same nature with his Father but to instruct us in that essential truth that Jesus is the Messiah...the Son of God in a sense of office and commission...which does not explain his nature, but his authority and power." Christ was divine by office but not by nature. The term Christ signified "that Person who was to sustain the place of God in this world," being the "bringer of the promise of life" and "with respect to his office, the true word of life...in the world as God's interpreter and the teacher of men." The phrase "Son of God" had been understood by all of the Apostles only in the sense of "Office and dignity." Neither "Christ" nor "Son of God" signified, as trinitarians claimed, "the eternal generation of our Lord Jesus from the essence of his father." The Holy Ghost had miraculously conceived Jesus and descended upon him at his baptism. The Holy Ghost was, however, only the power of God and not a person of the Godhead.[65]

It was "not without reason" Locke suggested "that St. John says that the word was in the beginning. Had he intended to teach an eternal Divinity he would...undoubtedly have expressed himself more emphatically." Jesus was the Christ, the Messiah, or the word from the beginning of the preaching of the Gospel. He was not the word from the beginning of the world, and therefore pre-existent, nor from the beginning of time and therefore eternal. The Fathers who had spoken of Christ's pre-existence and had made it agreeable to Plato's word had allegorized in order to gain converts. What started as a "Mystery of prudence" had then degenerated into "real and metaphysical doctrines" of Christ's pre-existence which were the mistaken foundation of trinitarianism.[66]

Although they did not explicitly deny the Trinity, none of Locke's works from the 1695 *Reasonableness* to his death set out a trinitarian theology or soteriology. The *Reasonableness*, published in the midst of a fierce debate about the Trinity known as the Unitarian Controversy, was silent about the Trinity and silent about baptism into the name of the Father, Son and Holy Ghost. It suggested that John's purpose in writing the Gospel was to show that Jesus was the Messiah. The union of Christ and God was described as "such an union that God operates in and by him." At all points in Paul's epistles cited in support of the Trinity, Locke's *Paraphrase* avoided trinitarian explications. The Trinity was not mentioned once in the entire *Paraphrase*, and neither Christ nor the Holy Ghost were referred to at any time as God.[67]

The *Reasonableness*, its *Vindications*, and the *Paraphrase* all omitted Christ's satisfaction for sin in the sense of payment for sin. They explained Christ's redemptive role in terms of restoring the possibility of eternal life, his teaching of the gospel, and the testimony that his death gave to its truth as a motive to holiness. Redemption meant deliverance from sin, not payment for sin; in this sense Christ redeemed all those who accepted the gospel. God did not accept payment for sins, but rather ignored them in accepting faith for righteousness. These works also rejected Arminian and Calvinist notions of original sin. Adam's fall had not caused "eternal punishment nor necessity of sinning" but mortality. Adam's sin had not corrupted the frame of his posterity and sin was charged only on those who committed it.[68]

VII

In many areas, then, Locke's thought paralleled and was undoubtedly much influenced by latitudinarian thought. Equally, however, on many issues Locke differed substantially from all of the latitudinarians.[69] Any full account of influences upon Locke's epistemological, ecclesiological and theological views would need to provide a much broader context for his thought than is provided by contemporary latitudinarianism. Locke's epistemology would have to be located in a skeptical tradition from Erasmus and Montaigne to Gassendi and Bayle, and against the background of contemporary European philosophy as a response to Descartes and others.[70] In ecclesiology Locke's most important influences included English Independent thought and the personal views of Shaftesbury. After 1683 Remonstrant and Socinian works were vital resources upon which Locke drew. In theology and biblical hermeneutics Locke was influenced particularly by Arminian and Socinian authors after 1683, but also significantly from the beginning of the Restoration by high church Anglicans such as Henry Hammond who were also constructing a "moral theology," and after 1680 by reading many patristic works.[71]

Adequate description of Locke's religious thought would have to capture not merely the delicate and changing balance of his own commitments and the many influences upon his views, but also the methodological eclecticism that he tirelessly promoted in his religious and epistemological writings and which he identified as the foundation of his own opinions. In the *Essay Concerning Human Understanding*, the *Reasonableness*, its *Vindications*, the *Paraphrase*, and the *Letters Concerning Toleration*, Locke assaulted the acceptance of authorities and claimed a personal catholicity of approach. He suggested that it did not matter to him what "the generality of divines" that he conversed with believed. It was not important "of what party" they denominated him because he was of the "party of truth." Truth he embraced "as far as I can attain to it, whether I find it among the orthodox or the heterodox." His religious views were not those of any sect of Christianity, he declared, but of a Christian who accepted the gospel and sought to understand it to the best of his ability. Some of this rhetoric was designed to avoid admitting to the Socinian complexion of his own views in the 1690s, but much of it was deeply felt. Seen in this light, Locke would not have been troubled by his agreement with the latitudinarians on many issues but substantial disagreement on many others. It would have been one more example of his eclectic pursuit of truth.[72]

Notes

1 This chapter summarizes part of my Ph.D. thesis, "John Locke in context: religion, ethics and politics," The Johns Hopkins University, 1989. I am grateful to the History Department of the Johns Hopkins University and to the Master and Fellows of Peterhouse, Cambridge, for fellowship support during work on this thesis. Professor J. G. A. Pocock and Dr. M. A. Goldie have provided helpful comments on a draft of this chapter. Place of publication London unless otherwise stated. Punctuation and spelling modernized.

2 Locke does not record his membership of Whichcote's congregation, long asserted by scholars. Le Clerc's *Life* of Locke, however, notes that Locke "very much admired some sermons he had heard from Dr. Whichcote ... which are now printed." Contemporary accounts place Mapletoft, Worthington, Wilkins, Barrow, Tillotson and Fowler in Firmin's circle. Locke's correspondence with Mapletoft indicates that he knew Firmin well. It is very likely that he was at least occasionally a member of Firmin's circle in the 1670s. Boyle and Wilkins were at Oxford when Locke was there in the 1650s and 1660s. Various diaries indicate that Locke dined out in London society with latitudinarians like Mapletoft and Barrow. From 1668 Locke was a member of the Royal Society. J. Le Clerc, *An Account of the Life and Writings of Mr. John Locke* (1713), pp. 52–53; H. Stephenson, "Thomas Firmin" (Oxford D.Phil. thesis, 1949), pp. 40, 74; H. R. Fox Bourne, *The Life of John Locke* (1876), Vol. I, pp. 309–11; M. Cranston, *John Locke* (1957), pp. 28, 75–77, 470; H. W. Robinson & W. Adams, eds., *The Diary of Robert Hooke* (1935), p. 155.

3 Cranston, *Locke*, pp. 28, 75–77, 134; Fox Bourne, *Life*, Vol. I, pp. 261, 309–11; *The Correspondence of John Locke*, ed. E. S. De Beer (Oxford, 1976–), letters 265, 348, 417, 1398, 1507, 1509, 1518, 1601, 1826. Thomas Grigg, husband of Locke's cousin Anne, was a rising London preacher at his premature death in 1670 and close to Patrick, Fowler, and Tillotson.

4 J. Harrison and P. Laslett, eds., *The Library of John Locke* (Oxford, 1965), entries under the names of Barrow, Boyle, Burnet, Cudworth, Fowler, Lloyd, Patrick, Stillingfleet, Tenison, Tillotson, Whichcote, Worthington, Chillingworth, Hales, More, and Smith.

5 A less sympathetic view would be that Locke often concealed his own debts to others, and frequently cited other authors only when he wanted to employ their prestige for a position they would not have defended.

6 *The Educational Writings of John Locke*, ed. J. Axtell (Cambridge, 1968),

pp. 262, 296, 305, 399, 403; Locke, *Works* (1801), Vol. IV, pp. 275–76, 281; Vol. VII, pp. 172, 179, 252, 276–77, 302, 361–62.

7 MS Locke f. 14, pp. 16, 19, 22–25, 28–29, 31–32, 35, 42, 46, 52, 54, 58–60, 62–64, 66, 68, 72, 74, 76, 78–80, 84, 86, 90, 93, 112–13, 116, 170; MS Locke d10, pp. 3, 7, 17, 23, 39, 43–44, 51, 59, 71, 81, 101, 131, 145, 149, 153, 155, 157, 159, 161, 169, 178, 189, 259; P.R.O. 30/24/5 pt. 3/278; K. H. D. Haley, *The First Earl of Shaftesbury* (Oxford, 1968), pp. 218–19; Locke, *Correspondence*, letters 312, 355; MS Locke f. 4, p. 95; MS Locke f. 5, pp. 23, 39, 52; MS Locke fol. 6, pp. 19–20, 50, 84–85; B. M. Add MS 15642, p. 113; MS Locke c. 33, pp. 20, 27–29; MS Locke c. 27, pp. 67–69, 157–60; MS Locke f. 30, pp. 1, 7–9, 43, 47–50, 83, 90, 93, 110, 118; MS Locke f. 32, pp. 15, 66, 119, 130, 157; Sir Thomas Pope Blount, *Censura Celebriorum Authorum* (1690), shelved in the Locke room in the Bodleian under 15.38, pp. 15, 19, 22–23, 40, 43, 54, 72, 100, 119, 125, 132, 138, 160, 200, 219, 221, 252, 370, 500–1, 532, 570, 572, 628, 636–37, 644–45, 652, 676, 684, 695, 701, 725, 745; *Le Nouveau Testament* (Mons, 1673), shelved under 9. 103–7, Vol. iv, pp. 4–5, 58, 82, 99, 102; *Holy Bible* (1648), shelved under 16. 25, pp. 28, 82, 88, 96, 102–3, 167, 183, 192, 219, 449, 455, 465, 496, 513, 529, 562, 667, 682, 689–90, 711, 729, 731, 733, 750, 754, 773, 787, 789, 791, 795–96, 807, 813, 819, 824, 828, 830–31, 837–38, 841–42, 844, 847–50, 852, 854; *Holy Bible* (1654), shelved under 10. 59–60, pp. 3, pp. 76, 88, 99, 151, 189, 245, 253, 329, 450; ii, pp. 536, 573. Dr. J. Milton provided useful comments on MS Locke f. 14.

8 Cranston, *Locke*, p. 1.

9 This was especially true early in his life. See, for instance, J. Locke, *Two Tracts Upon Government*, ed. P. Abrams (Cambridge, 1967), pp. 121–22; "Essay on Toleration" in Fox Bourne, *Life*, Vol. I, pp. 174–94; MS Locke c. 34, pp. 8–9, 54, 59, 104, 147. In his later works Locke tended to describe himself as a member of the Christian Church rather than of any particular denomination, but in the *Second Letter Concerning Toleration* in 1690 and in the *Third Letter Concerning Toleration* in 1692 he clearly declared himself (still) of the Church of England: Locke, *Works* (1794), Vol. V, pp. 99, 320, cf. 172–73.

10 Locke, *Correspondence*, Vol. I, letter 163 and p. 214. Anglican is used in this article (anachronistically) merely to indicate membership of the Church of England.

11 Haley, *Shaftesbury*, p. 311; MS Locke c. 44, pp. 1–23; P.R.O. 30/24/5 pt. 1/257; P.R.O. 30/24/42/59; P.R.O. 30/24/47/30, fols. 24–26. It does, however, seem unlikely that there was any ideologically latitudinarian dimension to these appointments by Locke.

12 Locke, *Correspondence*, letter 2202; Le Clerc, *Life*, p. 44; H. Mclachlan, *The Religious Opinions of Locke, Milton and Newton* (Manchester, 1941), p. 80.

13 Locke, *Two Tracts*, pp. 121, 128, 158–59, 161 and *passim*. Gabriel Towerson, perhaps the instigator of the *Tracts*, recommended John Pearson's *No Necessity of Reformation* (1660) to Locke in the belief that it would give Locke "Much content" for its assurance of reply to all "exceptions against the doctrine, discipline and ceremonies of the Church of England": *Tracts*, p. 11.

14 The change may have been influenced by an increasing perception that the Clarendon Code was divisive, by the persuasive example of a stable toleration on Locke's diplomatic mission to Cleves, and by the personal influence of

Boyle, to whom Locke's praise of toleration in Cleves was addressed. Probably most important, however, was the beginning of Locke's association with Shaftesbury. See ch. 3 of my Ph.D. thesis; also J. Dunn, *The Political Thought of John Locke* (Cambridge, 1969), ch. 4; R. Ashcraft, *Revolutionary Politics and Locke's Two Treatises of Government* (Princeton, 1986), ch. 3.

15 Fox Bourne, *Life*, Vol. I, p. 194.

16 Locke, Works (1801), Vol. X, pp. 200–2, 206, 215, 227–29. On Locke's role in composition of the *Letter* see Ashcraft, *Revolutionary Politics*, pp. 118–22. It would be unwise to presume that Locke subscribed to all of the views expressed in the *Letter*, but there seems no reason to think that he did not agree with its ecclesiological arguments.

17 MS Locke c. 34, pp. 6, 8–10, 36, 54, 59, 104, 147. The "Critical notes" is a somewhat awkward title for a 167-page manuscript, but is used in the secondary literature and does convey its character of a point-by-point reply to Stillingfleet. It is largely in the hand of Locke's friend James Tyrrell and is generally identified as a joint composition by Locke and Tyrrell. There are, however, several reasons to suggest that Locke was sole author. In March 1685 Locke wrote to Edward Clarke about papers that he had left with Clarke, including a parcel "whereof one part was of the Doctor's preparing … and the other of my own though for the most part marked by another's hand who was my operator when I kept my bed." The last phrase was written over "kept ill a bed." The Doctor referred to was almost certainly Stillingfleet, and the manuscript the "Critical notes." Locke was ill at Tyrrell's house in January and early February 1681, recording that he had left Tyrrell's house "after so long keeping my bed and being almost constantly in a breathing sweat," and reflecting in June that he had been "Constantly in bed for a fortnight." Locke's sole responsibility for the manuscript is also suggested by Tyrrell himself, who wrote to Locke in 1686 in an attempt to persuade him to revise the work they had "writ together": Tyrrell referred to it as "your discourse" on toleration and not as "our discourse." It is further confirmed by many of the passages in Tyrrell's hand which are very close verbal parallels to passages in Locke's other writings on toleration. Passages in Tyrrell's hand also discuss details of French protestantism that were known to Locke from his time there in the 1670s. The index to the manuscript was by Locke. Finally, it is suggestive that when Locke went abroad this manuscript went to Clarke and not to Tyrrell. Richard Ashcraft, who tentatively dates MS Locke c. 34 to May 1681, presumes that Locke's first journal reference to Stillingfleet's *Unreasonableness* denotes its arrival at Tyrrell's house. While Locke was ill, however, he made – uncharacteristically – almost no entries in his journal. It is therefore quite likely that Locke's first reference to the work reflects that he was still working on MS Locke c. 34 in May, but not that it had just arrived. References to various works in the later sections of the "Critical notes" and in Locke's journal also suggest that Locke worked on MS Locke c. 34 in May 1681. Locke, *Correspondence*, letters 615–18, 620, 815, 817, 820, 822–23, 889; Ashcraft, *Revolutionary Politics*, p. 491n.; MS Locke f. 5, pp. 7–9, 39, 68.

18 MS Locke c. 34, pp. 35, 51, 142–43.

19 E. Stillingfleet, *Irenicum* (1662), title page, preface sig. a2r, sig. a3r, p. 121.

20 E. Fowler, *The Principles and Practices of Certain Moderate Divines* (1670),

title page, pp. 333–34; *The Memoirs of John Howe*, ed. E. Calamy (1724), p. 33; Barlow's manuscript introduction to the Bodleian Library copy of *Several Tracts Relating to the Great Acts for Comprehension* (1680), p. xiii cited in Simon, "Comprehension in the Age of Charles II," *Church History* (1962): 442.

21 T. Birch, "Life of Tillotson" in Birch, ed., Tillotson, *Works* (1752), p. xxix; G. Burnet, *A Sermon Preached at the Funeral of … John … Archbishop of Canterbury* (1695), p. 31; R. Baxter, *Reliquiae Baxterianae* (1696), pp. 386–87; Burnet, *History of my own Time* (Oxford, 1823), Vol. I, pp. 323–24, cited in Cranston, *Locke*, p. 127.

22 See especially R. Thomas, "Comprehension and indulgence" in G. Nuttall and O. Chadwick (eds.) *From Uniformity to Unity 1662–1962* (1962), pp. 191–253; also Simon, "Comprehension"; H. Horwitz, "Protestant reconciliation in the exclusion crisis," *Journal of Ecclesiastical History* (1964): 201–17.

23 S. P[atrick], *A Brief Account of the New Sect of Latitude-Men* (1662), p. 11; J. Tillotson, *Works* (1820), Vol. VII, pp. 184–85 cited in L. Locke, "Tillotson: a study in seventeenth century literature" in *Anglistica* (1954), p. 78.

24 Fowler, *Principles*, p. 18; Burnet, *Sermon*, pp. 31–32.

25 J. Tillotson, *Sermons* (1688), Vol. I, p. 217 cited in H. R. McAdoo, *The Spirit of Anglicanism* (1965), p. 175; Birch, *Works … Tillotson*, p. cxix; Tillotson, *Works* (Edinburgh 1748), Vol. V, p. 253 cited in R. Sullivan, *John Toland and the Deist Controversy* (Harvard, 1982), p. 65; Fowler, *Principles*, p. 89; Tillotson *Works* (1820), Vol. III, p. 68; Tillotson, *Sermons* (1688), Vol. I, p. 25 cited in G. Cragg, *From Puritanism to the Age of Reason* (Cambridge, 1950), p. 78n; Tillotson, *Works* (1704), Vol. V, pp. 424–25.

26 Fowler, *Principles*, pp. 114, 117–30, 148–62, 188–89; Patrick, *Works* (Oxford, 1858), Vol. V, p. 277; Tillotson, *Works* (1704), Vol. IV, pp. 71, 142–45, 251–55; J. Glanvill, "Antifanatical religion and free philosophy" in *Essays on Several Important Subjects* (1676), pp. vii, 22; G. Burnet, *An Exposition of the 39 Articles of the Church of England* (1819), Articles 11 and 12. Stillingfleet was closer still to the main strands of sixteenth-century Protestant thought, insisting that works were the fruit of justifying faith. See generally C. F. Allison, *The Rise of Moralism* (1966); D. D. Wallace, "Socinianism, justification by faith and the sources of John Locke's *The Reasonableness of Christianity*," *Journal of the History of Ideas* (1984): 49–66.

27 Tillotson, *Works* (1704), Vol. I, pp. 8–9, Vol. III, p. 331; Patrick, *Works*, Vol. V, pp. 289–90; Fowler, *Principles*, pp. 114, 130, 239–40.

28 Patrick, *Works*, Vol. IX, pp. 418–19; Fowler, *Principles*, pp. 251–55, 287–97; Glanvill, "Antifanatical Religion," pp. 21–22; Baxter, *Reliqiuae*, p. 386.

29 This is slightly too synoptic a statement. While belief in God and in the importance of morality are palpable in Locke's early writings, from the *Essays on the Law of Nature* to the *Two Treatises*, with the possible exception discussed below Locke nowhere discussed soteriological questions at any length in these years. The evidence that does exist about Locke's views is surveyed in ch. 2–5 of my Ph.D. thesis (see n. 1 above).

30 Locke's one important but neglected work with a significant Augustinian (although not Calvinist) tinge was his translation of Nicole's *Essais de Morale*.

Locke's attitudes towards this work are discussed in ch. 4 of my thesis; see also section VI of this chapter. This translation is published by T. Hancock as *Discourses translated from Nicole's Essays by John Locke* (1828). For a very different view of Locke's thought see Dunn, *Political Thought, passim.*

31 I agree with R. Ashcraft (*Revolutionary Politics*, pp. 92–94) that this draft is of January 1667 rather than January 1666.

32 Ashcraft, the only other scholar to have discussed this evidence, describes it as "notes" that Locke may have taken at a nonconformist sermon that he attended (without any evidence that Locke ever attended a nonconformist sermon). Having read thousands of pages of Locke's hand, he gives no indication that there is any doubt about whose hand it is in. Whoever was the author, in terms of compositional flow it seems to me more accurate to call it a "draft" rather than "notes" on someone else's sermon: the frequent alterations, marginal additions, and transfers of passages to rhetorically more effective locations strongly suggest authorship by whoever wrote the draft itself. The draft is dated at "St. Andrews" church. On the level of pure speculation, one possible venue would be St. Andrew Undershaft, parish of Locke's relative Thomas Grigg (see n. 3 above). It is possible that the draft represents a sermon by Grigg, or, if the hand is Locke's, that it represents Locke at least considering giving a sermon to "try the pulpit" due to his recent consideration of clerical offers. In January 1667 Locke had only very recently (November 1666) been excused from the requirement of entering orders if he wished to remain at Christ Church, Oxford, but he had not yet decided to become Shaftesbury's personal adviser and friend or gone to London; the question of a clerical career was not necessarily completely closed, even if Locke's reluctance to enter such a career was certainly already palpable. Even if the sermon was by Locke, the tentative nature of the following comments on the draft needs to be noted. Only a part of the draft (pt. 3) survives, and there is little indication of the contents of the missing parts. Ashcraft describes the substance and language of the sermon as "distinctly sectarian and non-conformist." I do not agree. I cannot locate anything in the sermon which could not have been preached by Anglicans as well as nonconformists. Indeed, the arguments on faith being counted for righteousness and the combination of James and Paul (see below), without ascription of James's statements to sanctification rather than justification, were more characteristic of Anglican than nonconformist preaching. The mere usage of "brothers" and "saints" at a couple of points in the sermon is not exclusively nonconformist, as Ashcraft seems to imply. In fact, the broad definition given to "brothers" in the sermon is if anything more characteristic of Anglican than of puritan usage. See D. D. Wallace, *Puritans and Predestination* (Chapel Hill, 1982) and J. Sears McGee, *The Godly Man in Stuart England* (New Haven, 1976), ch. 5 for discussion of the differences in tone between Anglican and puritan attitudes. Various hints that also indicate that Locke was committed to a (very broad) moral theology from the 1660s to the early 1680s are discussed in my Ph.D. thesis, chs. 2–5.

33 MS Locke c. 27, pp. 19–20, 22.

34 MS Locke c. 27, pp. 22, 25–27.

35 Locke, *Works* (1801), Vol. X, p. 306; *Holy Bible*, shelved under 16:25, p. 791.

36 Locke, *Works* (1801), Vol. VII, pp. 13–14, 42, 48–51, 53, 90, 99–105, 110–13,

120–26, 186–87, 235, 285–86; Vol. VI, p. 6. For a comparison of Locke and the latitudinarians in this area see Wallace, "Socinianism."

37 Locke, *Works*, Vol. VII, pp. 128–51; MS Locke c. 43, p. 44; on man's motivation by desire for happiness or to avoid pain see especially, of course, the *Essay Concerning Human Understanding*.

38 Burnet, *History*, p. 324; Glanvill, "Antifanatical Religion," pp. 11–12, 14; more generally, H. G. Van Leeuwen, *The Problem of Certainty in English Thought 1630–90* (The Hague, 1963), *passim*; G. A. J. Rogers, this volume.

39 B. Whichcote, *Moral and Religious Aphorisms* (1753), Aphorism 130 cited in Rogers, this volume; Glanvill, "Antifanatical Religion," pp. 11–12, 19–20; B. Shapiro, *Probability and Certainty in Seventeenth-Century England* (Princeton, 1983), ch. 3.

40 Fowler, *Principles*, pp. 307–9, 314–18; Tillotson, *Works* (1704), Vol. III, pp. 62–63; Glanvill, "Antifanatical religion," pp. 11, 14, 25; Sullivan, *Toland*, p. 54; Birch, *Works ... Tillotson*, p. xxxvii.

41 See especially Shapiro, *Probability*, ch. 3; McAdoo, *Anglicanism*, chs. 5 and 6; G. Reedy, *The Bible and Reason* (Philadelphia, 1985), *passim*; Glanvill, "Antifanatical religion," pp. 42–43; Fowler, *Principles*, pp. 70, 96–7.

42 Fowler, *Principles*, pp. 314–17; Tillotson, *Works* (1704), Vol. III, p. 60; Vol. XII, p. 267.

43 See generally Van Leeuwen, *Certainty*; R. T. Carroll, *The Commonsense Philosophy of Religion of Bishop Edward Stillingfleet* (The Hague, 1975); J. Yolton, *John Locke and the Way of Ideas* (Oxford, 1956); Rogers, this volume. J. Biddle, "John Locke's 'Essay on infallibility': introduction, text and translation," *Journal of Church and State* (1977): 301–27; Fox Bourne, *Life*, Vol. I, pp. 174–94; MS Locke c. 27, p. 26; *An early draft of Locke's Essay*, ed. R. I. Aaron and J. Gibb (Oxford, 1936), *passim*, Locke, *An Essay Concerning Human Understanding*, ed. P. Nidditch (Oxford, 1975), *passim*; Locke, *Letters concerning Toleration* in *Works*, Vol. VI, *passim*. Locke and the latitudinarians differed substantially and significantly on innate ideas. See especially Yolton, *Way of Ideas*, ch. 2.

44 Locke, *Works*, Vol. VII, *passim*, especially pp. 227–29, p. 234; Locke, *A Letter Concerning Toleration*, ed. J. Tully (Indianapolis, 1985), pp. 56–58; Locke, *Essay*, Bk. IV; Locke, *Essays on the Law of Nature*, ed. W. Von Leyden (Oxford, 1954), pp. 272–81; Locke, *Essay*, ed. Nidditch, ch. 19; P. King, *Life of John Locke* (1830), Vol. II, pp. 75–81.

45 Axtell, *Educational Writings*, pp. 262, 296, 399; Locke, *Correspondence*, letters 2939, 3332.

46 On the latitudinarians' condemnation of persecution see, for example, G. Burnet, *An Exhortation to Peace and Union* (1681), *passim*; Burnet, *History of My Own Time* (Oxford, 1900), Vol. II, p. 222; Tillotson's preface to his edition of Wilkins' *Sermons* (1682); N. Luttrell, *Brief Historical Relations of State Affairs* (Oxford, 1857), Vol. I, p. 246; E. Stillingfleet, *The Unreasonableness of Separation* (1681), preface pp. lxxix–xcii.

47 E. Stillingfleet, *The Mischief of Separation* (1680), *passim*; Stillingfleet, *Unreasonableness*, preface, p. xxiii; Patrick, *Brief Account*, pp. 7, 11; Birch, *Works ... Tillotson*, p. xxix; Tillotson, *The Protestant Religion Vindicated* (1680), *passim*; more generally, see my "The ecclesiology of the latitude-men

1660–89: Stillingfleet, Tillotson and 'Hobbism'," *Journal of Ecclesiastical History* (1985): 407–27.

48 Stillingfleet, *Unreasonableness*, preface, pp. lxxii–xciii; Fowler, *Principles*, pp. 325–8; Stillingfleet, *Irenicum*, pp. 3, 39–40, 47–49; Glanvill, "Antifanatical religion," pp. 32–5; Patrick, *Works*, Vol. V, pp. 255–65; Carroll, *Commonsense Philosophy*, 18–38; my "Ecclesiology," *passim*.

49 Fox Bourne, *Life*, Vol. I, pp. 174–94 especially pp. 175–78, 189 together with the "Addenda and Corrigenda" to the "Essay on toleration" in J. Gough, *Locke's Political Philosophy* (Oxford, 1950), pp. 197–99. The fourth draft was less hostile to dissent than the first three drafts.

50 King, *Life*, Vol. II, pp. 108–19 at p. 116; Locke, *Works*, Vol. X, *passim* especially pp. 204–7; MS Locke c. 34, pp. 13, 43, 56, 64, 67, 102, 104, 132. See also MS Locke d. 10, 43–44; King, *Life*, Vol. II, pp. 99–101.

51 Fox Bourne, *Life*, pp. 174–94; King, *Life*, Vol. II, pp. 108–19; MS Locke c. 34, 1, 3, 5a, 7, 12, 14–15, 19, 21, 23–25, 28–31, 46–47, 49, 60, 65, 74, 76, 107, 111, 113–16, 118–22; Locke *Essays on the Law of Nature*, pp. 274–75; Cranston, *Locke*, 131–33. In the *Letter from a Person of Quality*, and perhaps in some ecclesiastical manuscripts of the early 1670s, however, Locke defended the King's Ecclesiastical Supremacy. On the letter see Locke, *Works*, Vol. X, pp. 200–46; on the manuscripts see ch. 4 of my Ph.D. thesis.

52 Locke, *Works*, Vol. VI, pp. 155–56, 261, 322, 328–30, 388, 422–23; MS Locke e. 17, p. 211; Locke, *Letter Concerning Toleration*, ed. Tully, pp. 21, 26–7, *passim*; Locke, *Correspondence*, letter 1182.

53 Locke, *Tracts*, p. 160; Biddle, "Locke's 'Essay,'" pp. 316–17; Locke, *Works*, Vol. X, p. 246; MS Locke c. 27, pp. 30c–30c.2.

54 MS Locke c. 34, pp. 5a, 6, 43, 88, 131, 148, 161.

55 Locke, *Correspondence*, letters 1480, 1672, 1684, 1702, 1745; Locke, *Works*, Vol. VII, pp. 135–40, 144, 149; King, *Life*, Vol. II, pp. 82–92; cf. "The conduct of the understanding," Locke, *Works*, Vol. III, p. 224.

56 Baxter, *Reliqiuae*, p. 386; Burnet, *History*, p. 323–4; J. Gascoigne, "The Holy Alliance" (Ph.D. Thesis, Cambridge Univ., 1981), pp. 49–50 (on Grotius); Fowler, *Principles*, pp. 228–29; Tillotson, *Works* (1704), Vol. IV, pp. 207–11; Burnet, *Exposition*, preface, p. XIV, article 17; Cragg, *From Puritanism*, p. 82.

57 Stillingfleet, *Works* (1710), Vol. I, pp. 414–15; Burnet, *Exposition*, Article 9; Tillotson, *Works* (1704), Vol. III, pp. 350–53, Vol. IV, 178–79, 183, Vol. V, pp. 325, 370, 451–3, Vol. VIII, 165, 347.

58 Stillingfleet, *Works* (1710), Vol. I, pp. 8, 24; Burnet, *Exposition*, Articles 5, 12; Tillotson, *Works* (1704), Vol. II, pp. 34, 60, Vol. XII, pp. 235, 238, 278–85.

59 Patrick, *Brief Account*, pp. 8–9; Fowler, *Certain Propositions* (1694); Burnet, *Four Discourses* (1694).

60 Carroll, *Commonsense Philosophy*, pp. 54, 80; Tillotson, *Sermons of the Divinity and Incarnation of our blessed Saviour* (1694), pp. 2, 14–18, 23–24, 36, 64–65, 77, 120–21.

61 Biddle, "Locke's 'Essay,'" pp. 322–23; Hancock, *Discourses…translated from Nicole's Essais*, *passim*; cf. ch. 4 of my dissertation (n. 1 above); also, Locke, *Tracts*, p. 141.

62 Cranston, *Locke*, p. 233n; cf. Le Clerc, *Life*, p. 24.

63 MS Locke f. 8, pp. 36–37, 41–42, 75; MS Locke f. 9, p. 82; MS Locke

c. 33, p. 27v; MS Locke b. 2, pp. 43, 44, 50–51, 81r, 84–86; MS Locke f. 29, p. 18. On the evidence surveyed in the following pages on Locke and Socinianism see my "John Locke and Socinianism" in M. A. Stewart, ed., *Seventeenth Century Philosophy in Historical Context* (Oxford, forthcoming).

64 MS Locke e. 17, pp. 175–223 at p. 175. This manuscript, largely in the hand of Locke's amanuensis Sylvanus Brownover but with marginalia probably by Locke, has to date been discussed only by M. S. Johnson, *Locke on Freedom* (Texas, 1978), pp. 150–51. His interpretation of its content differs from mine. See my forthcoming "John Locke and socinianism" (note above) for the attribution of this manuscript to Locke.

65 MS Locke, e. 17, pp. 183–84, 193–94.

66 MS Locke e. 17, pp. 195–97, 199–202.

67 Locke, *Works*, Vol. VII, pp. 4–9, 91, 101, 111–12; Locke, *Works*, Vol. VIII, *passim*, especially the paraphrases of and notes upon 1 Cor. 2:13, 1 Cor. 8:6; 2 Cor. 4:4 and 6; Eph. 3:9; Romans 9:5.

68 Locke, *Works*, Vol. VII, pp. 4–9, 267–71; Locke, *Works*, Vol. VIII on Romans 2:23–26, 4:8, 5:12; MS Locke c. 43, p. 46; MS Locke c. 27, pp. 111v–112r.

69 Space does not permit discussion of a number of other significant parallels between the latitudinarians and Locke, nor of many further areas of divergence. Both Locke and the latitudinarians were, for instance, much influenced by neo-stoic ethics. Equally, while the latitudinarians were energetic preachers of non-resistance during the Restoration, Locke was involved in planning and justifying resistance. On these issues see my Ph.D. thesis (n. 1 above).

70 Much of this account has been provided by the works of Van Leeuwen, Popkin, Carroll, and Bonno.

71 On all of these relationships see my Ph.D. thesis (n. 1 above).

72 See Locke, *Essay Concerning Human Understanding*, ed. Nidditch, *passim*; Locke, *Works*, Vol. VI, *passim*, Vol. VII, *passim* esp. pp. 171, 176, 309, 408, Vol. VIII, preface; Locke, *Correspondence*, letter 1901. There is an important sense, however, in which Locke's extended defense of theological investigation was in part caused by the need to convince himself that his own "heretical" beliefs would not prevent his salvation.

Index